Florida A&M University, Tallahassee
Florida Atlantic University, Boca Raton
Florida Gulf Coast University, Ft. Myers
Florida International University, Miami
Florida State University, Tallahassee
University of Central Florida, Orlando
University of Florida, Gainesville
University of North Florida, Jacksonville
University of South Florida, Tampa
University of West Florida, Pensacola

CARIBBEAN DANCE
FROM ABAKUÁ TO ZOUK

HOW MOVEMENT SHAPES IDENTITY

Edited by Susanna Sloat

University Press of Florida

Gainesville · Tallahassee · Tampa · Boca Raton
Pensacola · Orlando · Miami · Jacksonville · Ft. Myers

10 09 08 07 06 05   6 5 4 3 2 1

Library of Congress Cataloging-in-Publication Data
Caribbean dance from abakuá to zouk: how movement shapes identity /
edited by Susanna Sloat.
p. cm.
Includes bibliographical references and index.
ISBN 0-8130-2549-4 (cloth: alk. paper)
ISBN 0-8130-2904-x (pbk.: alk. paper)
1. Dance—Anthropological aspects—Caribbean Area. I. Sloat, Susanna.
GV1631.C37   2002
792.8'09729—dc21   2002020446

The University Press of Florida is the scholarly publishing agency for the State University
System of Florida, comprising Florida A&M University, Florida Atlantic University, Flor-
ida Gulf Coast University, Florida International University, Florida State University, Uni-
versity of Central Florida, University of Florida, University of North Florida, University
of South Florida, and University of West Florida.

University Press of Florida
15 Northwest 15th Street
Gainesville, FL 32611<n>2079
http://www.upf.com

CONTENTS

INTRODUCTION

In the twenty-first century, as in the twentieth, the world dances to Caribbean beats. From Sydney to Helsinki, Tokyo to Abidjan, salsa and reggae call out to aficionados. Londoners merengue and develop new dance rhythms like English ska or drum and bass out of older Jamaican ones; Parisians and Angolans borrow *zouk* from the Antilles. Rhythms derived from Africa return there and become newly Africanized rumbas and reggaes. Cruise-ship tourists on all the seas move to *soca* line dances. On stages all over, choreographers, even austere postmodern ones, may add a bit of Caribbean hip fluidity to Caribbean rhythms when they want to suggest sensuality or joy. African-Caribbean religions with dancing at their ritual core flourish not only in Cuba, Haiti, Jamaica, and Trinidad, but also in diversely Caribbean New York City. Caribbean rhythms, dances, and fragments of dance movement, even an attitude toward movement, reach beyond the islands, beyond the huge West Indian diaspora communities in North America, Latin America, and Europe, to be joyously embraced by the world at large.

Despite the wide-flung popularity and influence of Caribbean dance and the prodigious lure of the West Indies for the tropical paradise vacation experience, the complex cultures that formed these dances are insufficiently known. Each island has its own complexly layered history—of indigenous cultures vanquished by European takeover, enslavement, and disease; of, frequently, multiple conquests by different European colonizers; of Africans from many places brought over as enslaved people to work plantations; of slaves escaping to form Maroon cultures; of slaves and colonists and free workers moving from island to island; of slavery being succeeded by indentured laborers brought over from India, China, Indonesia, or Africa; of Syrians and Lebanese, Latin and North Americans, Europeans, West Indians from other islands, and others arriving at various times from a multitude of places.

Such a layering of influences over the past five hundred–plus years has given these islands dance cultures of a fascinating complexity. Dances of

African descent coexist with those of mostly European origins; dances born elsewhere with those mixed and creolized on the islands. Although modern commercial trends seem as if they might vanquish old traditions and do, in fact, lead to abandonment of some, while others survive only in the repertoires of folkloric troupes, dance traditions once assumed to be dying get revived in ways that might surprise their old exponents. In the past, European dances of the plantation owners were adopted and creolized by slaves and free people of African descent and became country traditions as the elite in towns took to social dances considered current at each particular era. Now rural dances such as the European-based Creole quadrilles and African-based Creole *bele* of Martinique may get taken up by fashionable urbanites; for several decades now intellectuals throughout the Antilles have been embracing the folkloric, which often means seeking to understand and celebrate rather than to downplay what is African in the culture. Markers of class and race can exchange places as what was once scorned is embraced. At the same time inheritors of dances, and of danced rites, whether remaining explicitly religious or with a spiritual element subsumed, may maintain them with devoted pride. In either case, and in many other situations, dance becomes a primary mark of identity.

As a legacy of competing colonizers, the West Indies is fragmented not just by water, but also by language. Spanish, French, English, Dutch, and a variety of Creoles (mixtures of African and European languages) are spoken. Certain historical inheritances such as Protestant hymns in the English-speaking Caribbean or the Spanish *décima* verse form where Spanish is spoken—and also to considerable extent the modern commercial musics that are now popular and the dances done to them—depend on whether Spanish, French, or English is the national language. But the European and African dances brought to the islands were, if not the same in every place, overall frequently shared and often carried with the movement of peoples from island to island where they evolved in somewhat different ways, but with a noticeable common dance language or vocabulary. Moreover, there is a great similarity in the most African styles of singing, the call and response chants and complex ways of harmonizing, between islands that may speak different languages and dance to different current rhythms. Still, language divisions remain strong markers of identity.

In setting its dances within the social contexts of each Caribbean island, the authors of this book over and over return to matters of identity, both personal and communal. Each island has dances that connote place

Fig. 1. Outline of Caribbean islands. Map: Don Burmeister.

and belonging, that have become "national." This can be particularly important in places that have not been until recently, and in some cases still are not, allowed the status of nations. Beginning mostly in the 1940s, pioneers on Caribbean islands began to codify folklore for onstage performance. Such codifications become a set of national dances that can be constantly revived, referred to, and added to. Particular communities, whether of place or affinity, attach themselves to particular dances. In the Caribbean, an arena of musical ferment where people love to dance, to achieve not only physical and aesthetic mastery, but also union with the divine with dance, individuals become passionately attached to the dances they do, whether they are those of the majority or of a subculture, in that way asserting their identity through movement.

Hence the subtitle: *How Movement Shapes Identity.* The title, *Caribbean Dance from Abakuá to Zouk,* suggests an arc from an old ritual tradition in parts of Cuba imported from the Calabar region of what is now Nigeria and adjacent Cameroon, down through the islands to Guadeloupe and Martinique, where zouk, a late twentieth-century commercial musical phenomenon, takes its name from a type of dancing party. The book moves farther south, to Trinidad and Curaçao, but it stops before reaching the continent of South America, or any continent. This is not because the islands of the West Indies are a dance culture unit in isolation, but rather because the phenomenon that most marks them—the confluence of African ways of moving and African ways of making music with European ones and hence the creation of Creole dances and music—is, in fact, too widespread to be dealt with in depth in one volume.

Wherever African slaves were brought—along all the shores of the Caribbean and the Gulf coast, up the Atlantic, and south along it past richly African parts of the Brazilian coast as far as Buenos Aires and Montevideo, on parts also of the Pacific coast from Mexico to Peru and Chile, and into continental interiors—dance developed based on African rhythmic concepts in conjunction with European influences and in some places Native American ones. Such complexes of rhythms and dances have many similarities with those of the Caribbean islands. But we have no room for them here, unfortunately, no room even for many of the islands of the Caribbean itself, each a dance universe of its own, with very small islands, like Carriacou with its Big Drum dance of many explicit African sources, no less interesting than larger places.

Caribbean Dance from Abakuá to Zouk: How Movement Shapes Identity is a book that hews to the islands, with excursions into the Caribbean diaspora. Its authors come from a variety of backgrounds and take a variety of approaches to describing dance, from the comprehensive ethnographic overview to the personal narrative, and the chapters reverberate with one another. It is this desired reverberation that has guided the varied selection of authors, so that the islands' dances can be seen from multifaceted points of view. The authors themselves wear many hats: they teach, dance, choreograph, administrate, lead communities, and write—from within the academy in various disciplines, and from without—as scholars, journalists, and storytellers. Their voices are distinct and individual. Most who write here about specific islands are from those islands, though many now live in the United States. Multiple points of view resound within the authors themselves and that has led to particular riches in this book.

Its scope ranges through every type of indigenous dance, from the folkloric, to the folkloric theatricalized and transferred to the stage, to contemporary choreographic creations that bring novel Caribbean approaches into the theater. The book attempts to set this spectrum of dance within its contexts: the often troubled settings of islands that have experienced repeated conquest, genocide of indigenous populations, centuries of slavery, colonization, and occupation, dictatorship and shaky democracy, natural disasters from volcanoes to hurricanes, the destruction of natural habitat caused by everything from plantations to overpopulation to too many tourists, and long-term economic exploitation and marginalization. These are islands that have suffered much, but that have developed cultures in which dance expresses spiritual depths as well as sensual joys. The literature on such dance is scattered and can be confusing; *Caribbean Dance* doesn't have an encyclopedic scope, but it is a centralized repository for information that can be hard to come by.

Although there are dances of European or largely European origin throughout the islands, it is the African element and the way it remains intact, whether in a genuine African retention, a neo–African-Caribbean creation, or a mixture of the African and European in proportions that vary greatly (but that can give even a largely European dance form a distinctive bounce and lilt) that sets the Caribbean apart, that, in fact, has set the whole world dancing to Caribbean rhythms. To frame the book through a lens that reveals the Africanness of the African content of Caribbean dance, we begin with Brenda Dixon Gottschild's illuminating "Crossroads, Continuities, and Contradictions: The Afro-Euro-Caribbean Triangle." Here Dixon Gottschild, as she did in her book *Digging the Africanist Presence in American Performance: Dance and Other Contexts*, sets forth a series of principles that underlie Africanist aesthetics of performance, building on the seminal work of another contributor, Robert Farris Thompson.

She finds rich examples of these concepts in two visual recordings of *Vodou* ceremonies by Maya Deren and Yvonne Daniel, but readers will note many more, from their own experience and in the course of reading about island dance in the other chapters of the book. See Thomas Pinnock's "Rasta and Reggae," for example, to find out how Jamaican youngsters in improvising "drop legs" competitions also exemplify the aesthetic of the cool, even surreptitiously washing away sweat to enhance the illusion. Or look to Gabri Christa's discussion of the *tambu* of Curaçao to see how, in a communal form that has lost its specific religious connections but maintains its purifying spiritual power, people dance for hours, "marathoning," as Dixon Gottschild calls it, in "spirit time." With this lens in place, one can see what is Africanist even about creolized dance forms in which the European contribution is significant or predominates. The world of dance, perhaps, for those for whom this lens is new, will never quite look the same.

In order to continue this shift of perspective, the book starts by attempting to look at Caribbean dance not from the inside looking out to Africa or Europe (as happens in sections of many essays in the book), but from Africa looking into the Caribbean. This is only a beginning, to be sure; others will have to continue this investigation. One would want to begin with expert eyes from Senegal and move inland to the peoples of the former Mali empire and down and around the entire bulge of Africa, including what is now Ghana, Dahomey (present-day Benin), and Yorubaland, among others, to the Calabar region of Nigeria and Cameroon, and then south, covering all of the areas that sent enslaved people to the West Indies.

We must look across centuries as well as span an ocean. Africa, like the West Indies, has undergone much cultural change since the first waves of Africans were forced across the sea. Its dance cultures are complicated ones, with confusion furthered by confluences and exchanges. But, as a bare start, moving to the Congo/Angola region of West Central Africa that sent very large numbers of people to the Caribbean from the sixteenth to the nineteenth centuries, we offer Nathaniel Crowell's essay "What Is Congolese in Caribbean Dance." Crowell, who dances with a Congolese company in New York, was investigating topics for an ethnomusicological dissertation in Angola when forced to leave because of continued war. He uses his experiences there, as well as in other parts of the Congo/Angola region (spelled Kongo/Angola in many parts of the book when referring to the cultural sphere of the Bakongo peoples), in the Caribbean, and in Caribbean New York, even in Peru, to look at some characteristics that distinguish the Congolese contributions and the chain that led from them to creole Caribbean dances.

Here, too, you will find some valuable long quotes from early observers of Caribbean dance such as Moreau de St. Méry and interesting correlations from Peru, Brazil, and Angola. The early naming of dances can be confusing—the same name may be used not only on different islands, but also for what seems like different dances (in part because the name may refer to a drum group or type of dance gathering). These names, such as *calenda* (or *kalinda*), *bamboula*, *chica*, *juba* (or *djouba*), are often still extant on various islands, describing various dances, and even names that appear to be different such as the *yubá* and *sicá* of Puerto Rican *bomba* may be variants of the old *juba* and *chica*.

Cuba, the largest island in the Caribbean, has a particularly complex dance culture with full-scale danced religions and many ritual retentions from Africa, immensely popular and influential creolized social dance and music forms, and notable performance traditions in folklore, ballet (important but outside our sphere), and modern dance that have been fostered by a cultural structure and educational emphasis formed since the Cuban Revolution. In "Cuban Dance: An Orchard of Caribbean Creativity," dance anthropologist Yvonne Daniel suggests the influence that Cuban dance and music has had throughout the Caribbean (as well as around the world at large) and gives a very valuable and thorough overview of all aspects of Cuban folkloric dance culture. We are fortunate to start with such a comprehensive article, which provides another frame for looking at dance of the region. Daniel discusses the structure of dance activity in Cuba, early reports of indigenous dance, importations from Europe, Haiti, and Africa—including an illuminating and extensive section on the danced religions and rites—and another equally interesting and extensive section on the many Cuban creations and their evolutions—in particular, the *son*, rumba, and *danzón* complexes.

Ramiro Guerra, first director of Conjunto Nacional de Danza Contemporánea, formed just after the Revolution in 1960, and a pioneering and innovative choreographer, is considered the founder of modern dance in Cuba, where he created a uniquely Cuban style of teaching and performing. With his career as a modern dance choreographer aborted when he fell out of favor with the government after eleven years as head of his Conjunto, he is one of the Caribbean's insufficiently known creative fountainheads. Melinda Mousouris's "The Dance World of Ramiro Guerra: Solemnity, Voluptuousness, Humor, and Chance," based on interviews and video viewing with Guerra in Havana, limns the fascinating arc of his career and discusses in depth some of the dances he made.

Guerra and associates developed the *técnica cubana*, a hybrid system of technique and teaching that combines dance forms, including Cuban folkloric elements, to make virtuosic and uniquely Cuban dances. It is not the only systematic technique developed to produce dance with distinctly Caribbean elements—the Jamaican national company has a technique, Lavinia Williams developed one in Haiti and Jamaica, and, of course, there is the powerful Dunham Technique that evolved in Katherine Dunham's company and school. But the técnica cubana is a major development and tool, and Suki John, a choreographer who learned the technique in Cuba, where she has also made dances, brings its story and that of Cuba's modern dance up to the twenty-first century in "The Técnica Cubana," in which she gives an extensive description of what might happen in a company class as taught by Danza Contemporánea's master teacher, Manolo Vásquez.

Rex Nettleford also talks about constructing a distinctly Caribbean technique to make distinctly Caribbean dances in "Jamaican Dance Theatre—Celebrating the Caribbean Heritage." Professor Nettleford, artistic director and chief choreographer of the National Dance Theatre Company of Jamaica, eloquently connects the dance of the company he helped found in 1962 to signal Jamaica's cultural identity simultaneously with the foundation of an independent state, with the other African-derived dance of the Caribbean, seeing this as establishing a classic tradition of its own. He notes that there are no English words to describe basic steps from such Jamaican dance traditions as *kumina* or *dinkimini* and suggests new ones as part of a celebration not just of many facets of Jamaican dance and of the people involved in it, but also of the entire community of Caribbean dancemakers from the 1940s to now.

A dance life begins in childhood and so does Thomas Osha Pinnock's essay "Rasta and Reggae," which flavorfully links his youthful "drop legs" competition days in the dance yards of West Kingston with the innovative dance works he choreographed after formal training and beginning a career as a modern dancer. In the process he reveals much about the social strata of Jamaica, the roots of Rastafari, and the development of distinctively Jamaican forms of popular music, culminating in reggae. With his Jamaican storyteller's flair, he makes you feel like you are there.

Smaller in area than Cuba, larger in the combined population of its two constituent nations of Haiti and the Dominican Republic, Hispaniola has a complicated history, shared and apart, which Martha Ellen Davis discusses in her comprehensive overview of the dance of the Dominican Republic. Henry Frank, a leader in the Haitian community in New York and an authority on Vodou, concentrates on the basics of that complexly syncretized danced religion with its diverse African roots. In "Haitian Vodou Ritual Dance and Its Secularization," Frank suggests that in Haiti even many secular dances have roots in the spiritual tradition.

Lois Wilcken enlarges this discussion in "Spirit Unbound: New Approaches to the Performance of Haitian Folklore." Here she ties a history of folkloric performance in Haiti and the diaspora from the 1940s and

1950s to a new concept of presenting folklore in a more direct way that she has been working on with the New York–based Haitian group, La Troupe Makandal. An ethnomusicologist as well as executive director of Makandal, Wilcken discusses patterns of presentation, including the folklore show and the exploitative "voodoo" show, and shows how they differ from Makandal's way of offering Vodou and *Rara* (a Lenten celebration) to the public.

Our thorough overviews, like Martha Ellen Davis's on the Dominican Republic, offer much that moves beyond the detailed examination of a particular dance culture. In "Dominican Folkdance and the Shaping of National Identity," Davis traces a trajectory of shifting identity, from an emphasis on the Hispanic heritage under the dictator Trujillo, who promoted a regional version of merengue until it became, and continues to be, a symbol of the country, to a current revival of interest, led by folklorists, in African-rooted music and the dance that accompanies it. In the process, she delves into the traditional culture of the country and how the folklore operates amid its social settings, from the Taínos and their *areítos*, to forms descended from those brought by African slaves, Haitian braceros, and Europeans, to the creolized social dances and their local variations, to the folkloric revivals, including the current one that is redefining Dominican identity as embracing African as well as European-derived heritage.

Postmodern performance artist Josefina Baez is also concerned with Dominican identity, in particular, the complications inherent in hers as a Dominican artist living in New York City, but she chooses to explore this using an unexpected idiom: *kuchipudi* dance from the South Indian state of Andhra Pradesh. In "A Dominican York in Andhra," an article excerpted from a longer essay, Ramón Rivera-Servera discusses Baez's work, "Dominicanish," and analyzes how she reveals the multiple meanings of her Domincanness through her performances in the homes of fellow Dominican Yorks, action including unorthodox kuchipudi dance, and text in the Spanish-English mixture she calls Dominicanish.

Alma Concepción's "Dance in Puerto Rico: Embodied Meanings," while concentrating on the island, also takes us back and forth between the island and the diaspora, particularly in New York, where the phenomenon of salsa was consolidated. This essay brings to the fore what this means to participants, as well as to those who dance or danced forms ranging from the nineteenth-century *danza* and *seis* to *bomba* and *plena*, up to the current generation of hip-hoppers and others now creating new dance forms, and conveys how a dance identity can embody both individual and wider social, even political, yearnings. In "Gilda Navarra: Before Taller de Histriones," Concepción, a member of that company during all of its existence, offers an evocative memoir, originally published in Spanish in the San Juan magazine *Postdata*, of the creation of the crucial piece that led Navarra to form Taller de Histriones to develop a new way of making dance theater, important work little known beyond its audience in the 1970s and early 1980s in Puerto Rico.

Puerto Rican bomba is a complex tradition that incorporates many influences from other islands among its multiple rhythms (like the *holandés*, the fastest rhythm, akin to the tambu of Curaçao), as well as those from Africa and Spain, within an overall approach making it the most African of Puerto Rico's dance traditions. The dancer directs the drummer, as anthropologist Halbert Barton explains in "The Challenges of Puerto Rican Bomba," in which he details his first wondering view of bomba, his initiation into it as a dancer, its history, its musical and dance elements, how it feels to actually dance the challenge, and its current revival, with the introduction of a new form of participatory bomba party, the *bombazo*.

Focusing on a smaller island, we can see all the components of a dance culture, down to the teachers whose students, like Cynthia Oliver, author of "Winin' Yo' Wais': The Changing Tastes of Dance on the U.S. Virgin Island of St. Croix," sometimes become professional dancers and choreographers. Opening with the exuberant "wining" and even more sexually explicit "wukkin' up" of St. Croix's Carnival, Oliver moves on to the diverse history of the multiply-colonized U.S. Virgin Islands, their continuing pinch between North American and Caribbean identities, the revival of the historical *bamboula* as a "nation dance" by folkloric groups despite persistent debate on what it looked like historically, and another "nation dance," the quadrille, still danced to the local *quelbe* music in public dances and private Heritage Dancers balls.

The French Caribbean (now two *départements* of France) centers on the islands of Martinique and Guadeloupe. In "Sa Ki Ta Nou (This belongs to us): Creole Dances of the French Caribbean," Martinican ethnomusicologist Dominique Cyrille offers a detailed overview of how such dances as the European-derived quadrille and the African-based bele dances, the *dans lalinklè* performed at wakes, and the fight dance *ladja* (formerly spelled *l'ag'ya*) of Martinique and the *léwoz* or *gwoka* of Guadeloupe developed and creolized within the historical circumstances of these culturally rich, plantation-based islands. Bringing us up to date with late twentieth-century cultural revivals and reinventions, Cyrille ends with a discussion of zouk and Creole identity.

To anyone who thinks of limbo as a party entertainment or nightclub spectacle, Molly Ahye's "In Search of the Limbo: An Investigation into Its Folklore as a Wake Dance" will be a revelation. A spiritual leader in Trinidad as well as an expert on the island's dance, Ahye explores the spiritual dimensions of a dance that was formerly a feature of wakes in parts of the island with strongly African culture. By interviewing exponents of Limbo and older people in the 1980s about the Limbo that they saw in their childhood, Ahye was able to gather valuable information about a practice that has faded as its ritual connotations are occluded by nightclub connections. Her search both for descriptions of Limbo at wakes and for the possible underlying meanings of the dance leads to absorbing insights into the folklore of Trinidad.

Trinidadian meanings beneath the surface, in this case those that lie behind what can be seen as Carnival display, are the focus of Patricia Alleyne-Dettmers's "The Moko Jumbie: Elevating the Children." Alleyne-Dettmers, linguistic anthropologist and carnival expert, delves into the African origins of these stiltwalking masquerade figures, danced by children now in Trinidad, discusses *Moko Jumbies* as part of the *Jonkonnu* tradition on other islands, and then begins a concentrated look at the meanings behind the costumes and dances of one particular band of Moko Jumbies in the 1999 Carnival, a band whose leader's ideas for their presentation encompassed the span of Trinidad's history and the many facets of its identity. Stepping inside the designer Francina Princesa Richards' head, as it were, in describing the Moko Jumbies, Alleyne-Dettmers gives us her distinctive Afro-Trinidadian view of how the past impacts the present.

Slavery and colonization have produced a need for forms of subversive resistance, met on many islands by song and dance forms that offer commentary in the ironic form of play. When a form is also a suppressed African ritual, as is the tambu of Curaçao, the irony—and the possibility of prohibition or overregulation—heightens. Choreographer and Guggenheim fellow Gabri Christa first fell in love with tambu and its forbidden aspects as a young teenager in her native Curaçao. In "Tambu: Afro-Curaçao's Music and Dance of Resistance," she tells us about the fascinating and little-known culture of this Papiamentu-speaking Dutch island, including summaries of Curaçao's other indigenous dance and music forms and much about the rapid hips and rhythms and hidden traditions of tambu.

The best of the older choreographies based on Caribbean themes have lost none of their beauty or their importance in history as pioneering explorations of a mixed idiom for the stage, which has rightly been deemed classic. Among the earliest pioneers of translating folkloric Caribbean dance elements to the stage is Katherine Dunham, who did anthropological research on four islands in the mid-1930s and returned home to the United States to begin choreography based on her experience. Her work, her training technique, and her company have had an enduring influence on African-American dance. VèVè Clark's "Katherine Dunham's *Tropical Revue*," first published in 1982 in *Black American Literature Forum*, explores the history of Dunham and her company, focusing on *L'Ag'Ya*, her landmark first full ballet from 1938. This Creole love tragedy set in Martinique, where Dunham had done research, uses Martinican and other Caribbean forms, mixing African and European elements into a well-structured drama. The dance and its implications are evoked in depth here.

More recent audiences had a chance to enjoy *L'Ag'Ya* as a highlight of the Alvin Ailey company's full evening, "The Magic of Katherine Dunham," produced in 1987. The islands and their performing traditions converge in pan-Caribbean New York City. Choreography seen there in the late 1990s is described by Susanna Sloat in "Islands Refracted: Recent Dance on Caribbean Themes in New York." While zeroing in on the explicitly Caribbean, she ends with an evocation, in the work of master choreographer Garth Fagan, of the sheer possibility for invention inherent in Caribbean movement itself.

Such possibilities of movement on the dance floor are brought to brilliantly vivid life by Robert Farris Thompson in "Teaching the People to Triumph over Time: Notes from the World of Mambo." No one will want to miss this final essay of the book. Full of his characteristic insights into the Kongo spiritual and movement elements underlying mambo, it takes us from city to city, from Havana to Lima to Mexico City, and finally to New York's Palladium in the 1950s, where dance innovators worked inventive changes and complications into mambo.

The extensive glossary, compiled of terms defined by the authors of relevant chapters (with, sometimes, variant spellings reflecting the choices of the authors for places where orthography varies or has been standardized in different ways at different times), and the combined bibliography are highly useful extensions of the book. Words are fixed in print, but dance, like identity, evolves. Think of this book not only as a useful and stimulating reference, but also as part of the evolution, a source book from which many further studies and more intensive investigations into the dance forms and culture of the Caribbean can emerge. Let *Caribbean Dance from Abakuá to Zouk: How Movement Shapes Identity* encourage such thought—and allow it also to provoke the desire to put some music on and get up and dance.

Acknowledgments

My thanks are incomplete here—many more people have been helpful than I can cite. I would like to begin by thanking my editor, Meredith Morris-Babb, for getting *Caribbean Dance* started and for being enthusiastic about it from the beginning. Grateful thanks also to others who were helpful in getting things going, including Bernadine Jennings, John Gray, Madeline Nichols, Alice Adamczyk, Jean Léon Destiné, Kate Ramsey, Barbara Palfy, Ben Jones, Ernesto Rodriguez, Boni Raposo, Tony Vicioso, Sandra Levinson, Kelvin Rotardier, Melle Randall, Suzanne Youngerman, et al. Thanks to Paul Mintus and to Margherita Davis of Country Dance New York for giving me the chance to go to the Playford Ball and see what English country dancing is like now. And thanks to all the friends, family, and acquaintances who were encouraging along the way.

Very special thanks to my husband, Don Burmeister, for being my in-house computer consultant (with occasional assists from sons Abe and Tobias Burmeister), and again most grateful thanks to Don for the many hours he spent computerizing and improving photographs and making the Caribbean map, musical notes, and the Yowa and Limbo charts.

Full body thanks, too, to all my dance teachers over the years of Dunham Technique and various Afro-Caribbean and African styles, including Pearl Reynolds, Pat Hall, Richard Gonzalez, Ricardo Colon, Xiomara Rodriguez, Norman Saunders, Esther Grant, Dele Husbands, Harold Pierson, Lygia Barreto, Bernadine Jennings, M'Bayero Louvouezo, Pedro Soto, and others.

And finally I would like to thank all of the authors, a group of extremely busy, exceptionally talented, invariably fascinating people who have taken the time and put in the energy to make this book a success.

.   .   .

Alma Concepción's "Gilda Navarra: Before Taller de Histriones" originally appeared in Spanish in *Postdata*, May 1996. Used by permission of *Postdata*. Portions of her "Dance in Puerto Rico: Embodied Meanings" are also part of "Dance and Diaspora," which will appear in *Musical Migrations*, edited by Frances Aparicio and Candida Jaquez, from St. Martin's Press.

VèVè Clark's "Katherine Dunham's Tropical Review" appeared originally in *Black American Literature Forum*, vol. 16, no. 4, Winter 1982, and was reprinted in *Caribe*, vol. 7, no. 1 and 2, 1983. Used by permission of the author.

Most of Henry Frank's "Haitian Vodou Ritual Dance and its Secularization" appeared originally as "A Survey of Haitian Vodun Ritual Dance" in *Caribe*, vol. 7, nos. 1 and 2, 1983. Used by permission of the author.

Most of the descriptions of dances in Susanna Sloat's "Islands Refracted: Recent Dance on Caribbean Themes in New York" were originally published in reviews, copyright Susanna Sloat, in various issues of *Attitude: The Dancers' Magazine*. Used by permission of the author.

Robert Farris Thompson's "Teaching the People to Triumph over Time: Notes from the World of Mambo" has also appeared in *First of the Month*, vol. 3, no. 2, 2001, under the title "Triumph over Time: Notes on Mambo."

◇ ◇ ◇

AFRICAN BACKGROUND

1

◇　◇　◇

Crossroads, Continuities, and Contradictions

The Afro-Euro-Caribbean Triangle

Brenda Dixon Gottschild

Here we stand, having crossed the threshold of a new millennium, at a moment in time when, performancewise, so much world beauty is at our fingertips that we might be ecstatic yet humbled by its sheer power. The world is our oyster, a global community. But it is also a market economy. Without questioning origins or rights, we have appropriated world cultural products as consumer commodities in a buy-and-sell, take-and-take environment. But what is given back? To whom? When? And how? I am speaking of the exchange rate that exists, generally, between Europeanist (that is, European and European-American) cultures and all other world cultures—and, specifically, between Europeanist and Africanist (that is continental and diasporan African) cultures.

There are some—seekers, students, scholars—whose work in bridging the divide between Europeanist and world cultures has acted as an antidote to expropriation and exploitation. A handful of them are represented in this book. In order to understand their work and the cultures they address, it behooves us to have an understanding of the philosophy and premises that underlie these gorgeous aesthetic treasures. In my book, *Digging the Africanist Presence in American Performance: Dance and Other Contexts* (Gottschild 1996, 1998), I discuss in detail and with various cultural examples the signposts of Africanist (and Europeanist) aesthetic standards. What follows is an extrapolation of and distillation from that hypothesis, this time as an application of Africanist aesthetic concepts to Caribbean performance, in general, and Caribbean dance, in particular.

These constructs are interrelated, interdependent, and inseparable. In practice, they cannot possibly be construed as discrete entities: they are interactive and processual.

Whether spoken, sung, sculpted, sketched, written, or danced, the Africanist aesthetic values process. How a thing is done is as important as getting it done—the journey as important as the destination. Language, sculpture, and visual arts are conceived as living, vital, motional concepts—moving movers, so to speak—which is why art historian Robert Farris Thompson could write his signature work on African visual arts and title it *African Art in Motion*. A stellar example of this premise is the fact that the deities of African and African diasporic practice are dancing spirits that come to life through the dancing bodies of the faithful. To use dance anthropologist Yvonne Daniel's wonderfully evocative term, these danced religions exhibit the principle of "embodied wisdom." (Note: Using Daniel's initiative I have removed the terms "possession" and "possessed by the deities" from my vocabulary. Instead, I refer to practitioners who manifest the deity through dance as "embodying" the spirit. This term indicates that the process is a form of cultural wisdom, knowledge, and education. "Possession," a term imposed by outsider perspectives, is biased toward a model of inconsequence and lack of control.) As Africanist scholar Sheila Walker pointed out, the fact that the spirit dances in/through the bodies of its believers is an affirmation and celebration of the fact that the universe is a dynamic process-in-motion, rather than a static entity (*Dancing* 1993).

Borrowing from and building on the consummate work of Thompson (1974), Kariamu Welsh-Asante (1985), and Susan Vogel (1986), I hope to designate a constellation of Africanist elements that are manifested in many forms of diasporan African dance, from South America to the Caribbean and the United States. It is important to reiterate the fact that these characteristics work symbiotically, do not exist as discrete entities, and are separated and categorized, here and elsewhere, solely for the sake of discourse. They indicate processes, tendencies, and attitudes.

In searching for specifically Caribbean danced examples of these principles, I utilize Haitian *Vodou* dance as demonstrated in the work of Maya Deren (the video *Divine Horsemen: The Living Gods of Haiti*) and Yvonne Daniel (the video *Public Vodun Ceremonies in Haiti*) to make my points. These two excellent films act as companion pieces and are essential viewing for anyone interested in this important form of sacred African diasporic performance.

Embracing the Conflict

In the broadest sense the Africanist aesthetic can be construed as a principle of contradictions and an encounter of opposites. The conflict, or paradox, that is innate to and insinuated by difference, disagreement, discord, or irregularity is embraced, rather than erased or resolved. The fact that this is a principle essential to the Africanist perspective is demonstrated by the importance of the crossroads as a symbol in African and African diasporic cultures. As Deren points out in her book *Divine Horsemen: The Living Gods of Haiti* (1991, 100n.), the crossroads is the site of the "coincidence of opposites." Accordingly, Africanist art forms deal in paradox as a matter of course, with irony following close on its heels. Contradiction is expressed in African dilemma tales, in music or vocal work that, to the untrained ear, may sound discordant or grating, and in dance that may seem unsophisticated, uncoordinated, or ungraceful to eyes schooled in the Europeanist aesthetic. This principle is reflected in the premises cited, below, and they, in turn, are reflected in it. Embracing the conflict is embedded in the final principle, the aesthetic of the cool, since coolness results from the juxtaposition of detachment with intensity. Both principles, as well as all the other aesthetic canons outlined herein, may manifest themselves as simultaneously comedic and tragic (and, occasionally, even self-mockingly so) in an attitude and style that is uncharacteristic of Europeanist endeavor.

Vodou and all Africanist danced religions are examples of Daniel's concept of embodied wisdom and embrace the contradictory, conflicting ethos of spirit world and body/material world. These two worlds do not join easily. We see the conflict in the struggle that occurs when the spirit mounts the body of the novice dancing practitioner. The struggle is allowed to occur, without onlookers attempting to suppress or subsume the process. The conflict is not regarded as "good" or "bad," "right" or "wrong"; it simply is what it is: the process.

Polycentrism/Polyrhythm

From the Africanist perspective, movement may originate from any body zone, and two or more areas of the body may simultaneously serve as centers of movement. Africanist-based movement is also polyrhythmic. The feet may maintain one rhythm while torso, legs, arms dance to the beat of different drums. This democracy of body parts is demonstrable in

Africanist dance forms throughout the Motherland and across the diaspora.

These confluent principles are demonstrated in Vodou's *zépaules*—the dance motif characterized by the beautifully subtle articulation of the shoulders that involves the rib cage in a concurrent but separate flow, with the feet moving to an independent rhythm far below.

High-Affect Juxtaposition

Movement, mood, or attitude disruptions that ensue abruptly, rather than with a transition phase, are the signature of this premise. A driving or somber mood may overlap and cohabit a light, humorous attitude; or, in another example, imitative movements (reflecting particular human or animal behavior) may be juxtaposed with abstract ones. The result of such contrasts may be comedy, irony, satire, double meanings, innuendo, and, ultimately, euphoria and exhilaration. It is true that all traditions utilize contrast as an aesthetic valence. However, Africanist high-affect juxtaposition is accelerated beyond the range of contrast that is acceptable, or "in good taste," in Europeanist criteria.

Their high-affect juxtapositions preserve Caribbean performance genres such as Vodou as a mystery—if not simply an example of bad taste—in the regard of the Europeanist-based outsider. How can a sacred ceremony involve secular dances, sexualized performance, and a deity such as Guede (the Vodou deity of birth, death, and fertility who jokes, plays sexual games, and generally wreaks havoc in his path), they ask themselves? Or how can a practitioner's face remain calm and mask-like as her body jerks and veers in a dance that seems to come from a force beyond her physical control? And how, indeed, can a spiritual practice be centered upon the very physicalized, sexualized human body? What are tears of joy, and how is it possible to laugh and cry simultaneously? How can a body express love and outrage in the same movement? The answer, once we leave behind our baggage of prejudice, bias, and inhibition, is simple: like Buddhism, this precept is part of a system that honors, rather than hides, the contradictions in human experience. It is a principle of "and," rather than "either/or": we are sexual *and* spiritual, body *and* soul, human *and* supernatural—indeed, good *and* bad—rather than one or the other.

Ephebism

This premise (*ephebe* was the ancient Greek word for a youth or young person) includes attributes such as power, vitality, attack, drive, and flexibility. You don't need to be young to demonstrate ephebism. In fact, the term is most frequently used when an elder dances and exhibits youthful characteristics. It's really not about age, but about using the right energy, attitude, and timing. Thompson (1974, 7) describes it as "the phrasing of every note and step with consummate vitality." Ephebism implies a supple, flexible torso, bending knees, and the ability and willingness to go down in order to be lifted up, literally and metaphorically: a flexibility that allows one to go with the flow and roll with the changes (of the dance, of life itself).

Ephebism is demonstrated in both Deren's and Daniel's field footage. In each we see examples of elders (particularly women) dancing with the ease, grace, and sensuality of youth, as well as countless examples of quintessential phrasing and timing in the dance of ordinary people who are capable of extraordinary kinetic moments.

The Aesthetic of the Cool

This principle is the circumference that holds all others in its thrall. It lives in the other premises, and they also reside in it. "The Cool" is the culminating step in an attitude that combines vitality with composure—or hot/engaged with cool/detached. To exhibit the cool involves dancing and presenting the self with clarity and lucidity. In a more spiritual sense—and the Africanist esthetic is ineluctably spiritual and physical—the cool has been characterized as "soul force," which includes "energy, . . . fiber, . . . spirit and flair" (Gay and Baber 1987, 11).

Vodou's Guede is quintessentially cool: he generally appears wearing dark glasses and either a derby or scarf on his head—accoutrements that inherently are associated with cooling processes. The dances of the *prise des yeux*, those practitioners who are adepts, are almost always a striking example of cool—their faces resembling ancient African masks in stillness, calm, and self-possession, while their bodies dance beyond their quotidian potential. Cool, however, is manifested in contrast with hot, which is its indispensable complement: the two illuminate each other in a symbiotic dance that is emblematic of the full spectrum of Africanist aesthetic characteristics.

With these basic principles laid out (and, to be sure, those listed above are in no way all-inclusive, but, simply, my way of making sense of a rich treasure trove whose manifestations, like the pantheons of deities or the stars in the sky, are too numerous to contain in any theory) let me, now, extend them in ways that I deem relevant to Caribbean dance. Again, Vodou forms a basic comparative integer.

Communication/Continuity Between Human and Spirit Worlds

Although this characteristic is cited inside the discussion, above, it also stands apart and on its own. The continuities between body/mind/spirit are so palpable in Africanist performance practices as to be almost tangible, literally. (For example, when a practitioner says s/he "feels the spirit," this is no mere metaphor.) What this means is that, even in a tourist performance of Vodou, practitioners are liable to truly embody the deities. It also means that, even in social dance situations, a spiritual experience may frequently occur. In fact, social dance "respites" are common occurrences in long Vodou ceremonies. Many of us may recall having entered a near-trancelike state in some social dance situation in our own Africanist-based realm of experience. And this is to be expected: the body movements, steps, postures, and motifs are the same in social and secular forms of Africanist dance; it is only through *Nommo*—the power of the word—that one type of experience is called ritual and another social. The music and dance are the same. As Daniel points out in her video, contemporary music groups like Boukman Eksperyans may make music at Vodou ceremonies and later incorporate that same music in their pop recordings.

Marathoning

Performances, festivals, holidays, celebrations, and rites, whether ritual or social, frequently involve dancing beyond natural capabilities and "normal" physical limitations of duration and energy at events that, themselves, may go on for twelve hours, two days, or even longer. To do what needs to be done takes time—not clock time, but spirit time. Again, this spirit work may just as easily occur in a social situation as in a ritual one. Thus, as Bernice Reagon points out, sometimes the way that one "finds" oneself after working a forty-hour or longer work week is, come Friday night, to take off the uniform, put on the dancing outfit, and dance until the wee hours of the morning (*Dancing* 1993). Although Reagon was referring to African-American social dance patterns, her comment is just as relevant to Caribbean performance.

Multiple Foci

In Africanist performance the circle reigns. Frequently it is manifested as a semicircle around a battery of percussionists. Even in line dances there may be a shifting circle of onlookers surrounding the performers. The circle stands in contrast to the fourth-wall, proscenium stage of Europeanist performance that emerged from the medieval Christian mass and continues today in the tradition of the concert stage. In proscenium form it is very clear who is audience and who is performer, because the two are separated by a linear arrangement: the performers are on stage; the spectators sit "in the house" and view the performance frontally. The energy and focus are targeted in one direction: toward the stage, by the spectators, and to the house, by the performers.

Where the circle rules, there is an abundance of energy, vitality, flexibility, and potential. For one, there is always the possibility that the person who is an onlooker may be drawn into the action and become a performer. In addition, since there is no proscenium stage separating audience from performers, spectators may choose where to focus their attention, and performers may choose where to locate themselves while performing. Frequently there is more than one "performance" going on simultaneously. No one person is capable of knowing/seeing all that is going on at any particular moment in time. But this is not to be mistaken for chaos (a cultural bias emanating from those who see linear structure as superior to other possible alternatives). Instead, this is a democracy of structure that is characteristic of Africanist-based performance modes.

Improvisation

This premise goes hand in hand with the circle, discussed above. When linearity is disrupted and the performer-audience divide is blurred, the force of the unforeseen gains ascendance. What this means is that, in Vodou, no dancer really dances like another. The steps may be the same for calling forth a particular deity, but each dancer performs them in her own unique way with her own special embellishments. Thus, improvisation is the name of the game, on the individual level, and it rules on the collective front as well. No one Vodou ceremony is like another, even though chants, motifs, dance steps, drumming patterns, and certain props and structures may be common in all. The improvisatory nature of Vodou is so deep that Deren claims to have never been to any two ceremonies that were alike, in spite of having attended some hundreds over a period of years.

Collective/Communal Trust

This premise serves as the check and balance for improvisation. One must have a sequestered space in order to "let it all hang out"—be it the Vodou temple, a communal courtyard, or a friend's living room on Saturday night. When the deities mount the bodies of the faithful there are arms and bodies of the community to catch them if they fall. When a dancer goes beyond the hot or the cool and performs in an "uncool" way, there is the communal voice to remind her that she has traveled beyond the fringe—drummers may cease to play, or the dance space may be emptied, with the person in question thus singled out by the collective. The community thus establishes and maintains continuity and respect for its cultural traditions, even while affirming and celebrating the power of improvisation.

Cultural Fusions/Inclusions

In anthropological jargon this principle is known as *syncretism*. What it means is that, without losing its root integrity in and adherence to an Africanist perspective, African-based cultures in the Motherland and in the diaspora have embraced the conflict of opposites that they have encountered in hostile, oppressive environments. So, for example, many Vodou ceremonies begin with the recitation of the Catholic litanies known as *actions de grace* by the *houngan* (Vodou priest). The Vodou deities, emanating from Fon and Kongo traditions of West and Central Africa, are identified with particular Catholic saints. Yet, they keep their Africanist characteristics. And the valence of water—so important in Africanist religious practice in the form of water deities and ritual immersion/cleansing in water—is easily identified with the Christian practice of baptism. Even the Christian crucifix is easily identifiable with the Africanist crossroads. So this brings us full circle from the beginning of this essay, readying us for the rich gems to follow in this anthology.

2

◇ ◇ ◇

What Is Congolese in Caribbean Dance

Nathaniel Hamilton Crowell, Jr.

Angola has been at war since 1961. First it was Africans fighting Portuguese; then it became the government, the MPLA, against the rebels, UNITA. Nonetheless, it's not because of the war that if you're in Luanda, the capital, at 4 A.M. on any morning and you're a light sleeper, you might be in trouble. Throughout the city there are numerous clubs and there are always parties. And the music as a rule is loud, very loud. Inside people dance to *soukous* or *kuduru*, or to the rage when I was last there in 1997, the *kizomba*.

Kizomba is puzzling. The music is new—*zouk*, sometimes straight from the Caribbean, sometimes from Angola—but the name (formerly spelled *quizomba*) and the steps are relatively old, harkening back to a dance cultivated a hundred years ago and probably long before. And it echoes in the traditional dances of Angola as well as in those of neighboring Congo-Brazzaville and Congo-Kinshasa. What makes it odd, though, is that the dance for kizomba is exactly like the dance done to *bachata* from the Dominican Republic; you do the same steps, at the same point in the instrumentation, with the same accents.

I think this is one reason it is hard, when you listen to Caribbean music and watch Caribbean dance, not to think there is a link between the Caribbean and the Congo—that is to say the homelands of the Bakongo peoples, Angola, the Republic of the Congo (Congo-Brazzaville), and the Democratic Republic of the Congo, the former Zaire (Congo-Kinshasa)—because so much of what is done in the Caribbean is done there too. After all, many of the rhythms of the Caribbean are straight— for example, zouk and dancehall and *compas:* there is no syncopation to the main rhythms, and the accent in a phrase always falls at the beginning of the phrase or at the beginning and right in the middle. And instrumentation based on straight rhythms is a hallmark of Congolese music. The congas or similar long drums are the key drums in several Caribbean music styles; in the Congo congas or their predecessors are the primary instruments and musicians in all parts of the region use them in a variety of music and dance styles. In Puerto Rican *bomba* and Martinican *bele linò* and *calenda ticano*, as is common in the Congo, the dancer leads the chief drummer in setting the rhythm. The isolations of the ball and heel of your foot that figure in toe heel in Jamaica and *méringue* in Haiti, touching the ground with just the ball of your foot or just the heel, are the same as those used in dances of the Congo. And winin' to Trinidad's *soca* and Jamaica's dancehall, the way that dancers mobilize their hips, quickly brings to mind the hip rolling and hip swinging that distinguish Congolese dance.

The style in which people dance several Caribbean dances also conjures up the Congo. In two of the main versions of Cuba's rumba, for example, men and women dance together in pairs. Much of the object of the rumba, *guaguancó*, is for the man to catch his partner in a compromising position, although she doesn't want him to and does all she can to avoid him. He tries to catch her with her legs open and get a leg, a hip between them, despite all her efforts to keep it from happening. She in turn keeps him dancing and keeps him attracted and interested. But, she does it on her own terms: that is to say, without letting him catch her when she doesn't want to be caught, without letting him score.

In effect, the partners challenge each other. And this type of competition is very common to Congolese dance. Even the very names of dances call up the Congo. The Congo of Haiti's Danse Congo only could come from the place Congo, just as Mayombe of Cuba's rite Palo Mayombe is the name of a region in the Democratic Republic of Congo.

The question then becomes how and why could Congolese traditions become part of Caribbean music and dance? In this article, I hope to begin to address this, to explore the process by which music and dance from the Congo would contribute to the development of the music and dance of the Caribbean.

Salsa provides a good illustration of how this could have happened. Salsa is perhaps the most widely recognized style of Puerto Rican music and dance, in part because its popularity has spread far beyond Puerto Rico and the various Puerto Rican communities in the United States. You hear salsa everywhere—Colombia, Peru, Senegal, Angola—anywhere people listen to Latin music.

The distinctive rhythms that became Puerto Rican salsa were cultivated in the 1940s and 1950s. In essence, despite a base in Cuban *son* and mambo, it is a combination of several music and dance styles. According to Dennis Clarke, "salsa is mainly derived from Cuban music, which contributed traditional Latin percussion (that is, timbales, congas, bongos), types of ensemble (*conjuntos* of trumpets and percussion, *charangas* with flute and violins, brass and sax-led big bands), clave (the basic rhythmic pattern) and numerous dance forms: son, *son montuno*, rumba, guaguancó, mambo, *chachachá*, bolero, *guajira, guaracha*. Salsa also embraces an international range of musics including Puerto Rican bomba and *plena*, Colombian *cumbia*, etc.; also fusion experiments with rock, jazz, soul" (Clarke 1989, 1033).

Salsa rhythms are layered and complex. But simplified, the basic rhythmic phrase for salsa is the following:

The main accents fall at notes 1 and 3. The time signature is 4/4, with the sixteenth notes before 1, 2, 3, and 4 serving as grace notes. To dance basic salsa you start out erect, with your feet about a foot apart and with your knees ever so slightly bent. By the time the musicians have played each of the quarter notes of the rhythmic phrase, that is 1, 2, 3, and 4, you will have finished marking out the steps that correspond to part of the phrase. In effect, you end the movements on 1, 2, 3, or 4. In the most basic pattern for the dance, you move first to the right, then to the left, touching just the ball of the foot for a moment before taking the step and swinging your hips out as you do. (Salsa footwork, however, can be complicated. Complications may be rhythmic, too. Dancers generally begin on beat one, but aficionados may start on two; many insert a hesitation, and the dancers may be dancing in syncopation to the rhythm.)

Salsa connects with some of the earliest Congolese-derived music and dance styles popular in the Americas. Again, Puerto Ricans adopted son, rumba, and a number of closely related music and dance styles. And the final product was salsa. Rumba provides an easy-to-see link to Africa.

Rumba is the name of a Cuban genre of African-derived music and dance styles. The name embraces a number of forms, principally guaguancó, *yambú*, and *columbia*. Except for the men's competition form, columbia, they are much alike, and in essence, they are variations of one set of instrumentation and one set of choreography. Guaguancó can serve as a model for the style. Again the rhythms are multiple and complexly meshed. But at its most basic, the pattern of guaguancó is:

a   1   2   3   (4)

The rhythm is straight, and the accents are at 1 and 3. The time signature for guaguancó is 4/4, and *a*, the note before 1, is a grace note. You begin the basic step of the dance with your feet facing forward a shoulder width apart, your knees slightly bent and with your arms bent so that your hands are roughly at chest height and at each note, a, 1, 2, 3, and 4, you do the corresponding step. As with salsa, the basic step involves an alternation, stepping to one side, then the other.

Key features of the choreography for men are isolation of the ball of the feet as at a and 1, and the isolations of the hips as at 1. Another major part of the choreography is the duel between the partners as described above.

When you compare salsa with guaguancó, you can see just how salsa preserves much of the rumba. Again, salsa is a straight rhythm with a 4/4 time signature and this is the case with guaguancó and rumba in general. The key phrase for salsa is just a variation of the phrase for rumba:

from

a   1   2   3   4

Effectively, Puerto Ricans used notes a and 1; they changed the grace note from an eighth note to two sixteenths and then repeated what they had made for the duration of the phrase. And the dance is similar: in both dances you basically step out to one side and then to the other. In addition, salsa maintains the isolation of the foot that you find in men's rumba, although in a simplified form: hence planting the ball of your foot for notes 1 and 3 of the rhythm. Also, salsa keeps the hip isolations of rumba; you consciously swing your hips to the left and right at 1 and 3, just as you would swing them out in rumba.

In turn, guaguancó and the other styles of rumba derive from much older Cuban social dances, dances popular a century or more ago. Researchers of Cuban music associate rumba with social dances such as *yuka* and *makuta* that were performed by enslaved people from the Congo and their descendants, and argue that rumba derives particularly from these dances. With its two lines of dancers who approach each other and retreat, yuka incorporates the rolling hips and the belly bounce (pelvic thrust) of Congo/Angola.

In the 1800s and even before, African-Americans throughout the Americas, from Brazil to Louisiana, danced similar dances. These dances had a variety of names—calenda, *chica*, *batuque*, samba—but they were variations of a common theme. Many features of the dances would carry on into dances like yuka, and from there to rumba. A description of the calenda as danced in the French West Indies at the end of the eighteenth century states:

One male and one female dancer, or an equal number of dancers of each sex push to the middle of the circle and begin to dance, remaining in pairs. This repetitive dance consists of a very simple step where, as in the "Anglaise" one alternatively extends each foot and withdraws it, tapping several times with the heel and toe. All one sees is the man spinning himself or swirling around his partner, who, herself, also spins and moves about, unless one is to count the raising and lowering of the arms of the dancers who hold their elbows close to their sides with the hands almost clenched. The woman holds both ends of a kerchief which she rocks from side to side. When one has not witnessed it himself, it is hard to believe how lively and animated it is as well as how the rigorous following of the meter gives it such grace (Moreau de St. Méry, quoted in Emery 1988, 22–23).

The isolations of the toe and heel in the dance prefigure the foot isolations of guaguancó.

A witness to a performance of the calenda in Peru in 1763, reporting in an article titled "Idea de las Congregaciones Publicas de los Negros Bozales" in *El Mercurio Peruano* of 16 June 1791, noted the following:

> [I]t is danced to the music of instruments and a song. The dancers place themselves in two lines, one of men, the other of women; the lines face each other so that each male dancer has a female partner and vice versa. The spectators make a circle around the dancers and musicians. One of the dancers leads the song, and the spectators pick up the refrain and they clap as they sing it. All of the dancers move about with their arms raised in the air, and they jump, spin, roll their hips as they continually come within two feet of their partners and then back away: they do this until the instruments or song signals them to get close to each other. At this point, the partners smack their bellies two or three times, and then they separate with jumps, and with lascivious gestures. [For the duration of the performance] they come together and smack bellies as often as the instruments or song tell them to. While they smack their bellies, they embrace, spin around two or three times, and kiss each other, all without losing the rhythm (my translation).

Here, in the rolls of the hips that the dancers perform and the belly smacks that they give each other, are the hip isolations that would become part of rumba.

As Moreau de St. Méry saw the chica in the French West Indies in the late 1700s:

> When one wants to dance the Chica, a tune, especially reserved for that type of dance, is played on crude instruments. The beat is very pronounced. For the woman, who holds the end of a kerchief or the sides of her skirt, the art of this dance consists mainly in moving the lower parts of her loins while maintaining the upper part of her body practically immobile. Should one want to enliven the Chica, a man approaches the woman while she is dancing, and throwing himself forward precipitously, he falls in with the rhythm, almost touching her, drawing back, lunging again, seeming to want to coax her to surrender to the passion which engulfs them. When the Chica

reaches its most expressive stage, there is in the gestures and in the movements of the dancers a harmony which is more easily imagined than described (Moreau de St. Méry, quoted in Emery 1988, 25)

And guaguancó would preserve this duel between the partners and later social dances this complex and passionate harmony.

Dances like the calenda derived from social music and dance styles performed in Congo/Angola. Not much is known about the rhythms of the dances, save that the musicians played drums and the *puita* or *cuica*—a membraphone that produces a deep groaning sound. As for the dance, nineteenth-century descriptions of the batuque and the quizomba of Angola give a general idea of how people danced throughout the region. Batuque and quizomba were the names of two dances performed in Angola and quite likely, as with the calenda and the chica, they were variations of the same dance. Here's a description of the batuque, which was danced in Brazil as well as in Angola:

> [I]n the land where it originated, batuque, probably derived from Portuguese, (perhaps from bater [to beat]) is the name of a type of dance, in which the Blacks, in a circle, dance zapateo, or tap dance, to rhythms marked out with handclaps and percussion instruments. In Luanda and other areas of Angola, one dancer goes in the middle, and after dancing several steps, he or she goes to give an embigada [pelvic thrust], which they call semba, to the person who he or she chooses to replace him or her: he or she then goes into the middle of the ring to dance (Ramos 1954, 128, my translation).

The tap dance of the batuque would yield the isolations of the toe and heel that became a feature of Cuban dance.

The quizomba is described in this way:

> [I]n the rural communities of Angola, people always dance the quizomba, and they dance it almost every night. No matter when you travel in the interior, after sundown you'll hear the cuica, with its monotonous groans, and the singing of the dancers. When they dance the quizomba, dancers form a ring into which a few couples go and do licentious movements and make indecorous gestures, movements and gestures in which voluptuousness competes with insolence for honors. Those who don't enter to dance provide the chorus for the music (Ramos 1940, 225, my translation).

And these "indecorous movements and gestures" are little more than hip rolling, hip swinging, hip shaking, that is, isolations of the hips. And of course, later these would figure into the chica and calenda and eventually the guaguancó, and many other Caribbean dances.

While nothing written describes challenges between partners, that doesn't mean that they didn't exist; rather, no one recorded them happening. Pursuit of a female dancer by her male partner, and her efforts to keep him interested but ineffectual, is very much a part of Congolese music and dance traditions, and it appears in some of the traditional dances of the region, such as Angola's *rebita*, as well as in contemporary dances, such as Congolese soukous.

In effect, features of the music and the dance of the Congo appeared (and appear) on both sides of the Atlantic. Dances such as the quizomba and batuque of Angola would give way to the calenda, to dances like yuka, and eventually to rumba and to salsa. There are basically two reasons for this.

First, the Portuguese arrived in Congo in 1483 and soon began exporting slaves, first to Portugal and, from the sixteenth century, to Brazil and to the colonies of other European powers, the Caribbean islands being prominent among them. If enslaved people from the Congo/Angola region were not always the slaves of choice, they did bring valuable skills and knew how to "work metal, to weave and make pottery, and to domesticate animals, including cattle" and, more importantly, they "seemed to be available in inexhaustible numbers" (Bowser 1974, 38). The slave trade from Congo/Angola continued for nearly four centuries, with other nations following the Portuguese in the trade. During its course, according to one recent historian (and others have higher estimates), three million enslaved people from the Congo/Angola region were sent to the Americas out of an estimated total of thirteen million enslaved people shipped from Africa (Thomas 1997, 805). They were an important part of the population on many Caribbean islands, still arriving in the nineteenth century and even after the slave trade ended, as indentured workers in Martinique.

Second, to the extent that they practiced their music and dance in Congo, as they attempted to create lives in the New World, they performed music and dance. And when they played, they played what they had played in Africa, and when they danced they danced the way they had danced there. Effectively, much of what we have now derives from what these millions of slaves from the Congo and elsewhere in Africa carried here with them, and what they and their descendants were able to maintain.

Some have argued that this could not be the case, that the Middle Passage and horrors of slavery stripped Africans of their cultures. So Africans would have brought little with them to the Americas, and found it nearly impossible to cultivate. A long line of scholars, however, including Herskovits, Thompson, Hurston, Dubois, and many others, have made clear that when Africans arrived here, they interpreted their experiences through the framework provided by their cultures; they gave meaning to the many new things they saw and experienced by comparing them to things they knew from home. Also, they consciously added to what they had learned already, and did so unconsciously, too. In reality, much of the African diaspora experience has been one of reinterpretation and reorientation. The Caribbean slaves from the Congo brought their music and dance with them and, to the best of their ability, they made it part of their reality. They added to them and took away, singing about distinctively American experiences and modifying the steps of their dances. From what they had had back home, dances like the calenda and yuka would develop; many years later, we had the material that would contribute to salsa.

The steps involved in the development of salsa were the same as or similar to those taken in the creation and cultivation of much of the Caribbean's music and dance, and much of the Caribbean's culture, in general. Therefore, whereas Caribbeans may look to Europeans and at times to Native Americans for some of the roots of their cultures, they must look just as much to Africans, including the numerous Congolese brought to Caribbean shores. For much of African culture—decidedly including the Congolese—is at the heart of the region's music, dance, religion, cuisine, etiquette, games, folktales—at the heart of its culture.

Editor's note: The Congo/Angola (or Kongo/Angola, as many authors prefer in referring to the region and culture of the Bakongo peoples) contribution to Caribbean music and dance is discussed by many other authors in this book. The most extensive treatment of the Congolese influence on Caribbean dance can be found in Yvonne Daniel's comprehensive chapter, "Cuban Dance: An Orchard of Caribbean Creativity." Discussing the Kongo/Angola tradition in Cuba, she calls it "the largest and deepest penetration of African tradition in Cuba." This extensive overview is also the place to go to learn about distinctively Cuban creations with a basis in Kongo tradition such as mambo and rumba.

How the late (second half of nineteenth century) entry of indentured workers from Congo/Angola influenced dance in the French Caribbean is discussed by Dominique Cyrille in her chapter on that area. Here too are interesting quotes from J. H. Weeks on Bakongo dancing in the late nineteenth century. The Congolese-derived long drums are mentioned prominently in Martha Ellen Davis's chapter on the Dominican Republic. Congolese etymology of Curaçaon terms is discussed in Gabri Christa's chapter about that island. See other chapters for mention of the Congolese component in Haitian Vodou, Puerto Rican bomba, and Jamaican dance.

Robert Farris Thompson is a noted scholar of Kongo/Angola traditions and their influence in the Americas. His chapter on mambo makes multiple Kongo connections, including the word *mambo* itself. Drawing on Thompson's work in her chapter, Molly Ahye cites a Congolese cosmogram and speculates on its possible resonances with Trinidadian limbo.

CUBA

3

◇ ◇ ◇

Cuban Dance

An Orchard of Caribbean Creativity

Yvonne Daniel

The Caribbean encounter of indigenous Americans, Europeans, and Africans has produced, to some degree, at least one similar dance/music form. On every island, people are accustomed to periodic social gatherings with highly seasoned food, potent drinks, and music and dancing. The common dance form that has been produced involves couple dancing, women and men, with lots of hip or pelvic action, whether hip circling as in the "wine" on Trinidad and Jamaica, or *méringue* in Haiti and merengue in the Dominican Republic, or hip swinging as in *mazouk* on Martinique, or rumba in Cuba. All such dances are performed to highly polyrhythmic music in which percussion drives the tone and the feeling.

It is in Cuba, however, that this rich, vibrant, and potent cultural mixture produced not simply one new dance/music form, but many forms and, in addition, many outstanding, creative dance/music artists who have affected popular music and dance formations internationally. Cuba is responsible for dance/music forms like *son*, rumba, mambo, *danzón*, and *chachachá*. Through such dances, its influence has been felt throughout the Caribbean basin, its neighboring continents, and beyond.

It has been from within Cuba that a huge "American" dance/music or music/dance tree has developed. (I use these terms, dance/music and music/dance, interchangeably and as equivalents, since they are so interdependent in the Caribbean and among the expatriate Caribbean enclaves that I study.) Cuban creation is American in the global sense (as the notion that the United States is the only "America" fades); thus, the American tree of dance and music traditions has heavy, weighty branches in Cuba. Not only does Cuba have its original Cuban creations, but it also houses multiple branches of distinct African-derived music/dance, as do few of its neighboring islands. Unlike in most other islands, large African ethnic groupings of *cabildos* (ethnic and religious associations) were permitted to congregate and preserve their customs. The distinctions among Africans were maintained and displayed in differing dances and unique music, among other practices. Thereby, Cuban dance distinctiveness is important to the Caribbean, to Latin American dance, and to the dance of the whole hemisphere.

Cuban dance/music is to the Caribbean as African-American dance/music is to U.S. American dance/music, an indelible and ever-present part of the broad, Caribbean cultural fabric (see Gottschild 1996). Cuban dance has affected Caribbean dance formation just as Cuban music has influenced Caribbean musical production, since Cuban dance emerged almost in tandem with each new Cuban musical form. The most significant difference between Cuban and non-Hispanic dance structure of the Caribbean is an amplified or embroidered foot pattern, beyond the basic alternation of walking steps. The amplified foot pattern dominates locomotion through the dance space. In many Cuban dance forms, a syncopated rhythm is created as a foot pattern instead of an even foot pattern and this is repeated, as in: "short (step), short, long—, short, short, long—" or "long—, short, short, long—, short, short" (in simplified dance traveling step instruction). The dance production of other islands is rooted in the alternation of walking steps, for example, merengue, *zouk*, *compas*, calypso, etc., that have "one, two" or "walk, walk" basic steps.

In most contemporary Caribbean and circum-Caribbean dance culture, for example, reggae, mazouk, zouk, *pachanga*, *kaseko*, *plena*, *bomba*, *bamba*, *cumbia*, salsa, etc., traces of Cuban dance exist. Ultimately, this stems from the early "settlement" of Cuba, as opposed to the "exploration" of other islands in the fifteenth and sixteenth centuries (Knight 1970, 1978; Perez 1988). Haiti showed signs of the first distinct Caribbean culture in the late eighteenth and early nineteenth centuries, but a genuine and fully "Cuban" culture formed shortly afterward in the nineteenth century. From the late fifteenth to mid-nineteenth centuries, however, Cuban dance culture percolated with tremendously varied cultural ingredients.

Because of the influence of Cuban music/dance since the nineteenth century, in the Caribbean and across the globe, I am amazed at the marginalization of Cuban dance that permeates the new, formidable collections of world dance on video. Today, video collections give us needed and easy access to dance around the world. Yet, generally, they marginalize, neglect, or omit one of the most influential Caribbean nations in the development of American forms and styles of music and dance. One reason for this may be that current political issues surrounding Cuban and U.S. interaction shape authentic dance documentation, competent and inclusive archiving of music, and the reality of Cuba's prolific output of dance/ music artistry. Another reason may be that the editors of several of the series are musicologists and they do not balance the contribution of dance.

In the video series *JVC Anthology of World Music and Dance* (1988), the two tapes on the Americas present a contribution from the Caribbean, including three examples from Cuba. This selection does not feature the range of contributions that Cuba has made to world dance, nor does it suggest Cuba's vast originality through its visual images. Furthermore, in *Music and Dance of the Americas*, produced by JVC/Smithsonian Institution in 1995, only three of the seven examples listed on the table of contents and jacket as Cuban are truly Cuban. The other four are from Haiti and Brazil, correctly identified only in the video itself. And the popular *Dancing* video series that was first presented on television by PBS in 1993 omits Cuban dance entirely.

Too often, the rich and varied world of Cuban dance has been compromised. In the 1930s and 1940s, when Hollywood, the music recording industry, and the general public confused a conga with a tango, a samba with a rumba, North African culture with sub-Saharan culture, Caribbean societies with Latin American societies, they did so out of laziness, ignorance, or bias. There is no excuse today, what with better knowledge of the world, instant technology to correct our errors swiftly, and the will to respect cultural distinctiveness. Credit is overdue for the many dances that Cuba has produced.

In an effort to reverse past omissions, I am eager to present an overview of Cuban dance. I first point out the important dance traditions or huge families of dances that are tightly related in terms of structure, instrumentation, song-style, and basic movements. There are several of these that were created in Cuba and several "foreign" traditions that have survived in Cuba for centuries. I explain how dance/music traditions combined to make Cuban dance culture, or what I have previously called the Cuban dance matrix (Daniel 1995, 26–44). In the process, I inform an interested public, balance the dance perspective on world music, and pay tribute to Cuba's contributions.

I am influenced thoroughly in this undertaking by having lived in Cuba during my original anthropological fieldwork, 1986–87, by my almost annual Cuban research trips since 1985, and by the dance/music history I received from Cuban scholars and the Cuban people, as they reported it to me. My first intent is to change the assumptions (and deductions) about Cuban dance that are distorted by encyclopedic references to world dance, which erase the site of distinct and dense traditions from reality. Then I attempt to reconcile these with the Cuban "regionalist" perspective that Cuban dance/music traditions are *the* most important in the newest New World, the twenty-first century (smiles).

Dancing Cubans

Today, despite all of the economic and political pressures that Cubans must absorb in daily life, they hold on to a sane social life, including dancing often. The sound of music playing is constant day and night, throughout large and small cities and across expanses of rural areas. I think a person would have to go high in the mountains or beyond the shore to escape music in Cuba, and then the quiet would last only for a while. Live performances, rehearsal patios, radios and televisions blast out expressions of joy, happiness, and relaxation from early in the morning to late, late evening. Occasionally, melodic laments are also heard, but often these are accompanied by sounds of stirring, romantic orchestration that cause listeners to focus away from work or conversation.

The stimulation of music in the air accumulates until it spills over into the need, the desire to dance. Whether a Cuban woman is in the middle of one of her daily rituals, mopping her floors, or whether a Cuban man is finishing a ten-hour meeting and must return home on a hot, sticky four-hour bus ride, they respond deeply to music in their environment—by dancing. It is not unusual for a Cuban to interrupt whatever is going on to raise his/her arms, perhaps close her/his eyes, and step rhythmically with accentuating hip motion to the surrounding magical sounds. S/he might even grab a partner in order to execute the dance more appropriately. Cubans love dance just as other Caribbean people do.

A big difference between the Cuban love of the dance and that of the rest of the world is that the Cuban government organizes support for dance and other artistic forms so that the arts flourish and nourish its people. Cuba is divided into large provinces, cities, towns, and, at the smallest level, districts, and each division has a vehicle for artistic expression, development, and enjoyment. The general public experiences dance (and other arts) for free as audience members in their own district community culture houses (*casas de cultura*). The public also enjoys performances in provincial and national theaters, for minimal cost (and even for free on occasion). Major directors, choreographers, conductors, cinematographers, etc., are paid to give regular performances on television, so an informed public experiences and also appreciates Cuba's artistic output. The public benefits immeasurably.

Of course, art as "tension-reliever of the masses" might be the first benefit, but in actuality, lively public criticism and educated analyses result, in the media as well as on street corners and in beauty parlors. Cuban dance, as an art form on stage or as a popular expression by amateurs in community culture houses, receives a range of commentary; dance performance practice—technique, execution, expression—is fully discussed and the performance content—social, political, or artistic—is intelligently analyzed. Cuban dance has a forum in which to grow; it is financed by the state for all to experience and enjoy.

Government support of the arts, and dance in particular, has other consequences. Not only does the public or audience benefit, but performers themselves develop as well. The Cuban government finances a rigorous dance training program that contains a philosophy, a concept, an assumption that everyone should/can/does dance. There is not simply a training program for specialists, but accessible dance training for the public (*el pueblo*), the amateur (*los aficionados*), and professional dance artists (*los profesionales*). Dancers are trained first in local courses and schools in folkloric, balletic, modern concert, *and* popular styles. The hierarchy among dance styles is muted by the serious study of all dance forms and styles. If dancers show promise and audition for the provincial dance program, they are eligible for a place in either the provincial or the national arts school. Further auditioning may result in placement in the limited slots of the national dance training division.

Upon graduation from the national arts (or less frequently, from provincial dance) programs, dance artists are eligible to audition for the six national dance companies. The national companies are: Danza Contemporánea—modern concert dance, Folklórico Nacional—traditional folkloric forms, Ballet Nacional—ballet company of Alicia Alonso, Ballet de Camagüey—ballet company of Fernando Alonso, Folklórico de Oriente—traditional folkloric forms, and Cutumba—traditional folkloric forms. Another recourse after graduation is to enter the large division of extravaganza dance. Cuban dancers in nightclubs and hotels are professionals and generally have more training than extravaganza dancers do elsewhere.

Cuban dance training requires competency in many types and styles of dance (Cashion 1989). Therefore, Cuban dancers are equipped early to begin a professional career in dance. If they succeed in national company selection, they tend to specialize in *danza* (a Cuban concert form derived mainly from twentieth-century United States), folkloric forms (antecedent forms that were brought to Cuba by differing cultures), ballet (a derived concert form from nineteenth-century Europe) or extravaganza dancing (theatrical presentations of mainly popular forms). Training is rigorous and thorough; competitive training yields exquisite technique and incredibly expressive performances. Young dance artists have models to look up to and mature professionals have challenges to face and responsibilities to maintain.

All trained Cuban professionals, including dancers, must do a kind of internship upon graduation. They give lessons throughout the provinces and teach the art form they know so well to budding professional and amateur dancers in community settings. In this way, amateurs get informed teaching, but also the casas de cultura organization provides rehearsal space and performance opportunities for amateurs. The amateur dance organization does not limit itself to individuals with love of or talent for dance, but extends to hospital workers, hotel workers, garbage collectors, school children, teachers, engineers—all sorts of associations of people who dance together regularly and who prepare community performances. In this way, the native love of dancing has a means to express itself in many ways.

In addition to professional and amateur dance, Cuba's nightclub and hotel industries provide space and time for public social dance. Neighborhood bars and small tropical taverns are sprinkled throughout Cuba and provide ordinary Cubans with a place to dance. They enjoy a jukebox with Cuban boleros or the latest Cuban rap and *timba* presentations. The youth tell me that there is a trend like "rave dancing" in the States, where Cubans congregate at changing addresses in houses, clubs, or dance halls and dance the night away. Most often, however, Cubans dance in their tiny homes with their relatives or they dance in community centers among their neighbors and friends. On birthdays, anniversaries, and other special occasions, they go to hotels and, into the dawn, dance all kinds of Latin dances (samba, *rancheros*, etc.) and U.S. fads or crazes (hip-hop, the butt, etc.), but mostly their own Cuban creations (*casino*, conga, chachachá, rumba, etc.).

Today's Cubans are well acquainted, both as performers and as audience members, with the varied roots of their dance culture. In the past, clear knowledge of all Cuban dance/music heritages was limited. Since Cubans now have opportunities to perform either as professionals or as amateurs, they can (and are quick to) critique what goes on in Cuban dance performance. Since they adore dancing for social activity and fun, they incorporate dancing into their difficult, daily life as often as possible. They draw upon their rich dance culture legacies, which are both broad and deep.

Indigenous Dance of Cuba

From time to time, Cubans acknowledge the indigenous dances of native peoples who first lived on Cuban soil. In contemporary choreographies, both professional and amateur dance companies utilize indigenous dance images as creative content in honor of ancient history and Cuban cultural legacy. Cubans give homage in a conscious manner to the eradicated roots of their dance/music and so indigenous dance performance is not entirely forgotten, despite its disappearance.

From October to December 1492 and from November 1493 to June 1494, Christopher Columbus explored Cuban waterways and lands (Perez 1995, 21–25). Like other, later *conquistadores*, he was more interested in the marketable resources he noticed and imagined than the awe that Cuban indigenous culture first summoned in his mind. He eventually disrupted native sites; the Ciboney and later, the Arawak (or Taino) communities were attacked, captured, and destroyed or dispersed by exploring exploiters. Native villages and food resources were overrun by herds of imported animals and native peoples died of malnutrition and suicide in massive numbers (Perez 1995, 14–30; Knight 1978, 3–49).

It is almost incredible, therefore, that descriptions of indigenous dance exist from the contact period (Dirección Política de las FAR 1972; Fernández de Oviedo 1851; Hernández 1980). Despite the fact that native dances do not presently exist in Cuba, we have ideas about how they might have looked and perhaps why they were performed due to these early unsuspecting dance chroniclers. The conquistadores wrote about massive group dances that were performed in their presence.

The chroniclers describe indigenous dances as group forms that demanded easy steps for hundreds, if not thousands, to perform in unison. The unison movements, however, were performed in intricate spatial configurations in order to secure good relations between the native peoples and their spiritual world. Line, circle, and zigzag patterns for both women and men or for men only or women only were examples of some of the many designs that the dancing produced. Often the performers danced in procession, holding hands or with locked elbows. The early chroniclers called these indigenous forms of Cuba *areítos,* meaning indigenous dance and song. We see similar dance performances today in areas that the native peoples of Cuba either came from or fled to at the time of conquest, and similar descriptions from related archaeological and cultural sites. In such sites (as in Jamaica, the Dominican Republic, Central and South America), the dances are called areítos or *taquis, mitotes,* or *batocos.* Descriptions of these dance forms approximate the descriptions the conquistadores gave of indigenous dance in Cuba. Cubans include this eradicated part of their dance/music as part of the mixture that results as Cuban dance/music culture.

Spanish and Haitian Dances in Cuba

European dance forms were "planted" in Cuban soil by Spaniards from southern Spain, mainly (Linares 1979, 18–31; León 1984, 95–118; Hernández 1980, 12–20; Chao Carbonero and Lamerán 1982, 23–27; Alén 1994, 5–27; Daniel 1995, 30–33, 37–38). Another significant selection was planted by French colonists, some of whom had previously settled on the neighboring island called Hispaniola (Española, Saint-Domingue, Santo Domingo), which is now divided into Haiti and the Dominican Republic. Other French colonists fled Louisiana Territory for Cuba when Napoleon sold it to the United States. These European colonists brought two distinct styles of European dance culture that contributed immeasurably to Cuban dance/music formation: Spanish *zapateo* and French *contredanse.*

The Spanish contribution came first in the form of the Spanish language and Spanish literary forms that have influenced music/dance in Cuba from the time of contact up to the present. The lyrics of songs that accompanied dancing were in Spanish and often the songs were organized in a manner that began in Spain and has forever influenced the literary production of the Caribbean and the European and South American continents. The structure of the Spanish song was based on a ten-syllable line within a ten-line stanza, called the *décima*. The décima songs, as sung poetry, accompanied rhythmic foot stamping, zapateo or *zapateado*, which was a signature of Spanish dance, particularly southern Andalucian dancing, where flamenco was forming also as a significant dance tradition. This structure evolved into a very descriptive (romantic) stanza that repeated a two-line or couplet refrain. The Spaniards also brought the guitar, the *bandurria*, *el tiple*, and *las bandolas*, string instruments that made up the sound background for early music/dance on the island. The emphasis on the Spanish language, the décima-like stanza with answering couplet verse, and zapateo continued on the island of Cuba as part of a growing matrix for what was to become Cuban, not Spanish, culture.

Additionally, from within Spanish culture (through Andalucians, Canarios, Castellanos, Asturianos, Gallegos, Catalanes, etc., an amalgam of regions and classes), a particular body orientation or stance while dancing was brought to the island. Spanish dancing characteristically utilized an elongated, uplifted upper body above the stamping or moving (running or jumping) feet. Extended arm movements that encircled the upper body in circular patterns accompanied the lifted chest. This upper body stance and the characteristic interest in rhythmic foot patterns were combined with some hip movement emphasis, which came from the Moors' invasion of Spain and the presence of North African culture *within* Spanish culture of the colonial period. As a result of the African infiltration of Spain, some Spaniards who came to Cuba were free, Spanish-speaking Africans. Later, an even stronger emphasis on the hips came to Cuba from sub-Saharan Africa, but it is important to remember this first African influence that came with the Spaniards within European culture itself.

French colonials (who had left Haiti either in anticipation or at the time of the Haitian Revolution, or who fled the U.S. dominion over former French Louisiana) brought the next European dance tradition (Alén 1987, 9–15; Knight 1970, 12, 33, 68–72). With the independence of enslaved Africans in one major island of the colonies, many frightened colonists escaped to Cuba, southern United States, or back to France. Those who came to Cuba brought a group of European dances that had also come with the Spaniards, derivations of European court dances. These colonists were French, however, and heavily influenced by the opulence of the historic French court. Instead of the Spanish emphasis on zapateo, their dance preferences approximated the look of the court forms, including dancing often on half toe (with body weight on the ball of the foot) in *los quadrilles* and *los minuetes* (quadrilles and minuets). It was hard, however, to replicate the dances exactly in a crude New World.

Of the French court imitations, the dance that prevailed more in Cuba had evolved from English country dance, which traveled to the French court and then to Haiti as contredanse. This form was a group of parlor or salon dances that relied on lines of couples who exchanged places and other partners in intricate floor patterns. Couples of women and men, often in four pairs, touched hands and fingers only occasionally as they paraded, promenaded, and crossed the dance space in rhythmic time to ensemble wind and string instruments. *Contradanza francesa*, its name in Spanish, relied on binary or two-part musical form (AA, BB), where each of two contrasting sections was repeated. The contrasts added dynamics and popularity to the dance. The first repeating sections were considered tranquil and the second two were rather lively. Even if New World conditions forced modification of the dance, the French Haitian contredanse was pivotal to Cuban creativity.

To summarize the European seeds within Cuban dance culture, I can say that Europeans from both Spain and Haiti were responsible for major elements of a new Cuban dance culture: straight back posture, touching of male and female partners, stanza with verse song-style, and interest in rhythm (seen in stamped foot patterns and some hip movement). With the demise of native dance/music on the island, European dance forms might have become the only sources of Cuban creativity. If it were not for the economic and political demands of sugar production, African cultures might not have entered the Cuban cultural mix as such indelible ingredients of Cuban dance/music or as such important branches on the tree of American dance as they are today. The African contribution would have come from only two sources, and both of these *within* strong European influence, replicating what happened to a great extent on other Caribbean islands. Until the nineteenth century—and as nowhere else in the Caribbean—Cuba was primarily a Euro-American way station for traveling Spaniards in search of gold who needed new supplies after crossing the Atlantic Ocean. For a significant time, Cuba was isolated and neglected by the Spanish Crown; white Spanish settlers with families and a few slaves dominated the terrain on cattle ranches and coffee farms, dancing in seasonal or intermittent gatherings and eking out a living.

Multiple African Dances

With the need for an increased labor force in the production and refining of sugar, Africans from the coasts of West and Central Africa were forced into slavery in staggering numbers and taken to Cuba, among other Caribbean ports. There was, however, a distinct source of African dance culture that came to Cuba from Haiti (Alén 1987; León 1984, 21–23; Daniel 1995, 37–38). A group of "African" dances came with black Haitians who accompanied white colonists as enslaved servants. Sometimes these colonists brought whole plantation populations.

Enslaved Africans and African Americans had been constructing an emerging "Haitian" culture from the sixteenth to late eighteenth centuries in Haiti. Their dances were different from the dances of enslaved Africans and African Americans of Cuba at the time. First, the dances were different because they were accompanied by the emerging Creole French language and not by Spanish. Second, these dances were different from other African forms that came to Cuba because they looked something like European courtly forms. But in contrast to the European contredanse, they were performed by African-derived people, and to drum accompaniment instead of the string and woodwind accompaniment of other court-like forms. These dances were performed by Haitian Africans in Cuba regularly and perceived as "their dances." In reality, their dance/music was a distinct mixture of colonists' European court imitations (of contredanse, quadrilles, minuets, and cotillions) and African imitations of these colonial forms. This music/dance tradition continues in Cuba today as *Tumba francesa* or French Drum—intact from the late 1700s to the present!

Other African influences in Cuba outnumbered tumba francesa by far, however. Four branches of huge and distinct African dance cultures emerged in the amalgam of perhaps hundreds of other African ethnic groups (Ortiz 1951; Chao Carbonero 1980; León 1984, 7–32; Alén 1994, 5–24; Daniel 1989, 60–97; 1995, 33–37). In Cuba, the four dance/music traditions or families are most often called (1) *Kongo* (or *Kongo-Angolan*, *Bantú*, or *Palo*), (2) *Arará*, (3) *Carabalí* (*Abakuá* or *Ñáñigo*), and the best known, (4) *Yoruba* (or *Lucumí*, *Oricha*, or *Santería*). These names for dance/music traditions of African descent are mixed geographical, ethnic, religious, and linguistic terms, but the alternate names have survived and are used interchangeably in Cuba. They are identified (along with tumba francesa) as the main stylistic traditions of African-derived dance/music in Cuba. While they have surely changed from their sources over the five centuries of African presence in Cuba, these four are considered African, and only secondarily Cuban by Cubans, since they are a result of original African creativity. Cubans and others commonly refer to them as Afro-Cuban traditions, for the Cuban influence that has shaped them since their arrival from Africa.

The differences among these four and between these and the French Haitian creolized form described above are great. Each is marked with special types of instrumentation and a general style among many differing dances within each tradition. (The descriptions of African-derived dance/music traditions that I summarize here are general. It is *very* important to keep in mind that each tradition has a wide range of differing dances. What I present is a broad, sweeping comparison in terms of dance style. What I emphasize are the differences between them that are most obvious as first visual impressions, and those distinctions that constitute the most important characteristics within a given dance tradition.)

The largest and deepest penetration of African tradition in Cuba is the Kongo tradition. While it is often considered the subtlest culture among the African cultures in Cuba, it has been one of the most pervasive in Cuba. Kongo-Angolan peoples have given Cuba and the Caribbean (in fact the hemisphere) many types of percussion instruments, including the *marímbula, catá* or *guagua*, but most importantly, conga drums—*tumba-dores*—the barrel-shaped drums we are most accustomed to in "Latin" dance/music. Also, Kongo music patterns form the base for long-lasting, indoor or outdoor, community social dance. Kongo rhythms permeate a great portion of Caribbean music/dance culture.

Kongo-Angolan dance was the means for and product of the basic social gathering not only in Cuba, but in most Caribbean and early Latin American nations. Its name, conga or *comparsa*, was used for colonial procession dances that displayed *cabildo* (ethnic or fraternal association) organization among Africans and followed Spanish Catholic practice among Europeans. The idea of processional dance was exceedingly important: each performer performed individualistically and yet, all performers were in effect creating a unified whole, a dancing line, a chain of interconnectedness, an ethnic community. The comparsas of Cuba were performed in a spectacular manner on January 6th of each year, the Day of the (Three) Kings. On this occasion in colonial times, all Africans were grouped according to origins and each cabildo or ethnic group paraded in procession for the entertainment of the season. Through cabildo organization and conga dance processions, Africans in Cuba maintained their distinct cultural identities and many African customs. I can only speculate as to why a Kongo name has been used for this celebration and for the familiar enthusiasm and vitality of international dancers when performing in a "conga line" elsewhere.

Another important contribution of Kongo-Angolan (Bantu) culture was a specific dance structure. Very often in Kongo dance, a dancing couple encircles each other and suddenly executes significant gestures. The timing of the dancers' gesture coincides with rhythmic accents from the accompanying drums. In Cuba's Kongo dance, *yuka* for example, male and female partners almost never touch, but they alternately advance toward one another and retreat, pushing both abdomens forward and then spinning away at spontaneous moments. A pelvic thrust, a navel bumping, or a throwing gesture toward the dancing partner's abdomen initiates the retreat pattern. The structure of many Kongo social dances throughout the Caribbean includes this Kongo dance pattern of couples at play. Other Kongo dance structures eliminate the pelvic thrust and focus more on rhythm, but they still concentrate on playful flirtation. Playful flirtation characterizes parts of many Kongo-Angolan traditions in the Caribbean and Latin America: in Cuba, *makuta*; in Haiti, *congo*; in Jamaica, *kumina*; in Brazil, samba; etc.

Kongo culture also gave Cuba a martial art/dance form, *juego de maní*, the peanut butter game (probably alluding to movements that were as slippery and smooth as peanut butter). This danced form is documented in the Cuban literature as late as the 1930s and 1940s, at least in terms of discussion and acknowledgment; however, the form died out in Cuba. It continued as Kongo-Angolan culture in Martinique, Trinidad, and northeastern Brazil as *ladja* or *damié*, *kalinda*, and *capoeira* respectively.

In general, Kongo-Angolan dance contains highly percussive, often sensuous, but generally nonlyrical movement material. The dancers' backs are usually bent forward, often exceedingly low, despite the fact of jumping and powerful, constant, all-body-parts movement. In fact, even though Kongo-Angolan culture is considered subtle in terms of visibility, its dance is rather dynamic, even explosive and powerful. The movements have a huge range of complexity, from the complicated independence of torso and limbs in simultaneous activity to the almost stationary movements during social events, initiated solely by the hips in gyrating circles or swings from side to side. Kongo dance/music is also associated with religious systems from Central Africa that are known as *Palo* or *Palo Monte* in Cuba; the entire division of sacred Kongo dances assists spiritual communication of believers.

The next African music/dance tradition of Cuba is Arará and originates with the peoples within and near the old Dahomey kingdom of West Africa, including the Ewe and Fon, among others. Arará has a relationship to other religious dance/music traditions in the Caribbean and Brazil called Arada, Rada, Ardra, Djedje, and/or Jeje. Like the Kongo tradition in Cuba, the Arará dance/music tradition in Cuba is also an amalgam of differing cultures but, unlike Central African Kongo, the amalgam came mainly from those that bordered the Bight of Benin in West Africa. The differing cultures coalesced into an identifiable Arará stylistic tradition in Cuba (Vinueza 1986). For example, the drums of Arará tradition are not barrel-shaped, but cylindrical or tubular and are accompanied by a metal bell or *ogan*. The drums are played with sticks instead of the hands, and drummers often stand as they play, with the drums leaning on a bench.

Arará dances are distinctive because they emphasize shoulder movements more than other elements. The shoulders are constantly rising and lowering or pushing backwards above all other complex body-part movements, no matter how or where the floor pattern directs the dancer. The body orientation can be low or high, that is, the dancer can be bent over or more upright, but the shoulders keep pulsing visually. The music of this tradition contains a dense and particularized group of rhythms. Arará is also associated with a religious system that conforms to some extent with several West African belief systems since many West Africans of different origins became known as Arará in Cuba.

The most distinctive African music/dance tradition in Cuba is called Carabalí, after its region of origin in Africa. It came with secret society members from ethnic and cultural groups (for example, Efik and Ejagham groups) along the Calabar River in parts of what are now Cameroon and Nigeria. Secret society organizations throughout the Calabar River area contain many masked dance forms, but Abakuá, as the society is known in Cuba, is the only surviving masked dance tradition in Cuba (Cabrera 1958). Enslaved Africans from this area replicated and maintained dance and drumming patterns, as well as songs and chants in the vestigial languages from the Calabar region.

The characteristic movements are smooth or sustained lunging stances that alternate with standing positions, requiring the performer to be high on the toes, pulled up tight, and contained. Intriguing, masked spirit dancers, called *Íremes*, *diablitos*, or *Ñáñigos*, perform the dance movements.

The Íremes have only eyes—no noses or mouths. Both the pointed, cone-shaped head of the mask and the tiny drum (*enkríkamo*) that invokes the spirit dancers further identify Abakuá distinctiveness. While the spirit dancers lunge to one side, they make gestures with short, handheld dance sticks or batons. Often and most characteristically, they kneel on one knee and make long sweeping gestures along the entire body or body part (leg, arm, or chest of the dancer), as if cleansing the body. These movements are preceded or followed by vibrations of the hips, the whole body, or, sometimes, simply a vibratory hand gesture. The dance movements, in sum, create an aura of "the strange," "the out-of-this-world," a nonhuman presence. There is little that has more effect than these awe-inspiring dances when a group of Íremes performs, either in genuine ceremonial performance or even in theatrical representation; the dance/music of Abakuá is incredibly beautiful and mysterious.

In addition to its distinctive dance/music tradition, Abakuá society members in Cuba are known to maintain a strong moral code. They have strict precepts of mutual aid, which secure swift and radical social action when necessary. Ideally, the male-only organizations expect members to be honorable family protectors and responsible community members. Membership is not given quickly or easily. Men must display and earn their eligibility through service to the larger community. When social injustice occurs in the larger community, it is often the wrath of secret society members that resolves situations. Abakuá members punish offenders and establish some sense of social justice. Their behavior is often severe, even brutal, and is accomplished by means of assured allegiance to the society from all members.

Although it is not generally discussed, women and families can dance portions of the secret society music/dance tradition in Cuba. A few individual women hold important ceremonial roles within the male organization. In separate formations, but without the masked spirit dancing of Íremes, women dance and sing their complementary Carabalí patterns, called *bríkamo*, lunging intermittently within the traveling rhythmic dance pattern and brushing their bodies with sweeping, cleansing gestures.

The latest Africans to arrive in massive numbers were called the Yorubas. In Cuba *Lucumí* became another identifying term for the many Yoruba groups and their language (Brandon 1993: 55–59). They came to Cuba in the nineteenth century, until the slave trade ended, from what is now southwestern Nigeria. The wars in Africa determined that the

Yorubas were the main enslaved groups of this period, although some of their subgroups had entered the Americas in smaller numbers earlier as well. Their dance/music tradition is familiar to many observers of Cuban culture and is often thought to be the only remaining African culture of Cuba because of its ornate visibility. We now understand it is one of four distinct African-derived traditions that continue in Cuba.

Yoruba dance/music is recognizable because of its impressive visual symbols and its diverse array of divinities. Divinities, called *orichas*, enter the bodies of worshippers and dance fiercely. Many specialists have focused on Yoruba culture and published on its elaborate altars, necklaces, and shrines, but have also commented on its ornate ceremonial practice (Ortiz 1951; Thompson 1974, 1983; Omari 1984; Murphy 1988; Daniel 1989; Drewal, Pemberton, and Abiodun 1989; Bólivar 1990; Mason 1992; Brandon 1993; Carnizares 1993). The dance/music comprises a continuum of varied, codified movement sequences and identifying gestures that represent differing divine personalities. The divinities dance as chartering characters of behavior that guard the many domains of human social life. In very general terms and in comparison with the other four branches of African music/dance traditions of Cuba, Yoruba movements are lyrical and often make the dancer seem to undulate vertically from the pelvic area up through the chest, shoulders, neck, and head.

The following information is condensed and taken from my book manuscript, "Articulate Movement: Sacred Performance in Vodun, Santería, and Candomble." Again, I caution the reader regarding the broad generalizations I make here, as I summarize a huge repertoire of dance. Yoruba dance/music tradition is a group of specific dances that personify the orichas, or divinities, in movement. Dance and music are performed as offerings to the divinities. The movement sequences depict portions of the lives of the divinities and visually clarify for whom the performance is created or to whom it is offered. When orichas appear as a result of the invocations and dances of worshippers, they also dance the codified gestures and signature movements that worshippers dance.

The oricha Elegba, for example, dances in red and black clothing and with a branch of a small tree; his movements are small-scaled, irregular patterns. He is perceived as a divine mischievous child or a wise secretive elder and so his body is low to the ground and his gestures shift and change quickly. He governs opportunities, chances, beginnings, and endings. His floor pattern often traces the four cardinal directions or the crossroad.

Another oricha, Ochun, dances like the divine river, sweet water flowing happily, bubbly yet carefully, over waterfalls and around embedded rocks. Her movements are sensuous, flowing, female-body-centered, like womankind in her most beautiful and alluring state, ready for social excitation and procreation. Crystal clear in direction and point of view, Ochun dances in golden yellow and giggles over the sounds of the drums.

The oricha Ogun dances in a striking pattern of diagonal slices, made with his machete. Ogun is a divine warrior, a protector whose force is equal to that within iron. His foot pattern clears a given space thrusting to both sides and constantly moving through and around. His arm gestures alternately slice, cut, or chop the forested area of his habitat or a perceived opponent. His movements are so strong that he shakes fiercely and vibrates forcefully with each accumulating gesture.

The oricha Yemaya dances and converts duple to triple rhythm so that the viewer senses the repetitive and soothing quality of the sea, divine creative source of life. Her dance traces the movements of waves and whirlpools, and of oars. Her force is as powerful as the ocean, salt water, and the sea. She is the omnipotent mother, maternal power—caring, nurturing, and incredibly protective.

Chango is another oricha, another divine warrior. He, too, is powerful and fierce, but his domain is not the forested area of Ogun. His sphere is communication, music, and intellect, and he dresses in red and white. His dance involves a characteristic kick that accompanies an arm gesture, symbolizing his extraordinary potency. With this gesture and kick, he brings the energy of lightning and thunder from the sky above into his body, his genitals, for ultimate protection of the nation or worshipping community. As he fights for survival of the group, he is the only dancing oricha who jumps (in Cuba). Many divinities use forceful runs and powerful turns, but it is Chango's dance that has jumps, tumbling, and kicks.

Oya is the female divine warrior, the oricha whose energy is that of air. She can dance with gentle charm like a breeze or with fire and force like a tornado or hurricane. She is woman all-powerful, totally shrewd and incomparably beautiful. She wears every color simultaneously, and appears at times and in places of extreme change—in the marketplace, at the end of the year, in Carnival. She fears nothing, not even death, so it is she who gallops everywhere. She guards the cemetery and communicates with the "living dead" or spirits of the ancestors. Her dance is provocative, unpredictable, and wild. She dashes and gallops across the space with the horse step, *caballo*, carrying a dark-colored horse's tail, often while screaming.

Ochosi is yet another oricha whose dance depicts a divine warrior. This warrior hunts with a bow and arrow, however, and is responsible for forest animals, and also for the distant future. His dance demonstrates the hunt, his search for a particular destination. His presence focuses long-range decisions. In his dance, he takes his arrow from the quiver, places it carefully in the bow, and calculates important dimensions of the impending shot. His body reacts in a jerking undulation from the force at the release of the arrow, the achievement of the chase, the accomplishment of all tedious and time-consuming preparation.

Obatala's dance symbolizes his position as the most powerful oricha, divine father of all the orichas and judge of humankind. He is elegant, cool, and stately. He does not move swiftly, but walks and dances bent over, in the determined and mindful manner of the eldest of elders. When he dances as a younger oricha, in his younger form, he gallops carrying a white horse's tail. His dance symbolizes a kind of peace, balance, and understanding, as do his white clothes.

Babaluaye's dance is also performed in a low position, but his is stooped, and he takes on the trembling and somewhat erratic movements of someone who is sick. Babaluaye is the divinity of smallpox and other diseases. He takes on the sickness and disease of the community as a leper or a smallpox victim and reaches for health as his dance cleanses the body, the mind, and ultimately the community.

The Yoruba dances are numerous and each has several contrasting sections, but those just described are the most characteristic. The Yoruba tradition has had influence on other African-derived traditions, for example on Arará and Kongo traditions in the nineteenth century. The Yoruba dance/music tradition gave ample movements and gestures as seeds not only for intra-African mixtures but also to European and African cultural blends.

As a group, the African traditions have commonalities among distinct movements and particular musical elements that they gave to the formation of Cuban dance/music culture. Percussion instruments (drums, shakers, and bells), and complex rhythmic interest (polyrhythms) are strong in all traditions and can be heard also in most Cuban dance/music. A singer consistently sings with an answering chorus in "call and response" pattern, with fragments or whole chants of archaic African languages. Again, this occurs among all four African branches and reappears within most Cuban creations on the tree of Cuban dance.

The dancing, while distinctive among the four families, accentuates a low-level position: that is, gently bent knees, feet firmly planted, back leaning slightly forward, in a "ready-for-anything" posture. Robert Farris Thompson (1974) has vividly described African stance as a "get-down" position, and Brenda Dixon Gottschild (1996) restates all of the important African dance elements, which dance teachers have passed on orally for six decades since Katherine Dunham, as "the blues aesthetic." In this ready position, the upper and lower torso can divide fully and move fluidly or percussively. In all of the African traditions, the hips are not constrained or obstructed and can circle in either direction, flex forward and back, or swing side to side, imitating the movements of life and symbolically representing the source of life and survival of the nation or ethnic group. Both the distinctions and the commonalities of African dance traditions have served as multiple seeds, available elements, for creation of Cuban—Afro-Cuban—dance forms.

Cuban Creations

Genuine Cuban dance/music evolved from the differing branches of the music/dance traditions previously discussed into five new families of Cuban creation. By the mid-nineteenth century, 1830s–1860s, the blendings of Spanish, French, French Haitian, Kongo, Arará, Abakuá, and Yoruba feelings, movements, instruments, and rhythms solidified, producing dances and musical forms that were neither European nor African solely, but Cuban (Alén 1994, 25–28; Daniel 1995, 38–44).

In Cuba, the original creations have been organized into broad categories, called complexes, of differing types, variations or branches on the tree of Cuban dance/music (León 1984; Alén 1987, 1994; Daniel 1995). *El son, la rumba, el danzón*, and *el punto guajiro o campesino* are the four dance/music complexes. There is one other complex, reserved for music that is not danced, *la canción cubana* or Cuban song complex. The new blended creations did not completely erase the European or African antecedents. As I have stated earlier, many of these continue alongside the new. Both newer and older dance/music traditions have incorporated change as it has occurred over time, but they have also retained distinctions that organize all dance/music traditions in Cuba. In turn, the Cuban dance/music complexes have become seeds themselves for even larger, related Caribbean dance/music complexes.

Son

Son is a major branch on the Cuban tree of dance, and also one that has become a pervasive seed for Caribbean dance/music. It has infiltrated all types of musical production, from folk, to popular, to symphonic music. It began, however, in the mountain farms and large, isolated stretches of cattle range, with a guajiro or campesino, a country farm worker, and his guitar. The Spanish farm worker sang his décima-derived refrains in a particular rhythm. Perhaps he accented his song by beating out the rhythm on the face of his guitar, imitating the zapateo of an absent stamping dancer. No one knows exactly how this music/dance tradition began, but its rhythm took a defined shape that became *son clave*. This is a syncopated rhythm that was organized to fit an ongoing series of counts, the clave, that kept all instruments and their improvisations within a repeated pattern of "one, two/ one, two, three//" or the reverse: "one, two, three/ one, two//."

This basic rhythm or son clave is intimately related to U.S. African-American basic song rhythm. In the States, it can be heard within the song "Hambone" and in the old rhythmic expression "shave and a haircut, two bits." Dr. Samuel Floyd (1998), a respected musicologist in the United States, has placed this rhythm within a family he named "Toussaint Rhythms," after the Haitian revolutionary, for their liberating and creative proliferation across the Americas. Son clave, as it is known in Cuba, is found throughout the main African-derived traditions of Cuba. It functions as the main musical structure or basic organizing rhythmic pattern. Researchers have traced it throughout the Caribbean and the North American continent in diverse musical contributions from African descendants.

Over time, the Spanish guitar accompaniment of the first *sones* expanded to include woodwind instruments, piano, and importantly, African drums, conga drums or tumbadores. The congas were played with bare hands on drum skins. Their barrel shapes with this style of playing pointed to a Central African or Kongo-Angolan legacy. As the family of varying sones developed and spread with the exploring/exploiting Spaniards and enslaved Africans to mainland Mexico and Peru and back to Spain as well, the complex, *el complejo del son*, was identified in Cuba as one of its own original creations. Son continues a separate evolution in other parts of Latin America, taking on local distinctions, emerging wherever the cultural mixture of Europeans and Africans took place. In Mexico,

Venezuela, and Colombia, and even in Puerto Rico, for example, Europeans and Africans from some of the same origins as those in Cuba mixed and lived together also. Differences in son development among the other places are great. For one thing, there was more Native American influence and more unobstructed European cultural dominance in other places in comparison to Cuba.

In the dance portion of Cuban son a viewer can see remnants of European and African cultures and their almost infinite, blended variations. The dance shows its European legacy with couples touching, not only their hands, the woman's waist, the man's shoulders, but as time goes on, both their chests and, sometimes, even their upper and lower abdomens. This is a definite European trait from the contredanse and the later *contradanza cubana*, where dancing partners were apart and facing one another or side by side with hands touching. African customs in general would dictate that the women and men dance separately and, if together, not touching. The other European element is the straight back, from the court and folk dance heritages, which opposes the African preference for bent and low back postures while dancing.

What is African in the dance is the heavy accent on the moving hips and an isolation of complementary rhythms in various body parts. An emphasis on the hips, and their articulation as they follow the rhythmic foot pattern, is constant in son and consistent throughout Cuban creations. The emphasis on moving hips permits the torso to divide its movement potential, and to create separate visual rhythms, polyrhythms between the upper and lower torso. The "divided" torso of son is African as opposed to European dance of the period, which generally used the entire torso as a stabilizer for arm and leg movement.

The nineteenth century's son was a fashionable, sensuous couple dance that satisfied the colonial desire for entertainment and provided opportunities for courtship. Because of its hip movement and closed, touching male and female dance position, it caused scandals in written accounts, but it was danced persistently and gained in popularity over time. It spawned many variants or types in each of Cuba's geographical regions. The type in western Pinos del Rio province is called *sucu-sucu*. Another, *changüi*, is popular in the easternmost Oriente province, and *guateque* is what it is often called in the central region and in parts of the east.

The son complex featured a growing list of instruments during the nineteenth and twentieth centuries. Adding to the sixteenth- to eighteenth-century sounds of guitars, clay jars that were blown, the twelve-string *tres* (smaller guitar), and a modified thumb piano or *marímbula*, it gradually accumulated string bass, maracas (hand shakers), piano, violins, flutes, and, later, its characteristic brass trumpet. Eventually, the bongo drums were highlighted, above the congas or tumbadores, because of their piercing soprano pitch and capacity for virtuoso rhythmic display. Thick musical textures resulted, with all instruments ornamenting and supporting the melodic line of the singer and the answering refrain of the *coro* or chorus.

The best-known variants of the son (particularly outside of Cuba) are the more recent descendants from the 1940s and 1950s up to the present: mambo and salsa. Mambo is a Cuban creation that emerged fully in the 1950s with a worldwide craze for many Cuban/Latin dances. Mambo in Cuba is very specific in particular gestures and sequences. The foot pattern switches son expectations (of short, short, long—) to a "touch, step" repetition that alternates from the right to the left foot. The toe of the right foot touches the floor momentarily and then the whole right foot takes a step; this pattern is repeated on the left and continues to alternate. Above, the hips (really pelvis) move forward and back with each touch, step of the feet. The hands and arms move alternately forward and back, each arm in opposition to the feet. The feeling and vision of Cuban mambo is bouncy, involving an up and down motion of the entire body and occasional shimmering shoulders. All sorts of catchy kicking patterns, quick small turns, and even little jumps are added. Mambo in Cuba developed among these strict, playful movements. As mambo traveled with Cuban musicians internationally (especially with Cuban-born Pérez Prado to Mexico and with Puerto Rican musicians to the United States), it retained the generic son foot pattern: short, short, long—; short, short, long—in contrast to its Cuban original. Instead of a bouncy quality as in original Cuban mambo, mambo outside of Cuba retained the suave and seductive sense of its earlier son heritage.

Both versions of mambo, inside and outside of Cuba, acquired partnering turns, which differentiated them from the original sones in each zone of Cuba, and demonstrates son's evolution. Instead of couples dancing in closed, touching position continuously around and across the dance floor, in mambo the woman was usually guided under the man's upheld arm in a series of smooth, intricate turns. The turns alternated with a closed dancing position that moved gracefully, rhythmically, and sensuously through the dance space. It was common in the international version to break the closed couple stance and for the couple to dance separated, but together—approximating an African stylization. At this time, both the man and woman could improvise with gestures of the arms, head, or chest, as well as rhythmically over the basic (son) foot pattern. Later in the dance, the couple rejoined and danced the basic son step to elaborate brass and percussion instrumentation, which also helped to classify mambo.

The dancing public was fascinated by Cuban mambo. It was a hit not only in Cuba, but everywhere in the 1950s. In Central Africa, where it was danced to Cuban recordings, African bands imitated it and identified with its Kongo traces, its African rhythmic origins (Malonga Casquelourd: personal communications 1987, 1994). Among partying francophone West and Central Africans, it was included in *la musique typique*. In Europe and in the States, it re-ignited ballroom dancing and joined the dance categories of ballroom dance competitions that continue internationally today.

In terms of music, the son complex reached another type of creative level with the incorporation of jazz instrumentation and the swing band sound of U.S. musicians in the 1940s and 1950s, and again in the 1970s (Roberts 1979; Figueroa 1994). Son added its Cuban percussion complexity and contagious song style to classic jazz band display in the African-American tradition of Dizzy Gillespie, Charlie Parker, Duke Ellington, Count Basie, and others, and made history as "Latin Jazz." Cuban percussionist Chano Pozo in Dizzy Gillespie's band, along with Gillespie and orchestra leader Mario Bauzá and his music director, Machito (Frank Grillo), both from Cuba, and Cuban-born arranger Chico O'Farrill were some of the most instrumental figures in the development of Latin Jazz.

Eventually, a new variant, the joyous and engaging salsa, was added to the development of son; this variant catapulted Cuban dance/music again, in the 1970s, into the international, commercial music industry. Salsa is a contemporary variant of Cuban son, but one that was developed outside of Cuba, particularly in the United States among African-Americans and most particularly among Puerto Rican musicians and dancers. The Cuban contemporary salsa dance is called *casino* and has almost endless variations. Salsa and casino are identified by their exciting fast pace, extreme virtuosity, and the almost continuous turning sequences of the dancing couple. They are both danced in son's basic foot pattern (and in the international style of mambo), but casino in Cuba has also developed into a group form, *casino de la rueda* (circle casino).

Usually, four couples dance in unison patterns within a circle. The couples alternate dancing with their own partners, with their facing partners, with corner partners, and circling until they have danced with each member of the opposite sex. A caller shouts out or signals dance patterns that may cause the partners to go into low level, that is, to bend their knees and lower their backs forward or, sometimes, to perform almost acrobatic feats while continuing the rhythmic foot pattern to the organizing clave. Planned sequences unfold, but also spontaneous calls create a series of "new steps."

The innovation that occurs constantly in Cuban dance stimulates new steps and, later, new types or categories of dances. It solidifies the types of dances by means of repeated dance sequences and repetition of distinct rhythms. More types amplify the family or tradition of dance. The multiplying of dances, in addition to the openness of Cuban culture to incorporation of musical innovations, have initiated variety within, and thereby continuity of, the son complex.

In 1998–99, there was a resurgence of older *soneros*, singers of son style, most noticeably in the recording and film titled *The Buena Vista Social Club*. These elders, *superabuelitos* of son and the sung tradition, *canción cubana*, have had sold-out performances, as well as successful recordings and movie videos, and are traveling worldwide. In Cuba today, there is an influx of professional Japanese, U.S. American, Scandinavian, and other international musicians who come to Cuba for lessons in Cuban popular and traditional dance/music and do so at the professional level. Also, the output of both Cuban and Cuban-influenced music is increasing. One of the most popular bands now in Japan is Orquesta de la luz; the group Africando is "making noise" in Senegal; and songs are being performed in Cubanized Spanish in Martinique, Spain, and France.

Thus, son illustrates the vibrant cultural interchange of Europeans and Africans in a new and constantly changing environment. It intrigues the listener as it combines European song form with African call and response singing, the Spanish language with multiple fragments of African languages. It places European horns, strings, and flutes alongside African percussive complexity and also African string melody and rhythmic interest. It alternates and combines upright, stable postures with independent, complex body-part isolation, and encourages profound feelings that result in musical and movement improvisation. Its popularity and continuity over centuries demonstrate the profound satisfaction son gives to performing artists and dancing and listening audience members.

Rumba

The next important complex that Cubans would cite is rumba. As opposed to son, rumba emerged in mainly African communities or where dark-skinned Africans and African-Americans lived, particularly near the ports in Matanzas and Havana during the early nineteenth century. Both Africans and Europeans came together, however, in urban streets, plazas, large verandas, and outdoor patios to relax after weeks of hard work, to avoid the heat and humidity of the crowded living quarters (called *solares*) of the urban poor in nineteenth- and early twentieth-century Cuba, to share news and gossip, and to sing and dance. Community members used both Spanish and African languages, the décima-derived song stanzas in African call and response patterns, and the rhythmic interest in musical polyrhythms and polyrhythmic movement: all the same ingredients that were used to create son. The results were not the same, however; rumba took on an equally vital, but different organization. In general, rumba had more pronounced emphasis on rhythm and the expectation of prolonged improvisation, in both the music and the dance patterns. The dance has become more complex and requires cultural immersion to really understand what is going on.

The structure of rumba was more constrained and yet more open than that of son. Its constraint lay in the number of instruments and dancing bodies that were involved; rumba uses only percussion instruments and human voices and generally is danced by only one performer or one couple. Its openness was in the duration of performance and the development of improvisation; rumba lasts as long as it takes for all singers to finish improvising their stanzas and as long as it takes for dancers to adequately display their expertise in the challenge of the form.

The musical timbre of rumba was limited to *claves* or sticks, drums, shakers, and human voices. The claves are two sticks that sound out the appropriate rhythmic pattern, also called clave. In rumba, the basic clave suspends, and thereby syncopates, the third sounded pulse of son clave. Instead of one, two, three/ one, two// one, two, three/ one, two// of son clave, the rumba clave shifts to: one, two——three/ one, two// one, two——three/ one, two// with an elongation of half a beat more within the total time of a pattern. Musicians would say that rumba clave and son clave have a difference of only half a beat. Performers do not always keep this ideal, but Cuban *rumberos* (true rumba performers) usually start with this precisely, and cite it as a differentiating element between the two music/dance complexes and the two claves.

Three tumbadores or congas are the main instruments that form the foundation of rumba sound. Instead of the drums being played in an African performance style, however, they are played in the European manner of high-voice dominance. Previously, the preference of African seed traditions was bass voice predominance, but in new Cuban creations, European concepts were blended into African-derived drumming practice. In rumba, the high voiced *quinto* or soprano drum takes on most of the singing and rhythmic commentary. The *tumbador* or bass and the *segundo* or mid-voiced drum anchor the rumba with repetition, even though they also improvise thick ornamentation within their own call and response patterns. The drums support the lengthening or stretching of the rumba clave in a complex display of improvisation.

Other percussion instruments are considered standard in rumba performance. There is a shaker, called *la madruga*, which is used to mark the main beat of the musical measure. The shaker functions during the song section to intensify the pace, to initiate the dancing portion of rumba, and to structurally divide rumba into its danced and nondanced sections. (The dancing doesn't begin until the instrumental and vocal sections are completed or reach a certain peak.) The other instrument is called *el catá* or *la guagua*. It is a cylindrical bamboo or wooden tube on a small platform that is played with sticks in very quick, repeated patterns. These patterns create a light but busy context and deepen the rich texture of total percussion.

Generally, the songs are sung in the same style and structural organization as in son. The difference is that there are many more phrases and fragments of African languages that punctuate the lyrics and particularly the coro or answering sections. The content of the songs is generally not as balladic, nor as romantic perhaps, as son music. Rumba lyrics often include old vendors' calls, laments, and homages to martyrs, famous rumberos, and cultural heroes, but consist mainly of sophisticated double entendres, joking and piercing commentary of a political or social nature. Just like related Caribbean music/dance (Trinidadian calypso, for example, or Curaçaon *tambu*), they form examples of sung social resistance and resilience.

The dance has developed from a basic step to several types of classified models. Basic rumba is simple, but complex. It does not take on the walking pattern I talked about at the beginning, but consistently repeats a one, two pattern. The rumba pattern in its simplest form is a step to the side with the right foot and then a return of the foot with feet together. The same pattern happens on the left and it keeps alternating. There is no way to describe all that goes on in the body as this foot pattern continues, but that is rumba's complexity. Suffice it to say, the objective of rumba dance is to augment, decorate, and ornament the rhythmic pattern or clave, in absolute time but with the utmost of syncopation, and with the use of any and every body part that can move, especially the hips.

With this basic understanding of the main step, rumba has three types: *yambú, guaguancó,* and *columbia.* The three have contrasting tempos—slow, medium, and fast, respectively—and they use varied and identifiable clave rhythms. The first two are performed by a couple *only,* one woman and one man, who are charged with executing total creativity above a relentless understanding of clave. (The clave is not always heard but is always implied.) The dancers are scrutinized by the entire community of spectators and, in that sense, take on the responsibility of representing all women or all men in the community. They dance with each other in the circle, but separated and with the lowest knee bends and the most forward back position possible. Both yambú and guaguancó involve a chase of the woman by the man. In guaguancó only, however, the man makes unexpected pelvic thrusts or random gestures from Kongo tradition, called now *el vacunao* (a pelvic thrust), toward his partner. She, in turn, hides or protects herself from being possessed or "vaccinated" by the man. The chase involves highly sensitive performers and skilled rhythmic display, descending from roots in yuka and other Kongo/Angolan forms.

The third rumba is called columbia, and historically was reserved for men. Unlike the two other forms, columbia is believed to have emerged in the rural areas of Matanzas Province, in Cardenas. There, in colonial times, the ratio of enslaved men to women was exceedingly unbalanced. As a result, the more numerous men danced together and developed a distinctive style of fast, rhythmic play in foot patterns, most often executed high on the toes and ball of the feet. The style also has remnants of the lunging and vibrating found in Abakuá or secret society traditions and has fragments of Abakuá secret society chants, among other African languages. In fact, it is within Abakuá repertoire that rumberos have identified the exact display of rumba clave, the sounded, sophisticated stretch of the identifiable half beat (Michael Spiro, from his interview in 2000 with Gollo Díaz and Jesús Alfonso).

The columbia adopted a competitive objective. First, each man who danced challenged another dancing male in a series of highly virtuosic performances. Additionally, each dancer was competing against the rhythmic skills of the soprano drum, in effect against the quinto player. Rhythmic conversations, movement dialogues, unfold in dramatic columbia performance. Men dance with knives while blindfolded, with glasses of water on their heads, and with walking canes in teeny spaces among rum bottles, to augment and dramatize their competitive advantage.

In the recent past, only a few older women have bolted across the all-men boundary of columbia and danced competitively among male dancers. Now, this is changing; more young (Cuban) women perform the intricate columbia specialized footwork. And, since they have expressed keen interest (and since Cuba takes advantage of all opportunities to obtain needed foreign currency), female international students who study dance in Cuba have been given some instruction in rumba columbia.

The most recent development of rumba complex has been in the combination of rumba instrumentation and *batá* drumming that comes from the Yoruba tradition. In this version of rumba, drummers combine two huge families of differing drums and distinct, but complementary, rhythms to form *batarumba*. Dancers have the opportunity to combine two dance traditions of multiple identifiable gestures and movement sequences with yet a third dance complex. In batarumba, dancers can perform any type of rumba, or any of the Yoruba oricha dances, and can include casino as well.

Rumba complex has developed over centuries and was considered a "museum" form by many Cubans, who thought that no one danced it anymore. It could not be erased from history, however, since its creators, mainly dark-skinned or Afro-Cubans, have never stopped dancing, drumming, and singing or commenting on their lives and their sociopolitical situation. Since the nineteenth century and despite the fact that Cubans, particularly light-skinned Cubans, stopped dancing or did not dance rumba, many dark-skinned Cubans have continued to dance rumba. Additionally, many Cuban composers and conductors, both light- and dark-skinned, have injected rumba form and passages into son-based popular dance/music as well as into symphonic music. Still, it is not as pervasive a dance/music form as son.

The Revolutionary government took advantage of rumba's connection to African roots and used rumba as a political vehicle for promoting Cuba's "new" identity as an Afro-Latin nation. In contrast to its lingering, but inaccurate, identity as a Euro-American island culture (which it was *only* before the nineteenth century), this new, more realistic identity was offered to the Cuban population and as an international image. The embarrassment over African cultures that existed in Cuba for centuries and the shame over African customs, including dances in lowered back positions with hips in motion to complicated drumming, were minimized as outmoded perspectives with the popularization of rumba performances and the knowledge of rumba history.

International dancers who love Cuban dance have routinely confused rumba and son. Rumba is, however, the "get down" signature dance of Cuba from an international perspective. It displays Cuba's roots, its *AfroCubanismo*, more so than son does. Cubans and knowledgeable international dancers and musicians respect the differences and enjoy them both immensely.

Danzón

The next distinct Cuban dance/music complex in terms of importance is danzón. It encompasses several variants that were very popular during the nineteenth century: contradanza, danza, danzón, *danzonete*, and *danzonchá*, and some authorities place chachachá in this family. These dances trace their heritage from the French contredanse and the Haitian Tumba Francesa, since they both stem from rows of women dancers facing their male dancing partners in very upright posture. The French trio of piano, violin, and flute acquired Cuban percussion and, starting with the contradanza cubana, as it was quickly named after its contredanse antecedent, produced a very light sound of elegant, rhythmic colors. Interestingly, the rhythm of contradanza cubana was first called *ritmo de tango* and, later, *ritmo de habanera* (Alén 1994, 82, 84). It was based on a rhythmic figure of five pulses (*cinquillo*) within a three-beat frame and has a relationship to the development of Cuban clave and to Toussaint Rhythm throughout the Americas. (The rhythm of cinquillo is the first part of son clave.)

The sweet sound of doubled and quadrupled strings, doubled woodwinds, and light percussion (*maracas* and *güiros*) incorporated the influence of the European waltz, and the dance placed the dancing couple shockingly close (for the period) in the romantic dance formations that developed. With the emergence of danza, couples were laced/locked together (*enlazadas*), rather than simply facing one another. A strict protocol surrounded the dance, however. For example, women placed their fingertips only on the palm of the man's hand in danza. In the next development, the danzón, dancing couples alternated between dancing and walking, for eight measures each. They danced enlazadas for eight measures and then the couple promenaded, talked with other couples, fanned, or generally rested for eight measures, before resuming the romantic, close contact. The dance structure came from Spain, walking elegantly to the music or *paseo*, but perhaps the walking pattern evolved also because of the "heat of the dance" or the heat of the tropics. Additionally, the danzón was characterized by a wonderful syncopation between the music and the dancers, permitting the dancers to accentuate the syncopation in the clave. Like both the rumba and the son before it, the danzón was vilified in written accounts, but it was also danced with great pleasure.

The distinguishing features of the entire danzón complex are that couples dance facing each other all the time and that the dances were identified with slight changes in the musical structure and in the instrumentation within the orchestra. At first, the orchestra was called *orquesta típica, orquesta típica francesa*, or *charanga francesa*. Later the term *orquesta típica* returned. *Mulato* (of both European and African ancestry) musicians were usually contracted to play for parades, balls, and small salon gatherings in the nineteenth century. The same musicians were aware of many African rhythms apart from the elite repertoire of their training and "infected" salon music with a rich rhythmic interest that became important to Cuban creation. They played the binary form that characterized the early contradanza structure, but due to their inventive compositions, another form surfaced. Miguel Failde composed the first danzón in 1879, one that had a returning theme for the reoccurring walking section, with contrasting sections in terms of melody and lead solo instrument (musically speaking, a rondo form or ABACAD etc.). The danzón constantly repeated the hip-provoking ritmo de tango or habanera. (Some Cubans teach danzón without any hip accentuation; they say the character of the dance comes from *doblar la rodilla* [to bend the knee], dancing with bent knees as if on the space of one floor tile.)

The next radical change in dance formation was chachachá. This dance was different, but its musical structure and instrumentation were very similar to the danzón, the danzonete, and the danzonchá, its related evolutions. With the chachachá, dancers marked the onomatopoeic phrase with three quick steps, followed by two slow ones. Partners danced the repeated rhythmic step in closed or open position, either holding on to one another or separated. Facing one another as all the dancers in danzón complex do, dancing partners alternate parallel dance patterns (going in the same direction) or contrasting dance patterns (going toward and away from each other). While the dance began earlier in the century, it was popularized by Enrique Jorrin's compositions in 1951. Since then, it has been danced until today throughout the Caribbean and Central and South America, and also in Caribbean niches across North America, Europe, and Africa.

Punto Guajiro or Campesino

The last Cuban music/dance complex is *punto guajiro* or *campesino*. High and low doubled and tripled guitar sounds, stanza singing with cries of "ay" and "eh," and zapateo dancing characterize Cuban country or folk music/dance. Campesino has permeated the countryside of the western-most part of Cuba and parts of the central zone. While it is rural Cuban music, its forms have penetrated the Cuban professional theatrical world as well. It originated at local festivals and celebrations, where families and neighbors congregated to socialize, as *punto libre* or free, independent, very elaborated song and dance in the west, and *punto fijo* or song set to fixed, repetitive accompaniment in parts of Cuba's central zone. The melodies have modal qualities that reference antiquity in Europe (and possibly North Africa). Texts are based in the Spanish décima tradition and often describe the landscape of the country, love, and comedic situations. The organization of instruments shifts from area to area, but includes the guitar, tres, claves, maracas, tumbadores, and güiro. In the west, they add a unique sounding, North African/Spanish string instrument, the *laúd*, and in the central provinces, they omit the laúd and add bongos.

The forms are danced with polyrhythmic, often contrapuntal, foot stamping or zapateo. The National Folkloric Ensemble replicates the dance form with dancers costumed as peasant farmers or military soldiers from a previous era, stamping out call and response rhythms with wooden sandals or *chancletas*.

Today, many of the elements of punto guajiro have been folded into son complex or compressed into canción complex, the sung tradition without dancing. At least, that is my impression, but I have not spent enough time in these regions to see if, like other small or less-known traditions, punto guajiro is still alive and kicking. In comparison to the vitality of the other four complexes of Cuban dance/music, however, it is smaller and the least formidable.

Conclusion

As I map the tree of Cuban dance/music and continue my studies in the Caribbean, I find that each island nation has its own diverse continuum or complement of dances, with minute classifications, but I also find connections and parallels to the dance/music of Cuba. Tumba francesa in Cuba has a relationship to *affranchis* in Haiti, to Big Drum Nation Dance in Carriacou, Grenada, and to *bele* in Martinique. Yoruba oricha dances parallel Haitian Vodou and Trinidadian Shango ceremonial dances. Kongo dances, like Kongo-Angolan yuka, Cuban rumba, Jamaican kumina, and Puerto Rican bomba have a relationship to each other. Cuban Arará is connected to Haitian *Rada*, as is Cuban *gagá* to Haitian *rara*. And son, kaseko, rumba, bomba, and soca's wining—all distinct branches on a Caribbean tree of dance—activate specialized dance movement such that *kaseko*, or "the body breaks" (from *casser corps*, meaning "to break the body"). When the body breaks—breaks out of its inertia, breaks out of its ordinary to its extraordinary articulation—when the body breaks into "Caribbean style," all the cobwebs are cleaned out, most stresses disappear, if only temporarily, and both the body and the person are left feeling good.

That is exactly how it feels to dance Cuban dance traditions, from Kongo, Arará, Carabalí, Yoruba, Tumba Francesa, son, rumba, danzón to punto guajiro—any one tradition, or all nine of them. Perhaps that is why I react so strongly when Cuban dance/music is marginalized. Cuban dance/music occupies a large tree of its own with roots that have spread throughout the Caribbean. It has potent cultures (Spanish, French, Haitian, Kongo-Angolan, Ewe/Fon, Efik/Ejagham, Yoruba, and Cuban) within its contemporary borders, and its music/dance traditions—four African-derived, one French Haitian, and five original Cuban creations (including the singing-only complex *canción cubana*)—have been rich sources of creative reference in the Caribbean and beyond, a true orchard of creativity.

Any definitive or general work—in print, video, or film—on Caribbean dance/music should include reference to the historical relevance and aesthetic distinctiveness of Cuba. If not out of respect for Cuba's prolific creativity, the inclusion should count for historical accuracy. There is vital, happy, creative music in Cuba and there is a whole lot of spirit-giving, spirit-restoring dance there also. Cuban dances are powerful and contagious, and affect natives and foreigners alike.

I am particularly grateful for the warm collegial environment and administrative support that I received as a scholar-in-residence, 1999–2000, from the Women's Leadership Institute of Mills College, under the direction of Dr. Edna Mitchell, as I wrote this chapter. In addition, I am forever indebted to Smith College for sabbatical time to contribute to scholarship on Caribbean cultures; in particular, President Ruth Simmons was responsible for my latest trip to the region and thereby, in part, for this reassessment of Cuban dance history.

4

◇ ◇ ◇

The Dance World of Ramiro Guerra

Solemnity, Voluptuousness, Humor, and Chance

Melinda Mousouris

Ramiro Guerra made a long, uncharted journey to self-discovery as an artist. In the mid-1940s he broke with family tradition and began serious dance studies during law school. While continuing his ballet training, he made an aesthetic leap into the modern dance movements of the United States and Europe. Although the concepts of Graham, Limon, and Laban opened new terrain, he still felt estranged from his natural way of moving. He pressed further to create a uniquely Cuban technique and aesthetic of contemporary dance.

In searching for a Cuban way, Ramiro Guerra unlocked the path for other dancers and is recognized in Cuba as the founder of Cuban modern dance. Alberto Mendez, one of the original dancers under Guerra's direction, voiced what many feel: "Although I ultimately became a ballet choreographer, it was Ramiro Guerra who showed me the potentialities of my body." Composer Juan Blanco summarized Guerra's influence in this way: "If Cuban modern dance has developed in such a short time, we owe it to Ramiro Guerra. All that we see today is the development of what he implanted. He was an authentic creator who developed new technique, new expression, original movement, and new dance stars. Thanks to him, too, Cuban music, traditional and commissioned new work, has entered fully into dance performance" (Pajares Santiesteban 1993, 25, 28, my translation).

As a result of the U.S. government's effective isolation of Cuba, Cuban modern dance is not well known in the United States. It has had a short but nevertheless tumultuous and impressive history. Prior to the Cuban Revolution in 1959, modern dance barely existed in Cuba, while European ballet traditions were heavily supported. A handful of pioneers led by Guerra were working in the area of modern dance. They wanted to build a repertory incorporating Cuba's Spanish heritage and its Afro-Cuban traditions. Cuba's Afro-Cuban traditions existed on the margins of society, where they were not accorded the official status of "culture." Initially, factions of the revolutionary government were wary of Afro-Cuban culture, which, because of its roots in Afro-Cuban religion, was perceived as competition to the political system for people's loyalty. Contemporary dance, too, had its Soviet-modeled critics, who labeled it a bourgeois, capitalist art and feared its influence in Cuba. But by 1960, seeing how passionate Cuban people were about their traditions, the government recognized the value of connecting these traditions with the state and founded two national dance companies, one folkloric and one devoted to contemporary dance.

Ramiro Guerra was appointed to create the contemporary dance company, Conjunto Nacional de Danza Contemporánea, and its repertory. Guerra continued the work he'd begun, exploring the complexity of Cuban expressions within the contemporary context that was modern dance. Because modern dance training was virtually nonexistent in Cuba, he invited dancers Elfriede Mahler and Lorna Burdsall of the United States, who were living in Havana, and Elena Noriega of Mexico to teach and dance with the Conjunto. Given a budget for twenty-four dancers, from open auditions he selected twelve black and twelve white dancers to form the new company. He recognized the different cultural heritages of his dancers and sought opportunities to use the possibilities of each one. This group began to study how the Cuban body moved, what made it different from bodies in other cultures, and what its movement could express. The result was La Técnica Cubana, which continues to produce marvelously fluent, powerful dancers who are open to improvisation. Under Guerra's direction, a cross-fertilization of the dancers' different backgrounds and capabilities occurred and the company realized an arresting common aesthetic in their productions.

However, the suspicion of contemporary dance continued to surface. In 1970, the artistic freedom of the 1960s was challenged when the ministry of culture placed control of performance companies in the hands of political officials, who knew little about art and perceived sedition in all they did not understand. Ramiro Guerra was one artist who was stripped of his directorship and not allowed to work. This period of repression lasted until 1977, when Armando Hart was appointed cultural minister. As a result of Hart's advocacy, the ministry of culture incorporated a broader understanding of art and shifted away from policing artists. During Hart's tenure Ramiro Guerra's reputation was rehabilitated.

Today he lives in an ambivalent embrace with his homeland that dates from the purge. The intersection of La Rampa and L Street is a hub of Havana life. On the southeast corner stands the Havana Libre Hotel, the former Conrad Hilton Hotel, expropriated by Castro's victorious government and used as its temporary headquarters, and still the city's business hotel of record. In a park diagonally across is a favorite meeting place, the futurist modular Coppelia ice cream shops. National television, the film institute, the foreign press office, and the university are all nearby. Two blocks north, approaching the ocean wall, Ramiro Guerra lives in semiseclusion in the tower of a once-elegant art deco apartment house built in the 1920s. Some Cubans still remember the building as the residence of Eduardo Chivas, opposition party leader to the Batista regime. A forerunner of the revolutionary movement that followed, Chivas had an exaggerated sense of honor. He shot himself on radio after a speech in which he apologized for not being able to deliver the evidence of the regime's corruption he had promised to the people.

The elevator in the apartment house shoots up to the twelfth floor like a sputnik and lurches to a stop. A winding metal staircase leads two flights further to the tower penthouse that is the sanctuary of Ramiro Guerra. His two-room living quarters exude both a strong sense of kingdom and the enclosure of exile. He lives amid artifacts of modernism from the 1930s through the 1950s intermingled with Afro-Cuban arts and crafts. Steep shelf-lined walls holding books, photo albums, and mementos are broken by a practice barre installed beneath a window and by a current-model PC on which he writes and publishes an international dance journal. The apartment has two slim balconies that open onto the Havana skyline. One looks out on the rocky coast and steely sea across which so many of his fellow artists have scattered, leaving behind the austerity wrought by the Cuban government's restrictiveness and U.S. government's punitive trade embargo. But Ramiro Guerra chose not to become an expatriate. Instead, after his ostracism, he retreated from Havana's daily life and cafe society—and never quite returned. He has no telephone. "Those people who want to find me know where to come," he told me.

In his mid-seventies and about five feet five inches, with a shock of white hair and an expressive, compassionate face, Ramiro Guerra may prize his solitude, but he is also a person who thrives on social contact. His warm, intelligent conversation kindles the atmosphere around him. He likes to relax at home in a tropical shirt and Bermuda shorts. They reveal a taut muscular physique and particularly strong legs. The strength, he said, was developed through ballet, and he retained ballet training as part of his dancers' regimen because "Cuban dancers tend to be a little lazy with their legs."

His equipoise and outward focus may have been grafted onto an essentially introspective, cerebral personality. He recalled as a child plotting in Cyrano de Bergerac manner the exploits of an older cousin, while he himself stayed inside occupied with solitary games. His attraction both to choreography and to the theater he recognizes in two of his childhood pastimes. "I adored marbles. I would watch them bounce into random patterns and then I would group them in arrangements around various pieces of furniture. I was fascinated by the designs light made passing through a stained glass parlor window."

While portraying himself as shy, he acknowledged his popularity as a social dance partner. His first idols were a neighbor, Carmela, who danced an Afro-tango in amateur shows; a Cuban dance team, Ortiz and Richard, who danced rumba and guaracha; and Astaire and Rogers on film. When he accompanied his girlfriend, a reluctant ballet pupil, to class, he instead recognized the potential for himself and summoned the courage to enroll. His first teacher was Alberto Alonso, the member of the famous ballet family who later proved to be the most interested in bringing Cuban identity into the form. Alonso now lives in the United States.

The Pro-Arte Musical Society, the theater and academy where Guerra began his studies in 1940, was the cosmopolitan cultural center of its time. Ted Shawn and Martha Graham performed there when they came to Cuba, and Guerra acknowledged that it was when he saw Ted Shawn that he began to shape an idea of a future for himself.

He was caught between his desire to be in the theater and an imperative not to dishonor his father. In 1943 he began performing in Pro-Arte productions, among them Fokine choreographies of Stravinsky's *Petrushka* and *Polish Dances*. He embarked upon a double life, finishing his law degree, but taking part in dance productions under the name of Edgar Suarez. "It so happened that I studied after law school with a friend whose two sisters followed the activities of Pro-Arte. One day, as we all sat in the parlor, they ridiculed another male they had seen taking dance class and excoriated men who danced on the stage. When I saw what lay in store for me, I decided to change my name and disguise myself. I always feared that one day I would arrive and they would say, 'I saw you on the stage,' but it never happened."

Guerra graduated law school in 1946, but soon left Cuba to work with a touring company of Ballet Russe. When he returned his vocation was no longer a secret. "My father made peace with my career," he said, "but he never surrendered his original ambition for me and continued to address me as Dr. Ramiro Guerra until he died."

Guerra related that it was through the classes of Nina Verchinina, a Russian ballerina who traveled the world with her British companion and had settled in Cuba in the early 1940s, that he began to acquire a true understanding of movement and develop as a dancer. Verchinina, he explained, belonged to a generation of "baby ballerinas" trained by Nijinska. She performed with the Ballet Russe de Monte Carlo beginning in 1933 and later with its successor the Original Ballet Russe. He evoked Verchinina as an unknown but avant-garde and far-sighted master. "She had an intense power of communication with her students. She demanded total concentration and we finished class exhausted. She didn't waste time on arm embellishments or contemplating stereotypic poses; she developed our muscles, aligned our postures, cleaned our movements. She had studied Laban's system and gave many exercises on the floor, training the torso and pelvis. She balanced a classical syllabus with the technique, equally demanding, for developing expressive freedom."

He also said that it was from Verchinina's example that he learned to teach his own dancers. "You can give a class to everyone, but you have to know each one of your dancers and take care of their physical and mental problems. Graham was more indirect. You had to learn from her."

When Verchinina joined as soloist a vassal company of the Ballet Russe from Brazil, she also brought Guerra into the company with her. The company traveled from Rio to Paris to New York, where the tour broke down. Guerra remained in New York. There he studied with Graham on scholarship, with Limón, and began to improvise with Francesca Boas, the daughter of anthropologist Franz Boas. He saw productions in which choreographers like Graham, de Mille, and Robbins utilized North American folkloric or urban material. Having arranged board by working as a brownstone building superintendent, he lived a frugal but happy bohemian existence that drew to a close when his visa expired.

Between Guerra's return to Cuba in 1948 and his appointment in 1959 as director of the dance division of the new national theater, he pursued a course of investigation and experimentation. Throughout his youth he had been accumulating knowledge of Afro-Cuban secular dances descended from the Yoruba and Congo peoples of Africa and from Afro-Cuban religious societies. In 1949 he traveled to Colombia to investigate Latin American folklore. At the same time he was examining techniques of developing character and narrative through dance, music, and stage-craft. "I now had a specific goal to which to apply the technique I had acquired in the United States, my studies, and my research," he said. "I wanted to translate my feeling of Cubanness into dance and develop themes and stories that I connected with Cuban roots."

Freelancing, he choreographed and performed in diverse theatrical contexts. In 1950 the Department of Education commissioned him to present folkloric dance programs. He mounted choreographies of Colombian, Panamanian, Venezuelan, and Mexican dances, as well as of Cuban *contradanzas* and *Abakuá* ceremonies. During these same years he worked closely with a theater group, Las Máscaras, whose founder Andre Castro, like Guerra, was influenced by Stanislavski. He choreographed dances and movement for the actors for productions of Garcia Lorca's *Yerma* and *Boda de Sangre*. In 1953 he worked with the Gran Teatro in Spain on further productions of Lorca and of Greek legend. He would return to Greek mythology later as director of the Conjunto.

By 1952 and 1953 Guerra began to create original Cuban ballets. In 1955 he created *Toque* and *Habana, 1930* for an experimental dance group formed by Alicia Alonso. "These ballet dancers knew nothing about the existence of modern dance," Guerra explained. "They were startled by the aesthetic and the music was as difficult for them as Stravinsky's 'The Rite of Spring' was when Nijinsky premiered his ballet." *Toque*, which portrayed a Santería service, ignited a scandal when Guerra incorporated a fertilization rite. The ballerinas' mothers protested to the directors. Guerra called upon Fernando Ortiz, Cuba's authority on Afro-Cuban religion, to lecture on the significance of the material. Parents satisfied, he was able to proceed and continued developing a modern dance group under Alonso's direction.

By the late 1950s Cuba was in the grip of civil war. The repression of the Batista regime escalated as it teetered on collapse. The government fell in December 1959. Not long after the revolutionary government came to power, it established a national theater. Ramiro Guerra was appointed director of its dance division. He now had the opportunity to build and direct a permanent troupe of dancers. In 1960 the dance division became two separate national companies, the Conjunto Folklórico Nacional and the Conjunto de Danza Contemporánea.

The celebration of liberation prompted patriotic art. Guerra created *Mambí*, a narrative dance celebrating the Cuban soldiers who fought for independence against Spain in 1898, a work inviting comparison with the rebel army's struggle against Batista. Two other initial works Guerra choreographed for the Contemporary Dance Company of the newly created National Theater were *The Pilgrim of Anaquillé* and *La Rebambaramba*, both from novels of Amadeo Roldán, with librettos by Alejo Carpentier. Guerra said he felt an obligation to premiere these works, but he sought liberty to revise several situations on which the stories turned whose romanticizing he found outdated. Carpentier agreed. "In these two works," Guerra related, "the primary tasks I set for myself were developing character and conflict. I think I succeeded in establishing a clear exposition and strong communication with the audience. However, I was still tied too strictly both to narrative and to music. In *Suite Yoruba* I achieved a balance between narrative and dance texture."

Suite Yoruba was a sensation when it premiered in Havana in l960 and continues to stand as a landmark dance. It was adapted for film in l962. The work, very simply, is a quartet of dances to orishas (*orichas* or divinities) in the Yoruba pantheon: Ochun, Chango, Yemaya, and Ogun. *Suite Yoruba* was performed to the authentic *batá* drum music and chant belonging to these orisha's ceremonies. However, Guerra was able to maintain the intensity of traditional dance at the same time as he expanded the dance movement and incorporated a mythological habitat. The late Elfriede Mahler, who danced with the company at this time, interpreted the work's impact: "It wasn't that Ramiro was the only one to synthesize modern and Afro-Cuban religious traditions, but that everyone felt that he did it right. You couldn't feel where the traditional left off and the contemporary began."

The dance opens with an arresting Afro-Cuban syncretism. The religiously transfixed face of a dancer appears in the oval cutout of a haloed, decorated painting of a Caribbean-represented Virgin Mary. She steps through it as Yemaya to dance with her attendants. In the original version, a curtain separated the dances. But in his filmed revision, Guerra eliminated the curtain and created thematic interludes linking the orishas. The movements of a mimetic rumba between Yemaya and Chango work narratively to recall that Yemaya is Chango's mother. From the duet Chango emerges with his warrior's personality. When first performed, the audience recognized dancers on all fours appearing with Chango as his dogs, never before depicted on stage. Ochun appears dancing over swirling river gods, Ogun, with dancers bearing the branches of his forests. Each group recedes toward the background as the focus shifts.

The dance builds to a climactic confrontation between Chango wielding his ax and Ogun his machete that seems to shake the forest to its foundation. Guerra utilizes musical stops and rhythm changes, ever tightening engagements, forceful ruptures, and leaping reentry into the fray. In the film version he closes in on the ferocity in the warriors' faces. He incorporates tumbling. The warriors somersault over each other, the raffia skirt of Chango flying like the feathers of two cocks devouring each other. Finally Ogun, the recognition of crushing defeat projected through his eyes, flees into the darkness.

Guerra prepared his dancers for their roles through the exercises of method acting, requiring that they integrate the technique with their own personalities. Some of his dancers practiced Santería and brought this added spirituality to their dance. Guerra stated that he found Eduardo Rivero incomparable as Ogun, but that he generally rotated the other roles in this and his other ballets. He did so, he said, to capitalize on varied personal qualities as suited to stage, television, or film, but also to keep the dancers fresh and always working.

Guerra had been developing in his technique classes the seamless movement of his company evident in *Suite Yoruba*. His appointment as director of the dance department of the National Theater had come with a mandate to develop a Cuban technique of contemporary dance as well as a company and repertory. The raw ingredients were: the theoretical base of the German school that grounds dance in the movements of daily life and establishes the dancer as choreographer of his/her own body; its direct expression in the embedded quality of dance, song, and instrumental music in Afro-Cuban life; the modern dance techniques of North America; and the discovery of isolations that perfected Afro-Cuban movements. Teachers of folkloric and modern dance worked in concert and from these ingredients an organic technique emerged.

Guerra dated his attainment of a language of dance through which movement possibilities perpetuated themselves to a period of close collaboration with Mexican choreographer Elena Noriega. Noriega had developed modern dance in Mexico and was embarked upon a search parallel to his own. "Before Elena," Guerra said, "I was like a horse with blinders. But with Elena, I could now analyze at the same time as create. I was able to focus on a multiplicity of possibilities and not surrender to the first solution."

Noriega taught technique classes to the Conjunto de Danza Contemporánea that brought Guerra closer to the core of Cuban movement:

> When I worked with Graham, I thought I was deficient at first. But then I realized that Cubans have something different in our bodies. We are not angular and set. The Cuban feeling is anarchic, emotional, improvisational—as in life. Perhaps we are also more open to discover physical possibilities and more adaptable to dynamic changes. The torso undulates and is in tension with the pelvis. The ground is different too. We let go; the emphasis is down, down, down.
>
> Working with Elena's experiments spurred me to work guided by my own personal experience. In creating technique I gave special treatment to oppositions that I consider to be the spiritual base and way of dancing of Cuban people.

The technique sequences he developed became the building material of one of his most eloquent dances, *Chacona*. *Chacona* also announced his entry into a period of purely abstract dance.

The movement of the preclassical *sarabanda* and *Chacona* and the history of their migrations had long fascinated Guerra. These dances, he explained, were first brought from the Americas by Spanish sailors to Seville, where they were assimilated in the style of other dances of seduction. During the Inquisition they were outlawed for their eroticism and dancing them could be punishable by imprisonment. These dances resurfaced, however, in the Spanish court, formal and de-eroticized. They crossed the ocean once more to the Spanish colonies, where the Afro-Caribbean slaves assimilated them by adding hip and torso movement and rhythmic complexity.

Chacona crystallizes this union of formalized European dance with the African body: undulating torso and rotating hips, restrained within a grave, disciplined body frame. Conjunto designer Eduardo Arrocha created Baroque-inspired black and white costumes with stiff high collars and puffed sleeves, contrasting with flowing capes or trains that enter into the movement. The dance, for three women and two men, shifts between duet, trio, and ensemble sections. *Chacona* has been performed most effec-

Fig. 5. From *Chacona*. Choreography by Ramiro Guerra. Used by permission of Ramiro Guerra, Havana.

tively in the Plaza de la Catedral in old Havana, where it has made full use of shadow and light, arcades and archways. Working further with oppositions, sections of it are danced in 4/4, but accompanied by Bach's "Chaconne" in 3/4 time.

Guerra stated that the fusion of styles from a multiplicity of sources—archaic, modern, African, Iberian—into his own movement brought him the freedom to open his narratives and greater freedom in music, to move with it and to move against it. He created two tragic love sagas, *Medea y los Negreros* and *Orfeo Antillano*. He had worked with the tragic fates and character of Greek heroes in his early days in theater and now wanted to narrate the dramas in experimental forms. In *Medea*, he divided the role of the heroine into parts to be played by three dancers, as mother, lover, and avenger.

In *Orfeo* he transposed the story to the Caribbean. Orfeo, a drummer, sets out in search of Euridice (a temptress in Guerra's version, not an innocent) through Santería, enlisting the aid of his orishas, who lead him to the kingdom of Ojá (death). But the Euridice with whom he is reunited is now an evil spirit. When he lifts the red fishnet cloaking her, he finds the skull of death, who tries to kill him. The final act returns Orfeo to a carnival that appears to be the same as in the opening section, but is the mad theater of his own mind. Spirits smother him. His lifeless body is returned to his spurned bride. Guerra set the hour-long work on a black stage to sever its unfolding from everyday reality. Its score combined live carnival music with electronic music, recorded natural sounds and voices, narration, and distorted speed changes.

The Conjunto under Guerra's direction performed works by other choreographers such as company soloists Geraldo Lastro and Eduardo Rivero; Elena Noriega, whose contemporary dance was based in Mexican folklore; Elfriede Mahler, who created works around political events; and Lorna Burdsall, who during this period mounted works of American choreographers and created new work with contemporary social content. Initially, the Conjunto de Danza Contemporánea had no previous experience working together, little repertory, and faced the further obstacle that modern dance had neither the prestige of ballet nor the following of popular entertainment. Within two years their performances acquired a chemistry that communicated very immediately with their Cuban audience. They contained themes and characteristics people could recognize, rich movement and visual art.

The Conjunto also introduced Cuban modern dance to enthusiastic audiences in Western Europe, the Eastern bloc, and China. Their tours, however, were fraught with problems that ranged from travel sickness and unreliable Soviet transports to political tensions and defections.

The 1970s ushered in a third, and what Guerra describes as an ultimate stage of development. "In this stage," he explained, "I was looking for new ways of moving. I wanted to make use of every space and surface. I wanted to exploit the outdoors. When I first saw Peking opera in 1960, which combined the theater and circus, all the ideas I had germinating came to life. They combined song, dance, narrative, acrobatics, and sometimes talk. I loved the music and the costumes."

His attention shifted to the spectrum of humor. "I became interested in developing metaphor, irony, satire, burlesque. I became more aggressive." His kinship with artists working in the atmosphere of social upheaval in the United States and Europe is apparent in this and in the further quest for openness. "I wanted to open my work to chance, freedom, and creativity."

Guerra developed his ability to satirize within the context of his experimental aims, which included leaving space for dancers to improvise and for alternative endings. In *Impromptu Galante* he satirizes machismo and the feminine mystique, inflected with peculiarly Cuban cultural habits. Whereas the tone of *Impromptu Galante* is light, Guerra described his last work for the Conjunto de Danza Contemporánea, *El Décalogo del Apocalipsis* (The Ten Commandments of the Apocalypse), as "evoking a tragicomic nightmare."

Décalogo was Ramiro Guerra's magnum opus, in which he endeavored to push the capacities of the dancers and the audience to their limits. The two-hour work with no intermission was set in the exterior facades of the National Theater, a modern complex housing two auditoriums, with multiple focal points, sculpture gardens, catwalks, and exposed stairways. The theater faces the sacrosanct Plaza de la Revolución, used by the government to address mass assemblies and behind which Cuba's most important government buildings are located. The National Theater was traditionally home to contemporary dance and Guerra acknowledged in hindsight that he did not take into account other possible implications when he chose the location for his iconoclastic work. The performance required the audience to move to twelve different sites in the vicinity, through construction work and the streets of a reputedly rough neighborhood on the other side of the theater known as La Timba.

With respect to movement, Guerra's aim was to create dance movement inspired by the architecture, close to the forms of the building, or suggested by contact with it. He wanted the dancers to explore moving on all the building surfaces, using varied body parts and centers of gravity, capitalizing on the elements of danger, disequilibrium, and recovery to create unusual images and rarely observed body action. The score is a multilayered collage that includes electronic sounds and an eclectic range of acoustic music. Some sequences incorporate live music, sounds and rhythms enunciated by the dancers, and text sung by them. Guerra described the production as partaking of the psychedelic aesthetic of the 1960s, into which archaic, Christian, and Afro-Cuban elements are incorporated. While the reference to the psychedelic art of the times is apparent, in his theatrical design and in the costuming by Eduardo Arrocha the spirit of Cuban carnivalesque pageantry is also unmistakable.

The subject matter evoked in *Décalogo* is the convulsive social change of the 1960s: the collision and confrontation of classes, interest groups, nations; the redistribution of power; the celebration of moral experimentation and the lifting of taboos in pursuit of hedonism or of new values. "A world howling, moving, changing, and exploding, eradicating identities to create new directions," Guerra wrote (Guerra 1999, 150). Guerra created

Fig. 6. From *El Décalogo del Apocalipsis*. Choreography by Ramiro Guerra. Used by permission of Ramiro Guerra, Havana.

the furious activity of a world gone mad, with his dancers climbing up walls like spiders, falling, leaping, or tumbling down from balconies and ledges like fallen angels, running through the streets, tangling in construction, bathing in fountains, dropping to the asphalt to stare at the stars.

Within this texture, ten vignettes, each an inversion or commentary on one of the Ten Commandments, are performed in various enclaves of the theater and vicinity. Four dancers identified as sibyls lead the spectators from one site to the next as through Dante's Circles of Hell or the Steppenwolf's Magic Theater.

The Ten Commandments are framed by a prologue and epilogue. The prologue, "Kyrie," is conceived to work minimally like a happening to blur the transition from ordinary life to theater. Ten dimly lit seated dancers move up a stairway intoning a Gregorian chant. The ceremonial uniformity is broken when jazz instruments using the same theme overtake the chants. The dancers' movements open to become increasingly anarchic, some dancers curling themselves around banisters as the group rises to the top of the stairway to recede from sight.

"Reign of the Sky," the epilogue, is set on the ledge that is the high point of the building—ten stories high. A dancer dressed as a cosmonaut appears lit by artificial fire. By a rope ladder leading up the side of the building, the celebrants of violence climb to join the cosmonaut.

The vignettes portray inversions of the Ten Commandments. Some, such as the inversion of the commandment against murder as a crucifixion in which a lynched Negro is carried on a cross to Golgotha, were noncontroversial in Cuba. Others, involving sexual behavior, triggered establishment indignation. In "The Foolish Virgins," Guerra depicted prostitution for luxuries. In "The Song of Songs" he suggested heterosexual orgy, homosexual abduction, and quasi-tribal phallic worship. The sequences are performed as an ironic counterpoint to biblical poems or as parodies, but each ends with a refrain from a poem of isolation by Jorge Zalamea that speaks of wandering and seeking what one doesn't find. In summing up his intentions, Guerra stated that he wished to conjure up a pre-reflective world, not to make moral judgments, but that he felt that burlesque and irony were embedded in the human activity shown, which the audience could reflect upon in retrospect.

Guerra and the Conjunto worked on *Décalogo* for a year and rehearsed on site before its anticipated performance in April 1971. Residents of La Timba, Guerra related, were among his most attentive observers, offering advice on viewing and staging vantage points. The National Cultural Council posted billboards inviting the public to attend the premiere. But two weeks before it was scheduled, the production was canceled on the basis of reports from its critics. Guerra was never to know how his work would have been received in its entirety. While he had tested the work's demands on his dancers, his questions about its demands on the audience would remain unanswered.

After the premiere of *Décalogo* was canceled, Guerra was removed from the Conjunto de Danza Contemporánea for unspecified political reasons. The company continued under other directorship, but the dances he choreographed were dropped. By the time he was permitted to work again, the dancers he had trained had retired or left for other countries. Guerra declined to implicate high government officials in the decision and held responsible the ministry of culture of that era, which, he explained, had been put in the hands of the military. "These men mistrusted everything that was new. They were weekend directors. They managed the performing arts companies for a while, sometimes removing valuables, and then moved on to other positions in the bureaucracy. I was kept from working for seven years, but my salary was not suspended, as happened to others."

Guerra seems not to have foreseen the response his work drew. Following his dismissal, his avant-garde output abruptly ceased. "I studied, wrote, and did what I had no time to do before." Apart from short trips to Colombia where he continued to research Latin American folklore, most of his physical and mental activity took place in his apartment. While he himself was prevented from working, he continued to follow the work of such choreographers as Meredith Monk, Trisha Brown, and Pina Bausch through videos sent to him and wrote about their work in essays on postmodernism. In 1977 Armando Hart was appointed cultural minister and made it his mission to improve relations between the government and the arts.

Eventually the government came around to a recognition of what Guerra had contributed. In 1988 an apology to Ramiro Guerra appeared in *Granma*, the official state newspaper. In speaking of the dismissal of "the acclaimed and then later maligned Maestro Ramiro Guerra," the author said, "In this arbitrary fashion, the intelligent, serious development of modern dance in Cuba was cut off. As a result the opportunity for it to mature harmoniously in far less time was wasted" (Rosa Elvira Peláez, *Granma*, 8/16/88, quoted in Pajares Santiesteban 1993).

Guerra, while he accepted the apology, did not attempt to resume his former life. "The company we had built had been destroyed and I did not want to start over," he explained. Instead he applied himself to folkloric research and presentation, concentrating first on the folklore of Oriente province. He mounted *Tríptico Oriental*, a panorama of traditions of the Haitian-influenced, eastern region of Cuba, including *gagá*, *carabalí*, *tumba francesa*, and carnival *chancleta* (clog dance). He created smaller programs devoted to a specific focus, such as a religious purpose, instrumental music, or an urban secular tradition. In the city of Trinidad he made a similarly comprehensive investigation of the folklore of Las Villas province and staged *Trinitarias*, a spectacular that lasted through the night.

In 1989 he published *La Teatralización del Folklore*, his theoretical base for preserving and presenting folklore. In it he asserts that while traditions cannot be resurrected with full knowledge because time erases meanings and origins, the goal of preserving folklore must be authenticity. Unlike the integration of folklore with contemporary dance in which creative liberty can be utilized, perpetuating and presenting authentic folklore requires the greatest possible precision, not blurring the boundaries of each tradition. He maintains that liberty can be taken with the staging, to avoid monotony, and with costume design, to enhance traditional dress for the theater.

Guerra returned to his old milieu in 1990 to create a television work to celebrate the Conjunto de Danza Contemporánea's thirtieth anniversary. This work, *Memoria Fragmentada*, is a biography in which the company's collective experience is reduced to fragments shown on stage and film. "It was my intention," Guerra said, "to rework, superimpose, and rearrange, as memory itself is prone to forgetting and reordering the past." Part of his audience remembered the repertory, and his challenge was to resurrect it in a new perspective with an element of surprise. He returned to his techniques of open theater.

Dancers from *Suite Yoruba*, *Medea*, and *Orfeo* appear in the theater lobby and disperse. They appear next on stage and, through an atmosphere of smoke and indistinct speech, a voice invites the audience to revisit the past in a mood of humor and burlesque. The dancers step in and out of character, moving by association between excerpts from their roles to autobiographical life situations. In a sequence near the end evoking the company's struggle against outside control, he evokes bureaucrats as invalids encircling the company in wheelchairs and as opportunists striding in their midst on stilts, carrying their suitcases, ready to leave the country. To recreate the period of tension of *Décalogo*, he had the dancers run in flight as though responding to an offstage fire or accident, and had an alarm sound, dislodging the audience for a long moment from its comfortable role as spectator.

When asked whether he had feared the consequences of pushing the government too far, Guerra replied, "They have to have Ramiro to fight with." More seriously he added, "I speak out against what I believe is wrong and the government has shown me respect." As the century drew to a close, the government took a more visible step to honor Ramiro Guerra. In December 1999, it reissued his book of essays, *Coordenadas Danzarias*, and awarded him the National Dance Prize.

While he says he has no need to work further, mentally he persists in entertaining choreographic ideas. It would appear that Ramiro Guerra's years as an artist are not over. While there was no escaping the consequences of the purge, the gratification he exudes when speaking of his years with the Conjunto de Danza Contemporánea is stronger. "I may have had my own problems," he said, "but my early years with the Conjunto were the best in my life. I was able to realize my personality in my work, with my people, in my country."

5

◇ ◇ ◇

The Técnica Cubana

Suki John

The *técnica cubana*, or the Cuban modern dance technique, is a unique mix of dance traditions, a powerful hybrid that is more than the sum of its parts. After the Cuban Revolution of 1959, Ramiro Guerra was appointed director of the Department of Modern Dance within the Teatro Nacional in Havana, with the goal of creating an indigenous Cuban modern dance form. Guerra had the foresight to bring together an eclectic group of amateur and professional ballet, modern, folkloric, and nightclub dancers. They culled their resources and training, and began to synthesize previously diverse dance forms into a truly Cuban *asíaco* or stew. The result is a technique that is tremendously athletic and expressive, a reflection of the African, Spanish, and Caribbean roots of Cuban culture within the theatrical tradition of modern dance.

The técnica cubana has played a major role in the development of this writer, who is also a dancer and choreographer. At the age of fourteen, in the mid-1970s, I went to Cuba with the intention of studying at the Ballet Nacional de Cuba, but instead ended up with my older brother in a Cuban brigade, building a school in the countryside. Apparently my father, a scientist who collaborates with a Cuban laboratory, had not sorted out the details. I was taken under the wings of several young Cuban women who taught me a little Spanish and a few salsa steps. At night, the men would play drums, *güiros*, and spoons, pounding out the rich syncopations of the orisha songs of Santería.

In 1988 I returned to Cuba for a two-week stay. A modern dancer by this point, I spent much of my time in the studios of Danza Contemporánea de Cuba. The company that Guerra had founded decades earlier had become a major artistic force in Cuba and abroad. The técnica cubana combined the strength of the Cuban ballet tradition, elements of the Graham and Cunningham techniques, and the sensuous fluidity and rhythmic complexity of Afro-Cuban folklore. I was amazed by the absolute physical mastery enjoyed by dancers trained in the técnica cubana. A typical combination would involve multiple turns (with and without contractions), dives to the floor, leaps to the rafters, and syncopated isolations of the ribs, hips, and head. Flexed sickled feet, raised hips, twisting torsos, and rolling heads identified the técnica cubana as distinct, even as it incorporated the extended lines and sailing turns of classical ballet and traditional modern. Guerra and his collaborators—among them Elfriede Mahler, Lorna Burdsall, Elena Noriega, and Manuel Hirán—had successfully created a truly Cuban technique unlike any dance form that I have seen elsewhere.

Most professional dancers in Cuba pass through a ten-year program in La ENA—the Escuela Nacional de Arte (National School of Art). La técnica cubana is taught alongside classical ballet and Cuban folklore. Dancers study all three dance forms, along with academics, acting, and music. Ballet dancers focus on ballet, just as modern and folkloric dancers begin to specialize as they mature. As in the Soviet system, some dancers are channeled into teaching while others are encouraged to perform. Upon graduation, dancers are chosen for the Ballet Nacional, Danza, the Conjunto Folklórico, or for one of the provincial companies or schools. Companies outside Havana include Danza Libre, founded by Elfriede Mahler in Guantánamo, and Teatro de la Danza del Caribe in Santiago de Cuba, directed by Eduardo Rivero, choreographer of *Súlkari*, a signature piece of Danza Contemporánea.

In 1991, I attended the Kuopio dance festival in Finland. The major draw for me had been the festival's inclusion of the Conjunto Folklórico and a small Cuban modern company then known as Gestos Transitorios, led by a soloist from Danza, Narciso Medina. Medina's arresting *Metamorfosis* had won the Prix de Lausanne in 1986. This particular piece, for three virtuosic male dancers, combined the raw athleticism of the técnica cubana with a sophisticated understanding of tanztheater. In the context of a European festival, the particular attributes of the Cuban technique and aesthetic—the Yoruba influence, the sinuousness of the spine, the ricochet moves to and from the floor, and the pervasively virile physicality—stood out in relief. After a vibrant performance that put the técnica cubana to wide choreographic use, I accosted the dancers at the stage door and was welcomed into their midst.

Fig. 7. *Metamorfosis*. Choreography by Narciso Medina. Photograph: David Garten. Used by permission of David Garten, Waitsfield, Vermont.

Throughout the 1990s I was lucky enough to choreograph for Narciso Medina's company on several occasions, and for Danza and the Ballet Nacional as well. A brilliant choreographer, Medina is also a pied piper of sorts. Dancers from all over the world study not only at Danza Contemporánea's semiannual workshops, Cubadanza, but also in the small academy Medina has built, the first independent dance school formed in Cuba since the revolution.

While in Cuba, I studied the técnica cubana, taking private or company class on a daily basis with the master teacher of Danza, Manolo Vásquez. Company class at Danza often begins with a freestanding center barre. The dancers start in parallel with the feet touching, knees pulled tightly together, hands clasped behind the back, and the head down. The first exercises open from contraction in parallel into first position, with or without an arch upwards. From first position, the heels pull back into a parallel second position, at which point upper body movement or hamstring stretches may be added. Often there is a variation that includes sitting into one hip and extending the torso and arms in the opposite direction. The arms have a soft, bird-like quality, as opposed to the rigid lifted-elbow mold required in ballet class. Relevés, head rolls, parallel tendues and ripples of the spine can all be inserted in parallel second. From here the exercise may return to the beginning and repeat on the other side. After working in parallel second, the legs are turned out to second position. A long sequence early in the warm-up might include arabesques, hip rolls, changes of weight, percussive drops to plié, and folkloric twists of the head and neck.

Many exercises are repeated in different rhythms, emphasizing contrasting dynamics. One of the identifying factors of a class in the técnica cubana is the use of a musical ensemble. Several drummers, a singer, and a flute or guitar player always accompany company classes at Danza Contemporánea. The music ranges from country melodies to the orisha songs of Santería. This attention to musical detail marries the dancing to its Cuban roots. It transforms the movement both rhythmically and kinesthetically. Take, for example, one staple in the center warm-up, a series called "Merce," after Merce Cunningham. Beginning in parallel, the legs turn out suddenly to first position and the head and palms open upward. A high contraction rolls the spine and head inwards, turning the arms over in their sockets. Then the spine is unfurled into a flatback in plié. From here a deep contraction in plié can lead to an extension of the leg in any direction, a low turn or a change of direction. The Merce is used as an introduction to other exercises, including at times the rapid dégagés à la second from first position associated with the Graham technique. When practiced to the rich syncopations of Cuban music, as opposed to a single piano or drumbeat, the exercises of both Graham and Cunningham take on a sensuous richness that invites embellishment in the head, pelvis and torso. While the work is clean and specific, the variations in dynamic and speed afforded by the rhythmic complexity of the music affect the feeling of the movement profoundly.

The warm-up follows a logical sequence incorporating pliés, tendues, dégagés, rond de jambes, and battements, but the exercises themselves are often long and filled with previously unmatched elements. These include: hip and head rolls; drops of the elbow; *ganchos* (an extended turned-in leg, hip lifted, with the foot flexed and sickled, usually with the torso in a spiralled contraction); ripples through the spine from base to head; shifts to the knee and back to standing; falls to the knee or floor; turns in spiral, contraction, on the bottom, or on the knee. A floor sequence may be included in the warm-up, often in the midst of an exercise that begins and ends standing. The floor work has a distinct Graham base, but includes more rippling flexibility in the spine and folkloric pecking and twisting motions of the head. It is not unusual to go from a Graham fourth position seated on the floor to a shoulder stand to a standing relevé balance.

Traveling work begins with turns and extensions, with the floor pattern often doubling back on itself in space. If the musicians play a familiar folk tune or orisha song, the dancers often join in singing as they wait to dance. Turns in classical attitude are frequently practiced with a high spiral of the upper body, while piqué turns are usually done in parallel with a contraction into the passé hip. If piqué turns are practiced turned out, it's not unusual for the dancer to go in and out of contraction in the course of one revolution on a plié in relevé.

Oftentimes the men will elaborate on the choreographed combinations, taking a standing turn to the floor, balancing on the tops of their feet, diving to their hands and sinking slowly to the floor, ricocheting back to standing, or springing into a huge second position split jump before walking off the floor. Cuban male dancers nurture their exceptional virtuosity with good-natured competition in class. While there is not a lot of attention paid to petit allegro, big jumps are a highlight of the technique. Leaps, Graham buffalo jumps, tours en l'air, barrel turns, and all sorts of air turns without names are followed by spectacular improvisation by the more pyrotechnical dancers at the end of class.

Company class in the técnica cubana usually ends with a low traveling step that is a variation on several orisha images, including that of the freshwater goddess Oshún observing herself in the mirror. These low stamping walks are followed by a rapid shaking of the rib cage as the dancer takes tiny steps in plié, vibrating from the tail bone through to the top of the head.

The técnica cubana includes a full set of floor exercises and a complete standing warm-up holding onto the barre. Both of these are used as the ballet masters see fit. Manolo Vásquez, who has trained a generation of Cuba's finest dancers, invokes martial arts and yoga in his teaching. Other teachers refer more specifically to Afro-Cuban sources, to Graham, or Cunningham. Some focus on footwork, speed, or balance. As more dancers graduate from La ENA, and others pass from performing into teaching, the technique evolves further. The técnica cubana is a living practice that continues to be expanded and refined by the master teachers and dancers working in this young and vital tradition.

The power of the técnica cubana, combined with the surreal imagination of the Caribbean and the urgent Cuban need for self-expression, has resulted in a vibrant dance culture that continues to flourish and expand. Contemporary Cuban choreographers—Medina, Lidice Nuñez, Lesme Grenot, Rosario Cárdenas, Isabel Bustos, and Mariana Boal, to name a few—continue to experiment with and enlarge upon the técnica cubana in which they were trained. Small companies burst on the scene across the island even as established troupes continue to work steadily, with and without government support. Despite material poverty, lighting outages, the lack of good shoes, costumes, technology, and vitamins, Cuban dancers constantly experiment with new choreography, finding ways to use their superior training to dramatic effect, creating riveting dances with the glowing raw material of their bodies.

◇ ◇ ◇

JAMAICA

6

◇ ◇ ◇

Jamaican Dance Theatre

Celebrating the Caribbean Heritage

Rex Nettleford

Jamaican dance theatre enjoys an ancestral pedigree dating back centuries. But as a conscious performance art it may be said to date back a mere fifty or so years, when Ivy Baxter and her Creative Dance Group caught the spirit of the self-government movement in Jamaica's nationalist urge not only to delink the centuries-old colony from its Mother Country, Great Britain, but also to find form and purpose on its own terms. Nowhere else would this spirit express itself more than in the creative arts generally, and specifically in the *dance* that played a central role in that awesome process of "becoming," shaped in the dynamic encounters between Africa and Europe on foreign soil, between plantation and plot, between Great House and outhouse, between martial law (massa's law) and the imaginative wit and creative resistance of chattels.

For the African slave discovered soon enough that his/her control over that prime instrument of expression, the body that encased the intellect and imagination, placed such expressions beyond the reach of the oppressor, who, in any case, needed that very instrument for the energy so vital for high productivity in the cultivation of sugar. Dance, through recreation, ritual worship, and nonverbal communication of the inner stirrings of the soul, became a survival tool that spoke to conquest over dispersal and denigration.

It, indeed, celebrated the *African Presence* in this part of the Americas, as well as the iconic stature of that Presence in the making of a definitive civilisation, as it had done time out of mind, both in antiquity in the Mediterranean and later in the Iberian peninsula before extending itself across the *mare tenebrosum*, the Atlantic, to the Americas.

So, on "August 6, 1962, Jamaica pulled down the red, white and blue flag of imperial Britain and replaced it with the gold, green and black flag of an independent Jamaica. A national anthem and other emblems also marked a break with the past" (Nettleford 1985, 39). But as a mark of the will to own a future that would make sense to Jamaicans and the rest of the Anglophone Caribbean, the National Dance Theatre Company (NDTC) of Jamaica was founded, with restrained enthusiasm and guarded confidence admittedly, but with a firm "purpose to secure for the Jamaican people one way of articulating their cultural identity and to build faith in a historical reality that was virtually denied them by the three centuries of British subjugation" (Nettleford 1985, 39).

Jamaica's NDTC was a cultural institution created not out of hubris, but out of "the genuine belief that in order to survive as a political entity, a nation, a people, must nurture the ambience within which the creative spirit of the people can enrich the polity" (Nettleford 1985, 39).

The founders of the company were all seized by the fact that this high-minded "political" objective had to be matched and bolstered by the achievement of excellence in the art of dance itself—whether in performance, in pedagogical discovery and transmission, or in its outreach into the wider community and the wider world. But none of this could happen without experimentation and exploration towards a truly distinctive vocabulary, technique or set of techniques, and style faithful to the Caribbean's sense and sensibility. The NDTC founders brought to the exercise tremendous energy, integrity, sustained application, dedication, and intelligence rooted in field investigation, in debate among themselves and with critics (none of whom has been indulgent), and in the building of arenas of action in an ongoing discourse through the establishment of a School of Dance (now a division of the Edna Manley College of the Visual and Performing Arts), as well as in community dance programmes through the annual festival competitions presided over by the Jamaica Cultural Development Commission (JCDC), and in nearly a hundred overseas tours to the United Kingdom, the United States and Canada, the old USSR, Finland, and Germany, various countries in Latin America, and the wider Caribbean including Cuba, Puerto Rico, and Martinique.

Besides being the nodal point from which other efforts have sprung both in Jamaica, where there are a growing number of smaller dance ensembles, each with its own "voice," and in the wider Caribbean (from the

Fig. 8. *Celebrations.* Choreography by Rex Nettleford. A Caribbean Creole dance-work inspired by the joropo and Carnival of Trinidad, the scarf dances of the French West Indies, Rastafari of Jamaica, and the coquette's dances found all over. Photograph: Denis Valentine. Used by permission of National Dance Theatre Company of Jamaica.

Bahamas to Guyana), the NDTC has remained something of a flagship of Caribbean dance, with the Jamaican sample being now, arguably, a mere variation on a theme.

So what is this theme? What is this Caribbean dance (theatre) that is so distinctive and recognisably an entity with its own inner logic and consistency? What does one look for in Caribbean dance-theatre as it expresses itself in Jamaica, Cuba, Barbados, Trinidad, and elsewhere in the region?

Caribbean dance, which is the dance of people nurtured over centuries in a dynamic Caribbean environment of nearly fifty million souls, is increasingly seeing the need to liberate itself from the narrow classifications that turn on the amount of melanin in the skins of those who create or perform dance in the Caribbean. For these categorizations indulged notions of predestined White domination and non-White inferiority. Caribbean dance cannot possibly accept the current classificatory scheme of dance-art (and all other art forms) into *classical* (meaning European), *contemporary or modern* (meaning White American with Martha Graham, Charles Weidman, and Doris Humphrey as chief historical icons and their European counterparts dating back to Mary Wigman), and *ethnic* (placed at the base of some cultural hierarchy and meaning everything else and especially the art coming out of people of African ancestry). A re-ordering and a re-defining are here mandatory, especially if questions of aesthetics, standards of excellence, and practice merely serve to prop up what needs to be released from current Eurocentric bias.

Caribbean dance, like other definitive genres of artistic expression, is demonstrably capable of multiple and interactive modes of expression, better perceived and described as *ancestral/traditional, contemporary/popular,* and *classic.* Just as Europe deeply mined its own national (ancestral/traditional) dances and lore and its popular expressions emerging from the urban streets, as well as the mannered "indulgences" at court, to create European classical ballet, the Caribbean for some half a century has been forging out of its traditional lore, for the concert stage, what can be called a classic mode. These dances all share many common elements, whether they are shaped by the creative artists working in Trinidad with Beryl McBurnie's Little Carib Theatre and in Cuba with Ramiro Guerra's work informing the Danza Contemporánea, or expressed in the work of Lavinia Williams and Jean Léon Destiné in Haiti, of Fradrique Lizardo in Santo Domingo, of the early Ivy Baxter in Jamaica, of the Barbados National Dance Theatre in Bridgetown, or in the extensive and internationally acclaimed repertory of the National Dance Theatre Company of Jamaica.

The emergent "classicism" in Caribbean dance art also has much in common with the traditions of American dance theatre identified with Katherine Dunham and Pearl Primus, pioneers of African-American dance, with Geoffrey Holder of later years and with latter-day exponents like Garth Fagan, the Jamaican-born and bred choreographer who is now creating waves in the United States with his dance company and his success choreographing the Broadway musical *The Lion King*. His company is seen by some as a modern dance ensemble with a "Caribbean impulse," in contrast to the Jamaican NDTC described by the critic Clive Barnes as "a Caribbean company with a modern dance impulse."

As Richard Long, in his well-researched and finely illustrated book *The Black Tradition in American Dance*, points out, all the above expressions in dance have a common source of energy in the ancestral/traditional dance and lore of the Caribbean. Ms. Dunham owes much to Jamaica and Haiti, Pearl Primus and Geoffrey Holder to Trinidad, and Garth Fagan to Jamaica, for inspiration, raw data, and ways of moving that are valid alternatives to the "approved" balletic forms that came originally from what some would see as essentially "White" sources.

Back in Jamaica and the Caribbean, forging a Caribbean dance-theatre genre out of the realities of Caribbean life, music, movement, and traditional lore became the commitment of McBurnie in Trinidad, Guerra in Cuba, and the moving spirits who founded and have nurtured the NDTC in Jamaica. As an art of discovery, dance demands continuing exploration and experimentation. The traditional sources, alongside the fecund and dynamic innovations of the contemporary urban streets, and along with all the inescapable influences from elsewhere, continue to inform the process of creolisation that began from the time the very first migrants set foot on Caribbean soil from the Old Worlds of Europe and Africa and started to become "new beings" on the Planet. Later arrivals from India and other parts of Asia in the nineteenth century have only intensified the process, especially in places like Trinidad, where the descendants of once-indentured East Indians participate in the annual Euro-African pre-Lenten carnival, while Black West Indians are to be found drumming or dancing in the Muslim Hosay Festival of the East Indians, whose own dance and music forms are undergoing creolised transformation as those of Europe and Africa in earlier centuries have done.

Debate as to whether Blacks are suited to dance White European ballet is irrelevant in a truly multiracial and culturally textured environment, especially when such debate is predicated on a denial of cultural legitimacy to non-Caucasian elements in a social complex whose dynamic is determined in large measure by these very elements. It is only fair to admit that in predominantly Black colonial societies as in the Caribbean, there are people who feel the debate is critical to their own sense of self-worth, since they may well have been taught to believe that things European are superior to their own achievements. So one is likely to get many Caribbean people and American Blacks arguing with deep conviction that no dance-art is valid without a thorough grounding in European classical ballet. The hyphenation of identities becomes irresponsible, if not offensive and limiting, as Black dancers functioning in societies that regard themselves as homogeneously White may well discover.

An understanding of this complex process of creolisation is critical to the understanding of Jamaican and Caribbean dance, coupled with an understanding of the myths, legends, cosmology, and ontologies that determine and characterise the emergent culture that is the Caribbean. Nothing in this is uniquely "Black," since the same process has determined time out of mind the development of all civilisations. The remarkable thing is that one is forced always to remind the wider world (and particularly the powerful North Atlantic), that this is so when applied to African civilisation and its offshoots in its diaspora in the Caribbean and the rest of the Americas or elsewhere.

The traditional ancestral repertoire of dance and music out of the collective Caribbean imagination is, for the most part, African-derived. And the products of early cross-fertilisation are varied and luxuriant. The rumbas and *comparsas*, the *beles*, merengues, *cumbite* (work) dances, carnival and festival dances, the quadrille and contredanse, the schottische and ring games are some of the creole sources that prompt from Caribbean choreographers movement-designs for the concert stage. No less vital to the creative urge are the rituals out of the African religious complex that have survived involuntary uprooting and transplantation across the Middle Passage. Kumina of Kongo origin and its syncretised form, Pukkumina, as well as Etu (a Yoruba-based rite) of Jamaica, the wide range of Kongo and Yoruba rites of Cuba and of Trinidad where Shango still thrives, the Rada and Petro rites of Haitian Vodou which are of Fon, Yoruba, and Kongo origin, like the "nation dances" of Carriacou of the

Grenadines, have all served as rich sources for what is called "Afro-Caribbean dance" by outside observers of dance in the region.

Contemporary sources follow the popular music forms such as calypso and *soca* (out of Trinidad and the Eastern Caribbean) and reggae and dancehall (coming out of Jamaica with strong diasporic counterparts in the United Kingdom). *Zouk* and cadence from the "French" parts of the region are also a source. Dancehall is supreme in Jamaica, spreading to all parts of the region, while variations of *son* remain a staple in a Cuba appropriately isolated since 1961 from the rampant cultural penetration that American (U.S.) pop culture (including televangelism) threatens these days. The contemporary pop forms offer challenges for distillation in the hands of the imaginative choreographer, and the NDTC, along with smaller ensembles in Jamaica and elsewhere, have in their repertory many works based on the pop idioms.

They have been integrated into a serviceable body of technique and dance vocabulary taught under various nomenclatures at home and abroad and developed within the region by a number of exponents.

Back in Jamaica and the wider Caribbean, the technique, research, and vocabulary-building for art dance gathered strength through research, ongoing experimentation in choreography, exploration in pedagogy, and exchange of teachers working mainly out of Jamaica (Rex Nettleford, Sheila Barnett, Ivy Baxter, Bert Rose, Cheryl Ryman, and Barbara Requa, who is currently dean of performing arts at the College of Visual and Performing Arts), Cuba (Eduardo Rivero of Santiago's Caribbean Dance Theatre and others from Danza Contemporánea), Haiti (Lavinia Williams and Jean Léon Destiné), and Trinidad (Beryl McBurnie of Little Carib Theatre).

The straightforward repertory of actual traditional dances is one thing. But the technical discoveries are strong in terms of the way Caribbean people move, whether in ritual, for recreation, or in reaction to everyday concerns; whether in jumping for joy, crawling with fear, writhing in pain, standing frozen in fear, or shimmying with anger. Very few of such locomotor responses are peculiarly "Black" or "Caribbean," but Caribbean people do express these emotions in body language that betrays a way of releasing energy and a vocabulary of "dance" that is distinctively different from that of other cultures.

A rigid back centered on a firm pelvis is bound to craft designs different from a supple undulating spine synchronised into a contraction-release signature of an equally supple pelvis. Therein lies one important difference.

The setting up of polyrhythms through simultaneous isolations in the body in axial splendour and the syncopated contouring of designs in the release of energy and the progression from point to point are signatures of cultural significance that speak to African continuities in the heritage of the region. Europe's heritage also persists, albeit in newly reconnected, long adapted versions of jeté, fouetté, arabesque, attitude, pas de bourrée, *pas de basque, sissonne* and so on, as can be found in the Jamaican quadrille with its heel-and-toe polkas, or in the Haitian contredanse with its elegant balance and waltz steps, which admittedly finally break out into earthy gyrations.

As I have said elsewhere there is a logic and inner consistency in the way Caribbean people move that gives to the commonplace crawl, hop, skip, jump, and walk distinctive aesthetic significance.

The emphasis on weight in the negotiation and shaping of many a movement-pattern finds kindred association with the fall-recovery, tension-relaxation complexes of some schools of American modern dance, as does the contraction-release complex, usually identified as a Martha Graham invention, but organic to all African dance, which predates American modern dance by a few centuries. Movement is moulded more often than attenuated. It is as though the material being worked on is clay rather than steel. Arms flow like rivers and torsos undulate like the outlines of rolling hills or the ebb-flow of the surrounding sea. These are technical foundations in the preparation of the body as the instrument of dance expression.

Caribbean dances, as I say in my 1985 publication *Dance Jamaica— Cultural Definition and Artistic Discovery*, emphasize the body's centre as if to celebrate life itself. These dances seem to recall a period when procreation and childbearing guaranteed men and women a sense of place and purpose. Building strength in the legs and feet is critical: strong feet and toes are needed for earth-centered movements, and sinewy calves will be resistant to the strains of marching and shuffling. Strong knees are requisite for attitudes of obeisance to the gods during ritual ceremonies, and strong thighs support a torso rippling horizontally while possessed of a particular spirit. The flexed foot is useful as symbol not only of hoe and pickaxe, but also of resolution, strength, and earthiness. The arms, like other parts of the body, must be able to describe the curve of mountains, the flow of rivers, and the ebb and flow of oceans, just as in other traditions the movements of swans and the shapes of Gothic cathedrals, skyscrapers, and pine trees piercing the winter sky have found correspondences in dance attitudes. Movement in the Caribbean is outward and open; in northern environments it is more contracted and self-centered, perhaps as protection of one's body against the wintry cold, or as psychological retreat into the caves of the heart, reflecting some kind of Freudian escape from a cruel world. Such spiritual imperatives are beginning to impinge on urban and middle-class life in the Caribbean, and a number of (NDTC) dances have portrayed them. But the natural environment, even if now more fragile, is less eroded and peasant sensibilities still abound.

The flow from toe to crown dictates technical training that encourages coordination of the total body, while it also allows for the isolation of different parts of the body to set up rhythmic counterpoint. There are many technical discoveries throughout the international dance world to aid Caribbean choreographers and teachers. It is not difficult to justify borrowing from established techniques of Western dance-art to serve the special needs of the Caribbean dancer. But indiscriminate eclecticism must give way to an integrated system of technical training. Much of this will be accomplished by conscious efforts in schools and studios, but the most satisfying solutions will inevitably be developed by means of innovative choreography addressing technical needs. Caribbean dance culture must therefore speak with its own voice; that is, it must move with its own kinetic force and aesthetic conviction. That voice is the summary utterance of a vocabulary that is served by the technique.

If only for the sake of convenience, I have also said that distinctive dance movements and gestures must have names. In the Caribbean the question immediately arises as to which language should be used. The European classical tradition settled for French, at one time the lingua franca and international diplomatic language, only recently eclipsed by English. The modern dance idiom in the United States has insisted on English terminology—such as spirals, relaxation, tension, contractions and releases, leaps, stretches, bends, falls, recoveries. But for many people steeped in the Eurocentric bias, a plié seems to suggest a more profound technical feat than the "deep-knee bend," and rising on one's toes is best accomplished by means of a *relevé*. An "extension" carries less prestige than a *développé*, and the "change of the back" may be considered somewhat inelegant when an *épaulement* succeeds in carrying out the movement. In Jamaica the question of language presents a problem in dance communication, especially for those who settle for the use of French, even when they lack a knowledge of European ballet technique.

Of course, the terminology of American modern dance is also acceptable since English is the official language of the entire Commonwealth Caribbean. Yet there are no English words that describe the basic steps from *Kumina, Dinkimini, Tambu,* and *Etu,* all indigenous Jamaican dances. Thus dance steps derived from Caribbean rituals are best described by native names. The low back-bend with pelvis forward and face up in the air on top of inching toes is called the limbo in Trinidad. In the Maroon community of Jamaica it is the *masumba,* which Sheila Barnett used effectively in her dance-drama, "Ni-Woman of Destiny." This inching movement using the toes on a flat foot firmly fixed on the ground has no name in traditional Western dance. Nor is there a word for the kind of port de bras where the arms are set akimbo—whether placed on the hips or overhead as if carrying a weight. There is no word for the extension—or twisted extension—of the spine into the shape of the letter S; in many classical ballet manuals this posture is even frowned upon. Nor are there terms for the countless movements of the feet or the pliant torsos of Caribbean dancers re-creating the throes of spirit possession (as in *Pukkumina, Shango,* or *Cumfa*) or imitating the improvisations of recreational dances.

For the purposes of codification, an analogy to Caribbean music may be instructive. The Trinidadians have added calypso to international music terminology to mean specifically the balladic musical forms that developed out of the ritual of pre-Lenten Carnival. *Kaiso,* the Creole term for calypso, is even more expressive. The Jamaicans created reggae and gave it a distinctive name that describes the music that emerged since the 1960s from the urban ghettos of Kingston. It is also creole in the strict sense of being native to a Caribbean country. Rumba, samba, cha-cha, mambo, tango, and merengue have also been Latin America's contribution to the vocabulary of music and dance throughout the world. As with jazz in the United States, the imprint of the African presence on all of them is incontrovertible. The rituals of Vodou, Kumina, Pukkumina, Santeria, Shango and masquerade have lent their names to specific dance forms, especially Haiti's Vodou complex with its panoply of rites. Jamaica's dance theatre tradition has drawn on the Haitian tradition as part of the sources of African continuities in the Caribbean.

Cheryl Ryman, a dance researcher and former NDTC principal, has isolated a core vocabulary that evolved and sustained itself over the nearly four decades of the National Dance Theatre Company's existence and now also informs Jamaican dance activities independent of the company.

Fig. 9. *Gerrehbenta*. Choreography by Rex Nettleford. The Jamaican NDTC work based on Jamaican "dead-yard" ceremonies. Dancers flank a horse-head marionette adapted from Jonkonnu, a major Caribbean festival art with deep roots in Africa. Photograph: Denis Valentine. Used by permission of NDTC of Jamaica.

She lists in detail many of the primary principles: contraction-release, rippling back or body waves, arched or hyperextended back, rib cage shifts (often with feet astride, as in second position), spiral and cross sit, flat back with side extension, low crouch turns, catch step, knee shuffles, off-balance leg extensions, slides to the ground, and hip side thrust, among others. Many steps based on traditional Caribbean movements are called by different names from one country to another, but Ryman has identified the *kongo* and the *bambosche* among others. Ryman also isolates the core forms in general terms: stretched, curved, and relaxed arms; held, stretched, cupped, flexed, and spread hands; pointed, flexed, relaxed, flat, inching, and "demipointe" feet. Patterns often occur in mass as a kind of visual polyrhythm, in columns of bodies deployed in straight or diagonal lines and circles, and in what she refers to as quadrille patterns, utilizing figure eight weaves. Obviously the vocabulary also takes into consideration certain peculiarities of dance expressions, such as the mechanical angularity of some modern dance forms, developed in the industrial United States, which produce effects palpably different from the rounded, ebb-and-flow, and deceptively lethargic movements of the still largely agricultural, seabound Caribbean.

It is, indeed, in the combination of music and modern theatrical devices that contemporary art-dance in the region can claim a Caribbeanism that is comprehensible, as well, in terms of an international language. The intertextuality of Jamaican/Caribbean life and living has indeed informed the creative spirit of choreographers like Eddy Thomas, Sheila Barnett, Barbara Requa, Bert Rose, Clive Thompson (formerly of Alvin Ailey American Dance Theater), and more recently Monica Lawrence, and the multitalented Arlene Richards, who brings to the dance her added gifts at costume design and performing prowess. They all have worked with me in the NDTC. Limited contributions by Thomas Pinnock and the late Neville Black in earlier times drew as well on the spirit, with Pinnock tuning into the "ching" and "cheng" of the urban rasta-reggae, ska-rocksteady complex specifically. Other Jamaican dance creators who have drawn consciously on the Jamaican/Caribbean cultural reality for their distinctive "voice" are Alma MockYen and her protégé L'Antoinette Stines, Monica Campbell, NDTC alumni Jackie Guy and Tony Wilson, as well as a large number of persons working in community dance, which received early encouragement from the NDTC and under the direction of NDTC's Joyce Campbell, herself the director of a youth dance group, the Jayteens.

Critical comment at home and abroad helps to situate the Jamaican dance-theatre, through the repertory of the Jamaican NDTC, in a genre that speaks to the artistic and aesthetic realities of a textured, multicultural, multiracial process "in motion." Alvina Ruprecht, after seeing the Jamaican company in Ottawa, had this to say in her CBC radio review on August 27, 1999:

> The pieces by [the NDTC's founder-artistic director] are particularly interesting in the way the choreographer works with the whole company of dancers in a form of total performance where costume, lights, music, singing, and body movement produce layers of meaning. The starting point is rhythm, . . . the beat of a drum, the chant-

ing of voices, and then the eruption of a complex musical form, jazz, calypso. In his piece entitled "Blood Canticles" he creates a cultural dialogue where borderlines are blurred and identities are redefined by setting up African tones next to a Protestant hymn based on music by Bach, pop musics with references to Arabic musics, Indian musics, and fused with hip hop and other modern rhythms, and it becomes a statement about the meeting and the fusion of cultures. The music translates into movement that has deep spiritual meaning.

The moments have such titles as "Song for Legba," the Haitian Vodou reference; "Gothic Canticle," a Christian reference; "Zion Revival," a Rasta or Jewish reference. "Song for Allah," brings us to Islam. . . . and into this soundscape—partly taped and partly played live—the choreographer has the dancers suggesting various forms of slavery and oppression in a postmodern meeting [of] movements that are classical, modern and traditional—rolling shoulders, quivering buttocks, certain movements of the lower body that suggest African dance without slipping into folklore, . . . movements that suggest East Indian codes coupled with universal gestures of refusal, or desire, . . . corporeal hieroglyphics which reminded me very much of the work of choreographer Maurice Bejart, creator of Les Ballets du XXeme Siècle.

The *African Presence* as a point of reference (and of power, even) persists. As Ruprecht observed, "there were suggestions of African costumes transformed into a generalised Eastern dress [descendants of Asian indentured servants constitute an important segment of the Caribbean population] . . . the ankle is attached to the waist by a bracelet and a rope . . . suggesting slavery and then there is a final movement where the dancers appear in glowing golden material . . . as they express the burden of physical and mental oppression under the lighting effect that brings out that burning heat and the blood."

The renowned poet and playwright Derek Walcott has described the NDTC's current artistic director's "revolutionary technique" as "defying abstract movement. He strains to challenge and contradict it, and finally he absorbs it so that two apparently different tensions become one ease, two cultures one metaphor," concludes Walcott in the *Trinidad Express,* August 20, 1971. The dignity, elation, and cool, which he further cites, are in fact dominant elements in Jamaican/Caribbean art of all kinds.

In less poetic but no less instructive language on August 3, 1976, *Wash-*

ington Post critic Alan Kriegsman, without a glimmer of reducing the work to the folksy exoticism of the "ethnic" genres, says of a performance of the Commonwealth Caribbean's major dance-group: "the stage was vibrant with *rolling* shoulders, *swaying* pelvises, *flitting* feet, and torsos *rippling* like windswept vines." And as I say in my book previously cited, "the emphases are mine because the words denote signatures of an emerging style that communicates the pulse of the Caribbean heritage"—in dance.

7

◇ ◇ ◇

Rasta & Reggae

Thomas Osha Pinnock

Poverty was like
A drum-beat
That encouraged dance
Steps into Rasta & Reggae
To fly away
Towards survival

I started dancing from a time when my head was below my granny's belly. She was a big woman who treasured the fullness of her breasts and batty. The rhythms of mento, rumba, and Congo-derived rhythms like Pocomania and buroo drums resonated through her formidable body. So when she said, "Come bwoy, mek mi teach you how fi dance!" she would take my hands and dance me around our one-room tenement dwelling in Jones Town, Jamaica. Then when I elevated in growth, she would press my head against her belly as she danced at weddings or ni' night ceremonies. Mi granny, Keturah Morrison, provided me with the sensory paradigm—the vital rhythms—by which, subsequently, to interpret Jamaica's indigenous contemporary rhythms like ska, rocksteady, rasta, reggae, lovers rock, DJ dancehall, and the formality of modern dance training.

Jones Town is part of a geographic conglomeration called West Kingston that includes Trench Town as its immediate neighbor to the west. Bob Marley made Trench Town famous with his "Trench Town Rock" and by the fact that he lived there and created seminal music with Peter Tosh and Bunny Wailer that spoke about conditions in the ghettos of West Kingston.

The prevailing rule of thumb to escape these conditions was to get a good education, have talent, or just be plain lucky. Plain lucky went with the other two most of the time in trying for this ghetto escape from one-room living with six or more occupants, bedbugs, pit latrines, parched yards that became rivers of mud during the rainy season, and leaky roofs. Or waiting in FAITH for something positive to happen. For some people, creativity took over during the "waiting" to ensure their survival: song-writers spilled their guts in ironic lyrics, handcart men built pushcarts to sell fruits, or, like my granny, a person waited on Mr. Folks to finish weaving her basket so that she could go sell her bread.

My granny sold bread as a way to make ends meet. She tugged me along all over West Kingston because she had to. Her favorite daughter, my mother, was dead. So I grew up with my grandmother, helping her to sell bread. I knew all of Jones Town and Trench Town and the rest of West Kingston and witnessed a process whereby the philosophy of Rastafari and the musical evolution of reggae took hold in the Jamaican psyche to continue the legacy of freedom fighters like the early Maroons: Juan de Serras and the legendary Nanny. And people like Sam Sharpe and Paul Bogle. And like Marcus Garvey, Alexander Bustamante, and Norman Manley. They all had been choreographing a dance of protest and resistance, set in motion from the first day an enslaved man or woman set foot on the shores of Jamaica.

Jamaica is
Land of wood & water
Jamaica is
Rock & yard
Jamaica is
Always stepping forward

My own dance of protest and resistance was happening between my granny and me. Saturday nights were the nights she collected money owed her. Then we would go to the movies, then walk past the dance yards on the way home.

I was spellbound by the dance yards. They came to be entrepreneurial ideas of sheer genius. A promoter would target an address of upkeep in the ghetto, approach the owner about rental for the night, and the dance was on. Some yards became regular rentals—thus owners of these yards, sensing an economic opportunity, paved the yards with concrete and called them "lawns." The lawns afforded easier dancing on the feet and prevented dirt and dust from flying on new outfits worn to the dance.

My granny's collection route took us past all of these yards and lawns and whenever we came upon a dance she would stop and listen to some music and then move on. But one Saturday night she moved on and I didn't. My head then had grown past her chest and she knew I was a young man bound for adventure. For that night—with speakers of the sound system blaring from the top of the roof for all of West Kingston to hear American hits from people like Louis Jordan, Roscoe Gordon, Fats Domino, Jerry Lee Lewis, and many other foreign artists—the dance competition was on in the streets. Competitors would just jump into a circle of onlookers and take on each other. That night, the competition came down to Jiggs, the reigning champion, and me. I "dropped legs" on Jiggs and won.

"Drop legs" was the skill and virtuosity displayed while dancing. The process also showcased your courage and creativity through improvising. Drop legs was jitterbugging with James Brown-like rubber-legged shuffle, shiver, sliding, gliding—punctuated with an imperceptible hop skip between steps—then tossing a handkerchief in the air while doing a "snap fall," catching the kerchief, then dropping into a split, to be up in a nanosecond dabbing at your face with the kerchief while remaining cool as a cucumber.

No matter how far
You climb
The more them see
You're behind
For top is bottom
And bottom is top
All depends on
Where you stop

Winning the street competition bolstered my adolescence and pushed me toward further inquiry about the rhythm of life in Jamaica. This rhythm played out its presence as a polarized dynamic between uptown and downtown that revealed itself as the colonial legacy of class status. Being from downtown, Jones Town, I felt the percolating pressure of this class status that permeated the society and served as a severe reference for the pursuit of excellence. For some, this "excellence" was the ability to move along a slide rule of social mobility to graduate from the dance yards and the concrete lawns of the ghetto to the clubs, party verandas, and grass lawns of uptown. And the reverse was true for uptown individuals seeking to immerse themselves into "roots."

Roots was
Is Rasta and Reggae
Flowering, blooming soft
Hard lyrics from
The depths of
Downtown rising
Over uptown to
The hills and heights of
Higher Heights

Roots was the teachings of Rastaman elders like Mortimer Planno and Brother Sam Brown in Trench Town, Brother Mug in Denham Town, Brother Phantom (George Williams) in Jones Town, Count Ossie in Rockfort, and all the other leaders of Rasta camps throughout the island. This teaching provided me with an alternate ethic to see God and to create a distance from the poverty brought on by the greed of "Babylon." The legacy of Marcus Garvey's philosophy centered on a Black ethos. Thus the Emperor of Ethiopia, His Imperial Majesty Emperor Haile Selassie the First, an offspring of the Tribe of Israel and a direct descendant from the line of King David, was identified as the returned Messiah. For Rastafarians he served as a living example of God in man and man in God. To be fully grounded in this thought process one had to participate in the ritual of a "Nyabinghi Groun'ation."

A Groun'ation is the prime event for all Rasta neophytes to attend and tune into the tenets of a spiritual system that embraces the ganja herb, the wisdom weed, as a meditative conduit to perceive more profoundly the cosmology of this African ethos. This is a revelation that calls for great rejoicing and celebration. Thus the Groun'ation celebrates the voices of Africa through the trinity of the Nyabinghi drums: the Funde that keeps the timing consistent with the heartbeat, the Bass Drum for anchoring the emotion of the heartbeat, and the Repeater that propels the soul and spirit toward Higher Heights.

A Rasta man in Higher Heights is in a meditative zone traveling to Mt. Zion to converse with the Godhead as he dances. He ritualistically bounces toward the sky with a hop/skip step, always shifting weight from

Fig. 10. Rasta man in Higher Heights from *Make a Joyful Noise*, 1980. Choreographer and dancer, Thomas Osha Pinnock. Photograph: Otto Berk. Used by permission of Thomas Osha Pinnock, Brooklyn, N.Y.

one leg to the other and poised in counterbalance to the movement cosmos while defying gravity. Or Rasta sees himself as a warrior defending himself and family against Babylon by rapidly shifting weight from back to front foot, mimicking the attacking steps of a warrior stalking prey or throwing a spear at his enemies, then signaling victory by twirling on one foot to remain rooted in Higher Heights.

But going back to roots wasn't accessible only through the province of the Nyabinghi Groun'ation. In a practical way, the dance yards were the ritual spaces that ensured the ongoing metaphor of connecting to the ancestors through regeneration from the pelvis. Sound system operators would scout and import the hottest records from the US of A, and boys and girls would lock hips and pelvis to the slow grind of The Platters, Mickey & Sylvia, Pérez Prado, Bill Doggett and his honky-tonk sound, and from a whole lot of other American recording artists. Each sound system operator tried to out-duel the competition with the latest hit records, so much so that he would scratch off the label for fear of the competitor hiring a spy to reveal the artist or label. Thus, in search of uniqueness, major sound system operators like Sir Coxson Downbeat (Clement Dodd) and Duke Reid started their own recording studios and recruited local talent to fill the bill. This was the beginning of the local recording industry that brought youths out of every town and village, with poverty in their pockets and a dream in their heads, to bleed their hearts in hard lyrics and song. And more importantly, to provide a viable alternative to the stranglehold of American pop music.

I hung out in the urban yards in Trench Town, which became the university for the development of Jamaican popular music and dance. Trench Town was defined by the government houses with red terrazzo tiles on the roof and long verandas connecting tenement dwellings that intersected with covered walkways that led to communal kitchens and toilets. One of these kitchens was located in a yard where Alton Ellis lived. He is one of the giants of Jamaican popular music. The kitchen in Alton's yard was abandoned by the tenants after dark. It was then occupied as a rehearsal room for new songs because of its excellent acoustics and was henceforth dubbed "The Kitchen." Folks like Higgs and Wilson, Skully and Bunny, Lascelles Perkins, Stranger Cole, Hortense Ellis, Baby G, Father G, mi brethren Moodie Jarrett, The Blues Busters—you name them—would pass through, smoke a spliff, and although inspired by the foreign sound, would riff on some group harmonies in trying to find their own original "yard" sound.

The dance yards/lawns became the Saturday night mecca to hear the new songs and to see a display of new dance steps. In my generation, Persian (Morris Samuels) was the leader of the pack in connecting to the dancing ancestors with his feet. Persian could drop legs bar none. He was the master of smooth, inheriting a mantle from popular dance masters Pam Pam and Fish, who set a tone in the early sixties for virtuoso excellence. Pam Pam was the consummate handkerchief dropper, the one who set the trend with his inimitable interpretation of the jitterbug and lindy hop.

Pressure drop
no more Lindy Hop
Take time out
Slow it almost
To a stop
Dub one dub two
Waistline rub-a-dub-rub

Jamaica's musical revolution was on when downtown youths became more interested in listening to The Wailers than to Curtis Mayfield and the Impressions. When they wanted to hear Jackie Edwards rather than Brook Benton, when they wanted to hear the Blues Busters rather than Sam and Dave. And when they really wanted to hear authentic melodies and ballads, they rocksteadied to Alton Ellis, Hortense Ellis, John Holt, Dennis Brown, Delroy Wilson, et al.

By the time Jamaica declared independence from Great Britain on August 6, 1962, the people of the dance yards had disconnected from an imported idea about partner social dancing re the proper etiquette of the waltz and the physically challenging swing dances like the lindy hop. They instead exhilarated in the solo tasks of replacing Chubby Checker's twist with the ska. The torso was angled forward with arms swinging to the up-tempo riffs from people like Toots and the Maytals. And when the dance yards tired of the persistent upbeat, Alton Ellis led the way in cooling down the pressure by ushering in the era of rocksteady.

The prevailing attitude in the dance yards was to defy the climatic heat by appearing ultra cool at all times. Some of us took it to the extreme by always carrying a bit of Lifebuoy soap, so that one could dash to the nearest standpipe to wash one's face and dry it off with toilet paper. The results: no matter how hot it got in the dance yard, one always appeared cool and sweatless. The rocksteady balladeers reflected this attitude by slowing down the dance beat to a pendulimic, minimalistic rock of the body.

Then Bob Marley symbolized the transition to reggae, where the rhythmic beat slowed to a "one drop"—a heavy accent on the downbeat—allowing the dance posture to reconnect to the ancestors and the idea of regeneration through pelvic interlock on the dance floor. This dance was popularly called "rent-a-tile"—because of the six-inch square space of tile that two people occupied while slow "grin'ing" to the music.

But the moral rectitude of Rastafari censored hip and pelvic movements, representing a classic case of acculturation: a process of borrowing useful traits to guarantee survival. Rasta borrowed Christianity's moral code and debunked the African-centered ritual traits like those of Kumina, Myal, and interrelated Yoruba traditions that facilitated communication with the ancestors by moving anticlockwise (to intercept time flow) while remaining connected to the earth with the shuffle of the feet and maintaining a language of spirit possession as the pelvis reacted to the centripetal pull of regeneration. Thus, the dance yards/lawns were the ultimate ritual space to release spiritual and secular conflicts.

In 1962, the year of Jamaica's independence, I was twenty. I enrolled to study dance formally. The movement attitude and social demeanor of the modern dance studios was far removed from the dance yards. The climate in the major dance studios was conditioned by the import of ballet and the Graham technique, despite the intellectual awareness that there were resources abounding from which to shape a dance language of independence. The irony for me was that I became so enamored with the Graham technique, I had to go to the source. I arrived in America in 1967, armed with a scholarship to the Graham School. Three years later a funny thing happened as I began to delve into thoughts of what would distinguish me as a Jamaican dance creator. I found out that I had to let go of Graham and fashion my own tool. By the time I returned to Jamaica in 1972, I knew there was a language already fashioned in the dance yards.

I had learned from people like Rex Nettleford, Martha Graham, and Katherine Dunham about the act of creating and codifying movement vocabulary. I learned from people like Talley Beatty how to tell stories through kinetic expressions, from Rod Rodgers how to warehouse movement phrases toward choreographic construction, and from Dianne McIntyre and Eleo Pomare how to create rituals out of current social issues.

As a Caribbean dance artist inspired by the milieu of the American modern dance movement, I felt that I could make a difference in the dance world by fashioning my own creative mould. With that in mind, the concept "Africa-Reggae Theater & Dance" came to the fore. Whereby, *Africa* is the touchstone of my physical identity, *Reggae* is the fulfillment of my generation's forging of a cultural tool, *Theater* is the environment in which all the rituals I ever witnessed were performed, and *Dance* is the eternal kinetic dynamic called movement.

I felt that reggae was as much a movement way of life as it was music— a mother lode from which to shape dance-theater choreography. So when Rex Nettleford, artistic director/founder of the National Dance Theatre Company of Jamaica, allowed me the opportunity to create with the company the first reggae dance work for the concert stage, I choreographed the work *Desperate Silences* in 1972.

The concept of the work was inspired by the dance yards. The decor and lighting replicated the mood and bare necessities of this urban ritual space: a bare light bulb hanging in the center of the space. Red Stripe beer cartons stacked high in one corner. The dancers exorcising the demons of poverty through their interlocked loins. The DJ's voice, urging release of the pressure, exploding from the shadows.

The drama of the work evolved within the time-space it took the DJ to change from one record to the next. This reflected a time before the advent of double turntables when the DJ had to "toast" the crowd to keep their attention. Toasting was the precursor to rap music. During this moment, one would anticipate the next record to be played and position oneself to get a dance with a young lady. If one was jostled out of position or out of favor, one was left to dance with oneself, sipping from and hugging a beer bottle. Or, during the silence, the hope was to escape the poverty and stress of everyday life and fly away on the banter of the DJ and the new lyrics of self-determination.

The work was constructed around seven episodes of silence. The dancers performed in silence based on an inner rhythmic "silent" count, enacting ghetto people surviving through silent hope against a background of despair, but celebrating life through the strength of their inner rhythms.

Desperate Silences became a watershed for me as an approach to my subsequent works. Armed with the experience of inhabiting the ritual spaces of Rastafari and reggae, I gleaned several performance modalities by which to solidify my approach as a Jamaican creative dance artist. Not the

Fig. 11. Noel Hall and Shirley Rushing rehearsing the duet from *Tenement Rhythms*. Choreographer, Thomas Osha Pinnock. Used by permission of Thomas Osha Pinnock, Brooklyn, N.Y.

least of which was the perception of how to utilize ritual breaths in tandem with the psychological use of space and time. In this ritual space of primal impulses, one seizes the vocal and movement outlines that come fully authorized by the cosmology of Africentricism. The emerged results led me to employ traditional ritual paradigms to house new vocabulary that speaks to contemporary issues and ideas.

Tenement Rhythms (1975), a work that I mounted on Choreo-Mutation, a dance company cofounded by Shirley Rushing, Noel Hall, and myself, featured the architectural shapes of the reggae dance yard landscape: the tilted stance of bodies anchored in the hip. With batty protruding, one arm dangled in relaxed existence, waiting to uncoil with index finger pointing in the air, while the other arm braced the backbone for comfort. A work like *Speng & Spar*, a male duet I created in 1975 on Noel Hall and myself, showcased the dynamics of male bonding as exhibited in the dance yards, where through primal body language men define themselves by varying stances of machismo: how they sound, how they look, how they express emotion toward each other. The piece was propelled not only by its dramatic subtext, but also by a narrative phonetic device, inspired by Pocomania rituals. The characters Speng and Spar would greet each other with "Wha g'wan?" (What's going on?), then transform the narrative syntax—through rhythmic repetitiveness—to its phonetic base to further engage themselves in a dialogue of rhythm and movement.

Fig. 12. *Hello Africa*, 1980. Choreographer, Thomas Osha Pinnock. Used by permission of Thomas Osha Pinnock, Brooklyn, N.Y.

My repertoire of choreography, which has garnered me fellowships and commissions, attests to the vision concept of ART & Dance (Africa Reggae Theater & Dance) as I continue to create and interact spiritually and secularly with all that's around me as I watch:

Birds fly from
Trees in the breeze
Dawg move
Cow sit
Donkey trot
Man just heng—
Woman womb
Just swell with
Creativity
To the heartbeat and
Drama of a culture

◇ ◇ ◇

HAITI

8

◇ ◇ ◇

Haitian Vodou Ritual Dance and Its Secularization

Henry Frank

Dance is the fullest expression of African cultures. That it occupies a very high stratum in the traditional African life is as true today as it was when the first African slaves were brought to Haiti in 1502. In contrast to the westerners who view dance solely as a recreative entity or expression of enjoyment, Africans use dance to express their grief as well as their joy, to reflect all their emotions and their religious beliefs. Upon their arrival in Haiti, they strengthened that concept and passed it on to their progeny. As a result, today still, dance is woven throughout Haitian life. Harold Courlander, a specialist in Africa and African-American folklore, giving an insight into the role of dance in the life of the Haitian people in his 1960 book *The Drum and the Hoe*, wrote: "Dance touches on virtually every aspect of life in Haiti. It plays a part in the supplication of loa, the placation of the dead; in the consecration of a hounfor, the installation of a houngan and the initiation of cult members; in planting, harvesting and building a house."

Courlander's observation, besides its accentuation of the close link between the dance and Vodou worshipping, gives us a strong hint as to why the Haitian folk dance is so full of excitement. It is actually extracted, to a large extent, from the rich repertoire of the ritual dances of this powerful religion, Vodou.

Vodou is a "danced religion," to paraphrase Alfred Metraux (1959), the well-known French anthropologist. Most of the deities of the Vodou pantheon have their specific dances along with specific rhythms of the drums and songs by which they are attracted during a ceremony. The dance, ordinarily, takes place in the peristyle of the *hounfor* (Vodou temple). The peristyle is the front part of the temple where public ceremonies are held. At its center, there is a pole called *poto-mitan* (center pole) through which the Vodou deities, the *loas* (spelled *lwas* in the current Kreyol, used in Lois Wilcken's following chapter), descend during the course of the ceremony and possess the celebrants (Frank 1982). The dance, in fact, constitutes an attractive force to the spirits, who manifest their presence by the possession of the worshippers. Almost anyone can attend a Vodou ritual dance, which is the most public aspect of this religion.

As a point of information, there are two major groups of deities in the Vodou pantheon: the Rada, consisting mostly of the West African spirits, particularly of Dahomean and Yoruba origins, and the Petro, comprising mostly local or Creole deities (Frank 1982).

Some of the most common ritual dances

Nago

Nago is the name given to the Yoruba, whose people mostly are from the southwest of Nigeria, by the Fon people of Dahomey (now Benin), whose influence is remarkable in Vodou religion in Haiti. The dance Nago is in honor of the Ogun deities, more particularly Ogun Feray, the deity of war and iron. The loa Ogun constitutes a large family. Some of the other Oguns are: Ogun Balinjo, Ogun Badagri, Ogun Batala, Ogun Panama, and Ogun Galone, including Shango, who in Haiti is also a member of the Ogun family. Actually this dance symbolizes the determination of the black man to control his destiny. The Nago dancer's arms and upper body movements simulate the efforts of the slave trying to break his chains. The Ogun deities are also honored by the *Mahi* dance, during which the rapidity of the feet is highlighted.

Zarenyen

The loa Guede Zarenyen belongs to the Guede family, the spirits of death. A devotee who is possessed by Guede Zarenyen would imitate the movements of a spider. This spirit has his own drumbeat, which is different from that of Banda, another Guede dance, described later. While the Banda dance and most of the loa of the Guede family belong to the Rada rite, Guede Zarenyen belongs to the Petro rite.

Zaka, Djuba/Martinique

These two dances are closely related. They are consecrated to cousin Zaka, the peasant deity of agriculture. The dance Zaka is a work dance in which the dancers mime the hardship of agricultural work, symbolizing the effort of the peasant to cultivate the soil. The Djuba, or Martinique, is a dance of flirtation depicting the elegance and the caprice of the peasant woman vis-à-vis the gallantry of the peasant man. The dancers are dressed in blue for both dances.

The Djuba dance is derived from an ancient African dance very popular during the period of slavery in Saint Domingue (that is, Haiti) called Calenda. Describing the Calenda in 1797, Moreau de Saint-Méry (1984), an eighteenth-century French historian born in Martinique who lived in Haiti for many years, wrote: "A male and female dancer, or several dancers divided into equal numbers of each sex, jump into the center of the circle and begin to dance, always two by two. This dance which varies little consists of a very simple step in which one foot is put forward after the other. . . . The dancers replace one another without respite." Moreau de Saint Méry's description is quite compatible with the dance Djuba or Martinique.

Yanvalou

The Yanvalou is a dance of supplication in honor of Agwe, the deity of the sea and Damballah, the snake god of fertility. In the execution of this dance the worshippers try to mime the undulating movements of a snake and the waves of the sea by moving gracefully, forward and back, their shoulders and the upper part of the body. The participants are often dressed in white during ceremonies honoring Agwe and Damballah. There are two types of Yanvalou: Yanvalou Doba (back bending) where the dancers bend forward and the Yanvalou Debout (straight) where the dancers perform upright. The latter is in honor of all the deities of the Rada rite.

Kongo

The Kongo rite is intermediary between Rada and the Petro rites. Kongo dance is in honor of all Kongo deities. This dance symbolizes beauty and love. There are many types of Kongo dances: Kongo Simple, Round Kongo, Kongo Mazoone, and Kongo Paillette. In a secular presentation the Kongo dancers use shiny and multicolored outfits.

Ibo

Originating in Nigeria, the Ibo dance characterizes the majestic temperament of the Ibo people, who have the reputation of being very proud.
This dance is for the celebration of all Ibo deities in the Vodou pantheon.
The dancers perform upright with great intricacy of movement of the
feet. It is not a fast dance, but it is full of elegance.

Banda

The Banda, which is derived from an old African dance called Chica, is in
honor of Guede, the deity of death. It symbolizes man's reincarnation.
The idea is that the person who dies and is buried will germinate into a
new life; therefore, there is no need for deep sorrow about someone's
death. Banda is danced by the devotees who are possessed by Guede, who
often appears at the end of a ceremony. It is also danced at funerals to
facilitate the departure of a dead person's spirit to the other world.

In this dance there is a great deal of hip twisting and abdomen rolling.
People who are possessed by Guede often dress in black or in black and
white with a black hat. Some people call the Banda dance, "belly dance"
Haitian style. Although visibly erotic sometimes, Banda is not to be
viewed as sexual exhibitionism, but as a sacred dance ridiculing death.

Petro

The Petro dance is the fastest Vodou ritual dance. It symbolizes the vitality of the black slave and his determination to set himself free. The movements of the shoulders, the arms, and the feet are extremely fast. The
Petro dance honors the Petro deities. One of the fastest Petro dances is
the *Kita* in honor of Tikita, a powerful deity. There is also the *Boumba*,
which is not as fast as the Petro proper and the *Kita* dances. During Petro
ceremonies people are often dressed in red, but there is no obligation to
do so.

Almost all Vodou dances have been secularized. Most of them are used
for divertissement, or diversion, especially after a *coumbite*. The coumbite
is a community gathering system of cooperative work instituted by Haitian peasants for mutual help. For example, after a hard day of labor in the
fields, planting, harvesting, or building a house, the family who has been
the beneficiary of the community's services provides food, drink, and music for the helpers. It is quite normal to expect the participants during
coumbite festivities to dance the Kongo, the Yanvalou, the Djuba or the
Martinique, and so on, with no religious implications.

Choreographers of Haitian folk dances extract most of their materials from the rich repertoire of the Vodou ritual dances. Banda, for example, is the most applauded dance at any folk dance festival when it is well choreographed and executed by an excellent dancer. Such dancers in New York, for instance, have included the late Louis Celestin, who was considered the king of Banda, Emile Saint-Lot of the Ibo Dancers of Haiti (a group based in New York), and Serge Saint-Juste. The Kongo, the Yanvalou, the Ibo, the Nago, the Petro, and the Spider (Zarenyen) dances as stylized by choreographers have become exciting additions to the repertoire of many folk dance groups and concert companies.

We must not overlook the richness of the secular dances in the Haitian folklore. Some originated from Africa; others are derived from European culture. For example, Le Bal des Affranchis (Ball of Free Men) is an imitation of the eighteenth-century quadrille, while the Mousondi (Battle Dance) and Tibaton or Battonie (Stick Dance) are basically African. Tresse Riban (Maypole Dance), a very popular organized dance during carnival, seems to have its origins in South America, but some Haitian ethnologists argue that it is a byproduct of the *Areitos* of the Arawak Indians who once peopled the island of Ayiti or Haiti.

Interestingly enough, a few secular dances are sometimes incorporated into the Vodou rituals, while most of the ritual dances, as we have noted earlier, have been used secularly. It seems safe to say that, in general, both Vodou ritual dances and Haitian secular folk dances have experienced some kind of symbiosis.

The richness of Haitian ritual dance is still very much alive today through practitioners of the Vodou religion. Moreover, modern choreographers have found in Haitian Vodou ritual dance a rich repository from which to draw for inspiration. Haitian Vodou ritual dances, transmuted and stylized by the imagination and artistry of these choreographers, have profoundly influenced black concert dance in the United States and in the Caribbean. Modern dance itself has been forged and shaped by many influences and not the least of these have been the ritual dances of Haiti. Jean Léon Destiné, Paulette Saint-Lot, Rex Nettleford, Geoffrey Holder, the great Katherine Dunham are just a few great choreographers of black dance who can testify to the above assertion. We should not forget either the beautiful works of the late Lavinia Williams, who lived and worked in Haiti for many years, nor those of Pearl Primus, or Alvin Ailey, or of many more departed giants of black dance in that context, that of those who have drawn richly from the well of Haitian dance.

9

◇ ◇ ◇

Spirit Unbound

New Approaches to the Performance of Haitian Folklore

Lois E. Wilcken

The first time [Makandal] did anything at Soundscape, last October, it took the group twenty minutes to end. They didn't know how to end. . . . They were trying to find closure in a situation that was very new.
Verna Gillis, interview, 1983

Traditional music and dance has inspired Haitian performing arts throughout the twentieth century and into the twenty-first. Examples range from a rhapsody on a folk melody in a piano sonata to the percolating Carnival beat of a commercial band set. None of the styles thus inspired has given as much attention to traditional dance as the one Haitians call "folklore." We can locate the roots of the "folkloric movement," a phrase found in the writings of Haitian scholars (Corvington 1991; Oriol, Aubourg, and Viaud 1952), in the years following the first North American occupation of Haiti (1915–1934). A distinct genre that married elements of classical European and modern dance with Haitian folk dance took shape during the 1940s and 1950s. Drawing on recent adventures within the genre, I shall argue that Haitian folklore continues to evolve in new and exciting directions.

What is Haitian folklore? Most broadly, it refers to Haiti's popular culture, but the word entered Haitian discourse in the context of nationalist movements in the early twentieth century. While folklore has its roots in folk tradition, its proponents have adapted it for the modern stage. The repertory derives its central materials from Vodou (service of spirits), *kanaval* and *rara* (rites of spring), and the *konbit* (labor cooperative in the current Kreyol spelling used in this chapter). Dances of European derivation occupy a lesser part of the repertory.

My essay sets the stage by revisiting the genesis of Haitian folklore. I examine the subtypes that developed within it and identify the forces that shaped these developments. The core of my essay explores the efforts of one company, La Troupe Makandal, to stage a form of Vodou (ecstatic) dance that presents truth without sensationalism. I recount and compare representative performances, eliciting the hard issues that have marked this form since its inception. In the end, I offer reflections on the social dynamics that shape this species of Caribbean movement.

Setting the Stage: The Genesis of Haitian Folklore

From an international perspective, the evolution of the folkloric genre in Haiti was bound to happen. A black consciousness movement swept through Africa, the Caribbean, and Latin America in the years between the World Wars, largely in response to North Atlantic hegemony over the entire Atlantic region. Black intellectuals tagged the folk musics and dances of their respective nations for the materials out of which they could fashion national identities. A resolution from a conference of directors of education of the American Republics that met in Panama in 1943, published four years later in a Haitian journal, sums up the steps deemed necessary to define and present identity: "Resolved that each nation intensify folkloric studies by means of public and private research institutes, . . . that diplomatic representatives aid in the development of artistic programs in state theaters where interpretive groups exhibit the best folkloric expression of the countries they represent" ("Resolution" 1947, 37–38, my translation). For many nations, including Haiti, the resolution outlined a process already underway.

The story of folklore's beginnings in Haiti comes down from several sources. Writer Jacques Roumain created the Bureau of Ethnology with government backing in 1941. The bureau collected, studied, and published on aspects of Taino (Amerindian) and African culture in Haiti. To demonstrate Afro-Haitian music and dance for visitors and students, the bureau organized a group of performers with the curiously Christian name Mater Dolorosa. At the same time, classical music instructor Lina Blanchet was taking her Legba Singers to Washington, D.C., to represent Haiti at a Pan American conference. Legba is a Vodou deity, and the group's repertory consisted of arrangements of folk songs. Group member Jean Léon Destiné afterward took up drumming and dance at the bureau, then incorporated these into Legba's repertory (Jean Léon Destiné interview, 1990).

A successful grab for political control by black power factions supported the nascent folklore groups. The coup d'état of 1946 placed Dumarsais Estimé in the presidency, ending decades of control by mulatto elites. The valorization of Afro-Haitian culture in the performances of such new groups as Haiti Chante et Danse, Troupe Macaya, and Aïda articulated the ideology of the new regime. Coupling a reciprocal support of the artistic movement with a perception that tourism would be good for the Haitian economy, the Estimé government laid plans for a grand exposition. Planners targeted 1949, the bicentennial of the foundation of Port-au-Prince, for the opening of a Cité de l'Exposition, a waterfront complex of hotels, casinos, and entertainment venues. Le Théâtre de Verdure housed the new Troupe Folklorique Nationale, directed by Destiné, an ensemble of musicians and dancers representing the best of existing groups. They debuted in December 1949.

The contradictions inherent to folk dance in the modern theater became apparent in the 1950s in Haiti. Guided by the values that shaped their own privileged upbringing, Haitian intellectuals influential in the government of Paul Magloire (1950–1956) expressed the need to temper Afro-Haitian dance with the aesthetic standards of ballet and modern dance. A delegation from the Bureau of Tourism traveled to New York in 1953 and recruited Lavinia Williams, an African-American dancer familiar with Haitian dance through her work with Katherine Dunham, to bring "technique" to the members of the national troupe (Williams-Yarborough 1959, 2). From then until her passing in 1989, Williams researched folk culture, established the Institute of Folklore and Classic Dance, and organized troupes for presentation of choreographed work. She brought her background in ballet and modern dance to her students and artists, but also scouted Vodou temples for talented initiates—to "get the vibrations and feeling of what is authentic" (Lavinia Williams, interview, 1987). The search for "staged" authenticity is an attempt to resolve the inherent contradictions of the genre. It has been an ongoing source of creativity and change.

Two books from the 1950s illustrate Haitian folklore in its heyday under Magloire: Lavinia Williams-Yarborough's *Haiti-Dance* (1959) and *Les danses folkloriques haïtiennes* by Michel Lamartinière Honorat (1955).

Taken together, they present a budding debate over authenticity. Williams's text gives origins and meanings of the dances but not details of movement. Photographs of her own company, many in color, dominate the pages. They depict elaborate choreographies, spectacular leaps and gestures, and lavish costuming in a nightclub setting. Honorat studied at the Bureau of Ethnology and uses photographs of Mater Dolorosa. In his introduction he notes that "certain artists take the initiative to transform our beautiful dances under the pretext of stylization" (1955, 9–10, my translation). Honorat's detailed descriptions of fourteen Afro-Haitian dances, three Euro-Haitian, and some dozen dances associated with the Carnival season demonstrate—and advocate—a fidelity to traditional movement.

To evaluate the various types of performance that have developed, I shall describe what I perceive as the common denominator, the *koregrafi* (choreography). I base my perception on nearly twenty years of work with folklore companies. In short, the choreography fuses traditional and modern elements. The Vodou drum and percussion set, or the Carnival band, sets the model for the music ensemble. To this accompaniment, a dance group, inspired by a corps de ballet, elaborates basic Afro-Haitian dance, creating new variations on traditional movement while outlining set floor designs. Interplay among performers is predetermined in rehearsal, and interaction with audience is minimal. A choreography that may bear the name "Ceremony" excerpts one segment from the full-scale Vodou ritual, but in a tight, stylized fashion. It typically presents a possession performance.

Presenters called on folklore companies to stage Vodou rituals from the beginning. Film director Abner Biberman left a priceless document when he included La Troupe Folklorique Nationale in his 1954 exotic adventure, *The Golden Mistress*. André Narcisse choreographed ritual segments and played the role of priest in the film's story. One segment invokes the serpent deity Danbala for a message concerning hidden treasure. "[I]t was time at last," says a narrator, "for the devil dance, the forbidden dance of the bewitcher, and the bewitched." About two dozen members of the Troupe, costumed in white, encircle the priest as he draws a sacred diagram on the ground. The dancers sing, their hands in a gesture of supplication. One rises to dance Yanvalou for Danbala, and another is possessed by the spirit. Supine, the possessed snakes toward the diagram as the other dancer and the priest guide her. They are receiving messages about the hidden treasure when an emergency disrupts the ritual. The layout of the piece is fixed and the movements of Yanvalou highly stylized, but Andrée Contant renders a realistic possession performance. The racist context unfortunately taints the segment. Yanvalou signifies purity. It is not a "devil dance."

During the Duvalier dictatorship many prominent dancers and musicians fled to the United States and formed new companies, but many remained, and during a short-lived liberalization period in the 1970s, folklore blossomed for a second time. Scholar Alan Goldberg (1981) describes two modes of performance from that period: the folklore show and the "voodoo" show. Most companies preferred the folklore show, with its suite of choreographies. The voodoo show claimed to be an authentic "ceremony," yet eschewed the structure of temple rituals (successive salutations to the nations, or divisions, within the pantheon) in favor of a focus on the spectacular—animal sacrifice and frenzied possession performances. Nightclubs provided the venue for voodoo shows during the 1970s and 1980s. A short study by Michelle Anderson (1982) refines Goldberg's model with the addition of an intermediary category of performance. Anderson visited a temple in Jacmel, a southern coastal town experiencing a tourist boom for the first time. Guides led tourists to temples where they could see an "authentic" ceremony for a fee. A community was present but "possessions were either wild parodies or semihysterical trances" (Anderson 1982, 110). Anderson placed the event on a continuum between the urban voodoo show and the real thing.

Haiti's liberalization, promoted by the Carter administration's emphasis on human rights as a condition for aid, ended with the election of Ronald Reagan in 1980. A brutal crackdown on journalists and political organizers sparked a new wave of emigration. Tourism collapsed, hotels went out of business, and performing artists were out of work. In 1983 a consul at the U.S. Embassy told me that in 1981 Haiti lost approximately 350 people through "stacked" folklore troupes, that is, troupes inflated with nonartists. These troupes secured temporary visas to perform abroad, but did not return to Haiti. The number the consul cited included La Troupe Makandal.

Changing the Face of Folklore: Experiments in the Diaspora

The first considerable wave of Haitian immigration to the United States hit New York City during the 1960s and 1970s, carrying with it prominent folklore artists. André Germain, Louinès Louinis, Arnold Elie, and

Paulette St. Lot all became choreographers/directors of their own companies. Destiné had established himself earlier. Community festivals ranging from modest church fundraisers to grand variety shows at Brooklyn College provided the venues for the new troupes. All favored the folklore show format, with its suite of choreographies. When asked why no companies staged Vodou rites, the late entrepreneur Firmin Joseph, pioneer of the Brooklyn College *spektak* (spectacle), explained that his audience preferred a product more polished than a ritual (Firmin Joseph interview, 1983). This suggests that it also preferred distance. Joseph saw his audience as "nostalgic of Haiti." Folklore would "remind them of home."

A more compelling approach was imminent. In the fall of 1981 Joseph presented La Troupe Makandal, a new company *directement d'Haiti* (directly from Haiti). This group of eight young people (some still in their teens) from the impoverished community of Belair in Port-au-Prince had named their troupe after a notorious eighteenth-century magician-revolutionary. The young artists challenged middle-class propriety with bold magic feats and risqué dance movement. They emphasized the Petwo rites of Vodou, performed for "hot" spirits that specialize in magic and the dissolving of social boundaries. Soon after arriving in New York, the Troupe had taken on as director Frisner Augustin, a master drummer who, like themselves, had experienced economic poverty but had a grounding rich in Vodou. Augustin shared the group's aesthetic of high spirit, spontaneity, and spunk. I was studying drumming with Augustin when Makandal arrived, and I began to spend much of my time with the artists. My doctoral dissertation and one of my publications sketch the story of Makandal's first months in New York (Wilcken 1991; 1998).

The convergence of Makandal, Augustin, scholars, and presenters brought the issue of authenticity to the foreground again. One year after Makandal's arrival in New York, I introduced the troupe to presenter Verna Gillis, and she immediately booked them for a show at Soundscape, a performance loft on Manhattan's West Side. Gillis asked Makandal to stage a Vodou ritual. "Do it just as you would at home," she explained. None of the artists had done this in Haiti; their preferred format was the folklore show, with choreographies. Absolute authenticity would be impossible to achieve, if only because a two-hour time limit precludes all the obligatory rites. It became apparent from the outset that any staged ritual would by necessity be an abridged ritual. Makandal's first attempt to stage a Vodou *dans* (dance, the preferred term for the all-night ritual in Haiti) prompted Gillis to make the remark quoted at the head of this essay. Staging Vodou is a bit like putting your size nine foot into a size four shoe, yet Soundscape's *Voodoo Theater* debuted, and went on to six more performances through April 1984.

The contradictions inherent to staged folk arts arise from the incongruities between forms that develop within communities and the modern stage context. La Troupe Makandal experienced such incongruities. I have already cited the first: time. Few, if any, venues would permit a full-scale Vodou dance. Salutations to the principal divisions of the pantheon span at least five or six hours, and they follow a logical order. Some performers who serve the spirits have expressed concern for offending excluded divinities. Second, staged Vodou uses unconsecrated spaces that lack the *poto mitan*, a center post with deep spiritual significance. Third, most of the public come to Vodou theater with little knowledge or experience of what they are seeing. Dances in Haiti place the initiated in the center while members of the community look on as spectators, but community members are familiar with the songs, the gestures and activities, and the spirits. Much of a dance is consumed in song, which tends to lose the attention of those who do not understand text. Stephanie Schmiderer (1990) and myself (Wilcken 1983) have studied audience identity as a factor shaping theatrical Vodou performances. The fourth and final problem stems from the esoteric nature of Vodou. Much knowledge belongs to the initiated only. I have heard charges that staged Vodou caters to voyeurism. Goldberg speculated that the less authentic aspects of both folklore and voodoo shows construct a "mask behind which performers may maintain a strong sense of themselves" (Goldberg 1981, 293).

Companies that stage Vodou dances despite these difficult issues share the deep and driving conviction that the performances have the power to de-legitimize racist stereotypes of Haiti. They might also reinforce stereotypes. The position of a performance on that continuum depends on how the artists resolve the contradictions I have named. Let's look at representative performances by Makandal.

On February 24, 1998, Makandal presented a dance for Ogou (a name attached to several members of the bellicose Nago nation) at Thread Waxing Space, a performance loft in Manhattan's Soho. The performance, one in a five-part series called Sanctuary: A Spiritual Music Festival, drew an audience with a keen interest in "danced" religions. A few Vodou initiates attended. The loft space afforded ample room for dance, and it placed the audience close to and on the same level with performers. The festival included an altar installation for performers' use. Makandal invited Luc Lacroix to play the role of *ougan* (priest). Lacroix was conducting Vodou dances in Brooklyn, and he had experience with the voodoo show in Haiti. Augustin led a music ensemble well seasoned in ritual drumming, while the dancers varied in experience. We oriented the audience with a one-page printed program and brief opening remarks.

Unlike the voodoo show in Haiti, Makandal's Vodou theater follows the structure of the community-based dance. A dance consists of a series of invocations to families or nations of spirits, although one particular spirit might be the focus of the evening. Port-au-Prince Vodou begins with the Rada nation (cool, air and water), then follows with Djouba (earth), Nago (iron, power), Petwo (fire, revolution), and the Gedes (pronounced gay-days; decay, death and regeneration). The cycle from Rada through Petwo moves from cool to hot, balance to upheaval. The final move to the Gedes proclaims dissolution but with the promise of rebirth. Each nation has its own dance or dances, accompanied by its own repertory of songs and drum ensemble patterns. Makandal's Vodou theater typically begins with opening prayers and the Flag Corps, a ceremonial orientation of the society's sequined flags toward the four cosmic cardinal points. We then present a series of invocations following the order I have described. To narrow the time frame, we focus on only one spirit in each nation—Rada rites might invoke fifteen or more. We omit a nation when time does not permit all.

The dance at Thread Waxing Space balanced structure with the spontaneity of community-based Vodou. Part One presented the Flag Corps and invoked two Rada spirits, so that Part Two could open with the focus of the evening, Ogou. Petwo rites followed, and we closed with the Gedes. Each segment featured possession performances, and such ritual movement as the pouring of libations, and orientations of ritual objects to the cardinal points. Performers involved the audience by touching ritual objects to their foreheads, encouraging them to dance, and inviting them to shake hands with the possessed. Haitian Vodou initiates in the audience stood up to sing alongside the musicians. The possessions and the audience involvement were not rehearsed. Makandal's performance, and the features of the space, succeeded in overcoming the lack of community that plagues much modern theater. It created a sense of spirit unbound.

Presenters have frequently called on Makandal to stage Rara, a processional form danced publicly in Haiti during Lent. Although timed with the Christian calendar, Rara links clearly with Vodou, and it extends the springtime celebration of rebirth that Carnival enacts. Rara bands are structured, but they create an impression of pandemonium. Features that distinguish them from Carnival bands include the dissonant hocketing of *vaksin* (bamboo trumpets) and the fancy footwork of a *majò jon* (baton major). The reader will find details of this rich and vibrant art in Gillis and Averill (1991), McAlister (1995), and Paul (1962, 167–177). Maya Deren's (1977) posthumously edited film *Divine Horsemen*, a critical source on Vodou dance, culminates in scenes of Rara and Carnival in the late 1940s.

Descriptions of Makandal's Rara performances vary according to the venue. Space does not always permit audience participation, a feature inseparable from authentic Rara. At a performance in Washington Square Church in April 1987 the group entered in procession. Dancers and musicians headed for a clearing in the center of the church nave and gave an electrifying performance surrounded by audience, but the venue and the presenters insisted that audience/performer boundaries be maintained. In June 1991 Makandal opened a festival in Central Park's Rumsey Playfield with a Rara procession. Led by a whip-cracking dancer, the artists snaked through the audience, picking up participants along the way, then headed for the stage, where they shifted to choreographies. At the 92nd Street Y in February of 1997 Makandal started its Rara procession during intermission from the dressing room. The milling public heard the band approaching and followed it, pied-piper fashion, back into the theater for the second half of the show.

Finding a workable context for "staged" Rara, while upholding its character as public revelry with sacred roots, stimulates presenters and performers to experiment. Both Carnival and Rara challenge the notion that we can successfully re-contextualize folk art. Honorat (1955) and Paul (1962) describe a sweeping spectrum of Carnival and Rara bands and dances related to neighborhoods, occupations, and religious themes. Few presenters or performing groups have the means to display such variety. Rara, like the Vodou dance, needs adaptation when taken to the theater, but relaxing the boundary between spectators and performers recreates what is most important about this spirited art.

Reflections

I leave the reader with several strands of thought that motivate this essay. My opening paragraph claims that "Haitian folklore continues to evolve in new and exciting directions." This argument responds to the unfounded perception on the part of some observers that this style of Haitian art is a dinosaur.

While some New York–based Haitian companies have dissolved with the deaths or retirements of their directors, new young companies have formed (Anacaona, Feets of Rhythm, Ti Ayiti, Tonel Lakay). I have not dealt here with the many opportunities in schools, museums, and libraries that the multicultural movement in education has spawned, but they have placed the services of folk artists in unprecedented demand. Aside from educational work, folklore companies continue to find a place in theaters, lofts, and other performance spaces. While it may be outside the mainstream, a tributary audience searches for kinds of music and dance it has never seen or heard. For many of us, the corporate culture's imposition of endless consumerism whets the appetite for a more intangible experience.

Haitian folklore companies thrive, too, because the contradictions between the modern stage on the one hand, and traditional music and dance on the other, demand resolution and lead to creative, not to mention healing, syntheses. Vodou dances, when cast as Hollywood "voodoo devil dances," become a tool for the perpetuation of bigotry and division. One can argue that folk artists bear a responsibility for presenting the dances to the public in a realistic manner that challenges racism. I close with an excerpt from the mission statement of La Troupe Makandal: "La Troupe Makandal seeks to enlighten the general public about Haiti through music and dance. Part of the company's repertory derives from the rituals of Vodou, widely known and disparaged in the United States as 'voodoo.' The Troupe's performances repudiate racist stereotypes while keeping the magic alive. In other words, La Troupe Makandal uses music and dance to represent a Haiti that is beautiful, dignified, and true."

❖ ❖ ❖

DOMINICAN REPUBLIC

10

◇ ◇ ◇

Dominican Folk Dance and the Shaping of National Identity

Martha Ellen Davis

"In Santo Domingo dance is the favorite passion; I think there is not another people in the world more fond of dance."
Father Jean Baptiste Labat, 1722

¿La tierra del merengue?

The Dominican Republic is popularly known as the "land of merengue" (*la tierra del merengue*) because the merengue is the dance genre that has come to symbolize Dominican national identity. However, the merengue is but one dance genre from one region—the Cibao or northern region— that has become ubiquitous throughout the country and now the expatriate communities, as well as internationally commercialized. Today, the traditional form of this merengue, called *merengue típico* or *perico ripiao*, which appears to have changed little in the past hundred years, coexists alongside an orchestrated merengue that is constantly evolving. The characteristic sound of the merengue típico—of accordion, *tambora*, and *güira*—represents a down-home, peasant identity, while the big-band style orchestrated merengue symbolizes Dominicanness within the modern, transnational context. The recent rise in fashion of the merengue during the last fifteen years or so, to become the hottest Latin dance beat in the clubs of Latin America and Spain, confirms for Dominicans that their country has taken its place in the modern world.

Many Dominicans relate to the dual symbolism represented by the two coexisting subspecies of merengue: the one of bucolic rusticity and the other of world-class cachet. This dual national identity through dance accurately reflects a sort of split personality and lack of definition with regard to social class and rural/urban sector. The ubiquity of the once-regional northern merengue and its symbolism as the national folkdance has marginalized other dance "species," obscuring regional identities. This is taken a step further in the expatriate context, in which, character-istically, regional and class boundaries are transcended by a national-as-ethnic minority identity, which serves as a common denominator. The national symbolism of the merengue—albeit creole (that is, hybrid) in na-ture and thus typical of national culture as a composite—also obscures the components of that culture, including and most deliberately its African-derived component, represented in the long-drums (*palos*) and their mu-sic and dance.

The phenomenon of a regional dance genre becoming symbolic of a larger national identity—sometimes entailing even the "invention of tra-dition"—is common in the modern world. In parallel fashion, specific re-gional dialects have become generalized as the standard, official languages for entire nations, displacing the other regional dialects. Today's standard Spanish, for example, is in fact the regional dialect *castellano*—Castillian—made the standard for a larger geopolitical unit and an arm of the con-quest of the Americas.

Political reasons are often behind the choice of dialect—linguistic as well as musical or choreographic—for standardization and role as cultural symbol. In the case of the merengue, dictator Rafael Leónidas Trujillo, who ruled 1930–1961, promoted the genre in the dancehall. As part of his agenda of weakening the oligarchy or landed elite of the Cibao, he must have taken special pleasure in promoting a peasant dance of their region that was associated with a seedy milieu, within the ranks of gracious waltzes, mazurkas, and *danzones*, which it ultimately did replace. This was facilitated by a structural adaptation: the addition in the 1920's of the *paseo* ("stroll")—adopted from the other ballroom genres such as the *danza* (Austerlitz 1997, 15–17)—to the merengue and *jaleo* (virtuosic figures) sections of the dance.

Trujillo promoted a cultural policy of *hispanidad*—the defense of His-panic heritage, both racial and cultural—as the authentically Dominican, a policy continued under his mastermind, Joaquin Balaguer (later presi-dent, 1966–1978 and 1986–1996). Hispanidad was juxtaposed with African influence, physical and ethnic, particularly that of Haitian origin (see below), which was viewed as a contaminant. In light of this policy, Trujillo's support of the merengue as the dance symbol of national identity is interesting, since this genre, like many other social dances, is not Hispanic. Rather, in style and instrumentation it is creole, born in the New World of various cultural components, European and African. Trujillo's support of the merengue as the musical symbol of national identity can be viewed as a sort of reframing of hispanidad—considering that, in this first colony in the New World, the five-hundred-year history of cultural contact and amalgamation has obscured awareness of which traits are in fact European, Native American, African, or other. This lack of consciousness of African heritage, in contrast with neighboring Haiti, has not been rectified by education because neither African nor African-American ethnography is taught. It is only in the past twenty-five years, mainly through the haranguing of certain anthropologists and folklorists, that the African heritage in Dominican music and dance has been begrudgingly acknowledged. The folk revivalists' search for and re-creation of Afro-Dominican music and dance serves as the antithesis to hispanidad.

Trujillo's promotion of the merengue also accelerated the trend toward the development of the orchestrated variety, with the addition of band instruments. This trend had already started with the alto saxophone in the 1920s; later, brass was added, reflecting U.S. big-band influence (Alberti 1975). Following the Trujillo era (post-1961), the orchestrated merengue has joined the ranks of other Latin American dances that have likewise become generalized and symbolic of national identity in their respective countries and, often, also internationally profitable. These include the tango of Argentina, the samba of Brazil, the rumba, mambo, and *chachachá* of Cuba (and regionally in the Hispanic Caribbean, the *guaracha* and *son*, and formerly the *danzón*), the *cumbia* of Colombia, the salsa of Puerto Rican New York. All these and other similar dances have three things in common, one social, one musical/choreographic, and one geographic: They are all social dances, that is, used for the social purpose of recreation and courtship. All are culturally hybrid, yet have fundamental African rhythmic influence. And many or most are urban, or became urban as a step in their rise to international popularity.

Meanwhile, what has happened with folk dances other than the merengue from the north? Within the past fifty years, most have rapidly declined in use and popularity, as musical and choreographic "dialects" displaced by the merengue and weakened by the impact of urbanization and modernization, including the mass media of communication. This article addresses the panorama of traditional dance of the Dominican Republic beyond the merengue, in historical and social context. It highlights the current effort by Dominican folk revivalists, including expatriates, to re-define national identity through the performance of certain music and dance genres of African heritage.

The Tripartite Heritage of an Island Divided

Today's countries of Haiti and the Dominican Republic, which share the island of Hispaniola, were originally a single country: Santo Domingo, the first colony in the New World. A tripartite cultural heritage—the na-tive Taíno, European, and African—was common to the entire island for its first two centuries following the European conquest and coloniza-tion.

The original Taíno inhabitants were a subgroup of the Arawak, one of the four huge language families of the Amazon region. Seafaring Arawak launched from the Amazon and Orinoco basins, populating the Antilles one by one and arriving at Hispaniola, which they called Quisqueya, more than four thousand years ago. At the same time as the Spaniards arrived, the Taínos of Borinquen (Puerto Rico) and Quisqueya were being con-quered by Caribs, another of the main language families of tropical South America. A more warlike people than the Arawak, they had already con-quered the lesser Antilles and were making incursions into and settle-ments along the Loíza River in northeastern Borinquen as well as along the Samaná Peninsula in northeastern Quisqueya.

The Taíno population on Quisqueya was large, estimated from as few as a half million to as many as four million. However, by 1530 they were all but decimated due to disease, conquest, exhaustion from enslavement, and even suicide. The culture of today's Hispaniola, in both of the two republics that now share the island, thus represents various mixtures of European and African elements.

The first two hundred years of history of the colony of Santo Domingo laid down a basic stratum of Spanish lore throughout the island. Its roots lay mainly in the south and west of Spain (Andalusia and Extremadura). They also undoubtedly included more Sephardic Jewish and Moorish in-fluence than is commonly acknowledged, given the impact of these ethnic components in pre-Conquest "Spanish" culture as well as the presence of these ethnic sectors among the early colonizers. The conquest and evangelization of the Americas in fact must be viewed in light of fifteenth-century Spanish history, for it was in fact an extension of the Catholic reconquest of Spain that expelled the Jews and the Moors just months before Columbus's first voyage.

The next stratum was African, starting as early as 1502, consisting of Christianized and Hispanicized Africans, called *ladinos*, who had resided in southern Spain for a century. Within just a few years, however, "heathens," called *bozales*, were brought directly from the African continent. The ladinos had established religious societies throughout the south of Spain, parish-based *cofradías*, a Mediterranean phenomenon that was originally guild-based. This sort of brotherhood was also established by blacks in the colony of Santo Domingo—and many other sites in Catholic Afro-America—as mutual-aid and burial societies (for example, the Cuban *cabildo* and the Brazilian *cofraria* and organizations in Venezuela, Panama, and elsewhere, parallel to similar phenomena among Native American populations of Central America and Mexico).

On the Spanish side of the island, cofradías, relics of the colonial slave society, are still functioning in many areas, although they are now in decline because they are no longer socially necessary. Today's cofradías are characterized by a patron saint (whose syncretism with an African-derived deity is not part of its members' consciousness), women leaders, and the use of long-drums (*palos*, *atabales*)—played for the patron saint's festival and optional individually sponsored, vow-based fiestas (*velaciones*) as well as death rituals of members.

At the same time as Africanized customs were taking root, slaves were escaping into remote rural areas to establish maroon communities, called in Hispaniola *manieles*. These communities became so numerous that the governors of Santo Domingo in the early 1520s feared they might unite and take over the island; this is exactly what happened more than 250 years later in the Haitian Revolution. In the regions of the manieles, Africans undoubtedly came into contact with Taínos who had also taken refuge from the Spanish. This contact is evidenced today by Taíno retentions in foods and forms of food processing—especially with regard to the root crops of manioc (genus *Manihot*), colloquially called *yuca*, and *guáyiga* (*Zamia pumila*)—conserved by certain Afro-Dominican enclaves of the south (Villa Mella, Santa María de San Cristóbal). These areas are known for the cassava (*casabe*) flat cakes made from grated yuca—an Amazonian food that does not spoil—and the *chola*, a dense sweetened and spiced roll, six to twelve inches long and two inches thick, made from the expressed starch of the guáyiga and eaten in slices as a snack.

Following the discovery of greater riches in the Aztec and Inca empires in 1519 and 1532 respectively, Spain turned its back on Hispaniola. Thus, France was able to take over the western third of the island, formalized in 1697 as their colony of "Saint-Domingue," the counterpart of the Spanish colony of Santo Domingo. Given the early demise of the Taínos, France developed St.-Domingue with an African slave labor force for production of agricultural wealth through sugarcane cultivation. When France took over the western third, the island was underpopulated, with about 130,000 people in all. However, during the seventeenth century, France imported perhaps one million African slaves into St.-Domingue. This led to tremendous demographic differences between Santo Domingo and St.-Domingue with regard to the number of Africans, the major African cultures represented (in Haiti, the Dahomeyan influence was predominant; in Dominican Republic, the Central African), the critical masses present from specific African ethnic origins, and the ratio between blacks and whites. The Spanish colony, in the meantime, continued to languish, underpopulated and primarily Hispanic in racial composition and culture, a place where master and slave had to work together to survive. This degree of contact led to intra-ethnic African and Afro-European cultural mergers to a greater degree than in Haiti.

A hundred years later, the African slaves of St.-Domingue revolted, winning their independence from France and establishing the second free republic in the New World (the first being the United States). In 1822, Haiti occupied Santo Domingo in an effort to free the entire island of European colonial control. Santo Domingo ironically called on Spain to oust the Haitians, and this was achieved in 1844. Dominican independence—not from Spain, but from Haiti—is celebrated on February 27th.

The trajectory of cultural divergence between the two neighbors of Hispaniola is reflected in music and dance—in style, accompaniment, and social context of performance. Nonetheless, Haiti is actually more European than commonly thought to be, and the Dominican Republic is more African. Haitian *Vodou* rituals, for example, begin with French prayers. Dances such as the archaic European stick dance and the maypole dance are performed. Social dances exhibit influences of some European ballroom and peasant dances.

At the same time, the African presence in Dominican dance is not circumscribed to the dance with the most African-influenced music, that of the semisacred palos. On the contrary, it is subtly or overtly present in the movement of many dances. The palos exhibit a certain European influence in the quatrain form of the sung texts, but, taken as a genre, the palos music is far more African-influenced than the associated dance, the drum dance (*baile de palos*), which has a number of European features, and in some ways resembles a Europeanized partnered folkdance.

There is also more shared culture between Haiti and the Dominican Republic than is commonly acknowledged, despite enormous cultural differences and an often adversarial political relationship. Cultural sharing is due not only to a common colonial past, but also to continual contact, given the fluidity of the border—disputed and altered during the nineteenth century and virtually unguarded in its rural extension during the twentieth. African heritage in the Dominican Republic can be attributed in part to the early colonial slave trade to Hispaniola, which contributed to the development of general Dominican culture. More distinguishably African cultural features are attributable to later phases of the slave trade as well as to the establishment of Haitian-derived extended families in Dominican territory, each associated with a family-based religious society or brotherhood.

Ties between the two countries have been fortified by such factors as the Haitian devotion and pilgrimage to the Virgen de la Altagracia, the Dominican extra-official patronness, in Higüey, in the eastern extreme of the island; the Dominican tapping of the presumably more powerful Haitian Vodou for acts of witchcraft and healing; the late twentieth-century popularity of Haitian commercial dance music, disseminated by the mass media; and, most important, the importation, during the mid- and late twentieth century, of thousands of Haitian braceros (seasonal farmworkers) to cut Dominican sugarcane, many of whom have stayed, joined by other undocumented Haitians seeking a better life. Their sugarcane community–based, Vodou-associated (*Pétro* cult) *rara* societies (pronounced "gagá" by Dominicans) of the Lenten season, with their carnivalesque music and dance, are becoming a Haitian-Dominican phenomenon.

Sacred Dance

The Taíno *areíto*

The *areíto* was the main musical and dance event on Quisqueya, as well as on Cuba and Borinquen. As described by various chroniclers, including Father Bartolomé de Las Casas, Gonzalo Fernández de Oviedo, Pedro Mártir de Anglería, Father Ramón Pané, and Francisco López de Gómara, the areíto was a large-scale sung dance ritual that could last from several hours to many days. Despite variations by region and social occasion, the main features included direction by a vocal and dance leader and response by an ensemble of dancing singers as large as three hundred men, women, or both. They were accompanied by the *mayohuacán* slit-gong, the counterpart of the Aztec *teponaztli* or the Mayan *tunkul*. (There were no skin-covered drums at all; the chroniclers noted that there was no animal adequately large to serve this function.) The dance movements in the areíto, as among living Arawak peoples, were probably vertical and earth-oriented, by groups linked in close formation, as described by chroniclers. The dancing singers played maracas; ankle rattles may have been used as well.

The areíto could be carried out for various occasions: as a petition, such as for fertility (for example, of the manioc crop) or protection from hurricanes (*huracán* being a Taíno word); to render homage—such as princess Anacaona's areíto for the governor of Santo Domingo with her three hundred maidservants as dancers; for the celebration of an important marriage or a victory in war; for a funerary memorial; or as a form of recreation. The narrative text of the areíto conserved, reiterated, and commemorated the past and the ancestors and their deeds, sometimes mentioning the way in which each died. Fernández de Oviedo documents a memorial for a chief that lasted fifteen or twenty days, with men and women singing in commemoration of his life's deeds and in praise of his rule. Chiefs and others came from afar to pay their respects, and in turn were given the late chief's belongings. There were also areítos with light or humorous texts. Some celebratory occasions included so much drinking that the event ended due to drunkenness, not uncommon in today's Native-South American fiestas.

The dancing chorus was positioned in linear, circular, or arch formation, maintaining close contact with one another by holding hands or linking arms. The soloist and chorus moved forward and backward with impeccable precision to the rhythm of the song text. The leader, called *tequina*, was either a man or woman and probably a shaman. He or she sang responsively with the chorus, which repeated the leader's every line, but at a lower or higher pitch, while he or she kept dancing in silence during the repetition. A soloist could be substituted, but without a break until the narrative song was finished. This could take three or four hours or even from one day to the next. The tune and movements could alter when a new soloist took over, but the narrative had to continue. For a new sung story, the tune could be the same as the former one.

On both sides of the island, Taíno dance has been lost, or in part assimilated. If there were Taíno retentions or syncretisms in music and dance, they would probably exist among certain Afro-Dominican enclaves of today. However, Taíno traits would be hard to discern given little documentation, cultural mixture and evolution, the loss of memory by the culture bearers of features of their Taíno past, and the inaccuracy of extrapolation from current customs of today's Arawak peoples of the South American tropical lowlands.

The baile de palos

Following the demise of the Taínos, the culture that has developed as Dominican is largely of European and African heritage, but most characteristically hybrid, the consequence of five hundred years of culture contact and evolution. In many instances, elements of both heritages have fused—as is characteristic of social dance and Dominican culture as a whole. However, in certain instances, either European or African components or both may have maintained their ethnic integrity. This is particularly true for sacred music and dance, which is slow-changing as part of folk liturgy and ritual. In fact, both European and African components may be present in a single event, such as the saint's festival (*velación*), without merging, a phenomenon this writer has called "native bi-musicality" (Davis 1994a). In this sense, the "traditional" music and dance culture is by nature bicultural.

The most African-influenced dance music is that for the sacred long-drum dance or *baile de palos* associated with Afro-Dominican cofradías, performed at the fiestas for their patron saints and at death rituals for their members. It is also performed at vow-based, annually recurring, all-night saints' fiestas of individual sponsorship in most of the country except the Hispanic central Cibao region in the north. Velaciones are offered in payment of a vow, a contractual relationship with a saint undertaken for divine healing. When healing has been successful, the mortal must pay what he or she promised or risk health and life itself at the hand of a potentially vengeful saint. If a velación is offered in payment of a vow, it often becomes an annually recurring obligation, in fact inherited by a father's eldest son or a mother's eldest daughter. Spirit possession by deities does not take place at velaciones unless the owner of the event is a *Vodú* medium.

Drum-dance events, when associated with spirit possession, have been censored since colonial times by proscriptive edicts (Davis 1976), which serve historians as evidence of the existence and nature of the events. The earliest documentation of African slave dance in Hispaniola may be the description in 1698 by Father Jean-Baptiste Labat (1663–1738) of the *calenda* (Labat 1722) (also spelled *calinda* or *kalinda*), a dance also widely popular throughout the colonial Caribbean, whose name may actually refer to various types of dance: Labat seems to refer to a line dance; today the Trinidadian kalinda is a stick dance.

However, a century later, M. L. E. Moreau de Saint-Méry (1750–1819) described the calenda as a dance apparently very similar to today's Dominican baile de palos or drum dance: an unembraced couples' dance that alternates a balancing step with circular turns representing ritual pursuit (Moreau de Saint-Méry [1797–1798] 1984). The balancing step entails side-to-side or front-and-back footwork in place, in which the woman challenges the man to catch her. This is followed by the tracing of the circumference of a circle, in which the woman "escapes" (*huye*) and is pursued by the man, until she turns back to face him again before escaping in the opposite direction around the circle. Actually, this pattern is replicated in several social dances (mostly in disuse within recent years), such as the *sarambo* and the *chenche*, and today in such embraced dances as the *priprí* of the east. So Moreau could have been describing another social dance, but with this characteristically Dominican pattern of the two-part choreography.

Despite regional variation in the accompanying instrumental ensembles, and in their rhythms and tempos, the baile de palos is similar throughout the country. To generalize, it is a couples' dance traditionally performed *suelto* (unembraced) as a *baile de respeto* (dance of respect) due to its sacred contexts of performance at saints' festivals and death rituals. Reflecting European influence, it is a dance of much foot movement, little movement of the arms, and practically no hip movement. The dancers maintain a formal, rigid torso, although with the non-European feature of keeping the knees and waist slightly bent. This posture and the lack of

Fig. 13. Drum Dance *(baile de palos)* of Monte Plata in the central-south region. *Palo arriba* rhythm; ritual pursuit step. At the town's novena (nine-night celebration) of the Virgen de la Altagracia, the country's and Monte Plata's extra-official patroness, January 1973. Photograph: Martha Ellen Davis. Used by permission of Martha Ellen Davis, Gainesville, Florida.

physical contact between the male and female dancers—except an occasional guiding hand on the woman's shoulder or waist by the man in pursuit—differentiates this dance of respect from Dominican social dance, which is described as *baile de regocijo* (a dance of enjoyment) and is often danced *agarrado* (embraced) and may use more hip movement. Regional variation is observable in the arm positions and props (as evidenced by the use of a handkerchief by the woman in the photo), as well as in the subtlety or overtness and vigor of the challenge and escape.

When danced unembraced, which is the traditional form, only one or two couples dance at a time at a saint's festival, while the public looks on. Participation in serial form is accomplished by cutting in during the circular step of pursuit (women, men, or either, depending on the region), and by the alternation of dancers from one piece to another. In some regions, such as El Seybo, the drum dance has changed or is changing to a couple dance, with simultaneous participation by more dancers. Likewise the polyrhythmically accompanied, non-liturgical *salve* of the central-south can be danced, according to current practice, usually embraced.

The character of the baile de palos is determined by the tempo, which in turn is dictated by the original function of the music. In the central-south, the rhythms of the lugubrious *palo abajo* and *palo arriba*, as well as the *congos*-drum dance of the Brotherhood of the Holy Spirit of Villa Mella, are associated with the dead, although they can be danced by the living. Here, as in the photo, the baile de palos of the central-south is a calm and serious dance, neither virtuosic nor exhausting. However, the drumming of other regions—which often have separate rhythms for the dead—is for the saints and hence livelier.

The most traditional areas with regard to the baile de respeto are the Afro-Dominican enclave of greater Villa Mella with its congos drums, as well as the long-drum-using community of Los Morenos just to the north of the town. These areas also have the highest incidence of funerary rituals with drums, for members of their respective brotherhoods—the *Espíritu Santo* (Holy Spirit) in the case of the congos and Our Lady of Sorrows (*La Virgen de los Dolores*, "*La Dolorita*") using the long-drums.

The main drumming events for the dead are the final *novena* of this nine-night prayer ceremony, called in the greater Villa Mella area the *rezo*, and the anniversary of death, the *cabo de año*, called a *banco*. The first anniversary is always celebrated, as well as a final anniversary—usually at the seventh year; others may be required if requested as needed by the spirit of the deceased, revealed through dream or possession of an heir. The rezo is like a second burial (a ritual known in many places of the world), in which the spirit of the deceased is dispatched, the material remains having been interred nine days earlier. In the rezo, only the deceased dances, by possessing a relative of the opposite sex, with a candle in the right hand. The movements entail a slow side-to-side swaying near the altar, a sym-

Fig. 14. *Sarandunga* dance (caught in the balancing step) of the *cofradía* of San Juan Bautista in Baní, Province of Peravia, during the processional visits to the homes of select members of the brotherhood on the return from the blessing at the river at dawn on the Day of St. John, June 1979. The dancers are Justiliano Mojica and Rafaela Germán. June 1979. Photograph: Martha Ellen Davis. Used by permission of Martha Ellen Davis, Gainesville, Florida.

bolic coffin called the *túmbulo*. This almost always occurs at the beginning of the ritual. In the banco, the deceased dances the first three pieces alone, then takes a partner for the rest of the event.

The livelier tempos of drums for the saints in the eastern, border, and southwestern regions call for a livelier dance. The main rhythms of both the east and the southwest are called *palo corrido* (running drums), suggesting the tempo and energy of the dance; in the southwest, this is also known as *palos del Espíritu Santo* (Drums of the Holy Spirit), patron of the huge and expanding Afro-Dominican brotherhood of the entire southwestern region. The dance is especially energetic in Las Matas de Farfán, in which large and rapid steps are used and the gestures of challenge, escape, and pursuit are overt, not subtle. The greatest extreme in baile de palos is the male virtuosity in the *sarandunga*, the dance of the Afro-

Dominican enclave of the Province of Peravia and its capital town of Baní. The man, during the balancing step, changes his weight from one foot to another in exaggerated fashion while characteristically surrounding the woman with his outstretched arms, flaunting a handkerchief in his courtship antics.

"Gagá"

The Dominican drum dance as well as its social dance strikes a contrast with the style of the Haitian dance of rará (pronounced "gagá" by Dominicans), introduced during the last third of the twentieth century by Haitian braceros, seasonal sugarcane cutters. The gagá is performed by Vodou-like societies in the sugarcane communities (bateyes), no more than one per community. The head of the society is a community and religious leader, usually male, who enters into a seven-year vow with its patron deity, of the Pétro family of deities (a subset of Vodou of Central African origin with perhaps local and even Native-American influences). The dance is performed to the Pétro drums with an ensemble of single-note bamboo trumpets of differing pitches, played in hocket (synchronization), accompanied by singing.

There are two types of dance or stylized movement: acrobatic maneuvers with batons by the four mayores, clad in multicolored skirts of attached scarves (each representing a deity)—actually a show as much as a dance; and the dance by the accompanying public (which can be worked into a brief routine by some members of a gagá society). The former, a routine coordinated among the four mayores, uses a walking or running step with abrupt stops and direction changes. There is a characteristic bend at the waist, but no hip movement whatsoever. The latter, women's dance, is openly lascivious in movement, accompanied by risqué text. The reason is that the gagá, done during the Lenten season culminating on Good Friday, is, like the Christian practice, a celebration of death-and-rebirth, that is, death-and-life. Hence it celebrates fertility, especially human fertility.

This dance is done by women and girls dancing alone or in ensembles of two or three, all positioned front to back facing the same direction and joined closely together. The legs are spread, knees bent, feet not lifted. The women dance in place, the weight alternated from one leg to another with an exaggerated lateral movement as the women wriggle up and down, reaching as high and low as possible. This is done in the middle of a packed entourage, so there is no space and no other movement. It is done during just a portion of a piece, as the gagá ensemble goes from house to house in the *batey*, like the Hispanic Christmas *parranda*, seeking rum or monetary donations. It is performed spontaneously by any female, or as a rehearsed showy routine with girls of the gagá ensemble, as part of the solicitation.

Social Dance

In the rural context, the velación, which serves an entertainment as well as a devotional function, and the brothel are the major sites for social dance and creativity. In the urban context, the taverns or mom-and-pop corner groceries/bars (*pulperías, colmados*)—often open-air and with no gender or age restriction—are popular venues. Whole families may enjoy a daylong, daytime Sunday event called a *pasadía* in a town's tavern. The elite dance in a town's exclusive social club (*club, casino*) is a selective courtship context to foster endogamy.

Social dance is a major vehicle of dialectical musical exchange between rural and urban sectors and the oral and literate traditions. Urban social dance of elite venues has often entailed fashionable foreign as well as national genres of folk origin, which are transformed and popularized in urban dancehalls. They may then diffuse back to rural areas and be conserved there in the oral tradition to this day. In the late eighteenth and early nineteenth centuries, the vogue was the English-French country dance (contradance) and quadrille and, later in the century, the Central European waltz, mazurka, and polka. Creole genres of Latin American origin became trendy in the late nineteenth century; by the 1920s, the rage was U.S. dances: the one-step, the two-step, and the foxtrot. In the 1920s, the Dominican merengue of the Cibao became more popular in the dancehall and was promoted by Trujillo after 1930. Trujillo's promotion of the merengue accelerated the trend toward orchestration of the genre, with the addition of band instruments that had started with the alto saxophone in the 1920s. Later, brass instruments were added, reflecting a U.S. big-band influence (Alberti 1975).

Since at least the time of the founding of the Republic in 1844, dance band musicians have served as a conduit for introduction of rural dance genres, albeit arranged, into the halls of the urban elite and, conversely, for transmission of urban fashion in social dance, often of foreign origin, to the rural domain. The dance band musicians, often members of a town's municipal band, are usually young men from the middle or lower class trained in band instruments at the local public music school (*Academia de Música*); the best are then hired by the municipal band (*banda de música municipal*). The flexibility of performance venue required by their profession and the need to make a living call for expertise in a wide range of genres and styles. So both dance and concert bands and their musicians serve as bridges between social classes, town and country milieu, and the oral and written traditions. At the same time, through music literacy, both municipal and military bands in Latin America also provide income and social mobility for their musicians, as does military service itself. The military theme in Dominican social-dance genres is further discussed below.

Virtually no documentation exists for social dance until the nineteenth century. A synthesis of Dominican rural and urban social dance starting at that time includes, in approximate chronological order of introduction:

Genres based on the *zapateo* (from the Moorish-influenced Spanish folk *zapateado*): These are the *sarambo* in the Cibao and *guarapo* in El Seybo (formerly the principal town in the east). These dances use the face-to-face step, where the zapateado occurs, alternated with the step of fleeing and ritual pursuit, a structure identical to the drum dance discussed above. An unaccompanied portion for virtuosic dance flourishes or *flores*, is called the *callao* ("silent") (Garrido de Boggs 1961, 12).

Derivatives of the seventeenth-century English country dance and the minuet, taken to France at the end of the seventeenth century (*contredanse*), and from there to Saint-Domingue (Garrido de Boggs 1961, 14) and Santo Domingo, are characterized by a caller (*bastonero*) as in a quadrille (*cuadrilla*), but are danced in a circle. They include the *carabiné* of the southwest (named for the Carabine rifle), presumably an imitation by Dominicans of the dance of Haitian troops (*carabinier*) during their border occupation of 1805 (Nolasco 1956, 317), and the pan-Caribbean *bambulá* (*bamboula*) still performed in the Haitian-derived (from about 1824) enclave in Tesón, Samaná. The *tumba dominicana* of the north (formerly more widespread) diminished the role of the caller and elevated couples' choreographic virtuosity. A much more complex version known in Saint-Domingue, the *tumba francesa*, was taken to Santiago de Cuba with the outmigration following the Haitian Revolution. The tumba was displaced in Santo Domingo by the rise of the merengue, ca. 1850 (Coopersmith 1949, 18–19).

Fashionable European dances of the mid-nineteenth century included the waltz (*valse*), the mazurka—perhaps becoming the basis of the *mangu-*

lina in the south—and the *schotis* (schottische), allegedly danced in the north by Spanish officers during the period 1861–1865, when the country briefly returned to Spanish control. The schotis was said to have been imitated by locals as the *chenche* or *chenche matriculado* ("matriculado" referring to "enlisted" men). Fashionable European dances of the later nineteenth century included the *pasodoble*, the basis, for example, of the *chivo* of Samaná, which is still known.

Hispanic-Caribbean creole urban dances of the late nineteenth century included the Puerto Rican *danza* and the Cuban *danzón*, presumably also derived from the *contradanza*, but with African-influenced rhythms (see Austerlitz 1997, 15–29). Austerlitz (1997, 15–17) points out their influence on the orchestrated merengue of the ballroom.

They also included the *son*—of possible Hispaniola origin, but attributed to Santiago de Cuba and possibly re-imported around the 1930s with the fashion for the Cuban *sexteto* ensemble. The son is performed and enjoyed by the Afro-Dominican lower-class sector of Santo Domingo and is also preserved in the Afro-Dominican enclave of Villa Mella, just north of the capital. Such popular dance music of the central-south region was and is played on a steel-stringed guitar and *tres*, while the accordion became popular in the north. The son gave rise to the popularity of the *bachata*, formerly referring to a noisy backyard musical party. More recently, starting in the late 1970s, the term began to refer to a commercial musical genre associated with the urban poor, which Pacini Hernández (1995) aptly terms a "music of marginality." Today it is commercially increasingly popular, second only to the orchestrated merengue in nightclubs. Another creole urban dance is the Latin-American bolero, for the slow dances in clubs.

Local creole rural dances, developed in the New World or Dominican Republic itself, include genres of various sources and time periods. The regional creole rural dance that is most popular and has diffused throughout the country, displacing other genres of rural social dance, is the merengue típico (also called *perico ripiao*) of the Cibao region, the dance that developed into the commercial, orchestrated merengue. An evolution of the folk merengue is the *pambiche* (the term from a cloth called "palmbeach" or perhaps the *bambouche*, the Haitian good-time dance), supposedly a musical adaptation of the movement of U.S. Marines trying to dance the merengue during the first U.S. occupation, 1916–1924.

Other forms of merengue include the *chivo* (or *chivo florete*) of Samaná, which allies a Spanish pasodoble with a merengue. In other regions, the colonial pan-Caribbean *juba* (*djouba*) dance is represented in today's *pripri* dance of the east/central-south region, and its accompanying juba drum, called in the Dominican Republic, *balsié*. The eastern/south-central balsié is a single-headed short drum laid horizontally on the ground, the player seated atop and dampening the skin with his heel as his hands beat and rub the waxed membrane on either side of his foot. In its wide colonial distribution and position of playing, its use is similar to that of the long drums in the bambulá. Other instruments of the eastern/south-central pripri ensemble are the accordion, the *güira*, and the Dominican marimba (that is, *marímbula*). The pripri dance, as observed today, with its small intricate steps and hip movement, is an embraced social dance, a sort of *merengue redondo* (round merengue) in which the couple pivots on an axis.

Another set of creole rural dances is performed in the southwest region. Each has its own origin, but today three genres are allied in performance: the carabiné, the mangulina, and either the valse (of the above category of fashionable European dances) or the danza (of the above category of Hispanic-Caribbean creole urban dances), depending on the region. The merengue adapted from the style of the Cibao may also be added to the set due to its current national ubiquity. The instrumental ensemble is also called pripri, though the instrumentation is different from that of social dance of the east: the accordion, a drum also called balsié but different in structure, a large tambourine with a laced head, and a güira (but no marimba). The southern balsié is half the size of a palo, with a single-laced goatskin head, and is held between the knees of the player, who dampens the sound by raising and lowering the drum against the ground.

More Merengue

The typical sound of the "typical merengue" (merengue típico) is of the accordion—the Hohner button accordion. However, the original melodic instruments were stringed, the guitar and the *tres;* these were replaced around the 1880s in the Cibao by the accordion, due to trade between Germany and Puerto Plata. The accordion of *norteño* or "Tex-Mex" music bridging northern Mexico and the United States has a similar German origin, and perhaps that of the Colombian *vallenato* does as well. The typical rhythm instrument is the tambora, a short, two-headed drum hung around the neck and played horizontally, beaten with the hand on one head and with a stick on the other. The ensemble also includes a scraper

Fig. 15. *Merengue típico* or *perico ripiao* danced in Santa María, province of San Cristóbal, at a fiesta during the Cuaresma Chiquita, between Easter and Pentecost, on the grounds of the *cofradía* of the Espiritu Santo, May 2000. The drum is the *tambora*. Photograph: Martha Ellen Davis. Used by permission of Martha Ellen Davis, Gainesville, Florida.

called the güira (a metal version of the gourd *güiro*) or *guayo* (grater). Since around the 1930s, to provide a bass, the marimba, which came in with the Cuban sexteto, has been added. Known in Cuba and Puerto Rico as the marímbula, it is a giant-sized Afro-Caribbean adaptation of the African thumb-piano, the *mbira*. The social dance ensembles from the east and the southwest (both called priprí as noted above) similarly use the accordion, though their drum types vary.

The merengue típico of the Cibao appears rather unchanging since the addition of the accordion. Within the continued traditionalism, current changes include a trend toward acceleration of tempo, and the addition, in the Dominican community in New York City, of modern instrumentation such as the conga drum and perhaps electric bass. There is also a current fashion of reverting to the string merengue, the pre-accordion, that is pre-1880s, Santo Domingo traditional accompaniment of popular dance, and this has been reinforced by an influence through the mass media of the similar Haitian *méringue*.

Key figures who have contributed to changes in the orchestrated merengue include Luis Alberti, composer and bandleader for Trujillo; the bandleader and singer Johnny Ventura, important in commercializing the merengue internationally; Joseíto Mateo, virtuosic dancer as well as composer and singer; Wilfrido Vargas; Milly Quezada; and others. Paul Austerlitz in his 1997 book *Merengue* and Del Castillo and García Arévalo in their 1992 *Anthology of the Merengue* provide a full discussion of the topic. Currently, Juan Luis Guerra, a musician and composer trained at Berklee College of Music, has tapped the merengue típico and the bachata and made these genres, of peasant and urban-slum identity respectively, palatable and even fashionable among the Dominican bourgeoisie. However, his merengue típico is too rapid to dance.

The structure and dance style are similar in both the merengue típico and the orchestrated variety. Both, of course, are couple dances, in duple time, in which the man leads—like other social dances and in contrast to the drum dance. The structure of both includes three sections: the *paseo* ("stroll"), for selecting the female partner and positioning oneself on the dance floor (added in the 1920s, if not before, but eliminated in today's orchestrated merengues), the merengue proper, and the *jaleo* ("fuss" or "good time"), which is characterized by virtuosic figures in the urban, orchestrated variety. As the merengue section begins, the pumping clasped hands of the couple (the man's left and the woman's right) serve to mark the rhythm and thus set the tempo for the dancers prior to launching forth with the feet. Like many other Afro-Latin American social dances, lateral hip movement is emphasized over foot or leg movements, except for the virtuosic movements of the male in the jaleo. In the típico version, there is more vertical movement and less hip movement.

In both versions, the feet are slid rather than stepped, the woman to her right, the man to his left. The steps are slightly retarded with regard to the music (the "off-beat phrasing" characteristic of African influence); salsa is also danced this way. In the típico version, according to current observations, each couple is autonomous. In the gracious, traditional setting of the dancehall (as opposed to the discothèque or night club), there is a collective pattern of movement around the hall in counterclockwise direction (as in all ritual movement of African origin!), with an audible slide of the feet on the floor on the second and fourth beats.

The jaleo is marked musically by the end of the soloist's stanzas and the beginning of a chorus section with shorter phrases and heightened intensity. In the merengue of the dancehall, the man directs the woman, then follows her, in figures of precisely executed turns under and around the couples' arms. The típico dance does not use these turns; rather there is an intensification, with a lowered posture, and accentuation of steps, a tighter embrace, and more pivoting turns as a couple. The orchestrated merengue, reflecting an international trend in urban music, shows a tendency toward an acceleration of tempo, so much so that dance is sometimes rendered difficult. In a set at a discothèque, salsa and the slow bolero will be represented, today bachata may be added as well, but most numbers will be merengue.

Lo Que se Pierde en Santo Domingo: The Study of Folklore and the *Ballet Folklórico*

Given the rapid decline of the varieties of Dominican folkdance, starting in the 1940s René Carrasco, a tailor and self-taught researcher and performer of Dominican folkdance, who died in 1978, assumed the mission of self-funded research and conservation through staged re-creation of the Dominican dance heritage. He titled his writings and series of home-industry recordings of his folkdance troupe *Lo que se pierde en Santo Domingo* (What is being lost in Santo Domingo). Although Puerto Plata bandleader Julio Arzeno was the first to publish transcribed Dominican folk music in 1927, and foreign folklorist Manuel J. Andrade was sent by Columbia University anthropologist Franz Boas to collect folktales in the late 1920s, Carrasco was probably the first to acknowledge the significant African heritage apparent in Dominican music and dance. The Négritude movement of the early twentieth century elsewhere in the Caribbean had bypassed the Dominican Republic. But, based on his readings, Carrasco often pontificated about the tripartite Dominican heritage: the native Taíno, the Spanish, and the African.

The only Dominican professional folklorist, Edna Garrido de Boggs (b. 1913), is also aware of the African heritage, although her training and interest have led her to focus on other genres. She points out that Dominican folklore has changed notably in her lifetime from predominantly Hispanic to more markedly African-based. The reasons undoubtedly stem from both a liberalization of proscribed practices and the changing demographic composition of the country with the substantial Haitian influx.

Unlike many countries, the Dominican Republic has never offered much governmental support for the conservation of the traditional cultural patrimony. Trujillo's government did support the pioneering field research and recordings, starting in 1947, of Edna Garrido de Boggs, whose father was minister of education. Carrasco, on the other hand, had no support. However, his pupils from his dance school in the colonial city, affectionately called the *Cueva Colonial* (colonial cave), have carried on the promotion of folkdance, albeit stylized.

Following Trujillo, during the short-lived progressive government of constitutional president Juan Bosch under the Partido Revolucionario Dominicano (PRD), there was a national folkdance festival in Santo Domingo in 1963 and support of a field research visit by the Argentine ethnomusicologist Isabel Aretz and her husband, Venezuelan folklorist Luis Felipe Ramón y Rivera (Aretz and Ramón y Rivera 1963). Fradique Lizardo (1930–1997) of San Cristóbal, involved in the festival and the research trip, launched his career as a self-made folklorist on his return in 1973 from self-imposed exile in Cuba. More gifted as a promoter than as a scientist or artist, he initiated a newspaper campaign to discredit other folklorists (such as Carrasco) and make his name as the première Dominican folklorist based on continual ethnographic "discoveries," capitalizing on the African component of Dominican dance heritage. He founded a folkdance ensemble and he published extensively. Eventually, by the late 1970s, he achieved the institutionalization of a national folkdance troupe with himself as director.

During the 1970s there was a proliferation of folkdance troupes. These included groups directed by the singer Casandra Damirón and the dancer Josefina Miniño. The ministry of tourism also founded its own ensemble, directed by a former accordion player with Carrasco's ensemble. The public university, the Universidad Autónoma de Santo Domingo, has its ensemble (actually now two), although around 1945 Edna Garrido de Boggs had founded one there as well. Following the return of the PRD to the presidency in 1978, there was an increased support of arts and culture, which had an impact beyond governmental institutions. Many research teams and folkdance ensembles were started by young people in neighborhood and small-town cultural clubs, a Caribbean phenomenon. However, given the centralization in the country, sometimes they were influenced by the urban-based "ballet folklórico" as a performance genre itself, and emulated the uniformed, synchronized folk troupes rather than the traditions of their own elders.

The Redefinition of Dominican Identity through Music and Dance

Today a number of Dominican musicians, of various class origins, are collecting and performing Afro-Dominican genres as an antithesis to hispanidad. Although they are mainly musicians, their performances also include dance. They have been inspired by René Carrasco, Fradique Lizardo, the folkdance troupe of the Universidad Autónoma de Santo Domingo, the musical group "Convite" (founded around 1975 by sociology professor Dagoberto Tejeda and now disbanded), and their local cultural clubs. They are motivated by the same human-rights ideology as those who, a short generation ago, would have performed the *nueva canción* or *nueva trova* with guitar. But they reframe this pan-Latin American social ideology to focus on the Afro-Latin American cultural sector. These musicians are different from many ballet folklórico performers because they actually engage in field research, albeit not systematic. Their purpose in "research" is to make shorthand recordings for imitation and to fraternize for inspiration and nourishment of the spirit. Pioneers in this vein include Luis Días, formerly lead musician of Convite, who taps the traditional sources for entirely unique compositions in both folk revival and Latin rock modes, rendering stylized drum rhythms on acoustic or electric guitar. They also include Tony Vicioso, formerly a rock musician who pioneered joint performances with traditional musicians. Others include José Duluc, Willian Alemán, Bony Raposo, Edis Sánchez, Osvaldo Sánchez, Roldán Marmol, and many more.

Given their human-rights and Afro-Dominican ideology, often expressed in mode of dress and hairstyle as well as in music and lyrics, they have been harassed by local police. And because of the lower-class origins of many, they have been marginalized from support and subsidy. Therefore, it is the expatriate musicians, primarily in New York City but also elsewhere, such as Duluc in Japan, who enjoy freedom for their artistic development and expression, as well as a cultural and economic milieu supportive of the arts. In New York City, where "black is beautiful" has long been an integral part of the ideological configuration, their message is well received, celebrated, and subsidized.

New York folk and popular arts organizations—the World Music Institute, the Center for Traditional Music and Dance (formerly the Ethnic Folk Arts Center), and CityLore—promote Afro-Dominican music and dance and musicians and dancers. Most notable is the CTMD's Dominican Community Cultural Initiative, which has led to a community-organized annual festival, "Quisqueya en el Hudson." Since 2000 it has become independent of the CTMD and is now organized by the association NewQuisqueyanos.

It is very possible that through music and dance, expatriate Dominican artists may influence the redefinition of Dominican cultural identity. It is already beginning to happen. In the nightclubs of New York City, Dominicans dance to orchestrated merengues, and in the typical restaurants, to merengue típico. In the last fifteen years, bachata has been added to the dance club repertoire as well, symbolizing a transcendence of social class. It is danced much like a Cuban or Dominican son.

The current trend in Dominican clubs in New York is live performances of palos between merengue sets. This is not a show, but another ensemble for dancing, and the public does dance. The regional style selected for performance in this context is the sprightly *palos del Espíritu Santo* of the Southwest region, the one Dominican drum rhythm that is expanding rather than contracting its base of supporters within the Republic, and now New York, thus becoming a sort of generic palos rhythm. The vogue of the palos in the clubs—as well as growing demand for spiritualist sessions called *manís*—has rendered the palos ensembles so much in demand that several new ones have been formed; their directors say they are doing well. At the same time, there has been a proliferation of CD recordings by these and other performers of Afro-Dominican music, some revivalist, some creative, some performed jointly with traditional musicians.

The Afro-Dominican movement is currently being channeled primarily through music. However, dance has also been a part of this awakening for many years, since the ensembles of René Carrasco and Fradique Lizardo. Lead dancers in this dimension of the movement in the Dominican Republic have been Nereyda Rodríguez of Lizardo's ensemble (starting in the mid-1970s) and, more recently, the dancer/researcher Marilí Gallardo, who directs a dance group called Kalalú Danza. In New York, Leonardo Iván Domínguez, another member of Convite, puts his Afro-Dominican ideology into practice as director of the Conjunto Folklórico of the Alianza Dominicana, the largest Dominican social-service agency. He views young expatriate Dominicans' development of expertise in, and performance of, Afro-Dominican dance genres as a form of communion with one's national identity, redefined.

A similar search for national identity and expression of an Afro-Dominican ideology is occurring in the visual arts. Like musicians and dancers, some visual artists engage in field research for inspiration and a quest for authenticity. Their work—viewed as cultural insiders—is very different from artists who paint or photograph Afro-Dominican figures as picturesque or exotic motifs. A pioneer in a research-based artistic representation of Afro-Dominican culture has been Geo Ripley, painter and installation artist of Santo Domingo. Contemporary painters also include Ricardo Toribio of Santiago de los Caballeros—formerly a professional photographer, who plays his field recordings for inspiration as he paints. Among expatriates, a leading artist is Charo Oquet of Miami, who is not only a professional painter and installation artist, but also a community leader in the arts; she organizes an annual Dominican Youth Arts Festival in Miami.

Therefore, as Afro-U.S. music/dance culture has become U.S. culture, one can foresee the same process underway in the Dominican Republic and its expatriate communities. Once exotic to the urban elite and bourgeoisie, the palos are being taken on as their own by a larger Dominican community beyond specific Afro-Dominican enclaves. As a result, the social function of palos music and dance is changing. Once they were the voice of the patron saint of mutual-aid societies of former slaves and marginal freemen. In today's transnational world the palos—including congos and *sarandunga* variants and the related Haitian-Dominican gagá—are becoming symbols of a revised Dominican national identity. As the merengue típico of the Cibao transcended region and the rural sector to represent the nation, and as the current popularity of bachata transcends class, so the palos are overcoming not only rural-sector, but also racial barriers, and gagá is beginning to overcome the more recalcitrant national barrier, superimposed on the racial.

As part of the process, within the regionally based palos variants, the semisacred music and dance of palos is suffering the same fate suffered by the merengue: as the lively palos del Espíritu Santo of the southwest becomes the generic palos rhythm and dance in commercial venues of dancehall, recording media, and the lucrative *Vodú* party known as the *maní*, it is marginalizing regional rhythms. Nonetheless, more significant is the growing national popularity of palos of whatever region. Their vogue implicitly broadens Dominicans' concept of their national cultural patrimony to embrace the Afro-Dominican. Thus, for both performer and public, Afro-Dominican folk music and dance are reshaping Dominican national identity.

11

◇ ◇ ◇

A Dominican York in Andhra

Ramón H. Rivera-Servera

It might come to the reader as a surprise that, in the context of a book on Caribbean dance and identity, the suggested geography for this article is India. A Dominican York in Andhra? The title evokes a transnational geography where the Dominican subject, hybridized through her now familiar experience of immigration in New York, performs an additional journey, reaching the far regions of South Asia. And what about the Caribbean? The Caribbean has indeed been influenced by a wealth of Indian cultural practices, primarily in the British colonies, through the import of Indian labor at the height of the plantation economy. But where then the connection to the Dominican experience, you may ask? Are we perhaps suffering from a transnational shipwreck?

Not exactly. Indeed, as many cultural critics have observed, transnational intersections have only increased with the continued demographic reconfiguration of the globe through the histories of migratory travels and the influx of new technologies that bring the world closer together. In this context, then, space is reconfigured, producing new localities that function as intersections where communities across the globe encounter each other and transform previous assumptions about the nature of cultural identity.

New York City functions as one such intersection: a place where the world meets and clashes, perhaps violently, but often productively, to constitute a truly hybrid cultural landscape. It is in a metropolitan setting such as New York City where India may encounter the Dominican Republic—through direct contact or perhaps through the longer routes of the British Indo-Caribbean diaspora—and set in motion an intercultural dance based on affinity and the hopes of recovering the story of their respective travels and histories to produce, in the present, a proud identity of survival. This article is concerned with such a dance by looking at *Dominicanish*, Josefina Baez's production, directed by Claudio Mir, at Dance Theater Workshop in New York City in November 1999. In this performance piece Baez utilizes kuchipudi movement, a classical Indian narrative dance form, as a strategy for exploring and critiquing the experiences of the Dominican diaspora in New York City.

Dominicanish, Baez's name not only for the piece but also for her mix of Spanish and English in her verbalized text, is invested in exploring, through the body, the changing geographies of the city and the transcultural experience of globality, in order to emerge renewed and to perform Dominican identity in movement. Baez's postmodern performance appears to take up a strategy in which the body engages in what has been called psychasthenic disorientation (Caillois 1984, 16–32; Olalquiaga 1992, 2)—losing a sense of itself while lost in a larger territory—but emerges recuperated, constituted out of the multiplicity of influences it encounters, thereby embodying the effects of a complex cultural moment, asserting an identity triumphantly.

Curiously, *Dominicanish* opens with the projection of a video clip of a group of dancers in Gagá, an Afro-Dominican carnival celebration that originated in Haiti and takes place during Lent. The bodies move in a polyrhythmic frenzy, accelerating in speed as the drums indicate a shift of pattern. This videoed rendition of the body serves as an affirmation of tradition and an identification with the performative manifestations of race in a country where discrimination based on skin color is rampant. The image on the screen, altered by the lens of the medium, also marks the distance between any idealized or utopian conception of home and the location of the performance in the metropolis. After a few minutes of footage, the image disappears and the stage goes dark and silent. In this opening scene the body is displayed in virtuosic prowess and is then abruptly absented from view. The video serves as evidence of the presence of a Dominican subject, a body to be recovered in the context of the performance, through travel into the memories inscribed in it. In *Dominicanish*, the body emerges as Baez utilizes the movement base of kuchipudi to present a complex solo piece about the pains and pleasures of the Dominican immigrant experience in New York City.

Josefina Baez's use of kuchipudi is grounded in a politics of affinity, one that honors the cultural origins and migration history of the performance form and relates to it a similarly complex history of travel. It is precisely this engagement with other diasporic communities that *Dominicanish* performs by embodying the dance tradition of kuchipudi as a vehicle to explore Dominican identity. Kuchipudi offers a series of elementary parallels to Baez's project: focusing on divinity, positioning the traveler-performer in a collaborative relationship to the community, and presenting a history of intervention by women in a space traditionally reserved for men.

Kuchipudi dance-drama developed from Bhakti devotional practices to Krishna at the beginning of the seventeenth century. As in most classical Indian theater, there are multiple stories of origin for this performance form. (For an introduction to kuchipudi in English, see Guru C. R. Acharaya and Mallika Sarabhai's *Understanding Kuchipudi*, 1992, New Delhi: Indira Gandhi National Center for the Arts.) The name of the dance form is said to derive from its origins in the village of Kuchelapuram, in translation, "village of the poor," in the South Indian region of Andhra Pradesh. For Baez, who studied it in Andhra, kuchipudi offers a performance form based on devotion, and although Baez's performance is not about religious reverence, and is, in fact, often irreverently funny, her focus is in exploring what she calls "the divinity" of the Dominican subject (interview with Josefina Baez, Nov. 1999). In the context of *Dominicanish*, this devotional practice constitutes a community affirming project, where Dominican identity figures as the celebrated deity.

Kuchipudi dancers developed parallel to the tradition of bhakta traveling performers. Bhaktas traveled throughout the southern region of India, performing their devotional dance drama from village to village and receiving their sustenance in return. Baez emulates this tradition in the performance development process for *Dominicanish*, traveling through the city in a series of open rehearsals, *apartarte/casarte* (apartment art/ house art), hosted at Dominican immigrant households throughout New York City. Through these performance events, Baez travels to the intimate space of the home to workshop her theater practice and solicit the community's input and support in developing her pieces. The development of the performance is thus housed at the site of community, serving then as a collective embodiment of diasporic history.

Traditionally, kuchipudi was exclusively performed by Brahmin men, who performed both male and female roles. Since their introduction as kuchipudi performers during the 1960s, women have taken lead in the performance and choreography of the form, significantly outnumbering men. A recent article in *Dance Magazine* further develops the history of this transition by incorporating the role of the diasporic community of women in the United States as a strong force in the continuation of Indian classical dance, including kuchipudi, and in furthering innovation into the choreographic possibilities of these traditions (Bleiberg 2000). Baez's approach to performance assumes a similar role in the recording of the Dominican experience from her location in the United States, while it develops a critically feminist intervention in the collective memory of her community. Likewise, her adoption of kuchipudi as a movement base for a performance about Dominican identity is a signal of how she makes a space for innovation in a tradition of theater about the Dominican experience that has largely remained restricted to the conventions of realist drama.

The adoption of Indian classical dance drama is thus a move toward enunciating an encounter between cultures in the metropolis and an active participation in the changing geographies of the city. These dynamics point toward a practice of coalition among peoples of color, and thus mark a significant difference in approach from the more problematic Eurocentric appropriations of culture by American and European theater practitioners.

The correspondence between kuchipudi and Baez's performance process, although extremely important in understanding her approach, remains, for the most part, obscured from the spectator. Instead, it is the use of kuchipudi on stage, with its distancing effect, that affects the spectatorship of the performance most successfully. It is specifically in this approach to the formal aspects of the staged performance that Baez performs a feminist politics of the body, demonstrating dance's capacity to produce meaning critically.

Kuchipudi movement is characterized by its rhythmic patterns, intricate gestures, and subtle employment of facial expression. The arms and legs maintain a triangular shape varied by their curvilinear movement. *Dominicanish* is strictly bound to the conventions of kuchipudi, though it abstracts it with a different emphasis and does not use all of the elements of the form, in particular not all of the elaborate array of emotion-conveying, story-telling facial and hand gestures, nor kuchipudi's jumps and turns. Baez's movement is dominated by contained standing sequences with the torso in vertical stress. Movement variation is primarily located in the extremities. Leg movement is limited to stomping and stepping in place. Most movement in *Dominicanish* derives from the basic four-step sequence below:

Standing position facing the audience. Feet are flat on the floor pointing away from the body and heels are touching (almost identical to ballet's first position). The legs are slightly bent at the knees with the toes raised off the floor.

The right heel stomps forward and slightly to the far side of the right leg.

The right foot returns to its original position.

The left heel stomps forward and slightly to the far side of the left leg.

The left foot returns to its original position.

This movement sequence is combined with a rhythmically paralleled opening and closing of the arms in a plane. Some variations occur to this basic structure. The body may rotate in place, changing the orientation of the dancer, or the stomping may be crossed in the front or in the back.

At times, the stomping sequences have forward or backward variations or progress across the stage in strong and directed phrases. Her legs are rarely raised with the exception of some across-stage marching. The arms extend outward to the side of the body and open and close at the forearm. The weight of the body is grounded at the abdomen. Shape transitions are concentrated at the limbs as well. The knees are kept straight or bent, never locked, to form a diamond shape in the lower body. The arms are maintained in sharp linear or angular shapes. Arm orientation is primarily in a plane, with some instances of cutting forward.

Dominicanish employs a wealth of gestural motifs, mostly using the upper torso, directly borrowed from the highly iconographic repertoire of Indian classical dance. The gestural phrases do not register semiotically for the audience, which is composed primarily of theater spectators without knowledge of kuchipudi's language. Baez does not utilize kuchipudi gestures for their iconography. The strict use of the movement pattern and its strangeness to the audience calls attention to itself in contrast to more recognizable movement sequences, establishing a distancing effect.

This enables the audience to engage critically with Baez's fragmentary and charged use of verbal language. As she states in our November 1999 interview, "If I give you the obvious movement you will get bored and I will lose you. Since my movement is alien to you and you have to work as an audience member, you are more likely to listen to what I have to say." The use of an "alien" movement base also evokes displacement, a central trope in Baez's treatment of the diasporic experience in America. However, this experience of alienation is critically employed and acted upon as a generative element in a politics of survival. The laying out of a distancing movement pattern helps to make the recovery of gestural intelligibility much more intense, and thus theatrically effective.

For example, when narrating the travel from the Dominican Republic to New York, Baez mimics with her arms the action of paddling a canoe. Her arms are bent at the elbow, gripping an imaginary paddle, the right hand is placed about six inches on top of the left hand and the movement is initiated from the right elbow toward the left side of the body. This gesture is recognizable because Baez identifies it in the spoken narrative about migration and because the movement, rupturing from the basic kuchipudi pattern, directly references the action mimetically.

Directly following the paddling sequence in performance, Baez transforms a traditional kuchipudi gesture through narrative contextualization, to function illustratively. Using a *hamsapaksha* hand gesture—thumb bent to touch the base of the first finger, little finger extending upward and the rest of the fingers bent to make the hand hollow—which refers to a goosewing in kuchipudi, Baez speaks of the return travel from New York to the Dominican Republic. This transformation of the kuchipudi source movement into a recognizable gesture illustrates a strategic vernacularization of the performance vocabulary, moments in the performance where the movement signifies important moments and/or ideas to the community, through an intelligible gesture.

In *The Signifying Monkey: A Theory of African-American Literary Criticism*, cultural critic Henry Louis Gates, Jr., locates African-American vernacular practices in relation to white America as a "simultaneous, but negated, parallel discursive (ontological, political) universe" (Gates 1988, 21). Gates makes a distinction between signification as the dominant discourse of whiteness and Signification as the African-American vernacularization of it. Baez's use of recognizable movement sequences within the kuchipudi-based performance Signifies Dominican cultural experience. Each significant break from kuchipudi occurs when Baez is either affirm-

Fig. 16. Josefina Baez in *Dominicanish*, showing the *hamsapaksha* (goose-wing) gesture, referring to travel. Used by permission of Josefina Baez, New York, N.Y.

ing community or addressing a crucial aspect of its experience: narrating travel, staging Dominican identification with African-American culture, or describing neighborhoods where many Dominicans live such as Manhattan Valley and Washington Heights.

Baez utilizes two different strategies to signify within the kuchipudi movement: recontextualization of a kuchipudi pattern through the verbal articulation of a narrative—illustrated by the use of *hamsapaksha* hand gesture described above—and a more confrontational juxtaposition of kuchipudi with a recognizable movement pattern. The direct confrontation strategy is best exemplified in the "Black is Beautiful" sequence where Baez alternates between the strong and direct planar isolation of the extended arm originated in the shoulder in a vertical axis position and a more inward and curvaceous isolation of the arms and shoulders, slight tilt forward of the torso, and circular motion of the head. The more flowing, soft movements evoke the bodily attitude of soul dancing and are further vernacularized by Baez's text. As she Signifies with her body she speaks affirmative phrases such as "Black is beautiful" and "Black is my color." The sharper movements of kuchipudi function dialectically to enable the heightened moment of community affirmation and establish a relationship of affinity to African-American cultural tradition in the United States.

In the "Isley Brothers" sequence, Baez performs another act of Signification. In this section Baez disrupts the back and forth direction of the foot pattern to a side-step–arm-swing combination characteristic of the Isley Brothers soul music act. Baez identifies the soul performers as her professors, establishing African-American popular performers, mainstreamed through shows like *Soul Train*, as primary figures of identification and influence to immigrants of color in New York City. Baez in performance says:

> I thought I'd never learn English never, nunca. I don't want my mouth to look all funny! Yo me se un chin: boy, girl love you, she does, she doesn't. Pero yo encontre mis profesores los hermanos Isley el sabado en *Soul Train*! Hermanos Isla . . . Hermanos Isley . . . los Isley Brothers! [I know a bit: boy, girl love you, she does, she doesn't. But I found my professors, the Isley brothers on Saturday in *Soul Train*! Island brothers . . . Brothers Isley . . . the Isley Brothers!] (Sings along to the music of the Isley Brothers.)
>
> Now I don't care what my mouth looks like. . . . I like what I say. Dominican miracle, writing sentences in perfect syntax. Poetry that they thought me . . . the Isley Brothers. (She raises her fist.) Fight the power!

In this section Baez parallels the language learning process with the learning of movement. The reference to *Soul Train* not only refers to the accessing of language through music, but is also a recognition of the world-making power of embodied culture; moving from a pleasurable identification with music, to an increased awareness of the power of language, to a full embodiment of the politics of radicalism. Furthermore, the identification with African-American popular culture enables yet another bridging with other marginal communities, thus confirming the power of coalitional politics, allowing for the identification with the marginal position of others. This positioning is not only spoken about, but also embodied in Baez's performance of the side-step routine. As she tells the story of gaining knowledge of the English language, the body gestures an identification with African-American popular music.

The performance style of this section is qualitatively different from the kuchipudi base in various ways. First, the step orientation is altered. Instead of following the four-step sequence illustrated above, the movement routine adopts a two-step routine to the side. A swinging forward movement of the arms and the isolation of the shoulder stand in stark contrast to the linear orientation of the kuchipudi base. Finally, the use of polyrhythms in this section is markedly different from the kuchipudi base sequence. The footsteps mark a different rhythm than the shoulders do.

I do not suggest that kuchipudi lacks polyrhythmic layering; in fact classical Indian dance is rich in its use of multiple counts, but the controlled usage of the form in *Dominicanish* doesn't exploit that possibility. Although Baez uses polyrhythmic isolation a few times in her kuchipudi sections, the orientation of the movement is always parallel to that of the base step. For example, when Baez moves her head in isolation over the basic step sequence, she moves it exclusively side to side, so that even when the head keeps a different rhythm, the movement follows the general directions and quality of the basic pattern. This is not the case with the Signifying sequences, where, although contained, the movement does not present as close a coordination among moving parts or clearly defined orientation of the movement. For example, in the "Pacheco" sequence, Baez describes the Manhattan Valley neighborhood through the people she comes in touch with; salsa/rumba rhythm and movement serve as the Signifying performance structure. As she marches across the stage, she says:

Hablo como Boricua y me peino como Morena
La viejita de abajo no e' viejita na'
El super se esta tirando a la culona del 5to piso
Jangueo con el pajaro del barrio
Me junto con la muchacha que salió preñá
Salgo con mi ex
Hablo con el muchacho que estaba preso
Garabatié paredes y trenes
City I pulled the emergency cord

[I talk like a Boricua (Puerto Rican) but comb my hair like a Black Woman/ The old lady from downstairs is not old at all/ The super is messing with the big ass from the 5th floor/ I hang out with the fairy of the neighborhood/ I get together with the girl that got pregnant/ I go out with my ex/ I talk to the young man who was in prison/ I tagged trains and walls/ City I pulled the emergency cord (my translation).]

In this sequence the recognizable city comes to life, offering a vivid portrait of life and staging for the audience the multiple bodies of the Dominican experience. The performance of the sequence is invested in pleasure, the sensuous undulations of a carnivalesque embodiment. Here, the body is recovered, not in the idealized image of the opening Gagá film, but in a similarly complex articulation of the body in motion. If the movement is somewhat more contained, the identities performed—the ex-convict, the old lady, the gay man, and the pregnant teenager—go about freeing any fixed imagination of a Dominican subject. This picture presents a marginal Dominican community. The sequence closes by pulling the emergency cord: a call to action.

The step pattern in this sequence offers an interesting comparison with the kuchipudi sequence because structurally it follows a very similar four-step trajectory. What differentiates this step pattern from that of kuchipudi is the side twist of the feet through the rotation originated at the hip socket. The general pattern is the same, but the salsa/rumba landing presents a freer quality and a lighter feel to the stomp. This freer quality of the movement is emphasized in the gyrating movement of the hips and the counterpoint breaks from the circular motion of the hands. The movement, because it flows more, gives the impression of being less restrictive.

Throughout *Dominicanish* movement is employed critically as an integral function of the performance. The kuchipudi pattern allows a distancing that forces the audience into a critical observation of the spoken text and creates a structure of movement that allows Baez's climactic insertions of the vernacular to be dramatically marked. These insertions Signify against the dominant movement pattern of the piece. Thus the body in movement performs an act of decolonization by reinscribing the vernacular, the language with which the marginal community historically identifies. The body in Baez's performance confronts its materiality, recovering a history that is at times painful, to travel assertively through the uncertain geographies of the global, while moving pleasurably to perform identity.

A Dominican York in Andhra, the diary notes of Josefina Baez in Andhra in 1998, is to be published in 2002. *Domincanish*, a performance text by Josefina Baez, was published in 2000. (Both works are published by I Ombe, P.O. Box 1387, Madison Square Station, New York, N.Y. 10159.)

❖   ❖   ❖

PUERTO RICO

12

◇ ◇ ◇

Dance in Puerto Rico

Embodied Meanings

Alma Concepción

There's a lot of Puerto Ricans out there that don't speak Spanish and aren't into the Spanish music, a lot of them and they're still proud to be Puerto Rican.
—Rick Rodríguez, Spanish-rap musician in Latin Empire

But if you don't know nothing about it, if you don't try to learn about it, you're gonna be lost in the sauce.
—Tony Boston, musician in Latin Empire

The 1970s New York–born musical and dance phenomenon called *salsa* has reached a broader audience today than ever as a new awareness has emerged in the United States and many other parts of the world about Latin American cultural expressions and their transformation in diasporic communities. This new awareness is not always accompanied by a historical or social understanding of the cultural background. As the twenty-first century begins, new technologies and globalization tend, in some cases, to minimize any need for understanding specificities and differences. And yet there is at the same time a growing tendency to look back and to look inside in an effort to chart neglected territories.

The recovery of memory and traditions is perhaps an aid for reconstructing identities and perhaps also for the rediscovery of deeper meanings beyond the here and now. A growing body of scholarship on popular culture in general, and on Latin American/Latino cultures in particular, poses new questions and new concepts for the analysis of musical and

dance traditions. Puerto Rican sociologist Angel Quintero-Rivera, for instance, in his 1998 book *Salsa, sabor y control,* explores music and dance
from a sociohistorical perspective that invites scholars to reconsider the
role of music in the forging of identities, especially in the Caribbean region and its migrations. This is precisely what I attempt to give in this
chapter: an overview of popular music and dance in Puerto Rico in the
context of Caribbean identities. This essay offers a brief historical narrative of the most salient aspects of dance and music, centered on the African legacy and on a broad definition of frontiers. I intend to point out the
importance of New York as a city of Caribbean encounters, encounters
that have generated the creation by the Caribbean-Latino population in
diaspora of new popular rhythms, such as salsa, as well as encounters that
have brought about new transformations and cultural practices of the
musical and dance heritage in the island of Puerto Rico.

What lies beneath these new or revived rituals of shared experiences?
Shaped to a large degree by diverse colonial powers and by the common
experience of slavery, Caribbean societies have undergone very complex
social processes in which many ethnicities in diaspora have come together.
Music, dance, and oral poetry have played a central role, particularly in
the maintenance and redefinition of identities and in the cohesion and
survival of cultural memories. To understand the complex context of this
experience, it is essential to look at Caribbean histories from a broad definition of "frontiers" and "crossings." Caribbean unity is not invariably
recognized as such, perhaps because of the many real linguistic and political differences. But, as artist and intellectual Rex Nettleford (1985) has
remarked in the initial chapters of *Dance Jamaica: Cultural Definitions and
Artistic Discovery: The National Dance Theatre Company of Jamaica, 1962–
1983,* the Caribbean as a whole hears the call to create for itself a coherent
reality—an existence—denied by history.

Puerto Rico is a case in point. The third largest of the Spanish-speaking Greater Antilles, it also belongs to the wider context of the Caribbean
archipelago. Since 1898 it has remained a colony of the United States, but
Puerto Ricans are also American citizens, moving (or migrating) frequently to the mainland. Part of an estimated population of almost four
million on the island and three million living in diaspora, Puerto Ricans in
New York City and in many other urban areas throughout the United
States have remained for several generations connected to the island.

For centuries music and dance have been an extraordinary expression of vitality and creativity. At the conclusion of the Spanish-Cuban-American War of 1898 there were at least three main musical and dance traditions in Puerto Rico: one in which Spanish roots were prominent; the second, derived from West African traditions; and a hybrid tradition resulting from what Quintero-Rivera and others call maroon societies. It is the African legacy that unites Puerto Rico to the Caribbean, while the Spanish musical traditions link the island with some of the Antilles and with the rest of the Hispanic world. In many ways Puerto Rico and the Puerto Rican experience belong simultaneously to colonial and postcolonial contexts.

At the end of the nineteenth century, the social elite in Puerto Rican cities danced to mostly European melodies, such as waltzes, mazurkas, polkas, and the Spanish contredanse or *contradanza*—forms soon transformed by the processes of creolization. The most eloquent example is the transformation of the contradanza. It is not clear if contredanse was introduced in Puerto Rico by the Spaniards, or by immigrants arriving from the English Antilles, or from Haiti. A figure dance, it was directed by a *bastonero*, a marshal in charge of calling the dance with a baton, and prescribed by fixed rules. Toward the middle of the nineteenth century, with the introduction of the Cuban *habanera*, dancers began to dance in couples.

The Puerto Rican *danza*, written on a 3/4 meter like the old contradanza, kept the same social dance rules, but was set to be danced in couples. After an initial arm-in-arm walk in slow tempo around the room, couples faced each other and initiated a somewhat quicker, but still moderate pace. Young people welcomed the new dance with its delicate motion and fewer rules, as it permitted closeness and an intimate conversation. Many musicians composed and still compose danzas. The danza retained a classical tone, but composers from the working class, many of them mulattos, were the ones who developed a uniquely Puerto Rican style. Many compositions are dedicated to popular themes. The danza continued to evolve, with Juan Morel Campos's nineteenth-century orchestrations attaining national prominence.

The influence of Spanish songs and rhythms is also most evident in the form called *seis*. The seis (and its many variations) is the most important musical dance form originating in the mainly rural, mountainous regions in the interior of the island. Danced by six couples, the Puerto Rican seis has a really remarkable similarity—which persists after centuries—to a type of Spanish song. There are many kinds of seises expressing a variety of moods and regional differences. Angel Quintero-Rivera points out that even though it has been argued that the seis is of Spanish origins, many of its variants evidence elements drawn from African influences found mainly in pulsation, syncopation, and Cuban rhythms such as *guaracha*, *habanera*, and *tumbao*. He underscores the fact that in Caribbean societies, and specifically in the Hispanic Caribbean, it is not possible to speak of pure influences, since these societies are at the core maroon societies, and the question of origins is always complex and uncertain. Although the majority of seises are no longer danced, the form is alive in the many Christmas songs called *aguinaldos* and in the *décima*, oral poetry in which ancient historical themes are expressed alongside present-day improvisations, and in which the voice resembles the falsettos used for regional Spanish songs. Some young people today continue to cultivate the improvised décima.

The bolero, a love song or ballad popular in all of Latin America, appeared in Santiago de Cuba toward the end of the nineteenth century. The dance, for couples, in European social dance position, is slow, romantic, and intimate. The slow tempo music and romantic lyrics address themes of love, hate, and separation. The bolero is a musical genre that has composers, interpreters, and lovers in many countries. In blurring national frontiers it has given all Latin Americans a sense of belonging to a culture far beyond national borders.

Popular music and dances were strongly influenced by West African traditions, especially along the coast and in sugar-growing communities. African and neo-African musical forms, centered in syncopated rhythms and percussive instruments, have been basic to meaningful social bonds. The origin of the music and dance called *bomba* has been associated historically with the lives and rituals of the slaves who lived in the plantations and has been tied by scholars to the survival of black identity.

The bomba, which had been a key means of expression for slaves living in Puerto Rico since the seventeenth century, shares traits common to the traditions of diverse African groups throughout the Caribbean. Percussive, melodic, and kinetic elements from ancient ceremonies still persist in bombas as they are performed today. As defined by Héctor Vega-Drouet (1983, 42) these elements include: a circle of performers and audience, the drum as the main instrument, the basic rhythmic pattern played by the second of two drums, the singer next to the drums and the chorus behind the singer, rhythm presiding over melody, songs couched in responsorial form, a dialogue between the first drummer and the dancer. Two additional characteristics are equally important: an improvisatory style and audience participation. The music is inseparable from the dance and the dialogue between drummer and dancer conveys a process that has been handed down from generation to generation.

The dance begins with a simple march in place, the women flashing their skirts from side to side, the men keeping their arms close to their bodies. Bodies are held inclined. The march is two-stepped and later three-stepped. The bodies displace themselves, but the most important element is the segmentation and movement of the body, which in general is almost stationary, with the dance stemming from a controlled movement of the muscles of the feet. Instead of following the beat as modern Latin dances do, bomba dances are structured within the improvised dialogue with the music. Because this knowledge is transmitted in community life, one has to belong to really dance well. Each individual dances in dialogue with the drum. Due to these distinct characteristics, African ethnic groups arriving at or from diverse parts of the Caribbean were able to maintain and provide their own variations to musical patterns.

These traditions were integral to the religious beliefs of many slaves. In Cuba, for example, the religion of the Yorubas continues to be practiced today along with its music and dance rituals. In Puerto Rico, the religious context is less evident, or less known. However, in my research I have come across various submerged systems deriving from Afro-Caribbean rituals that are not evident on the surface, and yet reappear cyclically, albeit in secularized manifestations. Some contemporary communal dance practices today retain elements that link them to ancient rituals as well as to new Afro-Caribbean experiences. Celeste Fraser Delgado and José Esteban Muñoz note

the drumming that connects not only the rumba and the mambo, but all Afro-Caribbean rhythms back through the cultural resistance of the enslaved peoples in the Americas to the religious practices of Western Africa. A frequent lack of specificity in the telling only makes that history more forceful in the living memory of Latinos today; the cultures of Africa survived the institutions of slavery and colonization and continue to survive, despite the institutions of capitalism and so-called development, in the sounding of the drums. In the times of our ancestors, the drums invoked the gods and the gods dwelled within the body of the duration of the dance. And they still do. (Delgado and Muñoz 1997, 11)

Subsequent to the abolition of the slave trade in the nineteenth century, Afro-Puerto Rican cultural traditions continued to develop, basing themselves on the retention of African elements, but through the processes of creolization and syncretism. Loíza Aldea in the north and the Barrio de San Antón in the southern town of Ponce are coastal enclaves of slave origins where the practice of bomba testifies to the survival of a culture, in spite of acute marginalization.

In Loíza, a town populated mainly by descendants of slaves and *libertos* (freedmen) cane cutters, there are still some recognizable ritual elements in the practice of bomba today. According to historian Lydia Milagros González:

(1) Although there have been many sites where *bomba* dances have taken place, there is one site that prevailed until very recently: the space around the tree where the saint was said to have appeared. (2) A performance of *bomba* always begins with the performers saluting the drum. (3) The dance is performed by individuals, not by couples; the dancer mounts his dance until his entire body is shaking, very much in the way dancers tremble when possessed by a spirit in ritual ceremonies. (4) Nobody interrupts the dancer; his or her time is respected and each person is allowed a space for freedom. (personal interview, Lydia Milagros González, 1995)

As historians have shown, Puerto Rico's economy, as in the rest of the Caribbean, was historically based in a large measure on smuggling and forced labor. It became a place to which many slaves from neighboring islands—Spanish, French, and English—came to settle, and where cross-fertilization of dancing styles occurred at an early date. In the early decades of the twentieth century, popular dances developed into a fusion of European, African, and Caribbean musical elements thoroughly transformed through the processes of creolization and syncretism. This was a dialectical process, resulting in dances that are mostly African (such as the bomba), others that are mostly Spanish (such as the seis) and the majority, which are multilayered expressions.

The *plena* is perhaps Puerto Rico's best expression of the fusion between the African and Hispanic legacies. The Spanish lyrics, mainly passed down orally, comment on daily life and events and usually incorporate street language. Instruments include the guitar, the *cuatro*, the *güiro*, the *pandereta* drums, and the *armónica*, which was later replaced by the accordion. Telling the news through music is an expression present in many Caribbean countries.

The plena has a contagious rhythm that incites listeners to dance and can be enjoyed by everyone, whether islanders or outsiders. The continuing pattern and repetition of a rhythm and chorus move the dancers. In the traditional dance, women usually move their skirts with a free flow of the body and slight jump to the side in a counterpoint step; men keep their arms behind whenever partners crisscross. Together with bomba, the plena has been one of the rhythms, along with Cuban and other Caribbean rhythms, at the core of the creation of salsa. During the 1920s plena became popular in the United States, mainly among Puerto Ricans in New York.

Twentieth-century mass communication technologies—radio, sound recordings, television, and film—radically expanded the diffusion of popular dance music. By the 1950s Cuba had become the center of Caribbean music through recording, film, and broadcasting industries. In Puerto Rico the most important development in African-derived music was the mainstreaming of bomba and plena rhythms through the voice of Ismael Rivera and the orchestrations of Rafael Cortijo, which earned immense respect in the island and in New York and, furthermore, won financial compensation for musicians from the *barrios*. Ismael Rivera and Rafael Cortijo deeply marked Puerto Rican contemporary culture, allowing us to further reflect on fundamental continuities. Their lives and musical influence embody the significant persistence and transformation of ancient African forms in contemporary Puerto Rican dance practices and their location as major links in the search for continuities between "tradition" and "modernity." This persistence in retrieving the roots and returning to origins, however transformed they may have become over time, coincides with the uneven social and political forces of modernization, which were accompanied in Puerto Rican society, as in the rest of the Caribbean, by massive migration and/or cultural exclusions.

It would be impossible to recount the history of dance without considering the implications of migration and diaspora. The beginnings of the great Puerto Rican migration to the United States date from the early years of the twentieth century, especially from the period following the granting of U.S. citizenship to residents of the island in 1917. Within the aggressive environments of modern and industrial cities in the United States, Puerto Ricans overwhelmingly retained their language, food, and music as a way of preserving their identity. Hispanic dance clubs, and Puerto Rican popular musicians, came into vogue in New York during the 1930s, preserving, transforming, and creating a variety of musical forms. Dancing, for example to Rafael Hernández's boleros and *guarachas*, interpreted mostly by trios, expressed the broad Latino Caribbean sentiment of an entire generation. The impact of the recording industry in this process and the contributions of Puerto Rican musicians in New York are studied by Ruth Glasser in her 1995 book, *My Music Is My Flag.*

Since 1952, with the establishment of the Estado Libre Asociado (or Commonwealth), Puerto Rico has undergone intense industrialization and modernization and new migrations. Over half a million Puerto Ricans migrated during the 1950s. Today about 40 percent of all Puerto Ricans have experienced massive displacements, always accompanied by complex and uneven encounters that, generally, force a continuous re-identification process, a process woven with bits and pieces of the past and the present. This, in turn, explains in part the creation of new "hybrid" forms. As scholar Néstor García Canclini points out, "the first hypothesis . . . is that the *uncertainty* about the meaning and value of modernity derives not only from what separates nations, ethnic groups, and classes, but also from the sociocultural hybrids in which the traditional and the modern are mixed" (García Canclini 1995, 2).

In New York the 1950s were characterized by a mediated sound imposed by the entertainment industry, featuring spectacular *cha cha cha* shows, with musical director Xavier Cugat as the media's star. Musicians such as the Cuban Machito were, on the other hand, preserving the Cuban *son*, from which most Hispanic Caribbean popular dance rhythms have evolved, and Latino musicians were transforming them. The popular Latin music of New York is rooted in layers of traditions combining Cuban, Puerto Rican, and other Latin American rhythms that interact with African American jazz, rock, and soul. This long process of musical and dance transformations and continuities, which had begun in the 1930s, culminated some forty years later, during the 1970s, in the Puerto Rican contribution to the uniquely New York-Caribbean dance phenomenon called salsa, already part of Fania, a record company and a well publicized commercial venture.

The musical and dance elements in salsa events belong to a cultural cycle. Angel Quintero-Rivera defines *salsa* not as a new rhythm, but as a new way of making music. In the face of the homogeneity of mass culture and globalization, salsa as a cultural movement portrays another perspective of time and space. As Quintero-Rivera aptly describes it, while Western youth were thumbing their nose at the "establishment" and its promise of "progress" and "well being" by pursuing an instant of gratification through their musical movements, young salsa musicians such as Willie Colón and Rubén Blades were dealing with complex notions of time to counter both the homogenizing aspects of modernity and the present-day vision of the counterculture. In the free combination of "diverse Afro-American rhythms—*son, guaracha, rumba, bomba, plena, merengue, seis, aguinaldo, reggae, cumbia, vallenato, samba, hip-hop, guajira, tamborito* . . . (combinations which define spatial territorial parameters of expression) . . . lies the testimony of another time, strung by displacements brought about from the margins of modernity" (Quintero-Rivera 1998, 199).

In salsa as in plena, the lyrics chronicle the lives of the dispossessed. The trials and tribulations of survival, displacement, and hope are interwoven with humor within multiple variations and repetitions building up to a climax. The music is composed in *clave*, a 3 plus 2 rhythmical base over which melodic variations and polyrhythms are created, and a salient and unifying feature of Caribbean musical structure. The dance is not so much a contagious easy step as in plena. When breaking the basic step down, one might mistake it for a simple one, but to be able to dance in rhythm with the music and in synch with a partner, a complex combination of musicality and virtuosity is required, as well as a great deal of versatility.

One can dance salsa according to one's own rhythm, that is to say, not everyone dances on the same note. But, at the same time, it is essential to step in tune within a variety of possibilities. The music, lyrics, and dance embody a complex syncopated fusion of elements that at first sight might seem easy to interpret. As in the bomba, dance gestures are centered on the freedom of the body, but dancers may move to a more fluid, less determinate free play of responses to the music. These elements, in their many crisscrosses of time and space, break away from the regularity of European traditional forms and are in that sense closer to, for example, flamenco or, perhaps, as Quintero-Rivera (1998, 190) suggests, to the Arabic *zéjel*. The incredible excitement expressed in sensual pelvic movements and fast intricate feet patterns is, however, revelatory of another context. Concerned with sexuality and the partnering relationship as well as with the recognition of its elaborate performance by an audience, salsa dancing reaches a climax in intensity similar to that of a cleansing and renewal ritual. Meanings are embodied in the dance.

For many Puerto Ricans salsa has been one way of bridging social differences, both personalizing and socializing its practitioners. Although the dance was initially practiced by those considered by the prevailing elites to be "vulgar" or "lumpen" (Flores 1993, 11), increased worldwide interest in salsa has made many reconsider their rejection, although not necessarily their denial of the constitutive role of the African legacy in Puerto Rico. Numerous salsa schools continue to flourish on the island. Results have been twofold: on the one hand salsa has given voice and dignity to a marginalized popular expression vis-à-vis the values of the dominant culture; on the other hand it is struggling to resist homogenization by the market of mass culture.

Music and dance have served to celebrate and to enhance their own values. Until recently some of the musical masters, such as the Fania stars, have resisted co-optation in the face of efforts by the media to impose images such as Ricky Martin's strictly commercial crossover as well as a Latin dance style that lacks the improvisational freedom and joy of "barrio" salsa. This new "Latin" sound resembles in some ways the 1950s, when Xavier Cugat was the media's star while Machito and Ismael Rivera were preserving and transforming the son and the bomba and plena.

Now manipulated by advertising industries, adapted for aerobics classes and videos, the music and dance are losing their original significance. As Juan Otero Garabís observes in the encyclopedia *Africana* (Appiah and Gates 1999, 1661): "This process of the homogenization of salsa developed what in the 1980's became known as romantic or erotic salsa, which simplified salsa lyrics in almost exclusively love songs, many of which were modeled on old romantic ballads." And as Katrina Hazzard-Donald comments in speaking about break dancing and hip-hop culture, "Most mainstream Americans will never see the subtle codes, gestures and meanings [. . .]" (Hazzard-Donald 1996).

Marketing strategies also necessitate some caution on the part of musicians and dancers who are entering the mainstream to pause and reflect on recent history. Says Hazzard-Donald about break dancing: "Movement into the mainstream negated its status as countercultural by redefining it from a subcultural form to one widely accepted and imitated, a move that inadvertently linked breakers with the society that had previously excluded them" (Hazzard-Donald 1996, 227). These effects are nevertheless "fluid and changing," to quote Raquel Rivera in her conclusion on mass consumption and social resistance: "What begins as indiscriminate consumerism can [also] lead to solidarity" (Rivera 1993).

The existential dilemmas and preoccupation with cultural identity have, with diverse emphasis, led many young musicians in Puerto Rican and U.S. neighborhoods to create their own free combination of rhythms. One outstanding example is the New York group called Latin Empire, which is inspired by African-American as well as Puerto Rican music and songs and which vividly reflects the multicultural experiences of New York ghettos. It is clear that music and dance are shared not only by Puerto Ricans who remain on the island and Puerto Ricans in diaspora, but also by other Latinos who find in dance a source of identity and hope, and a sense of belonging. The evolution of Caribbean rhythms into new dance rituals points to the ceaseless transformation of highly significant signs and symbols. As a matter of fact, the lyrics often express utopian politics of Latino unity. It is above all in the participatory arena provided by Caribbean dance and music where a greater sense of identity, direction, and purpose resides.

Portions of this essay also appear in Alma Concepción's "Dance and Diaspora," to be published in the forthcoming *Musical Migrations*, ed. Frances Aparicio and Candida Jaquez, St. Martin's Press, New York.

13

◇ ◇ ◇

Gilda Navarra

Before Taller de Histriones

Alma Concepción

Translated by Nadia Benabid

Gilda Navarra, one of the most important figures in the history of theater and dance in Puerto Rico and the Hispanic Caribbean, cofounder of Ballets de San Juan in 1954, created in 1971 a ground-breaking collective group she called Taller de Histriones. The new language of the body that Navarra elaborated incorporated mime, dance, and gestures as well as literary, musical, and pictorial reformulations. During fourteen years, the art expressed in mime-dramas such as *Ocho Mujeres* (1974), *Asíntota* (1976), *Abelardo y Eloísa* (1978), or *Atibón, Ogú, Erzulí* (1979) was able to reflect a myriad of human passions within a multiplicity of meanings that eloquently proclaimed Puerto Rico's cultural maturity and independence.

Of all my teachers at the School of American Ballet, Anatole Oboukhoff was by far the most formidable. He would descend the small staircase into the studio where our classes were held commanding us in his booming voice to "Dance, dance, dance!" He was aware of the circumstances that had brought me there—my recommendation from Ana García and the scholarship from Puerto Rico's Ballets de San Juan. One afternoon, I looked up to find him staring intently and persistently at me. I was already in a panic, wondering what utterance was going to pass Oboukhoff's lips, when he asked me, with his heavy Russian accent, "What is Ana sister

176

Fig. 17. Gilda Navarra, ca. 1960. Photograph: Faré. Collection of Alma Concepción. Used by permission of Alma Concepción, Princeton, N.J.

name?" "Gilda," I answered. "Yes," he murmured and continued to stand there, silent and lost in thought.

After that exchange, I became increasingly curious about the lives Gilda and Ana had led while studying at the School of American Ballet in the 1940s. Over the years, I have often thought about the historical significance of that period, but it was only a few months ago, on a stormy Santurce afternoon, that Gilda and I finally sat down on her terrace to talk about the importance of those years and of New York to her formation as an artist. Gilda said:

> The whole atmosphere was of utmost importance: Ballet Theater, El Marqués de Cuevas, the Ballet Russe. [Balanchine, with whom Ana worked in 1945 when Ballet Society was founded, was also there at the time.] Katherine Dunham was there, and at the American Ballet one took classes with people like Toumanova and Danilova and had teachers like Nemchinova, Muriel Stuart, and William Dollar. I liked William Dollar very much . . . and Oboukhoff, with all that incredible discipline and energy. But the one who had the greatest impact on me, the one who had the greatest effect hands down, was neither Balanchine nor anyone else—it was Antony Tudor. That was the first time I understood that acting and dancing could go hand in hand. For me, the premiere of *Pillar of Fire* was like an awakening into a new world.

Those of us who studied ballet and Spanish dance under Ana García and Gilda Navarra in the 1950s in San Juan had never seen hide nor hair of Tudor, but we had all been raised in the firm conviction that the magic of dance was inseparable from acting. The children who took part in the production of *La cucarachita Martina* grasped how a story, a Puerto Rican folktale heard time and again from grandmothers and great-grandmothers, could be dramatized with the Spanish dance steps Gilda had taught us. We also learned that before dance pieces could become part of the repertoire of the *Teatro del Niño* (The Child's Theater)—as Gilda and Ana had dubbed this project, many different kinds of artists had to be involved for that imaginary world to come to life. The contributors included Carlos Marichal, Jack Delano, Francisco Arriví, and above all else, Gilda, whose gift for the fusing and filtering of the various elements and whose unfailing taste could be distilled into a small artistic gem that was worlds apart from the forgettable recitals other children associated with the world of dance.

In 1954, Gilda Navarra and Ana García founded Ballets de San Juan. Gilda's many excellent choreographies drew on Spanish music and themes and were influenced by the exemplary work of the Spanish dancer Pilar López, for whom Gilda had only the highest regard. This particular phase of Gilda's creative itinerary culminated in her choreography for Suriñach's *Tientos*, an avant-garde piece that would remain unparalleled for many years to come even among Spanish choreographers. The seeds for what would, in time, be Gilda Navarra's greatest work from this phase—*La historia del soldado*, which premiered at the University of Puerto Rico in 1971 and immediately preceded the creation of Taller de Histriones—were already present in that earlier work. *La historia del soldado*, however, marked Gilda's break with Spanish dance. Stravinsky's extraordinary music and Gilda's pantomime training with Lecoq in Paris were to be the guiding principles for this new choreography.

At Gilda's request, I, who had been her disciple in Spanish dance, found myself interpreting the part of the Princess and dancing in the privileged company of Ernesto González, José Luis Marrero, and Rafael Enrique Saldaña, all of us joined in a marvelous quest for new forms of expression. *La historia del soldado* was for me what *Pillar of Fire* had been for Gilda in 1945; I was awakened to a new world of idioms from the theater, pantomime, modern dance, and classical ballet.

The plot—the story of a soldier who makes a pact with the devil in exchange for riches, love, and happiness—was pieced together by Gilda in close collaboration with a number of profoundly cultured artists whose respective talents and sensitivities charged Stravinsky's grand scheme with new life. The original text by Ramuz, conceived for a traveling theater, was intended for dancers accompanied by a small orchestra and a textual narration. A Spanish translation was commissioned from Esteban Tollinchi and an adaptation from Luis Rafael Sánchez. The orchestra, positioned stage left by Gilda, was conducted by James Thompson; the scenery, lights, and costumes were designed by Fernando Rivero, with whom Gilda had worked on several occasions. After endless hours of rehearsal and joint dedication, the dramatic tale began to shine through. Nothing was as important to Gilda as the discipline she learned as a child: "I was taught discipline by Oboukhoff and by my mother, period." Consumed by the intensity of the work at hand, and "taking our time," our effort to achieve perfect expression became the central axis of our meetings. The character I played was interconnected with that of the Soldier, played by Ernesto González, my partner in the piece, who had come from New York

Fig. 18. Ernesto González and Alma Concepción rehearsing Gilda Navarra's *La historia del soldado*. Used by permission of Alma Concepción, Princeton, N.J.

to dance the principal role. Ernesto was the Raúl Juliá of the day, bringing his distinguished credentials in film and theater with him. As it happened, he was also an excellent dancer, schooled in the technique of the brilliant José Limón, who had always been a major inspirational figure for Gilda.

The challenge at hand had less to do with our vision of the characters and the plot and more to do with an interpretation of the music and movement. Gilda did not aim to choreograph suitable steps for the music or to synchronize the narrator's voice with Stravinsky's score, but to enter the complexities of the music. Even though José Luis (who played the Devil), Ernesto, and I came from very different traditions, we awaited each day with a joyous readiness to see how Gilda was going to coax our movements into a new transformational synthesis. The steps or text were not merely something learned; rather, they were the product of a subjective yet collective voyage of discovery that was a necessary prelude to the plot development. In this process actors became mimes, dancers became actors, and the narrated accompaniment, delivered by Rafael Enrique Saldaña, became a counterpoint to the music, seeping into the sound of the violin and insinuating itself into the drumbeat—all working together to re-create the work's literary world.

Stravinsky, for his part, drew on a variety of sources for his composition—military marches, reminiscences of Spanish pasodobles, the waltz, the tango, and ragtime. Despite such musical syncretism, an undeniable musical style is clearly manifest. In a very similar manner, Gilda prodded the dividing line between classical and modern dance, and between theater and pantomime, to elicit a unity of style in the movement, gesture, and tone of the work. The future language of Histriones had already been launched—a "language" that is as difficult to categorize as that of any art. Be that as it may, however, I think we can safely describe it as a language of stylized gestures, of extreme contrasts of stasis and motion, of slow-going rhythms—a language that ranges through the polarities of the human soul and that breaks the boundaries of bodily limits.

Still, one cannot help but wonder by what magic such quality and grandeur are conjured up. Much is owed, no doubt, to discipline and collaboration as well as to the physical and musical talent of the participants. An even larger share falls to the choreographer's imagination and the director's vision, to the process of selection and distillation that gives the work its shape. But the key to it all is in the secret, the mystery of creative genius that José Limón best expressed when he said, "Sometimes I think we come already formed, like Athena, complete from the brow of Father

Fig. 19. Alma Concepción in Taller de Histriones's *Atibón, Ogú, Erzulí,* 1979. Used by permission of Alma Concepción, Princeton, N.J.

Zeus. Sometimes I believe that we are what we are from the very beginning" (Pollack 1993,2). That's how I think of Gilda, before and after Histriones, as a daughter of Zeus exercising her powerful art, cutting deep into the wood, taking her time.

Except for the first paragraph, this essay, originally written in Spanish, appeared in "Dossier Gilda Navarra," May 1996, in *Postdata,* a literary magazine published in San Juan, Puerto Rico. Used with permission of *Postdata.*

14

❖ ❖ ❖

The Challenges of Puerto Rican Bomba

Halbert Barton

Reto/Challenge

July 1990: a first impression. On the stage in the town plaza of Loíza was a *bomba* troupe playing music. One of the singers, a woman in an elaborate ruffled skirt, turned away from the crowd, faced and stared down one of the drummers, and began dancing using stutter steps and pulling the edges of her skirt outward. She continued the dance with a very serious look of concentration on her face, accenting her movements with ruffles of the skirt. Yet contrary to what one might expect in a carnivalesque atmosphere, there was nothing especially coquettish about the movements, postures, and gestures of the dancer.

As I saw more of bomba at the festival, I came to find that the tone of the presentation was quite different from the well-known recreational and courtship dances such as salsa, merengue, and rumba guaguancó that are commonly encountered at parties and music festivals in Puerto Rico. This was unlike any dance I'd ever seen before. The movements of the solo dancer were elegant yet forceful, but what got my attention most was the encounter between the dancer and the lead drummer. It appeared that the solo dancer and the lead drummer were attempting to synchronize sounds on the drum, but however much they exerted themselves they never seemed to achieve it. I noticed a subtle lag time between the movement and the sound, which at times approached synchrony and at other times there was a startling gap. For lack of an explanation, as neither I nor my Puerto Rican friends were very familiar with the nuances of the genre, I began to doubt the quality of the performance, and I wondered if the lack of synchrony was because the performers were rusty, or distracted, or unmotivated, or perhaps intoxicated. Yet the energy and concentration that both dancer and drummer appeared to be bringing to an encounter, which to my eyes had looked embarrassingly out-of-synch, left me deeply confused, as well as intrigued. The performance didn't translate.

This form of highly stylized spontaneity had me puzzled. Watching bomba in this way was similar to listening in on someone else's conversation—the words are audible, but the meaning may not be. While watching bomba is not exactly eavesdropping (to the extent that it's public), the performance certainly did not seem to be scripted or choreographed in any precise way. Raw improvisation, within a tightly structured framework of interlocking rhythms, seemed to be the rule rather than the exception. In this way, I came to see that bomba shared much of the spirit of jazz (cf. Jones 1963), yet with the percussive exuberance of tap, crossed with the passionately elegant posturings of flamenco.

Having had quite a bit of experience with popular dance in North American contexts, I was accustomed to seeing, and expecting, synchrony between movement and sound in dance performance, where lack of synchrony would be judged as incompetent regardless of what is being danced, whether it be classical ballet, jazz, modern, the hustle, or any of the proliferating variety of hip-hop dances based on African-derived principles of movement. Synchrony was for me, as for just about everyone I knew, a basic given of performance.

To add to the confusion, bomba is sometimes approached and performed as if synchrony were essential. Many of the stage performances of the Familia Cepeda, for example, exhibit such high degrees of synchrony between movement and sound that the untrained eye would not necessarily be aware of the central role that improvisation plays in performance. Over the years, as I've come to witness dozens more of the stage show variety of bomba, I've come to see the stage show as a special kind of face that bomba presents to the general public and the masses of uninitiated observers. But a more intimate portrait of bomba would have to include a more detailed study of the role of agonism (called *el reto* or *la controversia*) in performance, which also includes the possibility of going off-beat, throwing someone off, playing a trick on somebody (*el relajo, el vacilón*).

In this light, bomba dancing is a kind of performance best suited for musical daredevils, especially those with a taste for the freshness of live jazz and improvisational humor, those for whom mistakes are simply sources for the generation of further creativity. The dancer as daredevil risks not conforming to the standard European-derived expectations about what constitutes competent performance. The daredevil may also merge into a trickster image—one who toys with European cultural standards at a tangled juncture between multiple worlds—now you see it, now you don't, not so much sleight of hand as sleight of foot, torso, shoulders, eyes. Look out! Here I come! Oops, there I went! Gotcha!

Soberao / Dance Circle

The first time I danced bomba was also in Loíza shortly after the scene described above. It was in Las Carreras, where there were some incredibly vibrant street performances going on in a driveway off the side of a winding road that led to the beach. A tight circle of several dozen people was crowding around the thundering drums as dancers took turns stepping out of the perimeter of the circle and into the center facing the drummers. Occasionally, a dancer would challenge another dancer by mischieviously cutting off the other to vie for the attention of the *subidor* (lead drummer).

After I had watched this scene for several minutes from the margins and had seen dancers rotate in and out (with expressions that were somehow both gleeful and serious), one of the singers saw me and pulled me into the *soberao* (dance circle). He then gestured toward the drummer and had me follow his movements, to the amusement and delight of the crowd: stutter steps, short hops, cross-steps—the baby steps of bomba. And then it hit me that as my movements changed, so did the sounds coming from the lead drummer, and aha! I got the idea. Before I could get carried away, a five-year-old girl with a megawatt smile cut in front of me and grabbed the attention of the subidor. I couldn't wait to try it again.

As I returned again several times to the street bomba performances, it struck me how aggressive the performers were in including outsiders (aha, fresh meat!). I later found out that the ringleaders were the famed Ayala brothers. Once this crew got started, there was no place to hide; everyone, no matter how old or young, male or female, light- or dark-skinned, was coaxed and cajoled into playing the game of challenge the drummer. At one point, the lead drummer would even pick up the drum and follow people around with it between his legs (*caminando el tambor*), and he would not give up easily to the rebuff of potential dancers that he targeted. If one of the crowd members turned his back on him to walk away he would follow the person, marking his steps (*pappappap*), converting his every movement, every gesture into its own sound. Shaking the head—no, not me, not now!—would be turned into *papapapapapa*. Even toddlers who could barely walk and had little idea what was going on would be reeled in—step, step, wobble, plop down: *pappappapapaboom!*

While plenty of experienced dancers came to show off during the evening, especially as the air cooled down after midnight, it was made very clear to me from the outset that the soberao was for everyone, of all skill levels. In fact, the impression that I had was that during these street jams (*bailes de bomba*) or community bomba dances (*bombazos*), which are also the ritual context of a patron saint festival, full of carnivalesque inversions, the subidor turns the whole world into a soberao, ready to mark anything that moves as far as the eye can see—no longer a question of insiders/ outsiders, just a horizon of vision. Novices and foreigners, far from being brushed to the side, were not only encouraged to participate, but joyously hounded in, giddy spectacles to be playfully toyed with and subjected to lighthearted ridicule and boundless laughter.

A Brief History of Bomba

For more than three hundred years now, bomba has provided the foundation, or template, on which Puerto Rican music and dance continue to evolve. Vega Drouet (1979) traced bomba to a seventeenth-century royal court dance of the Ashanti, and it continues to carry a regal and majestic demeanor. Over many years of cultural mixture and immigration bomba has also acquired musical and aesthetic flavorings from subsequent new-comers from West and West Central Africa (especially in the late eighteenth and early nineteenth centuries from the Bakongo nations) and from many Caribbean islands—most importantly the French Antilles (*yubá, leró,* and *corvé* in 6/8 time, many with lyrics in Creole), but also the Dutch Antilles (*holandés*) and the former Danish Antilles (*danué*). The Congolese influence seems to have been important in the development of a movement aesthetic that has strongly shaped the foot movements and weight distribution in both bomba and plena dance. Yet from the waist up, bomba dancing appears to be all Andalusian flamenco in its elaborate arm gestures, upright postures, dramatic poses, flowing skirt movements for women, and elegant *figuras*.

Bomba developed in the lowland plains of the island where sugarcane was cultivated, the three main zones being Mayaguez, Ponce, and Can-grejos (the outskirts of San Juan, once covering a large area that included

Cataño, Santurce and Loíza). The labor-intensive process of cutting, hauling, and refining the cane created a huge demand for workers, many of whom were brought over as slaves from West Africa. These coastal areas became population centers where an increasingly mixed group of workers with African, Spanish, and Native American ancestry brought together their talents for singing, drumming, and dancing in the birth of Puerto Rican bomba.

The first written reports of bomba dancing date back to the early 1700s. They continued throughout the slavery period, which ended when slavery was abolished in 1873, when bomba served as both entertainment on the plantation as well as a camouflaged form of rebellion in which slaves could congregate without interference and relay communications about future insurrections. On several occasions in the early 1800s, likely inspired by the achievements of the Haitian revolution that led to an independent Haiti in 1804, bomba dances served as a diversion in which slaves were able to set the cane fields on fire and escape to the mountains. During the 1800s, bomba performances were highly regulated by the government out of fear of their rebellious qualities. The genre had not achieved wide acceptance beyond the coastal working-class areas, but Cangrejos, the site of the oldest free black settlement in Puerto Rico, became the mecca of bomba during this period.

According to oral historians Jorge and José Emmanuelli, drawing on research by Lester Nurse, by the early part of the twentieth century there were several extended family networks with well-established bomba traditions—the Pizarros of Cataño, the Almésticas of Carolina, and the Cepedas of Santurce. Whereas the Améstica family was known as the first family of bomba at the turn of the century, the Pizarro brothers (Flor, Yenye, and friends) became one of the hot bomba groups between 1920 and 1940 and were a strong influence on the young Rafael Cepeda of Santurce, the future patriarch of bomba and plena who died recently (interviews with José Emmanuelli and Manuel "Yenye" Pizarro, May 1998). By the 1950s, the Améstica family had stopped playing, and the Cepedas emerged as the premier bomba family, later challenged by the Ayala brothers of Loíza in the 1960s. With the establishment of the commonwealth government and the formation of the Institute of Puerto Rican Culture in 1953, bomba became a genre officially deemed folkloric (described as "vanishing" in a 1957 newspaper article), and the Cepeda family, led by the patriarch Don Rafael, set the tone for the professionalization of bomba performance as folklore.

Since the 1960s, Loíza has become synonymous with bomba, not because bomba originated in Loíza, but because it has been the town with
the most active bomba tradition, largely due to the charismatic leadership
of the Ayala brothers, who continue to win converts to their distinctive
freewheeling style. While community bomba dances ceased in the south
of Puerto Rico in the late 1970s (Dufrasne-González 1994), and in Santurce
as well (by the 1950s apparently), the music never stopped in Loíza and it
has been an integral part of the annual patron saint celebration, the Festival de Santiago Apóstol (St. James the Apostle) for a hundred years.

Only recently, since 1994, have community bomba dances reemerged
beyond the Loíza patron saint celebrations, that is, performed regularly
outside of a professional folkloric stage context. This has been in the form
of what is now called a *bombazo*, an informal performance mode in which
anyone and any number can participate and where the stage/audience
separation is obliterated, inspired both by the *toques* of Loíza and the community bomba dances of years past. Since 1994, the Cepedas and the
Emmanuelli brothers of Carolina, sparked by a sequence of birthday
bombazos organized by Yamil Rios and Juan Usera, have been hosting
and sponsoring bombazos with the intent of bringing bomba dancing into
a wider circle of appreciation and social acceptance. Dozens of bimonthly
bombazos throughout the San Juan Metro Area in 1998–1999 have
brought bomba dancing into the limelight as never before, and baile de
bomba has begun entering the clubs and pubs of Puerto Rico for the first
time in its history.

Pasos/Steps

Once I was hooked on the incredible energy that bomba dances generate,
I searched among my contacts for places where I could learn this dance in
greater detail, hoping that there would be some kind of institution that
offered regular classes. Back in the fall of 1990 there was only one such
place, La Escuela de Bomba y Plena Don Rafael Cepeda, in the Villa
Palmeras sector of Santurce.

Modesto Cepeda, the director of the school and oldest son of Don
Rafael, bomba's late patriarch, had (and still has) a class on Saturday
mornings that was open to the public. Somewhat to my surprise, I was the
only adult in the class and often the only male, but over time I managed to
learn the basic steps and rhythms and how to improvise, that is, *hacer
piquetes.*

What I came to understand as the basic elements, from tutelage in the Cepeda school and the Emmanuelli brothers, may be summarized as follows:

Instruments: (1) *el barril:* A goatskin barrel-drum, of which there are always at least two, the lower-pitched *buleador,* which plays the basic rhythm, *bomba larga,* and the higher-pitched subidor, which plays the lead drum parts, *repiques,* that answer the solo dancer's improvised movements, *piquetes.* Barriles are made from recycled oak barrels, once used for storing items such as rum or codfish, and have a greater sound range, more similar to a *djembe* than the Afro-Cuban conga drum that is often used as a substitute when the custom-made barriles are not available.

(2) *el cuá:* A hollow barrel or bamboo log played with two drumsticks, following the rhythm played by the buleador.

(3) *la maraca:* A large gourd rattle.

Vocals: Bomba songs follow a call-and-response structure, termed *coro* (what the chorus sings: a refrain) and *voz* (what the lead sings: verses on the theme set by the coro). The lead singer, who plays the maraca, starts with the chorus of a song (the call), and in the space of that chorus the drummers (in a bombazo context) must be able to determine the rhythm from the meter or swing of the lyrics. The drummers and chorus come in at the same time, followed by the lead singer in the next sequence, who often starts with a few well-known verses before venturing off into lyrical and melodic improvisation.

Rhythms: Bomba consists of three main rhythmic complexes: *sicá* and *holandés* in 2/4 time and the *yubá* in 6/8 time. There are a total of sixteen variations, called *seises* or *sones* (in the south), which are still known and performed today. The seises within each rhythm complex refer to a distinct metric of composition (the characteristic swing of the chorus) and performance style (whether *piquetes* are performed, whether sticks are used, when in the cycle of bomba rhythms it is performed, and how fast or slow).

The sicá complex is the largest and the basic rhythm is the most familiar to *salseros* and is often referred to as just "bomba." It consists of twelve variations called seises or, in the south, sones: *paulé* (the slowest), *gracimá, danué, calindá, cunyá, balancé* (danced without piquetes, that is, pure *paseo* with *repiques*), *cocobalé* (danced with sticks similar to Brazilian *maculele*), *bambulaé* (the fastest in this group), sicá (the namesake), *cuembé* (sometimes considered a separate rhythm, called *güembé* in the south), and finally *belén* (the "last dance," also played in honor of those who've passed away). In Loíza, which has developed its own distinct traditional bomba style, the corresponding rhythm in the sicá family is *seis corrido*, which is played similarly to cuembé but at lightning speed.

The yubá complex refers to all bomba songs in 6/8 rhythm: *leró* (the slower), yubá (the faster), and in Loíza, the *corvé* (fastest).

Holandés is its own rhythmic complex. It is the fastest of all the rhythms and the most challenging to play.

Unlike plena and danza, where dancers move to the music independently of the musicians, bomba dancing is integral to the music. Movements of the solo dancer's body correspond to sounds on the drum that the lead drummer must mark. In this sense, the bomba dancer is also a musician, similar to the way a tap dancer (or an orchestra conductor) may be considered a musician. In bomba dancing, the question is not so much how it looks, but how it sounds!

The dance begins with a basic step that corresponds to the main rhythm (sicá, yubá, or holandés) being played. This basic step (for example a toe-touch step for sicá, alternating left arm-right leg and right arm-left leg) is used during the paseo, or approach, before and after the piquetes or improvised segment. During the paseo, dancers may approach the drum alone, in pairs, or in threes (for example, a man with a woman on each side), but when dancers have finished the paseo and are ready to challenge the subidor, they take leave of their partners, sometimes symbolized by a twirl of the partner, and concentrate on their dialogue with the drummer.

Again in contrast to danza and plena (not to mention salsa and merengue), bomba is not strictly a couples or courtship dance. Dancers may approach the drum in pairs during the paseo, but pairing up is not essential. Moreover, even when pairs do approach the drum together, they go their separate ways during the piquetes, the solo improvisations that are marked by the lead drummer. Another way in which bomba and danza or plena part company is that during the paseo couples generally do not face each other except to signal a turn with hands raised overhead; rather, they perform the basic step, corresponding to the basic rhythm, side by side, facing the lead drummer, who is the actual center of attention for the dancers, not the dance partner. To put it another way: the subidor is the real dance partner.

Piquetes/Improvisations

Since the dance is integral to the music, bomba dancers understandably have an important role to play as musicians: *para subir el ritmo* (to raise, or lift up, the rhythm). The concept of subir el ritmo is to gradually increase the polyrhythmic intensity of the music by making combinations of dance movements, piquetes, that enliven the beat through fresh and unexpected changes in tone and direction, forming counterpoints by dancing counterbeats, coming back to the main beat again and accelerating, making sure to finish at a peak of intensity prior to the point of exhaustion, leaving everybody wanting more.

While there are significant regional variations in dance styles, there are some common denominators. For men, piquetes generally include sharply defined movements of the feet and torso. For women, piquetes include movements of the skirt (for the women who wear them), shoulders, and hips (especially in the Loíza style in which women usually dance in hip-hugging pants rather than skirts). While there are several dozen combinations of standard movements that are considered traditional bomba piquetes and thus markable by any good drummer, there is considerable room for freedom and creativity in the dance as long as one follows the cardinal rules of bomba dancing: *postura* (posture), *firmeza* (firmness), and *elegancia* (elegance).

Though the basic movements of bomba are simple enough that small children can learn them fairly quickly, what distinguishes advanced dancers from novices is their ability to subir el ritmo, to be able to dance for an extended period of time without losing the interest of the subidor. The dancer can hold the drummer's attention by putting out a continuous stream of fresh combinations that slowly build from the easiest to the most difficult steps to mark. If a dancer gives an especially bewitching performance, the subidor may tilt the drum horizontally as a salute to the dancer and continue playing from there. In this situation of heightened creativity (being "in the zone"), the dancer who gets the subidor to tilt his drum is called a *brujo* (wizard). Of course, becoming a brujo is easier said than done, and the drum-tilting rarely occurs in more traditional contexts, reserved for special moments and occasions.

In practice, even for people who have been dancing for several years, it is very difficult to make lively music with the body and follow the three cardinal rules of postura, firmeza y elegancia. Even experienced dancers can fall into a routine, having pet moves which become so predictable that the performance becomes overly repetitious, flat, and stale. (Hint: if the subidor can mark the dancer with his eyes closed, it's gotten stale.) To some extent, dancers rely on each other for new ideas and new challenges, and may cut off one another if a dancer feels that the other has gone on too long or is repeating the same tired combinations.

A good bomba solo generally starts with a calm and dignified paseo, followed by a *ponche* ("punch") on the first beat of a measure, a simple piquete done extra sharp as a wake-up call to the subidor. For men, a ponche may be a toe-touch done with flair, two quick steps, left-right, then left with the toe pointing down. For women, a good ponche would be a sharp flash of the edge of the skirt in the direction of the subidor. In order to get warmed up and get a feel for the skills of the subidor, a dancer may do a short series of ponches interspersed with paseo. After the initial run of paseo and ponches, it is the dancer's aim to mix in an increasing number of different kinds of piquetes and combinations, so that at the peak of the solo the dancer is putting out a kaleidoscope of piquetes that a good subidor, with quick reflexes, should be able to mark on the drum. The subidor may not actually mark all of the piquetes, but must at least make the attempt, as part of the game. In this sense, the subidor is in the position of the batter in baseball, who tries to connect on pitches that cannot, and should not, from the pitcher/dancer's viewpoint, be foreseen. A high failure rate (lots of strikeouts) may result in the batter/subidor being replaced, but does not end the game. Synchrony/connection is not presupposed, but rather a goal or target at which to aim.

When top-notch bomba dancers and drummers stare each other down and face off for a drum-dance challenge (reto), the excitement is palpable. The dancer who is performing at a high level is virtually unpredictable, executing a dazzling array of precise movement combinations, while a great subidor, who's usually also an accomplished dancer, can never be fooled since he's seen it all before—supposedly. So who will back down first?

When the dancer is female and the drummer is male, this contest can take on battle-of-the-sexes proportions, for the woman has the opportunity to publicly humiliate a subidor who prides himself on his dexterity by making him "strike out." The subidores who survive these repeated challenges to their skills generally have certain traits that enable them to endure. Ironically, but not surprisingly, the best subidores usually have the most humble, down-to-earth personalities—not all percussionists are able to leave their egos behind long enough to do a good job of marking a dancer's extended solo, let alone do it for hours on end. The supermacho drummer who lords it over as a cock-of-the-walk control freak finds himself with a bit too much to lose in a bombazo. Being a good subidor requires not only physical skill—excellent drum technique and superior hand-eye coordination—but also an encyclopedic knowledge of what movements correspond to what sounds, the artistic ability to interpret these movements with signature flair, and an inviting sociability that engages the dancers and promises to be a source of good conversation.

Not all bomba performances are ideal for dancers. For most of the past fifty years, bomba in the folkloric mode has been presented on a stage where musicians are separated from and elevated over the audience. Some folkloric groups have dealt with this problem by inviting people from the audience to climb up to the stage to dance. Added to this aesthetic of separation is the fact that the clothes that people have been wearing on stage—traditional bomba costumes, all white suits for the men, frilly dresses for the women—are markedly different from everyday street clothes, so that those who are brave enough to get on stage are "not dressed properly." Sometimes dancers are not even invited on stage and must struggle to get the attention of the lead drummer from down below (in the pit!), hardly conducive to a good conversation, but for lack of alternatives, the dancers keep trying. When bomba is presented as music first, as a form of, or in the context of, salsa or Latin jazz, implying that the dance is optional or secondary, then it understandably follows that the overall vitality of the music will suffer—not to mention that dancers, and almost by definition, most women, will be excluded.

At a recent event in New York, not unlike hundreds of bomba stage shows that I'd seen in Puerto Rico and elsewhere, a "fiesta de bomba" was announced that consisted of a group of jazz musicians on a stage playing music inspired by, and sometimes based on, bomba rhythms. The only bomba dancers allowed on the stage were members of the group and were presented in the conventional way, that is, as spectacles. The audience was seated in rows, classroom style, with a little bit of room to dance in front below the stage and in the aisles. As the band began a short segment of traditional bomba, I got up and found my dance partner, Awilda Sterling, across the aisle and brought her with me to approach the stage.

It's a classic situation given the context: bomba dancers come up to face the drummers and the lead drummer spots us and begins shaking his head vigorously from side to side ("no, no, no . . . don't do it . . . not now").

Having been in this situation many times before—snubbed by drummers in stage performances, we are not deterred and begin a paseo in pairs, preparing ourselves to challenge the drummer with an enthusiastic crowd behind us, cheering us on.

After we calmly dance the paseo, making eye contact with each other, responding to each other's gestures, I give her a twirl signifying that she will dance first—if he turns her down now, and fails to respond to the challenge, he will be scorned by the "real *bomberos*" in the audience, who know the codes, customs, and protocols. With gracious gestures, straight back bending slightly at the waist, she greets him *pidiendo golpe* (asking for beats to be marked). He makes a few beats in deference to her movements, showing that she's got his attention.

She begins her piquetes gently. For lack of a long bomba skirt, she does it Loíza style; she's wearing a hip hugging evening dress and uses it to her advantage. She steps slowly to the side, makes a brisk turn of the hip sideways toward the drummer, stops and poses, gives a shoulder shimmy followed by a sharp thrust forward with both shoulders. A little more paseo, a few more piquetes, and then it's my turn. I make a very wide circle in my paseo, making sure that the drummer and I are together before I start the challenge.

When I'm ready, I start with a ponche on one, a sharp piquete that signals the drummer to wake up—two quick steps, left-right, left toe touch. Then back to paseo, then another ponche. Okay, he's followed me so far, now I can go into some piquetes to loosen up, congo pose (right arm up and bent, left hand on the hip) with a torso rotation to loosen up the lower back. This move always shakes off any jitters I might have. Then I go into a "march" step (here I come!) toward the drummer: right step, cross, left step, cross. Okay, he's still with me . . . now I can apply a little more pressure with some combinations . . . oops, he's not following so I go back to some easier combinations and then back out with a ponche. Alexandra, the next dancer in line, approaches and I give her a twirl, she takes over, and Awilda and I return to the basic chorus step off to the side.

Bombazos, such as those organized by CICRE, which bring together professionals from dozens of folkloric groups and amateur dancers from throughout the island, are a great way to experience bomba dancing in its full range of expression, with people with a variety of skill levels and regional styles invited to participate. Whereas most bomba shows have the minimal and restricted audience participation I've just described, these events are organized with the explicit intent of optimizing the experience for dancers and die-hard bomberos in general.

All the activity takes place at ground level where dancers and drummers can see each other without obstruction; drums are taken off the stage and put on the ground, so the drummer is no longer literally "looking down" on the dancers. Dancers have the opportunity to do piquetes directly in front of the drummer, even over the drum, and have a better opportunity to get the ultimate recognition from the subidor, having his drum tilt toward the dancer he declares a brujo.

Hundreds of dancers have unimpeded access to the drummers in the course of the evening. The dance solos are projected on a big screen so that spectators, now often numbering in the five hundred to eight hundred range, can see clearly without forcing the dance circle to collapse and implode.

The music never stops; the songs are performed in a medley format with percussionists and *coristas* able to move freely in and out and rotate beach volleyball–style. Transitions between the major rhythms (for example between sicá in 2/4 time and yubá in 6/8) utilize standardized breaks that are led by the subidor and executed by a core group of pre-designated bombazo drummers (at least two in a group of four to eight drummers). The only break in the music is after a set that includes the full cycle of sicá/yubá/holandés songs. After the full cycle is played, the host will say his thank-yous over a slow sicá before the belén, or last dance.

Conclusion

Nowadays, perhaps more than ever with the increased attention to African heritage in Puerto Rican culture in recent years, to know bomba is to know how to dance bomba. A powerful reminder of its historic status as a West African nation dance with transcultural origins, bomba dancing puts the attention back on an enduring precolonial (and future postcolonial) aesthetic in which dance and music are completely coextensive and interpenetrated, a deeply invigorating modality of performance that not even the hyperalienating forces of slavery and the marketplace have been able to destroy. While there are still many more break-dancers (aka *raperos*) and salseros (aka *cocolos*) than bomba dancers (bomberos) in Puerto Rico, there are signs that these three key living, dancing symbols of urban black Latino Caribbean pride, though sometimes mutually divisive (for example, Nuyorican hip-hoppers and wannabes versus Island nationalists, new versus old, pop versus folk), can also be at times complementary, with bomba having an influence in the origins of break-dancing in a Boricua-heavy South Bronx and in the grand ballrooms of salsa. With all building on a similar grammar and vocabulary of African-derived movement, they might continue to reinforce each other in positive ways. Several of the top young bomba performers in Puerto Rico (the Emmanuelli Brothers, An-gel Luis Reyes and his son Otiko, et al.) come from a break-dancing hip-hop background, all having moved back and forth between New York City and Carolina, P.R., for significant periods during their formative years. And perhaps even more surprising, the Arthur Murray Dance Studio in the Miramar section of Santurce has proved to be a viable training ground for bomba newcomers, thanks to manager Tato Conrad, percussion teacher Raúl Berrios, and master bombero José Emmanuelli, where students and instructors of salsa, merengue and other Latin ballroom dances have been getting bomba classes for free since 1997.

More than thirty years after bomba's obituary was written in the Island newspapers, the dance is now alive and well (*San Juan Star,* June 24, 1999). The spirits of the ancestors, the eternal roots that just won't go away, will no doubt be getting the last laugh.

Special thanks to José Emmanuelli for his guidance and tutelage in the historical and practical nuances of bomba performance.

◇   ◇   ◇

VIRGIN ISLANDS

15

◇ ◇ ◇

Winin' Yo' Wais'

The Changing Tastes of Dance on the U.S. Virgin Island of St. Croix

Cynthia Oliver

I look for you
In the jouvert crowd before the break of dawn
as gleaming sweating faces and twisting hips bump and roll
I look for you
in the heat of high day
as the moko jumbies shimmy and shake balancing on air
I look for you
in the teams of bodies rushing to meet the street
as rum scorches throats and the sun bakes asphalt and weary feet
I look for you
in the eyes of lovers holding tight around each other's waists
as the calypso plays on in the colors of sequins and feathers
I see you
as the goddesses and gods of another time come to bless another year
Cynthia Oliver

Every year as the calypso blasted from trucks with speakers towering far above anything appearing close to safe, my family and I would wind our way down to a cool spot on the sidelines of either the wide streets of Frederiksted or the narrower avenues of Christiansted in St. Croix. I grew up here, to a native father and an African-American mother. Carnival was a tradition for ours and countless island families. And its accompanying dances were an anticipated treat. Watching brave and bold island men and women show off their skillful moves and demonstrate creative physical humor made us all respect the body moving as an art. Some moved in ways that were called "rude" or "wutless," signifying more than anything that they could "wine" the best. With an isolation of the lower region of the body shifting and slicing the air in figures of eight or circling round and round like there could be no end, these performers could stand any test. Wining or the more sexually explicit "wukkin' up" is important here. Both are symbols of one's sexuality and confidence, one's talent and abilities both on the dance floor and in the boudoir. Though wining is the cooler, more under-control counterpart to wukkin' up, they are both an important art, skill, device, as well as a measure of our values and condition, our class, social location, and upbringing. *Yo see . . . de elite don wuk up, dey does wine, or watch de res. De res could leggo, leggo wid out fear, leggo wid out consequence, just pure leggo.*

In my early days of carnival and festival watching, dancing was a means by which the world made sense to me, and still does. It is a way of defining and identifying a specific period in the island's social history, a way of connecting the movement of a nation, our unique brand of nation, with the movement of the bodies that comprise that nation. Here, I aim to briefly describe the movements of specifically St. Croix's popular dances, those of the masses, as its social and political conditions shifted and changed, as *it had mek de people dem sweat and weep, mek dem holler and burn, or even mellow and yearn.* From the dances taught and learned body to body, to those requiring more "formal schooling," I move from carnival and its accompanying calypso, to what has been labeled by some our traditional dance, the quadrille and its local accompaniment, the *quelbe*, and quadrille's historical counterpart, the *bamboula*. This is a journey through discontent and content, through slavery and freedom, through a rooted African and resulting Caribbeanness and an undeniable American presence and influence.

Carnival traditions in the United States Virgin Islands have been a cultural staple for decades. Some might argue centuries, if the masqueraders of traveling troupes moving from neighborhood to neighborhood in early eighteenth to mid-twentieth centuries are taken into account. The masqueraders of yesteryear were the precursors to our current Carnival. The sight of local people twisting and wining through the streets in revelry has been a classic feature of mass celebratory events. Local scholar Antonio Jarvis, in his "Folk Dancing in the Virgin Islands," mentions slave conditions and participation in recreational activities, saying the "underprivileged people did indulge in unpracticed and informal dancing, as in the masqueraders who marched about the streets in small bands called troupes" (Jarvis 1952, 3). These informal dance events occurred at different times during the year, but most notably during Crop Over, a harvest celebration, and Christmas and New Year's celebrations. These were similar festivities, containing itinerant minstrelsy, whereby slave musicians toured the town and played for various masters and either solicited money or were hired by the planters to play. Playing violins and goombay drums, the slaves entertained themselves and others with combinations of African and European sounds. Based on the instrumentation of local players, Neville Hall (1992), in *Slave Society in the Danish West Indies*, suggests that the music accompanying the festivities was a very creolized variant of European practice.

This creolized variant of which Hall speaks is the result of a particular formation of ethnicities in what is now the United States Virgin Islands. Residing at the gateway between the Greater and Lesser Antilles, this grouping of more than fifty, mostly uninhabited, islands is known by its three largest: St. Croix, St. Thomas, and St. John. With slightly varying histories, these are English-speaking islands with dialects that have been influenced by numerous migrations. The most prominent combination of peoples historically has been Spanish, Dutch, British, French, Danish, and of course the most visibly present, African. Known as the land of seven flags, St. Croix survived colonization by the above European groups, the Knights of Malta, and finally the United States. The indigenous peoples of Carib and Arawak ethnicities were decimated during early colonization by the Spanish. Various colonists fought and inhabited the islands at different times over the course of two hundred turbulent years. The Danes then purchased St. Thomas in 1695, St. John in 1717, and St. Croix in 1733. In 1917, the United States bought the entire territory from Denmark as a strategic military stronghold intended to prevent Germany from attaining territory in this hemisphere during World War I.

The entry of the United States into the lives of Virgin Islanders did not stop the mélange of cultures that mix and mingle here. We continue today to see, as we have in the past, migrations of South Asian, Asian, and Middle Eastern people as economic opportunity paves a way for increased travel. We see an influx of more and more North Americans of varying classes, often coming to work and help rebuild after devastating hurricanes hit the territory, then deciding to remain after these critical periods are over. Where once only the wealthy wintered or decided to relocate here permanently, the trend over the past fifty years has been the settling of vacationers who seek economic opportunity and favorable living conditions. Thus our dialects shift and move with the broad sound of a base in English and remnants of African languages or phrases peppered with Dutch, Danish, or French inflections upon our tongues. Our vocalities are vibrant reflections of our diversity, of the slippage between ethnicities as our peoples have mixed through the ages. Our physical practice, the moving of our bodies, reflects the same variance, though tinged with plenty of weighted history, as we move from one step to the next, shifting weight mercilessly from left to right as *de waist does wine and the face betrays nutting atall.* This weightedness of which I speak is the complicated currency of a negotiation I mentioned above, between our Caribbeanness and its meeting with our Americanness.

Gordon K. Lewis poignantly expressed our position when, in *The Virgin Islands: A Caribbean Lilliput,* he wrote:

> [O]n the one hand, Virgin Islanders, like Puerto Ricans, are grateful for American economic benevolence, in the form, for example, of the massive federal matching funds that help finance the embryonic welfare state in both communities; on the other hand, they lampoon American political arrogance as it treats their demands for rapid constitutional reform with indifference or at best a glacial pace of change. Their economic benefactor becomes, paradoxically, their major political irritant. Equally paradoxically, the economic largesse helps to blunt the temper of political agitation, giving rise to a spirit of happy indifference to public affairs that so many critics find disconcerting in Virgin Islanders. (Lewis 1972, 18)

We are always pinched between the two, North American and Caribbean identities, as we balance privilege with promise, who we are with who we are not, and choose one practice, one step over another in our particular brand of nation dance. I use nation here knowing fully that ours is a territory of the United States and not what is customarily considered a "nation." Nevertheless, I am interested in *nation* as Partha Chatterjee (1993, 6) uses the term, to connote a place virtually inseparable from political consciousness, one that includes a "spiritual domain," that area that manages to survive and thrive, not without the influences of "the West," or colonialism, but in spite of it. When I speak of spiritual domain here, I do not mean a nationally practiced religion; I mean a dominant commitment to the cultural practices of the area, the firm belief in a way of operating, of conducting formal and informal business, a way of speaking and being understood, in other words, a host of intangibles that are at once a unifying force that create community, engender practice, and sustain the group. This nation body is perhaps what Benedict Anderson (1995, 6), in *Imagined Communities*, calls an imagined political community, one that we collectively imagine and therefore make manifest. And while Carnival is a manifestation of another sort, not of a dance but of a celebratory event embedded with nationalistic undertones, its accompanying dance, the calypso, is one of our most visible and prominent dances, whose shape and execution may vary from island to island, but remains a signpost of Caribbean culture and practice.

Calypso, a product of Carnival, is a dance where the feet sometimes shuffle, sometimes lift gracefully off the floor as the upper body remains stoic and the waist and hips twist and bounce. Solidly identified with calypso music, whose components are the classic mix of African polyrhythmic expression in brass and rhythm section instrumentation, and European structural elements, the dance is a Caribbean staple. Originating in Trinidad, like Carnival itself, and moving through the region like countless forms of cultural expression, this communal production has become a part of our identity. While Virgin Island music is something quite distinct and significantly different, which I will address later, calypso has staying power. It is a foundation to our bodily practices.

Calypso dancing has its trends and flourishes that come with each season. It is a phenomenon, one that retains a "contemporariness" as it remains rooted in history. One year a popular calypso dance was called "the horse chip." This dance played on the calypso rhythm, but added a horse-like stylized gallop to the basic wind, or "wine," of the waist and shuffle of the feet. Like any trend, these dances come and go. What has become popular of late are "instructional" dances that accompany catchy songs that become the rage for a few months or weeks leading up to Carnival festivities, vie for the title of road march, the most popular song of the season, then disappear as quickly as they rise.

For the 1999–2000 Crucian Festival season, the calypso dance that captured local attention was called "shark-a-come." Sung by Onyan, the fast-paced, catchy tune "Swim" offered explicit instructions. The accompanying dance followed the direct demand of the song, instructing players to move "inna de watta, outta de watta, backstroke . . ." Dancers would then jump forward, backward, then mime a backstroke as they averted danger as men/women overboard in the imaginary sea. In between these movements, or when the singers performed a lyrical segment before the refrain or instrumental segment, performers would revert to basic calypso hip wining movements or depend on their own sense of flair and creativity. Another 1999 song of note, Derima's "Bounce to de ounce," instructed dancers to "raise up your hands and BOUNCE." These songs and their accompanying movements have great popular appeal, because of their sense of humor, sexual implications, and simple ability to make a crowd move. They are performed indoors at dance halls and outside in festival villages or streets.

While calypso dancing and music are remarkable for their longevity, they remain subject to the times. And these are times of fast changes, of fleeting fads. What we hear less and less, in terms of "the popular," are the political songs, the critically astute calypso commentaries that were historically imperative to political and social movements of the nineteenth and twentieth centuries. These were the songs that informed slaves in the fields of the goings-on in the various estates, the songs that moved newly freed workers to riot against unfair working conditions, or simply let the contemporary lay person in on particular political fast talking. They still exist, of course, but radio airplay has diminished as the faster and faster beats and catchy nonsensical tunes blow in and blow out, like the temperamental breezes of what have become all too frequent tropical storms.

Still, these "party songs" are not to be disregarded. Perhaps what these nonsensical routines provide is respite from the dramatic and encompassing greed and materialism that has infected the territory, from the halls of Legislature, as senators and government officials consistently negotiate deals purported to assist the economic development of the area, but that seem more often geared toward special interests and the proliferation of the wealth of a select few, to the fights of school children on playgrounds for sneakers and CD players. Amid economic uncertainty and a certain unspoken desperateness, the dance here becomes a unifying entity, like the unifying quality of carnival itself. The "great equalizer" it has been called, as it has historically drawn together the upper and lower classes for one celebratory event, one time of mas, bacchanal, steeped in a gratefulness for life and survival, and of hope for prosperity, social equality, and continued spiritual blessing.

These moments are recalled in the *Virgin Islands Daily News* special publication titled *The Times of Our Lives: 100 Years in the Virgin Islands 1900–1999*. In the article "Don't Even Try to Stop the Carnival," a play on the classic Duke of Iron calypso "Don't Stop the Carnival," journalist Lynda Lohr (1999) retells the story of St. Thomas local Ron De Lugo, a young man in 1952, who began reminiscing on St. Thomian radio about "old time" masquerades, the celebratory roaming about the streets I mentioned earlier. De Lugo said callers to the station offered many more stories and sparked, in him, an idea to "organize" the island's tradition of tramping, or the random marching down the streets to music, into a more formalized event. With the invited participation of Trinidad's Duke of Iron, and the able assistance of numerous local personalities, including Eldra Schulterbrandt, 1952 became the year of the territory's first Trinidadian-style Carnival event.

But St. Thomas was not the only island to assume a part of this trend. In St. Croix the Women's League, a group of civic-minded community women, took the initiative and were key to the organization of Carnival events there. This shift, of sensibilities and organization around Carnival, cannot be understood only as a nostalgic attempt to unite people of the territory. These events are part of a larger machinery that was at work in the area and reflected significant moves and shifts of local perceptions about our status as Caribbeans and a need to significantly change our economic condition while attempting to take advantage of our status as an American territory. This same era saw the development of government agencies that would direct energies toward moving us into modernity and take advantage of the shift to the movement of the middle class via air travel.

The 1950s brought structural changes in governmental policy to the islands. The Revised Organic Act of 1954 did away with two municipal councils that had prior jurisdiction over St. Croix and St. Thomas separately and developed a legislative body that would govern the whole territory. One of these reformative laws shifted the U.S. government's relation to the islands and dictated that the U.S. government would now match funds the territory collected, allowing those monies to remain in the Virgin Islands Treasury. In 1952, the Tourist Development Board was created and in turn helped to produce the annual Carnival to attract visitors to the islands' cultural riches. This "production" of Carnival organized the prior improvisational events of the masquerading sensibility in a more formulaic manner. And this formula was adopted by each island at differing times of year to capitalize on tourism and the movement of Carnival devotees.

St. Thomas, the territory's capital, conducts its Carnival in April or May. The events are structured in such a way as to extend the tourist season as long as possible without actually moving into the summer season. St. Croix's event is called "Christmas Festival," and it starts in the Christmas season, peaks at New Year's parade day, and ends close to what used to be a celebration of Three Kings Day, a holiday adopted in a spirit of brother/sisterhood with our Puerto Rican neighbors. St. John, often treated as the appendage of St. Thomas, holds its festivities over the July fourth weekend, but has shifted its focus to July third in honor of a more Afrocentric celebration of the slave rebellion on that island, one of the most notable in the Caribbean, where the slaves held the Europeans captive for six months between 1733 and the summer of 1734.

The restructured carnivals became more controlled festivals for the island locals, hosting two to three large parades with community involvement as well as the participation of the many immigrants who make the Virgin Islands home. Instead of having the loosely structured groups roaming through the town and country streets, the 1950s brought about the organizing of official parades that would occur in island towns, control wandering groups, appear more like the elite, planter celebrations in the eighteenth and nineteenth centuries hosted by Europeans in the territory, and cater to a nervous Continental (Statesiders) population with a seeming distaste for unguarded wandering groups of local (black) people. While the initiative for this revised Carnival may have been prompted by De Lugo and Schultebrant of St. Thomas, Wilhelm Samuel, a businessman and organizer from St. Croix described the festival event here in comparison to the events past, saying:

> [W]hen we started the celebration it was more cultural than today. The activities were centered around culture, not money. And people were more creative. The floats and troupes were more representative of old St. Croix. There were colorful masquerades, jig and quadrille dancers. Sugarcane workers paraded with sugarcane, canebills, and hoes. I can never forget the woman who sang cariso from her donkey-cart, while a scratchband followed behind, pumping music. Some folks were decked out in crocus- and flour-bag outfits. And Indians were a part of the scene, and as the kettle drums rolled, they danced like fire. And there were pirates too. There were other bands: Ivan "Tom" Roberts, Archie Thomas, and the Motta Brothers put down music like rain. (Schrader 1994, 52)

Samuel's recollection is beautifully nostalgic and his account is also valuable in terms of the loss of certain forms. What he neglects to mention are those forms that have survived, and, further, what has been borne out of the remnants of the past and the continuing evolution of a creole culture, ever informed by adopting and transforming that with which it comes into contact. While Samuel recollects a woman singing cariso from her donkey cart, there are few cariso singers today, singers who croon a cappella extempore about current events and custom. A precursor of the current calypso, cariso has maintained a purity of form. Performed most often by women of yesteryear, they were, as Harold Willocks (1995, 15) says in *The Umbilical Cord*, "composed about real life events and people, and were performed as spontaneous improvisations or well thought out compositions." Most notably today there is Leona Watson, locally anointed "tradition bearer," who prides herself in the retention of the tradition and the performance of songs exposing and espousing current political dilemmas and opinions.

Workers, also remembered by Samuel, still parade en masse, but in a form less related to their workaday lives. They indeed "tramp" or march in parades, but within the confines of Carnival's chosen themes and the parameters of the festival itself. We have for the most part seen the demise of the jig, though it may occasionally raise a leg in the body of an elder. This dance was most prominent from the early nineteen hundreds through the fifties when Dance Dramas were a popular occurrence. These dramas were based on biblical or fanciful fables and were enacted in the streets with the performance of the jig, the spoken word, and live music. They have since disappeared.

What has probably survived most has been the music. And while calypso may reign as the overwhelming King/Queen of festival events, and soca, salsa, and reggae rear their heads as well, the form that seems to hold calypso's hand is our "native" form, "quelbe," sometimes colloquially called "fungi" music, or "scratch." With instrumentation that includes any combination of guitars, quatros, an occasional rustic banjo, a bass pipe, forged steel triangle, tambourines, the guiro, and flute, scratch is played by popular bands like Stanley and the Ten Sleepless Knights or Jamesie and the Happy Seven. Quelbe or fungi bands have a long history of playing on their own, as added accompaniment to cariso, or as backdrop to festivals or quadrille dances. Alongside our particular brand of calypso festival dance, it is the quadrille that is most identified with quelbe music and as our local cultural dance.

Yet, quadrille has not been embraced without its own manner of controversy. This French-originating set dance has been under fire periodically, by some who favor the promotion of Afrocentric practices, as another European form adopted by blacks in our ever accommodating fashion. Nevertheless, Virgin Islanders, like all Caribbeans, have continued in our tradition of adopting and adapting practices of different cultures, thereby creating our specific creole expression. Thus, while we may be charged with having embraced Eurocentric tradition at the demise of our own, we have also applied our speech, our music, our style, and made it essentially ours, if indeed within the African, Afro-Caribbean, and very human practice of mimicry. I use mimicry here to connote a mindful reproduction of a form, in the process demonstrating a sense of humor, sophistication, innovation, and cleverness.

The quadrille is embraced by many because of a historical longevity that traces back to slave/planter roots similar to its cousin, the bamboula. These are two dances that are not operating at odds with one another— one acknowledged for its roots in Europe and the other for its African origins—but moving in tandem, albeit one as the less visible shadow informing the other. Like many early terms describing Afro-Caribbean dance, the bamboula has been described in numerous ways, many of which conflict. But Florence Lewisohn (1970, 136), in *St. Croix Under Seven Flags*, wrote that "dimly remembered tribal dances out of Africa vied with the bamboula, a gay and spirited dance which soon became the favorite of townspeople also. Originating on the Guinea Coast, the bamboula reached the peak of becoming a craze some decades later in the 18th century among the Spanish Catholics on St. Thomas and Puerto Rico." Lewisohn also describes a bamboula that was sacred, performed in the church by nuns. This sacred version varied from the secular in its lack of male participants. This sacred dance was short lived though the secular form withstood criticism. The church forbade the practice and preached against its performance under any circumstances.

Isidor Paiewonsky in his *Eyewitness Accounts of Slavery in the Danish West Indies* mentions an Andre Pierre Ledru who studied the bamboula and discovered it not only among the slaves and nuns in their "bamboula sacries" but also in the ballrooms of Danish West Indian planters. Ledru claimed the bamboula was performed by selected teams of talented slaves "as no white man could." This action that "no white man could" reproduce was nevertheless performed by the children of the planters who Ledru claimed delighted their parents in "their close imitation and near mastery of the wild rhythms and body contortions of the African slave" (Paiewonsky 1989, 153).

These descriptions, like that supplied by Virgin Island scholar Antonio Jarvis, are consistent with colonialist views of the movement of the African body, connoting hip movement with rampant sexuality and primitiveness. Jarvis (1944) in *The Virgin Islands and Their People* describes a scene whereby a young woman, surrounded by men, gyrates wildly using a snake and its tail as a phallus. According to him, she moves wildly until the climax of the action is the sacrifice of a young child. In the Virgin Islands, the sacred and the secular have long been separate. No dance or cultural practice has been noted for human sacrifice. What many of these descriptions provide, more than anything, is a demonstration of the writer's vivid imagination rather than actual events. Whether the bamboula was actually a separate dance, or as Lynn Emery (1988) in *Black Dance from 1619 to Today* speculates, a version of the chica, which has been described as "the rotation of the hips with an immobile upper body" accompanied by a two-headed or bamboula drum, is up to question. So much of West Indian dance requires the movement of the hips with a stoic upper torso that this description is, at the very least, common.

Whatever the condition of the bamboula, as the specter of an actual dance or a reality, there are those who maintain it exists, those like Dimitri Copeman and Stanley Jacobs who have claimed it is rooted in the Kingdom of Ardra on the coast of Guinea as a ritual dance accompanied by drums and chants (Willocks 1995,14), those who have sought it out in photographs and historical literature, and those who have tried to reproduce its physical vibrancy. In the 1999 *Virgin Islands Daily News* special issue *The Times of Our Lives*, articles by writers Marilynn Bailey (1999) and Mary Ann Christopher (1999) describe a bamboula that appears to be very much alive, particularly on the island of St. Thomas and in great part because of a woman lovingly called "Miss Clara." Clara Isabella Simmonds Matthias was recognized for having brought this dance back to life at that magical time, 1952. It was said to have died out, then once again revived in 1981, by a small number of teachers and interested students at the Joseph Gomez Elementary School. This group, Christopher states, founded what is now known as the Joseph Gomez MACISLYN Bamboula Dance Co., Inc., MACISLYN being an acronym for the group's founders. Still, no description of bamboula circulates on the page, in written texts, outside of what Bailey describes as "rapid-fire movement to the unrelenting beat of the drums." Bailey says the bamboula provides a strong spiritual link, to Africa presumably, and in her article local scholar Myron

Jackson claims the word itself may be related to the word *bomba*, "a spirit filled dance of Puerto Rico" that still survives and is having a renaissance.

Bamboula remains a shadow dance, one that is captured in faded photographs and an even more faded collective memory. Local dance companies have been known to attempt reconstruction of the dance from vague photographs and travel account descriptions of the seventeenth and eighteenth centuries. These, accompanied by social history of the times, provide a scant map of the steps, bare hints at the ways bodies may have moved when, and in response to what. The bamboula's mystery is pregnant with possibility, one that holds our Africanness. It is a shadow dance that breathes breath into every lilting step and rhythmic gesture. It is the quiet sister to our popular form, the quadrille, whose echoes of both Europe and Africa resound more loudly and with regularity on the thick wooden boards of St. Gerard's Hall's worn dance floor in Frederiksted, St. Croix.

At St. Gerard's the dance begins in two long lines, the men to one side, the women to the other. At these crowded dances, the quadrille continues at the discretion of the floor master. The basic step is a shuffle where the feet barely graze the floor before coming down on each of the three beats in a phrase. The upper bodies remain for the most part upright and move in one piece. When the dance gets a bit more lively in the later sets of the evening, the upper bodies initiate the movement by leaning forward from the head with the lower body following. The lower body, including the hips as well as the feet, is responsible for most of the additional movement or embellishment (unless the group is asked to clap or link arms), particularly if individuals decide to take their own liberties and get fanciful.

The floor master, or caller, begins with simple calls to slowly warm up the crowd. He speaks firmly into the microphone, calling "balance" to signal the start of the dance. The dancers approach their partners. To "tunez" they make a 360-degree turn and in "draw away," they back up a few feet. With the call "dance away," for a few moments the dancers have time to move with their respective partners. The evening builds in tempo and excitement as the calls get more complicated and the floor patterns and interactions between couples get increasingly intricate. There are often more women than men at these evening dances, but this is no matter. Some women choose to dance the male part and partner other women. Ages within the group vary widely, from stately older gentlemen and women to the young B-boys and girls and all that fall between. The quadrille is a contemporary dance and it is most certainly a historical one.

Fig. 20. Quadrille dancing in a Frederiksted, St. Croix festival, Carnival season 1999–2000. Photograph: Cynthia Oliver. Used by permission of Cynthia Oliver, Urbana-Champaign, Ill.

Introduced to the Virgin Islands centuries ago, the quadrille is perhaps, more than any other movement form, considered the territory, or nation, dance. Like any cultural practice emphasized for its value to the community, there is, on the one hand, a certain arbitrariness to this choice. However, on the other hand, the quadrille has been remembered, revived, and evoked more than any other physical practice in the area. While we often speak of the bamboula, it is a scarce practice. When it comes to moving bodies, the quadrille is the alternative to calypso, the alternative to reggae or salsa. It is one dance that has had a solid and recountable history, or at least an imagined and inscribed one, that has enjoyed a longevity in these islands that rises above other forms. Derived from the French quadrille, this set dance has a history tied inextricably to the social ebb and flow of the islands' populations. Lisa Lekis, in *Dancing Gods*, says:

Estate managers and the great merchants . . . imported favorite European dances of the era—the minuet, rigodon, lanceros, and others of the quadrille style popular during the first half of the nineteenth century. Slaves and mulattoes watched the dances through the open windows of the plantation houses and tried to imitate both the costumes and courtesies of the ballroom. . . . An acceptable performance of these dances became a requirement for both black and white society on the islands. (Lekis 1960, 181)

The mulattoes of whom Lekis speaks were classified differently because of their status as offspring of planter and slave relations. Often given freedom by their planter fathers, this group, as well as the few blacks called "free colored," who were granted freedom by their "masters" for years of faithful service or for a variety of undisclosed reasons, were key in the development of a middle class. Positioned between the planters and the slaves, mulattoes and the free colored occupied this middle ground and participated in the quadrille as a demonstration of their worldliness and sophistication. Lekis described this dance and its structure as "the stock in trade of the fiddle players and the dancing masters of the period. . . . In its original form, the quadrille was composed of a couple or two couples making up each side of a hollow square" (Lekis 1960, 182). The conductor of the dance was (and remains) the "caller" and directed the figures. The vision through greathouse windows was of "beautifully gowned women gracefully extending their right hands to their impeccably tailored escorts, the women making a low curtsy, the gentlemen bowing gallantly over their ladies' hands" (Lekis 1960, 182). These movements were carefully noted and reproduced by those outside the privileged greathouse.

While many scholars have argued that the actions of the slaves were mimetic, Neville Hall (1992), in *Slave Society in the Danish West Indies*, explored the possibility and likelihood of mimicry and exaggeration as an outlet for poking fun at the rigidity and formality of the "high classes." Hall states: "It might just as probably have been ridicule, and there is the third alternative that the slaves could have been investing the occasion with special significance by the adaptation of European styles of address and usage in contemporary 'society.' At any rate, the adaptations were subject to the slaves' own sobering sense of the appropriate, an eye for the absurd, and a capacity to poke fun at each other" (1992, 116). These behaviors were not invented in the Virgin Islands, but were more probably carried over from the African traditions with which the slaves had been accustomed. As Hall states in *Slave Society:*

> C. G. A. Oldendorp, who visited the Danish islands between 1767 and 1769, claimed to have observed a large number of "tribes": Fulani, Mandingoes, Amina, Akims, Popos, Ibos and Yorubas, corresponding to a geographical area stretching from the Senegal River to the Bight of Benin. Although he provided no figures for the Danish West Indies, he maintained that the "Amina" were the most numerous. Pauline Holman-Pope has sustained Oldendorp's observations by identifying large numbers of Akan-Amina speakers of Twi in St. Croix in the later eighteenth century, and a similar preponderance of this ethnic group in St. John. (Hall 1992, 71)

Africans from the Congo were also a distinct presence, particularly in St. Croix, during the days of human cargoes (Hall 1992, 71). These groups mixed and mingled practices and developed the very creole mix for which the Caribbean is most noted. And dancing was a crucial part of this mélange that became cultural practice. When slaves rebelled to gain their freedom in Frederiksted, St. Croix, in 1848, dancing was integral to the emotional and physical uproar of the battle for freedom. While it is not likely that set dances were performed during the freedom triumph, the use of quadrille dancing and courtly behavior in other social settings may have been an exercise in excess and levity for the black masses as well as a social leveler in planter and mixed-race or free colored communities. Its importance as a society dance could not be shaken. The ridicule of the pomp and circumstance surrounding the quadrille did not curb its impact on slaves and status-conscious free blacks and mixed-race "coloreds" alike. The quadrille became the dance of the time, performed indoors and outdoors by the elite, the free colored, and the enslaved.

Today, the collapsing of ethnic and economic barriers remains a feature of the quadrille. Quadrilles are attended by a variety of people, of many economic classes. The majority of attendees are Afro-Caribbean. Though quadrilles at St. Gerard's are also held at other times, they are most numerous and popular during the Christmas Carnival season, a time when social and economic structures and the separation between groups is still present, but perhaps a little less rigid. The Virgin Island community is a stratified community, acutely aware of privilege or the lack thereof; there are clear boundaries between middle, lower and upper classes, and between the races. There are inequities here, as the world over, with regard to privilege, capital, and power and these lines are clearly drawn in our day-to-day existences. But the quadrille is a setting where all of these weighty sociopolitical concerns fade to the background and the human spirit and the desire to move together rise to the surface as person by person, couple by couple, all shuffle, twist, turn, and sashay to the calls of the floor master and the sounds of quelbe. Now, unless it is a formal ball, or a parade presentation, the atmosphere is relaxed and the dress, casual. The sense of humor Hall indicated remains evident in the freedom and playfulness that appear both on and off the dance floor. The rigid formality of the visions through the greathouse windows Lekis recounted recurs only in the balls designed for a specific group where adherence to, and a reconstruction of, tradition and ceremony are the focus of the evening. What occurs at St. Gerard's Hall in Frederiksted, St. Croix, is the result of a successful revival project of many years.

While historically the dance continued to be a measuring stick for class and privilege, it lost its popularity for a period following the United States purchase of the territory in 1917 until the 1940s, when quadrille leader Vivian MacIntosh was particularly popular. In the 1950s quadrille re-emerged in the parades, performed by young children of the public schools. Some say its disappearance lasted even longer. But in the 1970s Milton Payne of Frederiksted initiated a significant resurgence. Teaching the concept and precision of the dance to local adults, he began what Bradley Christian continues to this day. Not only the star of the quadrille scene, Christian follows a long line of quadrille leaders and callers (though he calls only for his group, the Heritage Dancers, fancying himself more a dancer than a caller), from Adam Peterson and Alexander "Ciple" Michael, to Vivian MacIntosh, Milton Payne's Quadrille Group, Helen Joseph's Virgin Island Dancers, the St. Croix Cultural Dancers founded by Lillian Bailey, and a caller particularly popular today, Curtis Williams. As we enter the new millennium, only one of these groups continues to exist, the Heritage Dancers.

The Heritage Dancers group was founded by Henrique Santos in January of 1981 to, as Christian tells it, "preserve the culture of the Virgin Islands through dancing" (Oliver 1995, 124). When I spoke to Christian in 1994, he said that his group received no funds from the government, but managed to survive via monthly dues, bake and food sales, and raffles. Performing periodically at a variety of venues including hotels and cruise ships, their highlighting events are balls, which are given a variety of names and themes. These ball events—with titles like the Canary Ball, the

Snow White Ball, the LaFrance Ball, or the Champagne Ball—are a recollection of the pomp and circumstance of yesteryear. They commonly open with an invocation and a selection of a king and queen, a practice performed widely at a variety of island occasions. Honorees are presented with plaques for community service. Toasts are made, and the formal French Lancier and Grand Waltzes are performed, after which the honorees participate, indicating the opening of the dance for the general audience to join. Waltz, merengue, and other "cultural" music accompany the event. This "cultural" music may be salsa or calypso in addition to the quelbe. The music is live, played often by Stanley and the Ten Sleepless Knights, one of the few quadrille bands left on the island. According to writer/storyteller Richard Schrader, when the Sleepless Knights don't play, Blinky and the Roadmasters or the Native Rhythms strike the sounds. These bands follow in the long tradition of quelbe bands like Bully and the Kaffooners and Jamesie and the Happy Seven (Jamesie has pursued this native music for more than fifty years) and are instrumental in what Schrader calls "the march of cultural revival in song, dance and music" (Schrader 1994, 62).

It is significant that there seems consistently to be underway the project of reviving the past, an interest in securing specific cultural practices that can be identified as distinctly Virgin Island. These are projects continually under construction, under reconstruction, in process. While tourism, with its promise of economic stability and attraction of global industrial and corporate dollars, continues to be an influence in that regard, survival and identity are the pertinent personal and cultural elements at stake. As cable television and the computer age and its accompanying "information highway" encroach on the territory, the influences of not simply North American, but global culture impact the community and contribute to the further bleeding of forms. This too, is a process hundreds of years in the making, one that picks up speed like the modems on increasingly speedy computers.

Speed is important, as a colleague and friend with whom I spoke said at the festival village of the 1999–2000 Crucian festival season. Otis Alexander, a scholar, teacher, singer, and master dancer of numerous West African forms, has invested decades on St. Croix teaching young people in the public schools. Alexander has been committed, in addition, to presenting choreographed troupes of students during festival parades. I asked about the training of young people as we reminisced about days past when many of us were committed to daily dance training. Alexander responded in the language of technology, saying that this is the age of the internet, that everything is immediate, that no one wants to work hard for years to achieve anything. I thought perhaps that we could call this formulation "fast dance," the product of the least amount of training and simple choreographic patterns.

This lack of committedness of which Alexander spoke is not pervasive, however. There has been a consistent "formal" training contingent on the island beginning in the 1940s with Leona Barnes, a local Crucian who trained in modern, tap, and ballet stateside, only to return and offer instruction to local children on both St. Croix and St. Thomas. In the 1950s Atti van den Berg, a Dutch dancer and choreographer and former Kurt Jooss performer, opened doors to a school also committed to teaching young dancers. Van den Berg became a moving force in the community, establishing Theatre Dance, Inc., and training numerous young people who became professionals in the field. I am one of those professionals. In addition, she contributed significantly to the opening of artistic and aesthetic doors to the community and those outside as she recruited off-island dancers and companies to appear as guests and instruct youngsters on a master class basis. She was instrumental in bringing the current artistic director of the Caribbean Dance Company, Montgomery Thompson, to the island in the 1970s. The company has seen great success in the Caribbean and abroad. Thompson, a Trinidadian, has contributed many years to the formal instruction of ballet, modern, and Caribbean dance and folklore to island children.

Thompson's extensive background with Alwyn Boyens in Trinidad and abroad exposed him to the works of artists like Beryl McBurnie, Torrance Mohammed, Alex McDougal from Canada, and the Ballet Folklorico de Mexico (Oliver 1995, 119). Concentrating on Caribbean and Modern dance forms, Thompson follows in the footsteps of Boyens's experimental focus in researching groups from the Caribbean and abroad and portraying their practices creatively on stage. His vision has been to create a dance company that represents the panorama of Caribbean practice, not simply the Virgin Islands. His company, in this vein, has performed the Shango dance of Trinidad, the Masquerade of Montserrat, a "Calypso Rainbow," and certain historical dramatic dances of the Virgin Islands that portray key figures in the development and culture of the territory, like "Queen Mary," a powerful work demonstrating the influence and strength of a woman who turned the tides of the labor movement on St. Croix. As I mentioned above, the company has also attempted a reconstruction of the bamboula (Oliver 1995, 120). The Caribbean Dance Company's work continues, due in great part to the dedication of countless artists, particularly Curliss Solomon, veteran dancer with the troupe from its inception in 1977, and its managing director Jill Thompson, also a member from the group's inception. They conduct yearly performances on St. Croix showcasing new work, before heading off on their touring schedules, and have been a consistent presence in the Artist-in-Schools programs, teaching dance to young people across the community. Caribbean Dance Company is but one of the local organizations working with the young. And while Thompson's group covers the area of Caribbean dance, there are others covering different movement arenas.

In the 1980s Charlita Withey, a ballet dancer trained also by Theatre Dance, Inc., then as a professional with Ballet Florida, established Music in Motion Dance Academy, offering ballet and gymnastics to youngsters. And in the 1990s Sonja Dickerson and Heidi Wright founded Pointe Dance Academy, a Cecchetti institution. All have had measured success, as they sometimes compete for students or Arts Council dollars. Some have given up on official funding and opt to appeal to grassroots for support as they struggle to keep their doors open and make a living as artists in the community. And others still, like Adjoa Young-Hinds, master African dancer and teacher, have skirted these trappings altogether and gone right to the grassroots, teaching West African dance forms and drumming to men, women, and children in community halls and other public spaces.

These schools form the body of "formal" training available on St. Croix. Most have taken their cues from the U.S. mainland or Europe as they impress on youngsters the importance of a certain aesthetic line, tilt of the head, or lift of the arm. They stand side by side with the clubs in the junior high and high schools, which in the legendary fashion of the Doc James Talent Club of the 1950s to the 1970s practice and participate in the "fast dance," geared toward the entertainment at queen shows, talent shows, and, of course, Carnival. James, a renaissance man who was a physician, musician, community leader, and radio personality, spearheaded the most popular variety show event in the area, featuring dance numbers choreographed by club members to contemporary pop hits. While the variety show format has waned and talent club performances are more insular, geared specifically toward school audiences, Otis Alexander has utilized his dance club, Street Dance, as an avenue for dance to change shape and remain a part of Carnival's riches. Whereas his group was often known for versions of quadrille-like forms, they broke out in the last year of the century with something different, something "new," steps choreographed to Michael Jackson's "Don't Stop Till You Get Enough."

An oddity in the body of the festival parade itself with its jumping and twisting, bouncing and rolling to countless calypso currents, the group created a sense of excitement in the crowds. They did not choose hip-hop, something more contemporary, or Jamaican dancehall, something perhaps immediately more translatable to a Caribbean event, but rarely a choice for Carnival processions. Michael Jackson, an icon of American success and excess, becomes the symbol, the sound, the movement of a territory, an island, of bodies pushing relentlessly forward, propelling themselves into the next century. This song becomes the anthem for the last century, for an unquenched desire for freedom, or in this age, for material wealth, access, and ease represented by our American colonizer, a desire not stopped by the planter's lash, the worker's wail, the youth culture's beat, or the Rastafari chant. This song becomes the anthem for the present, a representation of who we have become, a community wanting, a community determined both by its materiality and by its struggle to hold on to the past while moving, moving, moving, quickly into an always uncertain future.

> I look for you in the step
> the beat
> the heat
> of tomorrow

Cynthia Oliver

Special thanks to Mr. Curtis Williams, Mr. Bradley Christian, and my family.

$\diamond$　$\diamond$　$\diamond$

MARTINIQUE AND GUADELOUPE

16

❖ ❖ ❖

Sa Ki Ta Nou (This belongs to us)

Creole Dances of the French Caribbean

Dominique Cyrille

We dance the maziouk without the pitché / We dance the biguine, but we do not swing / When we hear the Creole waltz we remain seated / But all these dances are our own / You should not borrow from others what will never be yours / You want kadans, bolero, and tango / But, my friend, you are lying to yourself / You must dance a fine biguine, a sweet maziouk, a slow Creole waltz / Take Loulou as an example, but do not imitate him
—**Eugène Mona**

These lyrics are an excerpt from a *maziouk* recorded in Creole by Eugène Mona, a Martinican singer popular in the early 1970s. This song, titled "What is yours, is yours" (*Sa ki taw sé taw*), was a warning about borrowing dance music from other islands, a custom that has developed in the French Caribbean. When this song was first recorded, the traditional *biguine*, the waltz, and the maziouk (mazurka) still constituted half the repertoire of Martinican and Guadeloupean receptions; the other half came from dance music borrowed from other countries of the Caribbean basin. Like many musicians in the 1970s, Eugène Mona feared that the custom of borrowing foreign genres would lead to the disappearance of the indigenous dance music of the French Caribbean. He chose the rhythm of maziouk to convey his message because it is considered emblematic of the cultural specificity of Martinique.

Much has been written about the use of music and dance to define both national and cultural identity and ethnicity in the Caribbean. Although cultural identity and ethnicity are not the focus of this essay, the social significance of dance in Caribbean cultures and societies cannot be overlooked. This chapter will describe the dances of the French Caribbean and will concentrate on the historical and sociological background of the repertoire of these islands. The various aspects of the creolization process will be discussed, from the acquisition of new political and social meanings that affected quadrille dancing to the camouflage of African customs using European styles and forms. As Mona feared, the biguine, the waltz, and the maziouk are no longer the main dances of French Caribbean receptions. Only a small number of maziouks and biguines are still performed and the waltz is disappearing. Ironically these changes were not a result of invasion from outside genres, but rather from within. They will be discussed in the last section of this essay.

Historical and Geographical Background of the French Caribbean

Guadeloupe and Martinique are French islands of the Lesser Antilles. Guadeloupe is made of two islands separated by a river creating the mountainous Basse-Terre or *Guadeloupe-proprement-dite*, and the flat Grande-Terre. Five smaller islands are considered dependencies of Guadeloupe: Marie-Galante, Désirade, Îles des Saintes, two small islands close to Guadeloupe, and St. Barthélemy as well as the French portion of St. Martin, which are neighbors of Antigua and Montserrat. Martinique is located between St. Lucia and Dominica, the latter being about thirty miles to the south of Guadeloupe.

Christopher Columbus discovered Marie-Galante and Guadeloupe in November of 1493 and Martinique in 1502. When, in 1635, both islands became part of the French crown, they were inhabited by the Carib people. After several decades of constant battle, few Caribs were to be found in Martinique by the end of the seventeenth century. This genocide of the aboriginal population was completed in the early eighteenth century. A small group, however, remained in a portion of Grande-Terre, Guadeloupe, where they slowly mixed with the Creole population.

The economic prosperity of these islands was based on the agriculture of sugarcane, which required large quantities of workers. The slave trade was established in 1640 to insure the economic growth of the French Caribbean islands, and over the course of a century Martinique became the wealthiest French possession in the Caribbean, partly because of its ideal geographic location. After 1640 the number of Africans enslaved in the

French Caribbean islands grew so rapidly that by the end of the seventeenth century they comprised more than 80 percent of the total population. The life span of the African slaves was very short because of malnutrition and brutal treatment, and the small number of births could not balance the high mortality rate among the enslaved workers.

Consequently, throughout the slavery era and up to the late 1860s, the Europeans constantly raided the West African coast to bring new workers to the Caribbean plantations (Daget 1990, 207–209). Between 1833, when the slave trade to the French Antilles was officially ended, and emancipation there in 1848, new African workers continued to be introduced into the French Caribbean through illegal trading (Curtin 1969, 234). In the 1850s and 1860s more than ten thousand African slaves bought in the coastal area of equatorial Africa were freed as soon as they boarded ships and then were transported against their will to the French Caribbean islands as indentured laborers (Nicolas 1996, vol. 2, 56). Slavery had already been interrupted in Guadeloupe from 1794 to 1802 under the first French Republic. This did not affect Martinique because the planters had given the island to the English in 1794. Martinique then was given back to France in 1802 as part of the Treaty of Paris, when the Consulate reinstated slavery in Guadeloupe.

The French began slave trading in the Senegambia in the seventeenth century and drifted slowly southbound along the western coast of the African continent. During the phase of intensive slavery and up to the mid-eighteenth century, a large majority of slaves were kidnapped in the Bight of Benin, in an area that went roughly from the greater Accra region in modern Ghana to Lagos and the Niger River in modern Nigeria. At times of war with other European nations, the French would capture their slaves either in the Bight of Benin or to the south of Cape Formosa at the mouth of the Congo River in order to avoid enemy ships (David 1973, 61). In the second half of the nineteenth century most Africans who came to work on the French sugar cane plantations were indentured laborers from the Congo basin (Debien 1974). These late arrivals had a strong influence on the dance culture of both Martinique and Guadeloupe.

Bal boutché, balakadri

It was customary for French planters to group newly arrived Africans with more experienced slaves who spoke the same language; they were in charge of accustoming the *bossales*, the newly arrived slaves who were not yet baptized, to life on the plantations. The Europeans also believed that certain African peoples were predisposed to certain technical skills and specific tasks (Moreau de Saint-Méry [1798] 1984, 48–54), and whenever possible they chose their slaves among them. Consequently, newly arrived Africans often found others who spoke their own language on the plantations, a situation that contributed to the maintenance of African cultural traits among the slaves. Many of these traits are still present in the Creole genres of Martinique and Guadeloupe, especially in the rural repertoires that have roots in both the Yoruba and Kongo traditions.

But Africa is not the only source of inspiration for Creole dances of the French Caribbean people. European genres also played a major role. During the centuries of contact with the Europeans, some African genres disappeared altogether. Other African genres, targeted by the planters because of their religious content, seemed to vanish only to reappear under another format. Although the dances had adopted external European features, the underlying African meaning was preserved. Quadrilles and other square dances arrived in a timely manner and served to camouflage many of the African danced rituals.

The European-derived quadrilles danced by Martinicans and Guadeloupeans were introduced in the eighteenth and nineteenth centuries by the planters. Some are choreographed for four couples in a square configuration, and others are closer to eighteenth-century French contredanse and are performed on a double column. All have a distinct dance routine for each element of the set. They were once reserved for the plantocracy elite, and although they are danced today by people from all socioeconomic backgrounds, quadrilles are still symbols of literacy and social elevation.

Until recently, they were the only genres performed in popular balls called *balakadri* in Guadeloupe and *bal boutché* in Martinique. Today, the European-derived quadrilles have disappeared from most popular balls and are mostly seen on stage during village festivals. Preparing for this, however, requires much practice, so that quadrille is still kept up by traditional dancing families in villages and new enthusiasts they have taught in towns.

From the earliest stages of slavery, some Africans were chosen to become domestics in the homes of the planters. By the end of the eighteenth century these slaves, who lived in close contact with the colonists, had integrated European music and dance into their repertoire, often under the supervision of Catholic missionaries. In the beginning, domestic slaves learned altered versions of European dances especially designed by seventeenth-century missionaries who wanted to suppress the "outrageous" postures of African dancing (Labat 1724, 53). These early European-derived genres were different from the contredanse of the late eighteenth century, and they are no longer found on the islands. It is my belief, however, that they provoked the integration of European elements into African dancing, which constituted the first steps toward creolization.

In the course of time, the domestic slaves adapted many aspects of European dancing into their African customs, creating distinctive genres that set them apart from the other slaves. They were forming a class somewhere between the European colonists and the laborers in the fields. Quadrille dancing thus became a symbol of their social elevation. At times they joined the others and danced with them to the sound of the drums; at other times they danced among themselves inside the planter's house in the European fashion (Dessalles [1834] 1987, 229). All three classes knew the ceremonial and educative value attached to the contredanse. Many free blacks were educated and some of the wealthiest had gone to France to complete their education. Newly freed slaves and black craftsmen had close contact with the whites, enough at least to know the social function and symbolic value attached to the planters' formal dances (Moreau de Saint-Méry 1802, 41). Therefore, whenever members of the lower classes borrowed the dances from the whites, political motivations were immedi-.ately inferred. Because of slavery, quadrille dancing became a symbol of power and freedom in the French Caribbean.

Contredanse had been a select element of French ceremonial balls for at least two decades before the French Revolution in 1789. At that time it was still danced in *pot-pourris*, or sets of two or three contredanses. When composers and choreographers began to conceive and treat each set as a distinct dance, it evolved into the quadrille. The dance became so popular that in the early nineteenth century as many as eight couples could perform together in order to give everyone a chance to participate (Guilcher 1969, 149). These dances became very popular in the Caribbean as well. Some elements of the quadrille were brought to the islands after the abolition of slavery and the domestics added them to their own repertoire as they had done before.

In the eighteenth century, the European-derived dances of the domestics were at first similar to the ones performed in the balls in France. The slaves had learned them by watching lessons given by dance masters whom planters hired from Paris (Moreau de Saint-Méry [1798] 1984, 69). In addition, the free blacks were careful to learn the proper attitudes and steps. They took lessons with the same dance masters as the planters and, according to Moreau de Saint-Méry (1802, 40), they surpassed many whites with their graceful manners and elegant gestures.

Soon after arriving in the colonies, the European dances were introduced to the receptions of the domestics, at times with some slight transformations. From the documents describing the receptions of domestic slaves and free people of color, it appears that the main changes were not so much in the music, but in the dance. Obviously the slaves' rendition of the ceremonial dances was affected by their African culture, which they never rejected completely. To the contrary, they sometimes participated in the drum dances with the field laborers, even when they were living close to the whites. These blacks acted as an interface through which European-derived genres circulated among all social classes in the French Caribbean. During most of the eighteenth and nineteenth centuries, the domestics danced the French contredanse and quadrilles with all the fashionable variations (Granier de Cassagnac 1844, 220).

In the Caribbean, the fashion of waltz and mazurka dancing grew in the early stages of the nineteenth century (Cyrille 1989: 25). However, it is the spirited rhythm of polka that has become symbolic of quadrille music in Guadeloupe and Martinique.

According to recent research, three types of quadrilles are danced in Guadeloupe. The *quadrille au commandement* (with calls) is performed on Grande-Terre and Marie-Galante. The French quadrille is danced in the western part of Basse-Terre, and the lancers are danced only in the town of Sainte-Anne (Uri and Uri 1991, 63).

The Guadeloupean version of the French quadrille comprises five figures. An introductory march serves as a prelude during which the dancers form a double column and prepare for the first figure, which is the waltz. It is followed by *pantalon, été, poule,* and *pastourelle* consecutively; these names are parts of the traditional quadrille as codified in the early nineteenth century in France. Then a *biguine* is added as a finale. A *commandeur* sometimes calls the steps and the figures; the couples shuffle, pirouette, cross, turn partners, etc. in response to his calls. The biguine/finale is danced by couples in a close embrace at the end of the set.

The French quadrille has produced two Creole dances in Martinique that do not require the calls of a commandeur. The first one is the pastourelle, danced in Sainte-Marie, and the other is *lakadri* (Creole for the quadrille). The pastourelle is composed of five figures that appear in the following order: a waltz, a *maziouk*, a polka, a pastourelle, and *polka-la-poule*. During the first three numbers the couples dance around the room. The figures end when the couples are back to their initial position. Then they dispose themselves in a square configuration for the pastourelle and the polka-la-poule. The fast and energizing rhythm of polka-la-poule gives the gentlemen an opportunity to demonstrate their virtuosity. The dancers call it *lanflanmansyon* because it is said to ignite the ballroom.

Lakadri is danced mostly in southern Martinique. Although it has much in common with the French quadrille of the nineteenth century, the dancers perform in a double column.

Haute-taille is the name for two set dances known only in three villages of southeastern Martinique. Although it is uncertain when this dance first appeared on the island, the name seems to be linked to the mid-eighteenth-century French contredanse (Cyrille 1989). At that time, *haute* and *basse taille* were other designations for dances that required bouncing steps or shuffling, respectively. This conjecture is corroborated by the existence of bouncing steps in the Périolat style. The haute-taille of Morne-Pitault, however, is shuffled and closer to nineteenth-century French quadrilles.

The distinctive feature of haute-taille is the presence of the commandeur who directs the dance and calls the steps. Both haute-taille sets are composed of five numbers, executed by four couples in the square configuration. In the Périolat area, the first three numbers are called contredanses and the last two are figures.

People from Morne-Pitault dance the first four figures following the commandeur's calls. During the fifth element, the maziouk, the couples turn around the dance area, as they do in the pastourelle.

Most haute-taille performers remind us that the genre is not their creation. They perform it, as one of my informants said, "because their parents and grandparents used to do so." My older informant, Monsieur Rosamond, who was ninety years old and still a renowned drummer/commandeur when I met him, told me that his grandfather learned it by watching the dance at the plantation house and taught him when he was a teenager.

The *réjane* is a set of contredanses also known in southeastern Martinique. There is no specified limit to the number of couples who can dance together. They form a double line and the music for each piece lasts long enough for all the couples to perform.

Today, European-derived quadrilles of the French Caribbean are danced to the sound of a melodic instrument (such as a violin or an accordion), accompanied by a shaker and a circular frame-drum (the Martinican *tanbou dibass* or the Guadeloupean *tambour basse*). A scraper (the *siyak*) and a triangle complete the band. Since quadrille dancing used to signal the social elevation of the free blacks and domestics, it has retained many European characteristics. Some quadrilles, like the lancers, are identical to the original dance. In the others such features as the number of dancers, the couples dancing in the middle of the square, the frequent use of the French steps *balancé* and *petit-pas*, and the instrumentation still preserve their European appearance.

The commandeur, however, is a Creole adaptation of the quadrille using calls because, whenever possible, the European traits were transformed to help preserve African elements that could not remain unchanged on the plantation. In Martinique, the drummer is also, at the same time, the commandeur, but in Guadeloupe he only drums. Despite this distinction, on both islands, the commandeurs call the steps and figures in a similar mixture of Creole and French. The orders are not as brief as their European counterparts; they are intertwined with remarks, sometimes caustic, about the dancers in the square. The commandeur delivers his speech in a distinctive manner; his phrases resemble rhythmic sequences. He stretches the prosody of the Creole language in order to create rhythms that complement the polyrhythmia.

To me, the rhythmic commands must be seen as a transposition of a type of drumming that was impossible to reproduce in the Caribbean given the linguistic diversity of the slave population. Many captives brought to the French Caribbean islands came from the Bight of Benin (Benoist 1975, 263). Drums talking to the dancers and commenting on their evolutions are frequently found among various ethnic groups who dwelled in that area. They exist among the Ewe (Nkétia 1968) as well as the neighboring Fon and Yoruba. The frame drum used for quadrille dancing did not allow the variety of pitch needed for drummed messages, and in any case, Creole is not a tone language. The commandeur assumes the function of the master drummer who in Yorubaland talks to the dancers while providing rhythmic support for the dance.

Quadrilles and Creolization

More radical transformations occurred among slaves dancing in the fields, away from the planter's sight. Dance was also very important in African culture, but for some entirely different reasons; it not only had a great social value, but also was part of the religious rites and worship. African danced rituals were not welcome in European colonies, and many elements of collective worship had to be altered in order to fit in the new environment. As I mentioned earlier, the Christian missionaries involuntarily facilitated the process by teaching altered versions of European genres to some of the slaves. When the contredanse arrived in the Caribbean during the second half of the eighteenth century, it combined many external qualities that allowed its metaphorical use in neo-African rituals, such as dancing in opposite lines, men and women face-to-face, and the clockwise and counterclockwise circling that began many contredanses. The opposite lines and the circle are the two dance formations that J. H. Weeks ([1882] 1914, 128) observed while studying the Bakongo people in the late nineteenth century.

In addition, the music for quadrilles and contredanses was interpreted with only two musical instruments: a flute or a violin and a tambourine or a frame drum. This, too, provided grounds for the blending of African and European traditions. Other qualities that allowed the merging of social European dances with African rituals are the association of a specific melody to a dance routine and the organization of contredanses into sets. It appears that a suite of dances, each with its distinctive music and steps, is a feature that most ethnic groups from the Bight of Benin—the area that gave the French Caribbean the majority of its slaves—have in common (Nkétia 1965, 5). Furthermore, in many Parisian formal balls of the nineteenth century, there used to be a queen and a king to open the dance and decide in which order the dancers would appear. I hypothesize that the transposition of this custom in Martinique helped the masking of rituals in quadrilles. Thus, when performed by the slaves, the quadrilles and contredanses served to mask what, to the French, were unwelcome African customs and, paradoxically, helped to maintain them in another form in the French Caribbean.

African-Derived Dances

The concentration of Africans with a similar cultural background in specific areas of the islands caused an uneven partition of the Creole genres. The steep hills of northern Martinique and of Guadeloupe-proprement-dite provided ideal shelter for runaway slaves. They re-created small African-based communities in the mountains and created new genres that would better fit their new lifestyle. This also contributed greatly to the maintenance of Africanisms in the Creole repertoire. In spite of the new roads that have opened communication between villages and neighborhoods since the 1960s, most musical genres of today are still confined to specific areas of Martinique and Guadeloupe.

As a result of their specific history, the links that tie the French Caribbean genres to Africa are more obvious in the rural repertoires. These dances are still called rural although today they are also performed in the cities. Up to three decades ago they were never danced by the intellectual and economic elite who lived in towns, but only by black peasants in the countryside. In the French Antilles, as in other parts of the Caribbean, music has always been an indicator of racial origin and of social status. The light-skinned urban population saw unwanted symbols of a shameful past in drum dances. They considered *gwoka* and *bele* a by-product of the underdeveloped dark-skinned peasants, and relied chiefly on European and European-derived music for their entertainment. The peasants, on the other hand, danced both the European-derived quadrilles and the African-derived genres.

Drum music is considered the genuine creation of the blacks in the French Caribbean. The rural songs carry the collective memory of the community and for a long time they were the only avenue of expression for people whose opinion was never sought. Once used for keeping track of events that affected the life of family members and neighbors, they now address issues that are important to the larger community. Many songs contain allusions to slavery and the African past. The rural repertoire is an important aspect of the Creole culture of the French Caribbean that has contributed to re-creating a sense of belonging that blacks had lost in the Middle Passage.

Bele linò

It is not known precisely when bele dancing first appeared in Martinique. Historical data have verified the constant presence of African dancing and drumming on the island since the beginning of slavery. However, the term bele does not appear in documents until the early nineteenth century (Dessalles [1834] 1987, 229). Even then, it referred to slave songs and not to dance or the drum. It has been possible, however, to relate many ancient descriptions of slave dancing and drumming to modern bele genres. In addition, some of the oldest songs that are still in use contain foreign words that appear to be derived from African languages (Cyrille 1996, 555).

There are two distinct set dances that are called bele in Martinique. Both are performed to the sound of the one-skinned conical drum known as *tanbou bele* (bele drum). The most famous is *bele linò*. It originated in the northeast and today has spread throughout the island. The best drummers and singers of bele linò come from the region of Sainte-Marie. The other genre is *bele lisid*, found solely in southern Martinique. Both beles are usually performed in informal *swaré beles* and sometimes onstage during village festivals.

The quadrille configuration has been adopted for the bele linò of Sainte-Marie. This set comprises as many numbers as the performers desire, although dancers usually execute five or six pieces before being replaced. Sets are made of bele, *bélia*, and *gwanbèlè* arranged in any order. According to my informants, bele dancers in the region of Sainte-Marie, the first piece of the set had traditionally been a gwanbèlè. The choice of song or dance performed is the privilege of the *kriyè* (lead singer), who is always the first musician to start. Usually, a small number of bele, or bélias, or gwanbèlè are performed successively. But sometimes, in a loose attempt to introduce some rhythmic variety, a bélia, or a gwanbèlè in triple meter is performed in between two *bidjin bele*, which are in duple meter. It may happen that a *bele twapa*, also in triple meter, would replace a bélia, but this piece is rarely heard in a swaré bele.

All bele linò songs are in a call and response pattern. The kriyè's (lead singer's) first melodic phrase is repeated by a chorus at regular intervals and becomes the response. Together they sing two or three sentences a cappella; then the *tibwa* (pair of sticks) sets the tempo with a recurring rhythmic sequence that will not stop before the end of the piece. Once a steady beat is established by the tibwa, the drummer introduces complex rhythms to reproduce the steps of the best dancer in the ring. He improvises his sequences by combining the appropriate rhythmic patterns developed in conformity to the bele drumming tradition. This procedure renews the songs and the dances with every performance and develops the creativity of both the dancer and the drummer.

When the dance begins, eight dancers form a single line, consisting of alternating men and women. They circle the dance area counterclock-wise, then clockwise to the sound of the drum, which plays a rhythm called *kouri lawond*. At a signal from the drum, the eight dancers form a quadrille (square) and begin dancing, two couples at a time, then one couple after another. They end their performance with a curtsy to the drum, and the male dancer guides his partner back to her initial spot. When the set is finished, all the dancers leave the ring in single file after having circled the dance area as they did at the beginning.

Despite the obvious influence from the French quadrille, bele linò is not a European-derived genre. The dancers constantly lean forward and keep their knees bent when they perform. The serious faces, the specific movements of the arms and hips, the bent contour of the bodies are dis-tinctively African and are in sharp contrast with the upright stance of Eu-ropean-derived quadrille dancers.

Each piece has distinctive steps. The bidjin bele is the most frequently played at the swarés because it affords great variations in tempo. Most Martinicans from the northeast refer to bidjin bele simply as bele. It is called *douss* when played at a slow tempo and *pitché* when it is fast. Bele douss is a seductive dance with slow, shuffled steps. This contrasts with the energizing bele pitché and its bouncing steps that allow demonstra-tions of agility. A third type of bidjin bele is *bele kourant*, which has a mod-erate tempo and moderate movement that supports a wide range of steps so that many dancers find it convenient as a form in which to develop their personal style. There is a specific drumming pattern for each of these variations of bidjin bele. The rhythm played by the tibwa in bele kourant has become distinctive of the biguine, where it is played with melodic instruments.

Gwanbèlè affords great rhythmic complexity. It requires a total inde-pendence of the arms, feet, and upper body on the part of the dancer. The drummer and the dancers express distinct sequences, but all evolve in triple meter. The rhythmic sequences of the tibwa constantly alternate between 9/8 and 3/4, but the dancers consistently move on a 3/8 beat. All my informants have stressed that in gwanbèlè, the movements of the dancer contribute to the polyrhythmia, as do the drum and tibwa.

In bélia as well, the movements of the dancers are an important part of the polyrhythmia. The dance, in 6/4, is in triple meter, but is accompanied by drumming sequences in duple meter (3/4). The distinctive bélia steps go alternately backward and forward, then the dancers spin and start again. They describe a circle around a virtual centerpole. Their motion is

Fig. 21. *Bele* on Martinique. Bidjin Bele, first quadrille. Photograph: Dominique Cyrille. Used by permission of Dominique Cyrille, Bronx, N.Y.

Fig. 22. Gwoup Matjoukan (Matjoukan Group) of Martinique, Bidjin Bele, first quadrille, from overhead. Photograph: Dominique Cyrille. Used by permission of Dominique Cyrille, Bronx, N.Y.

Fig. 23. *Bélia*, salute to the drum, in Martinique. Photograph: Dominique Cyrille. Used by permission of Dominique Cyrille, Bronx, N.Y.

comparable to that of the *laplace* (priest's helper) and flag bearers opening a Rada rite in Haitian Vodou. In 1797 Moreau de Saint-Méry described a dance similar to the bélia sequence:

> [I]t consists of a step where each foot is alternately extended and withdrawn, striking the ground hard, first with the toe, [then] with the heel. It is somewhat similar to the step of the Anglaise. The man turns either around in the same spot or around his partner, who also turns and changes her place, while shaking the two ends of a kerchief which she holds. The man continues to raise and lower his arms while holding his elbows close to his body and his fists almost closed. This dance, in which the play of the eyes is important, is fast and animated, and an even beat adds grace to it (Moreau de Saint-Méry [1797–1798] 1984, 63; my translation).

Bele lisid

Bele lisid of southern Martinique is composed of two numbers only: bele and gwanbèlè. In spite of the similar names, these dances have little in common with their northern counterparts. The songs are in call and response style, but the chorus sings longer sections than in bele linò. Southern gwanbèlè is in 2/4, and bele is in 3/4. Today, the music is played with two drums, a tibwa, and a *chacha* (shaker), but just a few decades ago, it included an armpit drum made out of a tin box that the drummer played with the fingers of both hands. The tibwa, which is often added in modern instrumentations, seems to be a recent addition. Evidence from the past suggests that two drums and a shaker were the common instrumentation in colonial Martinique. A description from Father Labat (1724, 54) indi-

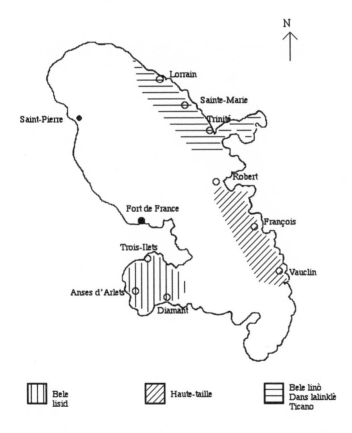

Fig. 24. Outline map of Martinique, showing areas where certain dances are done.

cates that at the end of the seventeenth century African dances required "two drums made out of two hollowed tree trunks of different sizes." The presence of shakers was documented by Moreau de St. Méry (1802, 44) approximately a hundred years later.

Drumming techniques have not undergone drastic changes either. Again, it was Father Labat (1724, 54) who remarked that "the drummers placed their instruments between their legs or sat on them; they beat them with four fingers of each hand. The one with the big drum beats calmly, whereas the one who touches the baboula beats as fast as he can." Indeed, one drum plays recurring patterns while the other elaborates rhythmic variations based on the dance.

The influence of French contredanse and quadrille is not predominant in bele lisid choreography. Rather, this dance shows influences from Kongo traditions. The dancers perform inside a circle of spectators, either one couple at a time or as a group. The steps in *gwanbèlè lisid* of Martinique resemble those of Trinidad bele and Puerto Rican bomba. Both the music and the dance are identical to Haitian Kongo dance. Furthermore, this description of xica (chica) by Moreau de St. Méry could still apply to modern gwanbèlè lisid:

> The skilled female dancer can move her hips and lower part of the body while keeping her upper body in a relative immobility undisturbed by the quiet movements of her arms, which balance a kerchief or the hem of her petticoat. A male dancer approaches her, rushes forward suddenly, and falls to the beat, almost touching her. He moves back, rushes forward once more, and provokes her into the most seductive struggle. The dance becomes more animated and soon it depicts a scene in which all elements are voluptuous at first, and then become lascivious. (Moreau de St. Méry [1797–1798] 1984, 64; my translation)

Guadeloupean *Léwoz*

African-derived dances of Guadeloupe and Martinique are comparable in many ways. In Guadeloupe, *léwoz*, also called *gwoka*, is the name of a set dance that includes an element called léwoz. The genre seems to have originated in the mountainous areas of Basse-Terre, where, according to Lafontaine and Carnot (1986, 61), the best gwoka drummers come from. Guadeloupean musicologist Françoise Uri has documented the existence of African dancing from seventeenth-century written documents. Although no names are mentioned, the descriptions of slave dances match that of modern léwoz.

Significant variations were later introduced due to the influence of the French quadrille. Eight dancers in a square configuration were guided by a commandeur and danced one at a time in the middle of the square to the sound of the drums. At the end of their performance, the commandeur guided them back to their initial spot. This variant, called the *léwoz-au-commandement*, coexisted with other creolized versions for a long time, until its disappearance in the 1960s.

The léwoz is a set of seven different rhythms, each corresponding to a specific dance with a distinct meaning. According to Françoise Uri, léwoz is a warrior and incantation dance, whereas *tumblak* and *kaladja* are for seduction purposes. The rhythms of *graj* and *kadjenbel* are used to coordinate hard labor. The *woulé* recalls aspects of the waltz, and *menndé* is closer to carnival rhythms used for street parades (Uri and Uri 1991, 34).

The léwoz is danced to the sound of three drums, two *bulas* and a *makè*, which are joined by a shaker. Today, local variations may allow more than two bulas. Instruments with similar names are found in Haiti. They are used during Vodou ceremonies and are part of the Rada and Kongo drum ensembles. For this reason, and also because the music of léwoz resembles that of the Kongo *mason* of Haiti, it is believed that the dance derives from Kongo secret societies that existed in colonial Guadeloupe (Uri and Uri 1991, 52). In addition, and in accord with popular belief, spirits will come to the dance when a gwoka drummer gives an outstanding performance. To Françoise Uri, this strongly suggests a sacred function for ancient léwoz.

Dans lalinklè

In northeastern Martinique, there is a series of dances that were performed at funeral wakes, the dans lalinklè (moonlight dances). During the night following a death in a community, neighbors, coworkers, friends, and relatives gathered for a wake at the home of the deceased. Inside the house, usually in the largest room, the deceased was laid in an open casket. Close family members surrounded the coffin and mourned silently. A few yards away, a small number of men and women sang old *cantiques* in French and Latin and offered prayers from the Catholic liturgy. Outside the house, a crowd of friends and neighbors listened to traditional tales of life and death in Creole. The performance of the storyteller consisted of singing as much as of telling stories. The songs, in call and response style, were accompanied by hand clapping from the audience.

After about three hours, the crowd usually dispersed, and the dance began later. It was performed to the sound of the bele drum and tibwa and strictly reserved to close friends and relatives of the deceased. Each dance had a distinct choreography and rhythmic pattern. The songs were in the same melodic style as bele linò. Today, only one song is remembered for each of them, except the *ting-bang*, for which several melodies are still used. Their performance as part of a wake has become a rare event, but they are sometimes included in swaré bele. The African elements are largely predominant in all the moonlight dances. Although these genres have lost most of their religious content today, many features remain that reveal their connection to the neo-African cults of the ancestors. These features will be described later in the essay.

There are six dans lalinklè: *woulé mango, karesé-yo, bénézuel* (or *véné-zuel*), *kanigwé, ting-bang* and *mabélo*. Karesé-yo is a recent addition, introduced some sixty years ago by Siméline Rangon. The mabélo, which is the last dance of the night, as informants Paul and Benoit Rastocle told the author in Sainte-Marie in 1995, offers striking resemblance to the "calenda," frequently described by travelers since the beginning of slavery (Labat 1724, 53), and also to a Kongo dance described by J. H. Weeks in the late nineteenth century:

> Two lines are formed—one of men and the other of an equal number of women. The drum is placed at one end of the line, and all begin to clap, chant, shuffle, and wriggle together. A man then advances dancing, and a woman from the opposite line advances, a few paces and they dance thus a few moments, usually a yard or so apart, but sometimes they approach nearer and strike their abdomens together, then they retire and others take their places, and so on right down the lines; and thus they proceed over and over again. (Weeks [1882] 1914, 128)

Woulé-mango, karesé-yo, and ting-bang are circular dances. In the kanigwé, men and women face each other from two opposite lines. During the bénézuel, everyone dances at the same time.

Woulé-mango and karesé-yo do not have specific steps, but both allow close physical contact between the dancers. They begin with a circle of alternating men and women holding hands. In woulé-mango, one dancer comes inside the ring and slowly rolls his (or her) whole body against the chain of dancers in a counterclockwise motion until he arrives at his initial spot. The next dancer to the right does the same, and so on.

Karesé-yo is another seduction game. The person inside the circle chooses one individual of the opposite gender for a partner. They proceed to the center of the ring where they dance to what the kriyè orders: *Karesé-yo / Bouch dan bouch / Vant dan vant / Pyé dan pyé* . . . (mouth to mouth / belly to belly / foot to foot . . .)

At a signal from the drum, a new partner is chosen by the last dancer who entered the ring while his/her former partner goes back to his/her initial spot. By the time the dance is finished, everyone has performed with two different dancers.

Although a circular configuration is also adopted for ting-bang, close physical contact between dancers remains purely accidental. The dancers form a wheel comprising equal numbers of men and women, which moves slowly counterclockwise. Instead of looking toward the center, the men and women face each other; all the men look in one direction and all the women look the opposite way. At a signal from the drum, they begin to dance and make a half-turn on each step, facing alternately the person in front and the person behind as the wheel turns. The distinctive step of ting-bang consists of raising the right foot sideways, then lowering it to strike the ground vigorously with both feet simultaneously. The half turn is made when the dancer stands on the left foot; this step is called *fwapé*. There is a dance described by Father Labat (1724, vol. 2, 54) in *Nouveaux Voyages* that could be related to ting-bang.

Opposing lines are chosen for kanigwé, a feature that has allowed the inclusion of elements from eighteenth-century contredanse in the last portion of the dance. However, other African-derived steps and the fwapé are part of the kanigwé as well.

Calenda ticano and *ladja*

Calenda ticano and ladja can be opposed to the bele and to the dans lalinklè because they are not included in a set. These dance routines do not seem to be corrupted by the inclusion of European features. Calenda ticano is danced only in the northeast, in the same area as the lalinklè dances. In spite of its name, calenda ticano does not bear any resemblance to mabélo. It is a solo dance in which the drummer and the dancer emulate each other; the drummer transforms the dancer's steps into musical sounds, and in this regard, ticano is comparable to bele linò. Ladja is found throughout Martinique in urban and rural settings. This highly acrobatic fight-dance, called interchangeably ladja or *damié*, is performed by two men to the sound of the drum. The instrumentation for both ticano and ladja consists of the bele drum and a tibwa. The kriyè and a chorus sing in reponsorial style, as they do in the other genres found in the northeast.

The ladja is performed mostly for entertainment today, but had a more serious meaning thirty years ago. It was customary to see it performed after a hard day of work, or in front of a church at the end of Sunday mass. This is the only Martinican genre for which people openly admit to using supernatural powers: before any serious ladja fight. They call this practice *achté an pwen* (buying a slap). If for some reason, the expected fight does not occur, one needs to strike a tree or any inanimate object to diffuse the supernatural powers. According to ladja fighters, the powers must be used soon after they are received, otherwise the recipient might lose the use of his arms or legs.

The skilled drummer follows closely each of the fighters' movements. It is said that his drummed sequences can reinvigorate the men in the ring or weaken one of them down, if he wishes to change the outcome of the fight.

The origin of the name damié is unknown, but researcher Josy Michalon has documented the existence of a genre comparable to ladja in the modern Republic of Benin (Michalon 1987: 39). This dance, which the Basantche people of Benin call *kadjia*, is performed at yam festivals and is also a means for warriors to develop their fighting skills. According to Michalon, those who cannot dance/fight in kadjia-style cannot get married.

The use of ladja in rites of passage is still alive in a Martinican event called the Holy Saturday ladja. Once a year, on the last day of Lent, ladja fighters meet after sunset for a nightlong competition. Until the mid-1960s these meetings took place on riverbanks and on the seashore.

Damié and ticano are not the only Martinican genres that are alive today and linked to rituals that may have disappeared. In lalinklè dances, especially in the mabélo, the metaphor for sexual insemination contained in each dance celebrates the renewal of life and reminds us that death and life are part of the same cycle. In the preceding descriptions, I presented some of the elements revealing a sacred function for both bele linò and lisid. But besides the external features of the dances, there is much to say about their underlying meaning. Bélia, for example, is often danced to carry a wish or a prayer; gwanbèlè linò is sung in honor of a deceased, at burials, and during commemorative ceremonies. Although possession dances have not been documented in Martinique since the eruption of Mount Pelée in 1902, some people imply that bele is sometimes still practiced with the purpose of summoning the spirits for help.

Further evidence is found in the name bele, which to me has little to do with the suggestion that it is a corruption of the French "bel air." In Martinique, "bel air" is adopted only by literate people foreign to the bele tradition. Old bele practitioners say "bay-lay," or *lele* "lay-lay," and do not recall ever hearing "bel air" in their communities. Furthermore, recognizing that all African-derived genres of the French Caribbean have names that are also of African origin, it seems to me, to the contrary of common belief, that "bel air" is a corruption of the African name for the syncretic danced-rituals of Martinique.

Most important, there are Kongo words that can be linked to the Creole bele, such as *boela*, of which Weeks says, "The Boela is a circular dance to the beating of a medium-sized drum. The cloth worn for it is first held under the armpit, then the belt is tied tightly round the waist, and the upper part of the cloth is allowed to fall in folds." (Weeks [1882] 1914, 132) There is also *mbele*, Kikongo for sword (Craven and Brafield [1883] 1971, 148). Although I limited my presentation to bele as a dance genre, Martinican bele is also work music. Most people born in the bele tradition of the northeastern part of the island refer to it as work music to accompany the sugarcane harvest, which requires a cutlass with a sharp blade. In 1995 informant Simonette Rotzen told the author: *"Bele sé travay, moun ka dansé anlèy tou"* (bele is work music, [but] people dance it too). This information was corroborated by Paul and Benoît Rastocle and other old bele practitioners. Given this, I hypothesize that the Kikongo term *mbele* may have been adopted as a name for a Martinican genre that involves the use of a sharp blade.

Zouk and Creole Identity

To most French Antilleans, the terms rural and urban, when applied to their traditional repertoires, indicate more than just geographical origin; they also contain sociological and historical implications. Although most of the genres are commonly practiced today, they are perceived as a heritage from their past and symbols of their dual identity. In the 1970s the rural repertoires were considered endangered. The European-derived quadrilles were deemed to be genres of the mulatto class and supposedly a threat to the black identity. Therefore, tradition revivalists focused on bele and gwoka and decided to introduce them in Fort-de-France and Pointe-à-Pitre, the main cities of Martinique and Guadeloupe. In the last decade, however, under the growing influence of *Créolité* scholars and writers who advocate recognition of all the constituents of the recomposed Caribbean Creole identity, quadrille dancing has grown significantly in favor. As a result, in both islands all traditional genres have become highly fashionable. Today they are danced by peasants and middle-class people together in *swaré bele*, *swaré gwoka*, and quadrille dances, held mostly during the weekend. These events gather crowds of over a hundred participants and spectators. The bal boutché has become a rare event, but is not completely forgotten. In fact, once a year for the past five or six years, people in a neighborhood of Fort-de-France have begun re-enacting a complete bal boutché ceremony on the anniversary of the community.

Besides traditional dancing, French Antilleans have private and public receptions held frequently during the weekend, the Carnival, and other community festivals. These nightlong dances, to the sound of either live bands or recorded music, are commonly called zouk. The music played during these parties is generally called *mizik zouk*, meaning "dance music," regardless of the type or origin of music. Mizik zouk comprises all Caribbean genres from the Cuban *son* and *guaguancó* to the Trinidadian calypso.

In the mid-1980s, a new genre appeared in the French islands that synthesized numerous influences from other Caribbean islands, although its distinctive component is the street carnival music of the French Antilles. This new popular genre, created by Kassav, a band of Guadeloupeans and Martinicans, was an immediate success on both islands. It was named zouk after the dance parties for which it was created. Today, it has been divided into two subcategories: *zouk love*, characterized by a moderate to slow tempo, and *zouk béton* (concrete zouk), with a fast tempo. Like the biguine and the maziouk, zouk love is danced by couples in a close embrace, but zouk béton is for individual dancing. The zouk step is like a simplification of the biguine.

To the contrary of traditional swarés reserved for adults, there is no age-group limitation for zouk participation. Adolescents and their parents dance zouk, though not generally at the same parties. In Martinique, zouk is performed at the receptions of adults along with maziouk, biguine, and other Caribbean music. Young people, on the other hand, do not dance the traditional genres, but only the latest zouk and other fashionable Caribbean genres.

Conclusion

The custom of borrowing dances from other islands to introduce variety into the balls of the French Caribbean is very old. A new genre was introduced to the islands of Martinique and Guadeloupe during practically every decade of the twentieth century. At times, the new genre was so well liked that it was inserted into a compatible indigenous genre. This happened with *pasillo* music, first introduced to Martinique in the early 1920s. By the end of the next decade, this rapid rhythm had become the central portion of the Creole waltz, and this genre is now called *valse-pasillo*.

More frequently, however, when the need for novelty had commanded the introduction of a new dance, the previous genre remained in the repertoire and was occasionally danced. Nevertheless, the traditional biguine and maziouk were always performed in the balls, and new pieces were often composed for that purpose. A true change was introduced in the mid-1980s with the advent of zouk. The biguine and waltz have since become so rare in the parties of young people that most of them no longer know the specific steps. Although the maziouk has remained a favorite number in modern balls, the one played most often in teenage gatherings has borrowed rhythmic elements from zouk and is now shuffled rather than danced with the pitché step. Traditional maziouks remain unchanged in quadrille music and in adult receptions, but the new maziouk-zouk is also performed.

The fashion for zouk grew at a time when the Creole culture of the French Caribbean was being redefined in an attempt to take into account all of its cultural components, not merely those coming from Europe and Africa. As a result, although this music was not at first connected to the concept of Créolité, people began to see it as the symbol of the new Creole identity. Thus, zouk has caused the creation of a new repertoire of dance music that meets the needs of the new Creole society.

In summary, these changes have resulted in three distinct dance repertoires in the French Caribbean today. The first one, the rural repertoire, originates from African customs and represents the powerful contribution that the enslaved ancestors made to the specificity of French Caribbean identity. The second repertoire, comprising biguine, maziouk, and waltz either separately or in quadrille sets, was developed during an era of violent social conflicts and drew most of its components from European traditions. It illustrates the social elevation of black people and their access to freedom. Finally, the modern zouk is a reflection of the new Creole identity, which is trying to make peace with its troubled past and be open to all of its constituents.

◇ ◇ ◇

TRINIDAD AND TOBAGO

17

❖ ❖ ❖

In Search of the Limbo

An Investigation into Its Folklore as a Wake Dance

Molly Ahye

The Limbo in years gone by was performed during ceremonies for the dead such as wakes and, in particular, the ninth and fortieth night after death ("nine-nights" and "forty-days"). This dance activity was one of the various ceremonial expressions performed during the period of funeral rites and mourning. Traditionally, a wake among people of African descent in Trinidad and Tobago is almost a festive affair in spite of the personal grief that the immediate family experiences. Much thought is given to the soul of the deceased, as friends gather with family to celebrate death, as it were.

This, of course, is one of the West African traditions brought over during slavery. For the people in today's vanishing rural areas in Trinidad and Tobago, the practice is still very much in evidence despite the effects of modernization as well as Christian religious restrictions that govern and control the behavior patterns of their adherents to some degree. Added to these influences has been the inevitable passage of time, which serves to devalue old customs and traditions as each successive generation gravitates closer to a world community with rapidly changing mores.

For those who maintain the old tradition of drumming, singing, and dancing as part of the funerary rites, there is a legacy—rich and colorful—that they nurture and hand down as part of a complex belief system that has its counterpart wherever people of African descent are concentrated. In some areas only the memory remains, or, if they are lucky, folklorization and transmission into artistic manifestations, publications, archives, libraries, and museums attempt to provide continuity, if only by references. Researchers and chroniclers enlighten us about these vanishing customs and give clues as to their meaning and origins even if they must surmise or deduce in most instances.

It is by now well established that "Africans attach great importance to funerals, believing that a dead man's send-off will affect his status on the other side" (Roberts 1973, 48). John Storm Roberts has found numerous examples of the role that dance and music play within this context and offers the practice of the marching bands in New Orleans as a testimony. He cites Benjamin Latrobe, who remarked on this practice on a visit to New Orleans in 1819 (Roberts 1973, 64). Well over a hundred years have passed and this custom is still alive. This writer was fortunate to witness a presentation by the oldest marching jazz band that keeps the funeral music alive and found a remarkable similarity to the hymns sung at wakes by the Afro-Christians of Trinidad. The Young Tuxedo Brass Band was featured in concert at the Caribbean Cultural Center's Expressions '85—A Celebration of Africa in the Americas on October 12, 1985, at Hunter College in New York. This is worthy of mention because of the connection between the southern United States and the Caribbean. As a matter of fact, there is an area called Princes Town in the south of Trinidad—the Company Villages—of lands made available for the settlement of four military companies of ex-slaves who fought in the American Civil War against the North.

The descendants of these early settlers from the southern United States have continued traditions that weave a strong Kongo influence with that of other "nations" of West Africa into those of the Afro-Christian Baptists. A reverse flow also took place; there is documented evidence of dances and music going from the Caribbean area to Africa. This connection is important as we seek the origin of the Limbo as a wake dance or any mention of it having existed at all. Without going too far afield to find similarities in attitudes of people of African descent toward their departed loved ones, we find ready reference; for example, "the lavishness of black U.S. funerals may reflect the African idea that the status of the shade in the other world is affected by the style of his going" (Roberts 1973, 62). This lavishness is seen in Trinidad and Tobago among the middle- and upper-class blacks in particular. It is also true that persons of modest means provide the best *turnout* for their departed loved ones.

The interment is not the final part of ritual, as Trinidadians share with other Caribbean peoples a rejoicing in the knowledge that the loved one is not far away, but will join the ancestors to become a guiding force in their lives from a world beyond. But, first, they must pass through several stages and the spirit must be appeased so there will be no reason for it to return in anger or discontent. This is the occasion for prayers and hymns followed by games, storytelling, secular songs, and vibrant dances.

Food and drinks are provided by what is termed a *gayap* effort as neighbors and friends contribute to the family in cash or kind during this period of community bonding. The men are available to construct a tent of bamboo covered by corrugated galvanized tin sheets with makeshift benches for seating. The women are on hand to do the cooking, washing, cleaning, and consoling. A liberal supply of strong coffee and alcoholic beverages is always at hand to keep them awake and in good spirits.

The Limbo was first seen as part of this scenario along with another dance of strength, the *Bongo*. Several other dances are performed such as the *Pique* and *Bele*. Holly Betaudier, a prominent folklorist and television host, recalled an occasion during his childhood when he experienced, for the first time, the dancing of the Limbo. Around 1936, on his parents' cocoa estate in the village of Manzanilla and many miles from his hometown, Arima, he, with his parents, attended a wake that was announced by the traditional blowing of a cow's horn (the old form of communicating a death in the rural areas).

Betaudier gave a vivid account of what he remembered, mostly because of the strangeness to him, coming from a staunch Roman Catholic town where such "carrying on" was not engaged in. Another much older man, Jose Ramon Fortune, corroborated this idea when he added that at that time the burgesses of Arima were mainly of Spanish and Carib descent. They abided by their customs, which fell within the parameters of established Church doctrines. He was reticent on the subject of dancing and drumming at wakes (telephone interview with Jose Ramon Fortune, Jan. 10, 1982).

Betaudier mentions the prayers, the singing of *sankeys* (creolized folk hymns), and Bongo dancing, but most of all he remembers the Limbo's being danced with a bamboo pole held at each end while the dancer passed, bending backward from the waist. He speaks of the consternation registered by the men when a woman decided to pass under the bar, lifting her dress to accommodate the movement. She was promptly admonished and thrown out by the men, who saw her action as the "height of indecency" (interview, St. Anns, Trinidad, Feb. 26, 1982).

In the absence of any solid documented material on the Limbo, one must piece together the smattering of information to enable a little more than speculation. This in itself is not by any means foolproof as the dangers lie in the contradictions and irregularities that are part of the oral tradition. For example, in the foregoing account we see it was taboo for women to dance this dance. Yet in other areas it was an accepted practice, as the women also competed with men, and the words of a version of the traditional song attest to this (telephone interview with Blanche Talma, Jan. 10, 1982):

> I want a woman to Limbo like me
> Limbo, Limbo like me.

However, in a short television documentary on the Limbo, Ben Jochanan, noted scholar of black history, said that it is only in Trinidad and Tobago that women dance the Limbo. He said that this was not the case in Africa; there, the Limbo was a dance done to strengthen men for war (*Limbo* 1983). It was a pity that he did not enlighten us as to where in Africa the Limbo was danced but rather used *Africa* in such a general sense that it could absorb any possibility without question.

On this same tape the Senegalese drummer Mor Thiam said that there was one "tribe" in Senegal who used sticks for dancing and he alluded to the premise that they danced the Limbo; he mentioned a name that sounded like Sande (*Limbo* 1983). We tie this in with an investigation by Julia Edwards while she was on tour in Senegal for the First Festival of Arts and Culture in 1969. She came up empty-handed as none of the African participants could identify the dance as coming from their area. An opportunity for a more in-depth investigation presented itself during the Festival of Arts and Culture (FESTAC) in Nigeria in 1977, when this writer was engaged in reviewing the dances of the sixty-two participating countries for the Nigerian Ministry of Culture and Information.

It seems, up to now, that all traces have been obliterated from that area, if in fact it did exist in Africa. In looking at dance in Brazil over the years, it has struck me as odd that not once did I see a trace or suggestion of the Limbo, in a country that has preserved some of the purest African traditions from the West Coast of Africa as far down as Angola. Haiti has no record of this dance, nor any form that vaguely resembles it. However, we do have two references to the dance as having been known at some time among the Maroons (runaway slaves) who made their home in the mountains of Accompong in Jamaica. Baba Rowe, "father of the ex-colonel of the Maroons," on looking at the way the Limbo was taught, took the stick and told the group that it must be put at the navel. "Thereupon, he took over and went under the stick himself (aged over 80 years) and two or three other old men followed him" (Baxter 1970, 150). He called the dance *mazumba*. Rex Nettleford also mentions a similar incident (Nettleford 1985, 184).

Perhaps this was a case of memory being stirred by the old man's seeing the dance performed, because Katherine Dunham's (1946) *Journey to Accompong* makes no mention of a similar dance. Whatever the circumstances surrounding the disappearance of the dance in Jamaica, I discuss the significance of positioning the stick at the navel later in this chapter.

There are several theories that have circulated for years regarding the origin of the dance itself. From among the exponents themselves I have collected quite a few, among which are the following:

1. It was a dance of puberty to show the strength of the young males (interview with Carlton Francis, Jan. 14, 1982).

2. The slaves on the ships were made to come out of their spaces in the holds by bending backwards and coming out by their legs first. (Several informants—this theory has existed for many years.)

3. The Spaniards, who then colonized Trinidad, punished the slaves by starving them, then tied their hands behind their backs and made them bend backward to eat bread, which they dangled on a string held over their mouths. This bobbed up and down and they were flogged if they did not try (interview with Julia Edwards, March 15, 1981).

The last theory was passionately refuted by the late Edric Connor, renowned Trinidadian singer and folklorist, who migrated to the United Kingdom in the 1940s. On one of his visits to Trinidad in 1956, he gave a lecture in the public library in Port of Spain, under the auspices of the librarian, the late Carlton Comma. Holly Betaudier (interview, Feb. 26, 1982) mentioned that Connor argued strenuously against this theory of the dance for bread. Details are not available as to his reasons for objecting, but, considering the information documented about slaves being made to dance against their will, it may not be so far-fetched after all. Lynne Fauley Emery (1972, 102) quotes several writers on this subject and mentions that "in the dark, dank slave pens, or on the banjo-table—another name for the auction block—the slaves were forced, again, to dance."

There is one suggestion offered with a good deal of seriousness: the Limbo started during the passage across as the slaves were made to bend backward to come out of the hold of the ship. From an anatomical/physical point of view, this idea does not seem feasible considering the weakened condition of the slaves, without proper nutrition for months and the little use of vital muscles during their restricted positioning en route. It is most unlikely that they would have been able to muster up the strength to perform such a feat. Besides, what crew member would have had the time to wait for the slaves to do this? They would have had to spread their legs very wide to execute such a movement and it is doubtful whether the exit could have offered so wide a space.

Origin of the Name *Limbo*

Now we come to a most fascinating topic, one which elicits a number of speculations. One interviewee was quite serious when he offered the explanation that lim-bo is simply a matter of the limbs forming a bow in passing below the pole (interview with Rodney Arneaud, Jan. 9, 1982). Others have also suggested this from time to time, but they add another explanation that finds the name analogous to having a limber body to perform the dance—Limbo and limber seem a logical relationship to them.

This writer and others, who include exponents, have given the matter serious thought, and in the absence of more concrete information to the contrary, we are inclined to believe that the name *Limbo* evinces significant religious connotations. Limbo has to be seen in the light of religious beliefs that were forcibly imposed on the slaves by their masters. Particularly around the late eighteenth and early nineteenth centuries, with a heavy Spanish and French influence in Trinidad, the dominating religion was Roman Catholicism.

Doctrines were imposed in the conversion process and the slaves, who were mostly illiterates, depended a great deal on visualization to make these teachings practicable. The catechisms elaborated on a definition by which the concept of the danced Limbo could easily be equated with the new Christians' understanding of Limbo—the intermediary place between heaven and hell where the soul, after leaving the earth plane through death, pauses for a while before the resurrection or before a period spent in purgatory.

This concept would not have been too difficult for them to perceive if it could, in honesty, have been identified with the cosmology of their own belief systems. For example, in *Flash of the Spirit*, Robert Farris Thompson (1983) details a very clear picture of Kongo cosmogony as he illus-

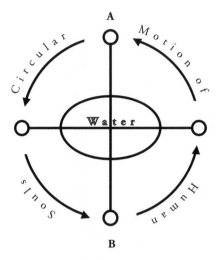

Fig. 25. *Yowa:* the Kongo sign of cosmos and the continuity of human life. *A* represents: God—peak of strength, noon—light, maleness—north. *B* represents: femaleness—south, midnight—darkness, dead—outerworldly strength.

trates the *yowa*—the Kongo sign of cosmos and the continuity of human life. Somehow I see a relationship between this concept and the Limbo.

In elaborating further on this mystic symbol, Thompson cites the work of Fu-Kiau Bunseki, from that author's privately published *The African Book Without Title* (1980):

> The horizontal line divides the mountain of the living world from its mirrored counterpart in the kingdom of the dead. The mountain of the living is described as "earth" (*ntoto*). The mountain of the dead is called "white clay" (*mpemba*). The bottom half of the Kongo cosmogram was also called *kalunga,* referring, literally, to the world of the dead as complete (*lunga*) within itself and to the wholeness that comes to a person who understands the ways and powers of both worlds. (Thompson 1983, 109)

Thompson cites other sources to affirm what is already known, that is, a Bakongo belief in accord with the Christian belief in a Supreme Being—Nzambi Mpungu. This also corresponds to the Yoruba's Olodumare. The indestructibility of the soul is another common tenet. Thompson, here, begins by quoting from Janzen and MacGaffey's (1974) *An Anthology of Kongo Religion: Primary Texts from Lower Zaire:*

'Bakongo believe and hold it true that man's life has no end, that it constitutes a cycle. The sun, in its rising and setting, is a sign of this cycle, and death is merely a transition in the process of change.' The Kongo *yowa* cross does not signify the crucifixion of Jesus for the salvation of mankind; it signifies the equally compelling vision of the circular motion of human souls about the circumference of its intersecting lines. The Kongo cross refers therefore to the everlasting continuity of *all* righteous men and women. (Thompson 1983: 108)

Now, let us dance this concept. Just think of the Limbo pole as the horizontal bar of the Kongo cosmogram, below which is the region of death. The symbolic passage through that region, defying death and rushing through the waters to reach the Godhead, is the moment of victory when the soul passes from midnight (darkness) to the peak of the sun (light). After speculating about this theory for many years, I offered these thoughts about the dancer passing below the bar: "At this point the body is balanced in a state of agonizing distortion, remaining in animated suspension until the moment when it eventually rises in triumph" (Ahye 1978, 111). Julia Edwards, who is considered the foremost innovator of the Limbo in its secular form, substantiated this notion when she excitedly related her experience as a young dancer going to a wake with Geoffrey Holder and other members of their dance company. The year was 1949 in Belmont, an area now part of the capital city of Port of Spain.

In this wake the Limbo was danced by one man who was a relative of the deceased. It was a more solemn affair, with people chanting the rosary while kneeling around the dancer, who appeared to be in trance. He repeatedly passed below the bar while prayers were said in patois (a dialect common to French-speaking areas of the Caribbean). As the drums increased the tempo, the man would salute the drummers—as he cleared the bar—by going toward them; at the same time two people would lift the bar/pole to the heavens and then bring it a little lower. When asked why this routine was being done, they offered the reason of lifting the soul to the "higher heaven."

Julia added the observation that, with the supporters around, there would always be a lead person acting as mover or guide to the proceedings, urging on the bender and guiding the movement with encouraging words, especially just before the head cleared the bar. Isn't this reminiscent of Charon, mythological boatman in Greek mythology, taking the shade safely across the Styx?

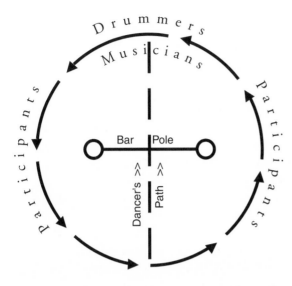

Fig. 26. Setting for Limbo at wakes.

Another point worthy of mention is the speculation about the Limbo and its relationship to the rite of passage in the simple ceremony that united slaves in matrimony. "Jumping the broom" was significant of union, a promise of new life—the regeneration of the species. It is looked at almost laughingly by some, but perhaps the symbolism runs deeper than the eyes can see.

Observe now the passing below the bar and its significance. It might well be the reverse order, portending disruption on the earth plane, the struggle and suffering in order to gain rewards. Also, by this interpretation, the passing under of one instead of two emphasizes the individualization of the soul of man. He is not really alone in the true sense, however, as his friends and family are there to cheer him on this time as well, with much singing, drumming, bamboo stamping, and hand clapping. The traditional chant suggests that his/her self-assurance will guarantee safe passage:

I want somebody to Limbo like me
Limbo, Limbo, like me (chorus)
Not a man, not a woman can Limbo like me

Limbo, Limbo like me (chorus)
Limbo boy, Limbo gul [girl]
Limbo, Limbo like me (chorus)

(interview, Rodney Arneaud, Jan. 9, 1982)

The fact that special attention was paid to going under the bar at waist or hip level, and never lower than the point of the navel in true tradition, must have had ritual implications. Edric Connor drew attention to the violation of this tradition when he saw the Limbo bar progress to a lower level through modernization. So, too, did Baba Rowe, the Maroon of Jamaica who was authoritative in pointing out this detail.

There is no clear-cut answer as to the particular reason for this, but I do know that Robert Farris Thompson, in a lecture at New York University on April 18, 1986, described *kundu*, the navel among the Kongos, as a seat of power, a region of secrets. Although the meaning may be obscure among Trinidadians and Tobagonians, the navel remains important. Up to the present time most mothers bury the umbilical cord of a newborn baby at the foot of a lofty tree, or plant a tree over the spot. To stress the reality that one is a true native, especially in a dispute, the phrase "my navel string is buried here" will frequently be used.

Without knowing the details, I always felt that the reason they did not go lower with the bar was because they did not have enough practice between wakes to develop the skill. In discussing this aspect with exponents of the dance such as Julia Edwards, Carlton Francis, Bill Trotman, and Andre Etienne, I was made aware that passing through at waist level is actually the most difficult. The spine bears the entire weight of the upper body, including the almost dead weight of the head, whereas at the very low levels, the thighs and hips function to keep the spine in a neutral state, distributing the weight more evenly.

Breath control is decisive in executing this passing beneath the bar. In order to maintain buoyancy throughout, the breath must be in and sustained between the crucial points of bending backward, traveling through, and rising up. Here again is symbolism at work. The apparent cessation of the breath as the body, weighted by sin, goes through the cleansing process while it passes through the mythical waters, to rise clean and free from sin and pain, is surely an emblematic action of hope.

The Limbo exudes an aura of mysticism, and when observed in a serious phenomenological context, it just cannot be dismissed as light entertainment. One young Roman Catholic priest, Father Terry Julien, offered his interpretation in 1974 while speaking at the graduation ceremony of the St. Francis Girls' College in Belmont, Port of Spain. In addressing the young women, he spoke of the past and of the challenge in building a new, stable nation. Trinidad and Tobago was only twelve years old at the time.

He presaged that "no longer is the challenge that of getting to the top of the plantation." He cautioned that in reaching to the top, they too could "become oppressors and exploiters of their own people," and suggested that "they identify themselves with the uneducated, the poor and the underprivileged." Here he was dealing with sociological problems and he included the psychological aspects of history to use the Limbo as an allegorical reference. The reporter of the article, "Priest Sees Message in Limbo Dance," discussing this speech in the *Trinidad Guardian* of March 11, 1974, wrote:

> Referring to the Limbo dance, he said that there was a lot more to the dance than just being a tourist attraction. He [Fr. Julien] added that there was a deep message depicted in it. Fr. Julien said the first phase of the dance where the performer danced around, making different actions before going under the bar, demonstrated the African woman crying out and shouting when she was captured by slave masters. In that stage she screamed and refused to go, knowing that she would never see her offspring again.
>
> The second phase—going under the bar—indicated the middle passage [in which] she was pushed, oppressed and squeezed to the bottom. The third part of getting from under the bar showed the woman landing in a new country.

This theory is very fascinating, especially coming from a Roman Catholic priest, but this was the late twentieth century and he is a native of the country. Incidentally, Father Julien left the priesthood not long afterward.

Areas in Which the Limbo Was Popular

There is a relationship between the areas in Trinidad where the Limbo found popularity and concentrations of people of African descent. The research omitted some areas, but informants who were much traveled, through their occupations and otherwise, could not recall seeing it in those areas when informally asked in conversation.

Rodney Arneaud, who died in 1985, lived in the region of Petit Valley, Diego Martin, in the northwest part of Trinidad. He gave some colorful

accounts of the Limbo as he had seen it danced at wakes in that area between the late 1930s and early 1950s. He sang the songs and told of a man
who was a Limbo champion of the area at that time. Arneaud described
the man as a Spanish/Chinese/Creole by the name of Lai Fatt. This is
interesting, because while continuous mention is made of persons of African descent, what is not stressed is the fact that the products of the mixing
and melding between the various ethnic groups in the country, especially
in Trinidad, defy any simple categorization.

Another elder, Blanche Talma, who died in 1986, spoke about wakes on
her father's estate in the La Brea area and included information about
Siparia as well. This is in the southern part of Trinidad, in the area called
the "oil belt." She was in her nineties, so her account dates back well over
seventy-five years. Blanche Talma observed that both men and women
danced the Limbo at various heights. The men wore red head kerchiefs
and the women wore their traditional *douillette*, an adaptation from the
nineteenth-century plantocracy. She was not sure, however, if the bar ever
went below the hip level, but she said it started from the chest.

Information about the Limbo in the San Fernando area, also in south
Trinidad, came from a renowned field naturalist, Urban Cross. His recol-
lections went back to circa 1935, when he saw it at a wake in the area called
"The Coffee." Cross lived in Mayaro earlier than that and he recalled for
me the wakes he had seen in his childhood. He said that Limbo was not
danced in Mayaro wakes, but could not offer any reason. Mayaro is in the
southeast of Trinidad (telephone interview, Jan. 10, 1982).

Urban Cross's account coincides with that of Michael Anthony, a nov-
elist and historian specializing in the history of Trinidad and Tobago. Anthony, who was born in Mayaro, said that the Bongo as a wake dance was
popular, but the Limbo was not done. Carenage, a fishing village at the
northwest point of Trinidad, is another African area with a rich history of
the culture. Carlton Francis, a choreographer and Limbo exponent, was
able to fill in the information for this area. He mentioned that during his
youth he attended a few wakes at which he had seen the Limbo being
performed.

Going further northwest to the tip of the island, which is just about
seven miles from Venezuela, one found thriving fishing villages and ver-
dant agricultural lands with a concentration of Africans, some of them
Maroons from other islands. This, of course, was before World War II,
when this whole area called Chaguaramas became a U.S. Navy base. The
point that juts out into the sea is called Pointe Gourde and there the vil-

lage of Hart's Cut was located. Wilfred Ahye, whose grandfather came from China and ran a dry goods store in the area, gave vital information regarding wakes at that time.

Ahye said that the Limbo was danced at wakes around the area, and the champion of the area was a man called Alexander. He mentioned that they did not hold the bar lower than the waist. Teteron Bay, nearby, was where they lived, but they were cleared from the lands and offered alternative lands in the north at Maracas Bay. Alexander, who still lived there in the late 1980s when he was well over seventy, carried on the tradition of Limbo dancing along with others at Maracas and the surrounding areas of La Fillette and Las Cuevas (interview with Wilfred Ahye, April 6, 1984).

Near Port of Spain, which is rich in history, the East Dry River area still bears evidence of the barracks-type structures of the emancipated slaves. It is an area where much of the rich folk culture developed over the years. The steel band and calypso had their early beginnings there, and the Carnival, which attracts tens of thousands each year, evolved around the lamplights of the early masqueraders. Many of the well-known artists and politicians were born in this area. La Cour Harpe (Harp Place), which has been renamed Teshea Terrace after a lady politician, was the scene of many activities, including the most rousing wakes.

Ruby Poon Quing (née Leotaud) was born not too far from there in Gonzales-Belmont. As mentioned before, this whole area was an African settlement, but it also boasted a mixture of several ethnic groups, descendants of French and Spanish people who came from other islands. Ruby Poon Quing was one such mixture; her family formed a solid core of talented musicians and folk artists. She gave a graphic account of life in the area from around 1923. What concerns this article is her mention of the Limbo in wakes. Much of what she said was a reiteration of others, but she mentioned the women who were known as *jamettes*, more or less women of easy virtue who matched the men in overt behavior. Some of them were known to be dreaded stick players in the dance game/fight known as *kalinda*, which was also done at wakes in this area. The women wore elaborate dresses and petticoats, which they had to tuck up in order to go under the bar. They were given cognomens that put fear in the heart of some men, such as Bea Bar the Devil or Bar Twenty, to name a couple (interview with Ruby Poon Quing on May 29, 1984). These women may have been seen as representatives of Mother Earth.

We have come to a crucial point in the discourse, which seeks, through historical and ethnographical perspectives, to trace the Limbo to its legendary home—Africa. So far, much evidence has been provided to support its religious and ritual function in its new home—or is Trinidad and Tobago its true home? Theories are answered by other theories. For example, the Maroons in Jamaica: were the carriers of the tradition of the dance mazumba so insignificant in numbers that their tradition was occluded to a point of extinction? Could there be a possibility that people who had been living in Trinidad joined them in the hills?

Ivy Baxter, deceased dance exponent of Jamaica, seems to think that this happened in Jamaica because "the intensity of movement and the compulsion of the dance and song often sensitized the bodies and minds of the participants beyond the limits needed for changing modes of life when the old social units broke up" (Baxter 1970).

These Jamaica Maroons went into isolation, but so too did the Djukas and Saramaccas of Suriname. There, however, the old customs have been retained and strengthened. The more I think of the Kongo cosmogram, the more hopeful I feel that someday the pieces of the puzzle will finally fit. It is well known that the Yorubas of Nigeria are the dominant African culture group in Trinidad. Their belief system—Shango—is well recognized. The Kongos are in evidence in subtler ways. For example, similar cosmograms are seen among the Shouter (Spiritual Baptists) of Trinidad and Tobago.

In his paper "The Yoruba Ancestor Cult in Gasparillo," Dr. J. D. Elder gives a vital clue as to the existence of the Kongo influence and its importance to this study:

> For the Congo group, we have less evidence of their identity but the place names in nearly all the village communities testify that in the past a Congo group of "Africans" skilled in magic, sorcery, and rain-making rituals, lived in the locality. Apart from this, the house-spots and derelict settlements compounds bear numerous names beginning with the "Congo." Informants in the present age-group of 60–90 have given personal accounts of these Congos and their magical feats. On one of the house-sites on Congo Hill at Mayo, several "thunder stones" (neolithic celts) belonging to a famous Congo magician were found by one of my field assistants. (Elder 1969b)

This opens another door in the search as we consider Thompson's examination of the cosmogram while he cites Fu-Kiau Bunseki:

> Members of the *Lemba* [emphasis inserted] society of healers had initiates stand on a cross chalked on the ground, a variant of the

cosmogram. "To stand upon this sign," Fu-Kiau Bunseki tells us, "meant that a person was fully capable of governing people, that he knew the nature of the world, that he had mastered the meaning of life and death." (Thompson 1983, 109)

This discourse concludes at a point at which it should be starting. The magical word is now *Lemba*. What does this mean? The sense of loss experienced by the Jamaica Maroons fuels a commitment to provide data for a fledgling society. There is much work to be done as this study has just chipped at the tip of the iceberg. The Limbo is like the Janus in the world of dance: there is another more exciting visage to look upon. Verity lies in the following statement: For a whole society to lose its sense of history would be tantamount to giving up its civilization.

18

The Moko Jumbie

Elevating the Children

Patricia T. Alleyne-Dettmers

As Balanchine said, "I want you to 'see' the music and 'hear' the dance."
—**Peter Minshall**

We have a voice to add to de song of de universe.
—**Peter Minshall**

Introduction: Setting the Stage for Carnival

To the strains of "stampede: mash up de place," one of the favorite soca tunes for 1999's Carnival, the Moko Jumbies, masqueraders on stilts, practically rolled onto the Savannah stage. The stilts ranged from six to twelve feet high and one had to look up into the sky to see these figures. Because they towered over the human frame, it was almost like we were seeing the music before we could actually hear the dance. They created beautiful silhouettes in the twilight, and as I looked at them I saw our broken histories high up in the air.

I saw the dancers reinventing their fragmented histories. There were blue devils, with the little girl, probably not more than five years old, leading them. There were clowns as well as a character carrying the Death Devil—a skull, enchained. I thought about Death—natural Death—and enforced Death in slavery. Who was it that dared to enchain us? Who was it that took away our gifts and our cultures? As the Moko Jumbies continued to wend their way across the stage, I realized that the dancing figures were children. I saw the children dancing their jigs and doing their flat-footed shuffles. There were one-footed, nimble, acrobatic Moko Jumbies as well. There were also hibiscus flowers, fish, and the national flag of Trinidad and Tobago. Everything was thrown together—a big mishmash as to what we are—and what we are still to become. This was decolonization in theatrical form. This was a creative attempt to rectify our marginalization and to emerge into the brightness of light with a return home—to the beginning and to the spirit of the ancestors.

I thought about Trinidad and Tobago, the land of my birth. Every year, we celebrate Carnival before the start of the Catholic season of Lent. We begin by washing and cleansing ourselves with the mud of Jour Ouvert (from French, meaning open day). We parade in the wee hours of the morning. There are no French-styled pretty costumes here. We decostume. Caked only with mud, we no longer recognize ourselves. We return to the belly of the ancestors, to Mama La Terre (Mother Earth), bearing witness to the gift of life even after the horrific traumas of slavery and colonization. In the darkness, we dance to the cacophonic music of biscuit tins. We move deeper to emerge into the depth of our Carnival world, to meditate on the altar of healing that we have carved for ourselves. And thinking of this and of how children figure in Carnival, I set down this chapter.

It presents a case study of contemporary Children's Carnival as enacted on the streets of Port of Spain, Trinidad. Its major focus is Carnival's performance context within the genre of Carnival. This refers specifically to the Trinidadian people's aesthetic cultural representations (Alleyne-Dettmers 1998)—masquerade themes that are kinesthetically *played* (enacted, portrayed, and displayed) in dance and *mas* (theatrical unscripted costuming) at Carnival time. The case study examines a band of Moko Jumbies that appeared in 1999's Children's Carnival. Through this medium, I explore the novel ways in which Children's Carnival designers engage in presenting and *re*presenting Carnival's history and, by implication, the islands' history.

Through a re-creation of one of the most powerful masquerade traditions of the African/Caribbean experience—the stilt dancing Moko Jumbie figure—these designers, the bandleader Francina Princesa Richards and Andrew (Moose) Alexander, who carried out her ideas, have succeeded in finding a way to re-historicize. They have found a way to revitalize the fragments of an African past denigrated or denied through the traumatic confrontation with the institutions of slavery and colonization. Since these Carnival portrayals were performed solely by children dancing on stilts, the designer has utilized this transformative played disguise and transcendental potential of the African masquerade form to recreate a sense of identity grounded in historical reality. By this conscious return to their history, the children reconstruct their ancestral past that was destroyed. In this way they configure their own sense of history and heritage, thereby forging a sense of identity for themselves. The children's voices are thus manifested through the music of their dance. The children become elevated.

Cultural identity in this context is not a static given, but something that develops out of the collision of the diverse historical narratives that are restored. The (re)construction of these historical narratives through Moko Jumbies' sculptural iconography provides the medium to interrogate, or get at, the kinds of historical moments, or the types of encounters, that determine who we are as a people and what we are becoming. Carnival thus provides the forum for the implosion between actual and metatropic realities, which leads to the artistic creation of novel and potent historical formations and transformations.

Moko Jumbie: Origins, Nomenclature, and a Description of Features

> In Trinidad and Tobago, if you should ask a Moko Jumbie where he/she comes from, he/she would say: "I have walked across the Atlantic Ocean, far far away from Africa. Even though I have endured centuries of brutalities . . . I have remained high, high, high against the Caribbean sky."

Moko Jumbie's origins seem to be clearly African, as evidenced in historical records, nomenclature, and Moko Jumbie's dance and costume. Scholarship (Elder 1969a; Herskovits 1990; Higman 1979, 1984; Public Record Office, Slave Reg. Returns T 71, cited in Liverpool 1993) clearly demonstrates that the enslaved Africans brought to Trinidad were principally Mandinka, Fulbe, Kwaka, Yoruba (including those Yoruba from Benin, formerly Dahomey), Hausa, Igbo, and Kongo peoples, who had their own African masquerades and masquerading traditions (Liverpool 1993; 1998, 34; Riggio 1998). To provide detailed documentation of these traditions is beyond the scope of this chapter. However, one can briefly introduce some of the more common of these African masquerade traditions to provide a broader picture of the origins of Moko Jumbie despite the impossible task of trying to pinpoint direct lines of origin between Africa and Trinidad, given the wider ramifications of the institutions of slavery and colonization.

Among Yoruba people, there are three ancestral masquerade traditions: the Egungun, the Efe/Gelede mask societies, and the Epa/Elofon. According to Doris Green, "Egungun is essentially an ancestral society which governs relationship between the living and those who have passed on to the spiritual world of the ancestors" (Green 1998, 22). These masked dancers, embodying a variety of shapes and forms, dance at funerals and also perform at the annual Egungun festival. Green further states that some of the masks are made "from yards of material, solids, stripes, patchwork panels and different African prints . . . [that] are fashioned into elaborate costumes that conceal the wearer" (Green 1998, 22).

Ryman, another source on the influence of the Egungun masquerade in the Caribbean, describes them as wearing masks representing the spirits of the ancestors. She further states that Egungun "specifically refers to the masking tradition among the Oyo Yoruba, but the term has been used to describe a wide variety of related traditions throughout Yorubaland" (Ryman 1984, 57). In this context, she mentions the Yoruba Gelede masquerades as having similar traditions to the Egungun. They also appear in the streets and also include female impersonators, comic figures, and entertainers (Ryman 1984, 57).

Another source makes reference to another tradition, the Gagalo stilt dancers from a Ketu town in West Yorubaland, and links them to the traditional Moko Jumbie stilt dancers who also thanked both their gods and ancestors for the harvest to come. Liverpool (1998, 34) states that "Gagalo stilt-dancers come out at their annual festival to honor the supernatural protector of the town 'Orisa Oluwa.' At this festival yams are offered and stilt dancers perform before the harvest begins."

From this evidence, it is important to stress, Moko Jumbie is not, and cannot be, ascribed to any single African model or source. However, these Afro-cultural masquerading traditions and others described below are extremely useful, since they collectively elucidate common African characteristics that have appeared, and still do even today, in the Moko Jumbie masquerade form.

Nomenclature: Etymology of the Term *Moko Jumbie*

A number of sources on origins of the term *Moko Jumbie* have served merely to confuse rather than to clarify its etymology. The earliest source (Young 1793, 258) suggests that the origin of the term is probably *mumbo jumbo*, a Mandinga phrase from West Africa. Young had seen a stilt dancer on St. Vincent at Christmas 1791. He called him *moco jumbie*, noting that the phrase was derived from mumbo jumbo of the Mendenges. A second fairly early source refers to *moko* as a Kongo word meaning "curer" (Bentley [1887] 1967, 350–371), especially when it is used together with the term *nganga* as in *nganga a moko*. In this context, it refers to a doctor who has been called to treat a specific illness and is not linked to stilt dancing in any way.

In her article on Jonkonnu, Cheryl Ryman makes the claim that the stilt-man, *moko-jumbo* or *moko-jumbie*, found within the Caribbean masquerade tradition, is a well-established figure in West Africa, particularly in Nigeria and Liberia. She also states, "The name, from which Moko-Jumbo is thought to be derived, Mumbo Jumbo, is offered by Judith Bettelheim (1979) and is found in the area spanned by Senegal, Gambia and Mali. It is associated with a huge vegetal masquerade, now known as *Fara Kankurang*, who presides over circumcision ceremonies and has power over female wrongdoers" (Ryman 1984: 55).

It seems, therefore, that the stilt-dancer Moko Jumbie from Africa is mirrored throughout the Caribbean. In contemporary Trinidadian Carnival the word *jumbie* signifies a dead spirit, while *Moko* "according to oral tradition . . . is known as the god of Vengeance. On the other hand, there is Omoko, an Ibo Ancestor spirit who is known as an appeaser of disputes" (Ahye 1978, 29).

Moko Jumbie: A Description of the Costume

The traditional Moko Jumbie's costume was generally made from yards of African print materials with solid stripes and patchwork panels. Daniel Crowley described the Trinidadian Moko Jumbie costume in this way:

> Moko Jumby, the stilt dancer, is known throughout the West Indies. . . . In Trinidad he was played, nearly always by men, on stilts as high as 10 or 15 feet. The stilts were brightly painted in stripes, and the masquer wore a long full skirt and a jacket or "eton" of brightly-colored satin or velvet. His hat was made of tosho, and dried pulp of

Fig. 27. Traditional Moko Jumbie costume portrayed by a contemporary Trinidadian masquerader. Photograph: Dr. Christian Dettmers. Used by permission of Dr. Christian Dettmers, Hamburg, Germany.

> the wild cucumber . . . which was fashioned into an Admiral's hat with long peaks in front and back and with the crown of the hat decorated with feathers. Moko Jumby was sometimes accompanied by a dwarf in similar costume but without stilts, to accentuate Moko's height. (Crowley 1956, 198)

There is concrete evidence that traces this costume (without stilts) back to the Egungun masquerades in Yorubaland. Ryman paints a similar picture of this costume for the Egungun: several panels of cloth, with red being the predominant color. She also states that the bits and pieces of the cloth may be sacred. In effect, the costume covers the entire body of the dancer (Ryman 1984, 57). During performances these figures embody the spirit of their representative ancestors and deities. Robert Farris Thompson (1974, 219) has described these figures as "the whirling return of the eternal Kings of Yorubaland."

This costume, however, also has its complements in stilt-dancing traditions in other parts of Africa. Doris Green describes the Chakaba stilt-dancers of Senegal, Gambia, and Guinea:

> My first encounter with these towering masked figures was in the late fifties and early sixties with Guinea Ballet. These towering figures were called Gods of the Sacred Forest, and actually frightened some of the younger people in the audience. . . .
>
> The Chakaba figure can be found in West Africa in several countries from the coast of Senegal to Mali. These stilts vary in height ranging from five feet to ten feet. Chakaba wears a headdress with side fringes. His body is clothed in an African print costume that covers the body to the top of the stilts. The legs of the stilts are covered in the same material that covers the body. Some Chakaba wear a fiber or raffia skirt and carry a whisk. There are those Chakaba that have only one leg. It is mystifying to see this figure enter the dance arena on one leg, then all of a sudden spring up on the stilted leg. Some of these stilted figures not only dance, but jump rope. (Green 1998, 25)

Another African stilt-dancer figure, similar to the traditional Trinidadian Moko Jumbie figure, is the Gue Gblin stilt figure of the Dan (Yacouba) of the Ivory Coast. As described by Green:

This figure has a black headdress with a plume of animal skin, topped with feathers projecting from the headdress. The headdress has red side fringes and the face of the mask is black, with a corded black tassel in the nose area. Gue Gblin wears a black and white striped costume with matching pants that cover the legs of the stilts and carries a black whisk in each hand. He is accompanied in dance by sets of triple-headed Sangba (Djimbe) drums and slit-lot drums. His dance routine is somewhat acrobatic and agile for a stilt figure. (Green 1998, 26)

In the early nineteenth-century carnivals in Trinidad, a black-and-white-clad Moko Jumbie figure was a prominent one. He functioned, like his African counterparts, as a mediator "between the world of the living and the spiritual world of the ancestors" (Green 1998, 25). Because of their height, these figures were able to intercede on behalf of the living to make special requests. These included rain to save the crops or blessings on the land.

In later years, according to Crowley (1956, 198), Moko Jumbie was generally seen "dancing through the streets, collecting money on a plate from people crowded in second-floor windows and balconies. Thus he tapped an audience out of reach of the street maskers" (Crowley 1956, 198). But Crowley further states that the figure virtually disappeared from the carnivals because of danger to such a tall figure passing under the many high-voltage electrical wires strung across the streets of Port of Spain.

Although this had been the case, in the 1980s Moko Jumbie made a dramatic appearance in Trinidadian Carnival, this time with children dancing on the stilts. This revitalization was necessary since the authorities feared that Carnival's traditional characters—especially the figure of the Moko Jumbie—were becoming extinct because of the huge masquerade bands thronging the streets. The resurgence of Moko Jumbie, particularly as children now dance it, facilitates this type of aesthetic historicizing—as will be demonstrated later with the case study. This is of paramount importance for revisioning a sense of history and heritage for the children.

Today the stilts measure between six and twelve feet and only the more experienced male dancers are allowed to dance on the tallest stilts. The children's designer explained that this was done in the interest of safety of

Fig. 28. Contemporary children's Moko Jumbies in black and white. Photograph: Dr. Christian Dettmers. Used by permission of Dr. Christian Dettmers, Hamburg, Germany.

Fig. 29. Pitchy patchy clowns and African Moko Jumbies. Photograph: Dr. Christian Dettmers. Used by permission of Dr. Christian Dettmers, Hamburg, Germany.

the very young children—the youngest stilt dancer was a six-year-old girl—and to reduce the possibility of children's falling off the stilts. The stilts are also carefully made in that their weight matches the child's body weight (interview with Francina Princesa Richards, February 1999). The children are also encouraged to do exercises to keep their leg and back muscles in shape before dancing on stilts.

The traditional Moko Jumbie's costume as described by Crowley has been somewhat changed. Although the basic body costumes have remained essentially the same, a number of them depict traditional Carnival characters. These include the blue devils of the early Emancipation Carnivals, *pitchy patchy* clowns (whose costumes are made of bits and strips of cloth), or the African forefathers from whom they actually evolved. The costumes can also be very innovative, depicting a variety of themes running the gamut from slavery to the natural flora and fauna of Trinidad and Tobago. The case study will highlight these contemporary changes.

A Description of Moko Jumbie's Dance

> The dance is strong magic. The dance is a spirit. It turns the body to liquid steel. It makes it vibrate like a guitar. The body can fly without wings. It can sing without voice. The dance is strong magic. The dance is life.
>
> **—Pearl Primus, "African Dance"**

This quotation from Pearl Primus aptly describes Trinidadian Carnival dance and what "playing mas" entails, African-Trinidadian style, for dance activated by music realizes the full artistic intention of the Carnival mas as multilayered, magical, kinesthetic symbol. Trinidadians speak of "the spirit of Carnival," which entails being possessed by the "spirit of the mas," that is, taking on the actual spirit of the persona embodied by the costume. This dates back to the Emancipation Carnival of the slaves, in which playing mas was the slaves' attempt to literally come out of themselves to confront the mask of the oppressor—and to function behind that mask of oppression to re-create *mas of the spirit*, a reaffirmation of the traumatized spirit inside. This fosters reconciliation, healing, and that reconstruction of self and spirit, even of community, leading up to ethnic empowerment and a sense of cultural wholeness. The Moko Jumbie mas and its accompanying dance forms are no exception.

Moko Jumbie masqueraders generally dance to emulate the particular spirit of the costume they are supposed to portray. Robert Farris Thompson aptly describes stilt and other dance patterns in the African context as a fulcrum on which African experience revolves and a logical extension of African philosophies:

> If spirits challenge gravity by moving on stilts 12 feet in the air to dance rhythms in the forest villages of Liberia; if athletes in Nigeria can carry nearly a hundred pounds of carved wood and shoulder this burden for a quarter of an hour while dancing before the king; if Dahomean initiates into a society honoring the collective ancestral dead can spin and spin and spin and spin and spin . . . until the very concept of human dizziness begins to lose its force—then anything is possible. (Thompson 1974, 14)

Moko Jumbie's dance steps encapsulate this undying strength, energy, and fluidity described here. The dancers' torsos are generally tilted forward as if on the threshold of the world. Then the dance begins—a type of call and response rhythm similar to that of the call and response songs of Africa.

The torsos then incline slightly forward and, with bent knees, flat-footed shuffles, and sweeping curves, the dancers dance. The dance is, thus, centrifugal—emanating and exploding outward from the hips. The dance is also flat-footed and favors gliding, dragging, or shuffling steps—what Trinidadians call *chipping*, which relates to the union of man to the earth, where the feet embrace the bountiful ground to give praise and draw from it additional power and strength.

Moko Jumbie's dance has been described in earlier literature as "jig like, changing to long strides and stamping movements, punctuating the beat of the music" (Ahye 1978, 29). However, what I witnessed with the children's Moko Jumbie dancing did not correspond to jig-like dancing. The children were dancing in accordance to the different gods and spirits that they were supposed to portray. As such there was an acrobatic energy and power, characterized by high forward stilt-legged kicks, jumps, and even pivots, that was rapid and repetitive, with ball-feet stamps, followed by a sudden rapid split in the dance.

With the rapid shuffles and acrobatic kicks, the dances escalated in fury as they became fused with ancestral presences, impelling us to embark on visual, kinesthetic journeys through particular moments in Trinidadian/Caribbean history. Then as the dance steps changed to flat-footed gliding and shuffling, Trinidadian chipping, there was a melting and slowing down to facilitate a pause, a breath, to recover. Through the medium of the towering stilts of the Moko Jumbie figure, the entire band of dancing Moko Jumbies performed a kind of offering—a call of "purgation," according to Rohlehr (1999, 248–293)—to the ancestors.

Moko Jumbie's Appearance on Other Caribbean Islands

Any examination of the Moko Jumbie figure would not be complete without brief attention to the figure on other islands in the Caribbean. From accounts discussing Moko Jumbie's name, there is evidence that the figure appeared as a feature of the Jonkonnu Christmas celebrations in Jamaica, St. Vincent, Bahamas, Bermuda, Belize, St. Kitts, and Antigua. According to Rosita Sands (1989, 143), at "one time Junkanoo appears to have been a pan-Caribbean celebration" and Judith Bettelheim (1988, 39) says, "Variations on this festival occur in many British-influenced Caribbean nations. . . . In no two places are the festivals exactly the same. . . . contemporary Bahamian Junkanoo shares only a nomenclature with the Jamaican practice."

Daniel Crowley (1956, 198) states: "Moko Jumby, the stilt dancer, is known throughout the West Indies, as a feature of John Canoe and other Christmas and Carnival fetes." While this may be so, the only festival that bears any resemblance to the Trinidadian Carnival in this regard is the Bahamian festival and even then there are differences. Literary scholarship on Jonkonnu in Jamaica is copious, but also suggests differences from the Moko Jumbie figure in Trinidadian Carnival celebrations. (For more on Jonkonnu [Junkanoo, John Canoe] see: Barnett 1979; Bettelheim 1976, 1979, 1985, 1988; Bettleheim and Nunley 1988a and b; Cowley 1991, 1997; Ryman 1984; Sands 1989.)

Sands provides the best definition:

> The word "Junkanoo" refers to a ritualistic celebration associated primarily with end-of-the-year holiday festivities, in particular, Christmas and New Year's Day. It is also commonly referred to in the literature as the "John Canoe" festival. In the Caribbean, it has been associated with the British holidays of Boxing Day (December 26th), Guy Fawkes Day (November 8th), and a festival known as Goombay in the English speaking Caribbean. (Sands 1989, 143).

Sands also states that because Junkanoo is celebrated at Christmastime and New Year's, as well as the fact that it begins at 3:00 A.M., it is different from the pre-Lenten Carnivals celebrated in Trinidad, New Orleans, and elsewhere. But Sands also claims that the Bahamian festival is "akin in style to Trinidad's Carnival and the New Orleans Mardi Gras" (Sands 1989, 143).

According to Sands (1989, 143–144), the Junkanoo tradition is characterized by lively music, free-spirited dancing, and flamboyant, colorful costumes and masks. It is a common feature in the Bahamas that every child rises early on Christmas morning to see the Junkanoos. They consist of costumed groups, similar in style to "bands of masqueraders" in Trinidad, who go from house to house begging for contributions. Not a door is missed where there might be a penny or a glass of rum. The climax of this mobile costume parade comes when the groups break out into dancing to the sounds of maracas (*shak shak* in the West Indies), scrapers, and a variety of drums—bongo drums, congas with goatskin heads—and cowbells. Moko Jumbie used to be a part of this entourage, but when the Moko Jumbie started to disappear from Trinidad Carnival as early as the 1950s, it seems as if the figure also began to die out of the Junkanoo bands. However, Moko Jumbies are still present today on some islands besides

Trinidad and Tobago. Today Bahamian Junkanoo bands are organized around a theme depicted in costumes, very much as with the Trinidadian Carnival bands.

We may now turn our attention to the Moko Jumbies' case study.

Something

Something, performed by the Watusi Carnival Cultural Caravan in 1999, was a novel Carnival portrayal. *Something* illustrated other innovations taking place on the Carnival stage with punning, ironic inversion, and myth. The pun was embedded in the simple but profound title of the Carnival club's name, *Watusi*, which signified "what you see." Thus, *Something* could refer to anything, based on what the viewer perceived. With the use of this innovative linguistic technique and the larger-than-life presence of the Moko Jumbie's masks, *Something* was a subtle Carnival (re)presentation of important movements in Trinidad's history. This mas portrayed the *designer's* (creative artist's) return to antiquity to pay reverence to the ancestors destroyed through slavery and recalled in this type of aesthetic geometry. *Something* showcased various historical fragments of a checkered history, bits and pieces portrayed as a quilt, yet newly re-assembled, a metamorphosis, *something* revalidated and reborn into the aesthetic landscape of the Carnival's present. The bandleader, Francina Princesa Richards, described it this way in a 1999 interview: "Anything is something. Whatever you see and think it is, then it is something. All these Moko Jumbies are something . . . everything."

The band was divided into two distinct segments. The first part re-envisioned colonization and its legacy of destruction, dispossession, and negation of both those indigenous to the island of Trinidad—the Arawak Indians—as well as the Africans coerced to make the Middle Passage trek to the Caribbean. These were the masks of colonial oppression. Part two sought to reconstitute those destroyed ancestral presences—to recreate mas—through a reaffirmation of that past, leading up to healing, reconciliation, and, eventually, a sense of cultural wholeness—a process of de-colonization.

The following descriptive analysis of *Something's* Moko Jumbie masks is based on detailed interviews with the bandleader, Francina Princesa Richards.

The first Moko Jumbies to appear were the fish, the music note, the anchor Jumbie with fishhooks for hands, and the spinning wheel. These depicted varying stages of the period of Spanish Conquest, incorporating that sense of dislocation and uncertainty, with three of these masks bearing direct association to the sea. The fish Moko Jumbie's mask portrayed the peace-loving Arawaks, one of the indigenous peoples on the island before the Spaniards came. The fish was a literal symbol of the Arawaks' fishing industry, their principal form of subsistence. However, the fish also conjured up notions of the Caribbean Sea, proclaiming the power of life—the ancestral presences—within the depths of the ocean. Thus, the fish and the other sea masks provided the medium for transcendence of the ordinary world to the realm of the extraordinary: the spiritual world of the ancestors.

The symbol of the sea, with its flowing waters, becomes the mask of discovery of the New World by the colonizers, yet it is also a powerful recall of the beginning of new existences in the New World. The sea thus reconstructs the omnipresence of ancestral memory, not only in its transportation and preservation of the cultures of Africa and the indigenous culture of the island, but also as a symbol of metamorphosis—the development of the life of the West Indian in a new environment. The masks thus depict the designer's ingenuity in recreating and celebrating the power associated with both spaces on the Carnival stage.

The next Moko Jumbie to appear was the music note. This one choreographed the Western tradition of conquest in all its diversity—Spanish, French, and English. The Spaniards came and anchored themselves in the Caribbean, to the detriment of the Indian. Later the French and the British came with their enslaved Africans. The symbol of the music note depicts Western culture, which the Spanish and French brought with them—the Spanish *parranda* (the house-to-house singing of Christmas songs to the accompaniment of guitars and cuatros, called *parang* in Trinidadian creole) and the celebration of the version of Carnival brought by the French.

Paradoxically, these cultures are recreated within a non-Western space and as such they are totally decentralized. What takes center stage is the dance and music of ancestral presence—the ritual music of the African drums destroyed, denigrated, but recapitulated, engendering a pause for the holy space of reconciliation and recovery. The music Jumbie thus signals rebirth of the African muse, but it is also a new beginning since the African muse is now rooted and anchored in the Caribbean homeland.

The Moko Jumbie with the anchor and the fishhooks for fingers recalled the period of piracy and buccaneers in the history of the Caribbean.

It is said that when the pirates were caught raiding other trade ships, as a form of punishment their fingers were amputated and replaced with hooks and they were left on the island to die. Metaphorically, the pirates may have been symbols of the unsung heroes of Trinidadian history.

The wheel Moko Jumbie, although still related to European imperialism, was a slightly different portrayal, representing another vivid image of the ravages of the colonial experience. The wheel is circular and thus Caribbean people are depicted as being trapped and enmeshed in the labyrinth of colonization with no sense of direction and no way out. Colonial dispossession brings in its wake uncertainty, confusion, and placelessness, which Caribbean peoples must make sense of for themselves. The wheel, however, is a medium for steering, and as such it was explored as another symbol of hope for that new dawning, that quest for black redemption and spiritual survival after colonial genocide.

The Amerindian Moko Jumbie was the next to appear. The designer evoked those Spanish settlers, Spanish Creoles, and other Venezuelans who migrated to Trinidad between 1814 and 1817. They resided in the foothills of the northern range, their chief duty being to plant cocoa. They were referred to as "peons" and were staunch Catholics. Their contribution to Carnival came with the prominence of the Amerindian bonnet with feathers, a common form in contemporary Carnival, which also has African connotations. According to Robert Farris Thompson (1988, 25), masks with feathers symbolize flying beings; a feathered person is thus a tangible being and a spiritual force. In the Kongo world, according to Thompson (1988, 25), feathers worn on masks or headpieces depict confidence and strength associated with the limitless power of flying. Through this Amerindian mask, therefore, the oppressed/powerless can rise—that is, literally fly out of physical oppression into full spiritual awareness, to revitalize that potentiality inside destroyed through the Indian demise in the Spanish Conquest. The colors of the feathers embodied in this Moko Jumbie's costume are of paramount importance. White in Kongo represents the "call of the ancestors" (Thompson 1988, 25). It is almost a re-communion with them. When this reunion is made, we get resurrection, rebirth, and reconstruction of the destroyed self. Red depicts waves of good fortune granted by the ancestors and the green symbolizes rebirth.

Feathers on masks are powerful mediums for attracting the positive attention of the ancestors in Yoruba culture as well. Thus this Carnival image of the Amerindian feathered bonnet provides a mask for multiple

ancestral tributes, so that Blacks pay tribute to the noble indigenous inhabitants of the Caribbean islands, honor the African ancestors who were
coercively brought there, and, by extension, pay tribute to their own
selves.

The next set of Moko Jumbies set the stage for the ritual return to
Africa and a reconnection to the vitality of an African past that was taken
away from the enslaved in the Middle Passage crossing to the Caribbean.
In the first instance, the designer invoked the creative and protective powers of three powerful African gods by reinstating them in the Carnival
aesthetic landscape. Ogun, Eshu, and Shango re-choreographed Africa's
denigrated history on this contemporary Carnival stage through the
dance movements of these African Moko Jumbies. Ogun led this section
of Yoruba orisha Moko Jumbies. This was a Moko Jumbie dressed in
white, carrying a golden waistband. According to the designer, the color
gold was used to depict the sharpness of the iron blades and the precious
nature of this symbol associated with the god of war and iron. Iron symbolizes the forceful nature and the vitality associated with this god. He
clears the way for the safe appearance of other gods. Margaret Thompson
Drewal described him in this way:

> In any ritual where iron or iron implements are required, Ogun must
> be dealt with first, for iron itself is Ogun. It represents Ogun's vital
> power, and his capacity for quick, forceful overt action concretized
> in iron tools and implements of all varieties. Iron implements are a
> symbol of Ogun's worldly achievements whether those are destruc-
> tive or productive, whether they involve the iron cutlasses, arrows
> and guns of warfare, automobiles and motorcycles, the blades of cir-
> cumcision, the hoes of farming, or the adzes and knives of carving.
> Iron implements and Ogun get things done quickly and forcefully.
> (Drewal 1989, 210)

The hoe, axe, and gun are all Ogun's symbols (Thompson 1983, 53). In
this Caribbean environment, however, even symbols of destruction such
as the axe and gun are paradoxically symbols of African survival and its
resulting protection, all needed for the reconstruction of spirit, self, and
the developing sense of community in the New World. Most important
was this Moko Jumbie's dance, which recaptured the vital nature of this
god's power. Like Ogun's initiates, the Jumbie's head was kept calm. In
contrast, the shoulder blades were raised and lowered repetitively in
quick, sharp, exaggerated movements consistent with the explosive en-

ergy of Ogun. Knees were then flexed, after which the torso was pitched forward from the hips at approximately a 45-degree angle. From this position, and with active shoulders, a number of different stepping patterns and rhythms were performed (Drewal 1989, 217). This Moko Jumbie demonstrated a type of stalking step. High up in the air, his movements started with a quick strong step, restrained, which burst forth again, sustained, then burst forth with a leaping explosion of energy, ending up in a type of crouch. In this way, we knew that Ogun had appeared. The path was now cleared to facilitate the entry of the next god, who works hand in hand with Ogun.

This was Elegba, or Legba, the divine mediator, who must receive the first invocations and sacrifices, and who is also known as Eshu, the trickster deity of the Yoruba, Fon, and other peoples of southwest Nigeria and Benin. He is the "god of the crossroads," who takes messages from the other gods on behalf of people in this world. He thus personifies the intersection between this world and the other world and is generally perceived as guarding the gateways of communication. This Moko Jumbie appeared in the form of a huge black and white spider.

In the Caribbean the figure of the trickster is a familiar one, including not only the Fon Legba/Yoruba Elegba, but also another common figure in Caribbean folktales known as Anansi the spider, originally from the Akan people of Ghana. This Moko Jumbie represented both, something that would be clear to most Trinidadians. As Richards explained, "I chose one Jumbie to portray the African trickster and the orisha Legba because I see them as complementary facets of each other. One cannot separate one from the next since they represent a regeneration of African history on both sides." Despite Legba's characteristic *anansyism* (a creole term in Trinidad parlance used to refer especially to the trickiness of politicians), this god's creative powers were invoked. As a Caribbean figure, Anansi, too, carries both creative and protective power. Thus he reconstructs and transforms, weaving, like the spider he portrays, the disparate and broken strands of the region's history into a novel whole, which ultimately becomes the source of new perceptions and new strengths.

Again the highlight of this presentation was Anansi/Elegba's dance. Elegba was invoked by placing the left foot forward. According to Drewal (1989, 208), the left side is stressed to symbolize entry into the realm of the spiritual. However, the masquerader danced a type of acrobatic dance on one leg to indicate the force of Elegba's power, conjuring up the Haitian version of Legba as the old man carrying the cane. This was particularly powerful here, since in Yorubaland a one-legged person is treated even more respectfully because he is said to have double the power of a two-legged one.

After Elegba's invocation, hope for the Caribbean person was further envisaged in the designer's evocation of Shango, the warrior god of thunder, lightning, and energy. Another white-clad Moko Jumbie, enshrined in a red flowing cape, choreographed Shango. What was important in this deity's portrayal was this Moko Jumbie's forceful dance. The masquerader danced first with a series of movements as if he were missing his steps. Then the dance was repeated with fast-paced, jerky, angular movements connoting a forceful release of energy, evoking in its speed the dynamics of lightning and thunder associated with Shango (Drewal 1989, 202). Throughout the dance, the Moko Jumbie first pointed the cape toward the sky and then brought it down to earth in short, diagonal movements, indicating possession by the god Shango (Ajayi 1998, 190–191n.).

The Shango god of thunder was selected to re-contextualize and re-create the energy of the thunder god, destroyed through slavery. From Ajayi's description of the *gbamu* dance, it is clear that one of the functions of Shango's dance movements is the calling down of thunder and lightning. The Shango Moko Jumbie thus becomes the medium for assessing the realm of the spirit—or the realm of the divine. This mask provides the cover for looking into the eyes of the Spirit. Shango thus becomes imbued with what the Yoruba call *ashe* ("spiritual command, the power-to-make-things-happen" [Thompson 1983, 5]), so that the body becomes transformed. His body becomes thunder. He thus rekindles the energy of the spirit within, which energizes and mobilizes; by so doing he recaptures that powerful energy that was destroyed in slavery.

The Shango Moko Jumbie's costume was probably the most important in the recall of the African gods, since it stylized and summoned up the temperamental characteristics of Shango's personality as well as the energy associated with the god of thunder and lightning. Shango effects creation—new beginnings and creativity. Through Shango there is rootedness and reconnection, a Caribbean community awakening to itself.

After the recall of the African gods, another set of Moko Jumbies appeared representing powerful African tribes, symbols of rootedness and the home continent that was wrenched away. The first of these conjured up was the Masai tribe of Kenya. These people live in the Rift Valley area and their dance is accompanied by chanting. The Masai masquerader, dressed in green and gold costume, danced with a series of vertical jumps

Fig. 30. Shango—Orisha of Thunder and Lightning *(the cape is red)*, with the Wheel Moko Jumbie *(left)*. Photograph: Dr. Christian Dettmers. Used by permission of Dr. Christian Dettmers, Hamburg, Germany.

like those of the Masai people he portrayed. Doris Green provides a description of the Masai dance: "The Masai concentrate on one kind of jump, from both feet to both feet with some gestures in a vertical plane" (Green 1998, 15).

The Zulu Fan Dancers closely followed him. By rejuvenating these powerful African tribes in the Moko Jumbie mas, the designer transported us back symbolically to the soul of Africa. These Moko Jumbies functioned as translators in the artist's attempt to sever the boundaries created by the powerful colonizers and the powerless Africans. The Fan Dancers' opening-and-closing-of-the-fans dance functioned in two ways. Literally, it illustrated the participatory nature of African dance. In addition, the image of dance was used to re-establish ritual dances associated with the African warrior tribe. The rhythm of these dancing Moko Jumbies, in response to the call of the African drums, was also an artifact, a reminder of that dark barren past in which drums were restricted and forbidden and from which the folk art of drumming emerged. With these Moko Jumbies, the designer created a Caribbean re-envisioning of human dignity by compensating for the lost history and culture of the Africans taken to the New World. In this way, Caribbean people become refreshed and re-energized.

The Skull of Death Jumbie was the final Jumbie of the "African recall set." This was a Jumbie enveloped in chains, who recalled the horrors of slavery. The enslaved people were doubly traumatized, in that they were alienated from their ancestors, from a sense of their social heritage, and they were cast away from their own communities, leading to a people's separation, dislocation, and isolation from their sources of identity. Death in the mind of the African, however, does not signify the end of human life, but rather ancestral reverence and communion. This, in turn, signals rebirth, celebration, and resurrection. In death, therefore, there is always renewal—the message that is disseminated here on the Carnival stage through the elevated figures of the children.

Here history is sculpturally recreated through the towering figure of the Moko Jumbie of Death. Change, regeneration, and redemption thus become possible, to re-establish that sense of cultural rootedness. This Moko Jumbie was almost ceremonial in his portrayal. He ritually reenacted the pain of the dead ancestors through his conjuring up of the limbo dance motions. However, through the meta-mask of Death, devastation, and the fragility of life, lie reconciliation to the situation, regeneration, reconnection, and new beginnings. Death thus informs a new sense of identity and becomes a dynamic metaphor for regenerating and revising African and Caribbean history. The Moko Jumbie of Death mobilized the masqueraders through his limbo dance routine, providing them with the medium for an anchoring of the new Caribbean self within the Carnival present.

This emerging Caribbean sense of salvation came in the song of praise to Haile Selassie, which was Richards's conscious celebration of African ancestral achievements. Salvation comes in a re-acceptance of ancestry. The artist thus returned to the past to honor the Lion of Judah, Haile Selassie, Emperor of Ethiopia, with a Moko Jumbie bearing the Emperor's colors—red, green, and gold. With this masquerader the process of decolonization had been put into motion. The stage was set for part two of the pilgrimage of history—the road to cultural wholeness.

Canboulay and the Emancipation Carnival:
The Sugarcane Moko Jumbie Queen

This section began with the Sugarcane Moko Jumbie dressed in gold, the Queen of the Moko Jumbies' band. She re-choreographed a ritual journey back to the sugarcane plantations and the enslaved people's Emancipation Carnival when in 1838 slavery was abolished. The slaves took to the streets with their Canboulay Festival to celebrate their newly found freedom from the shackles of slavery and to reclaim that celebratory space of the streets, both literally and metaphorically. In this sense the Sugarcane Moko Jumbie Queen (the woman's costume) was a metaphorical restoration of the broken pieces of Trinidadian/Caribbean people's shattered history. By capitalizing on the power of Emancipation portrayed in this mas, the Sugarcane Moko Jumbie provided political and sociopsychological strategies to re-address the daily psychological tensions and fears with which the African Trinidadian peoples are confronted in their constant attempts to come to terms with themselves as blacks and with their African past.

Important here is the color gold of her costume, and the circularity of the image of the sugarcanes that she carries on her back, as well as the fact that she is Queen of the band. What is happening here is that with Emancipation, sugarcane—symbol of enslavement—now becomes a symbol of freedom, since it implies victory and freedom from colonial rule. That she is female hints at the notion of giving life back to the powerless and the

Fig. 31. The Sugarcane Moko Jumbie in gold, Queen of the band performing *Something*. Photograph: Dr. Christian Dettmers. Used by permission of Dr. Christian Dettmers, Hamburg, Germany.

displaced. Women here thus epitomize female strength and power through the female's role as creator, facilitating the process of personal and national recovery for Afro-Caribbean peoples.

The Sadu and Chinese Moko Jumbies

With the abolishment of slavery, other non-African sources of labor were once again sought to continue work on the sugarcane plantations. Between 1845 and 1917 approximately 117,000 Indians (Hindus and Muslims mainly from Uttar Pradesh and South India) were brought to Trinidad as indentured laborers. Unlike their African counterparts, Indian families remained intact on the sugar plantations, and, as such, even though displaced, they remained close to their cultures of origin. As a result, a type of rural village developed centered on the extended family and a reformulated sense of the Indian caste system. The very popular Sadu/Babu Moko Jumbie pays tribute to the Indian indentured workers. Babu also depicts the Hindu priest, the mediating force between god and his earthly subjects. Here he was dressed in a white wrap or *dhoti* (as it is called in Hindi) and wore a beard and headwrap.

The next Moko Jumbie played at the identity of the Chinese who also settled throughout the island. Unlike the Indians, they tended to avoid work on the sugar estates, preferring to set up their own businesses. The Chinese businessman, however, operated originally at a peasant level. He planted rice. As such was the Chinese man featured as the Chinese Moko Jumbie. He was wearing long pants, a smock with a long braid, and a lantern-shaped hat. Of interest here were the scales he carried in his hands, with the domino game of chance represented by the dice showing the figures three and five.

According to designer Francina Princesa Richards and another informant, Wayne Alleyne, who looked at the band, the figure five recalls the main ethnic groups that provided the contours of Trinidad and Tobago society: indigenous Carib and Arawak Indians; Western European colonizers: French, Spanish, English; the African enslaved peoples; East Indian indentureds; Chinese and others who came after Emancipation. The figure three, however, symbolizes the Trinity, linked to the naming of the island of Trinidad by Columbus, and as a result, to the chance discovery of this island by the colonizers. Three on the scale is tipped higher than the figure five, indicating the merger of the five ethnic strands, which constitute the rich cosmopolitan milieu of contemporary Caribbean society.

Flora and Fauna Moko Jumbies

The next three Jumbies depicted the flora and fauna of the island—the hibiscus, the *Anthurium* lilies, and the scarlet ibis, national bird of Trinidad and Tobago. These recalled the natural habitat and the innocence before the land was ravaged by colonization. On a metaphorical level, the designer used the flora and fauna Jumbies as metaphors to re-create and convert the decadence and destruction of the land into dynamic symbols of reconstruction and new birth. They function like landmarks, which provide the necessary movement out of the pain of self-negation and dispossession into a New World of self-affirmation.

The National Flag Moko Jumbie

With this Moko Jumbie we have come full circle, in that we have experienced all the important historical movements of the islands of Trinidad and Tobago: from *nothing*—colonial settlement and slavery, the despair and geographical dislocation of the African peoples, through their emancipation and the ensuing indentureship of the Asian population—to *something*—national culture depicted in the outstanding colors of the national flag in this Moko Jumbie's costume. The colors of the flag of Trinidad and Tobago are red, white, and black. The red represents the vitality of Trinidadian, and by extension, Caribbean peoples. Black is the color of strength and purpose. White is the most dynamic symbol here. It depicts the sea—water being the source of the Caribbean heritage (the Middle Passage crossing to the Caribbean)—since water carried European settlers, African slaves, and indentured Indian laborers to the Caribbean. Water reflects discovery through ancestral presence—Columbus's discovery of the island, the indigenous Amerindian demise, the African's coerced trek to the Caribbean, and the docking of the Fatal Rosack with the first Indian indentureds. Water is also a traditional African symbol of washing and purgation, re-evaluated to signify an act of creation, since water can also refer to the fluid in the mother's womb from which all human life emerges. Water as a symbol of eternity and timelessness thus provides the foundation for birth and eventual growth.

In conclusion, with the Moko Jumbie band's presentation of *Something* we have literally moved from Nothing to Something. With *Something* the designer has offered another perspective for an understanding of history and, consequently, the reconstruction of self and the formation of an ethnic identity. Through the sculptural form of the Moko Jumbie figure, *Something* has presented Carnival as a powerful vehicle for restoring and revising the fragmented Trinidadian Afro-Caribbean historical past—its ancestral presences. It was as if *Something* were a Carnival meta-ceremony in which ancestral presences re-entered the present, thereby unlocking the pain and suffering of the past. The dancing Moko Jumbie children masqueraders thus provided the masks for the manifestation of ancestral presence. Their dance created the means for a type of sociocultural re-habilitation process, a reconstruction that processes off trauma and dis-integration, not conjured up negatively, but rather as prerequisites for engendering reintegration, reconstruction, and new growth. History thus acquired meaning through playing Moko Jumbie mas since it provided an outlet for memory rooted in the meditative, healing, and reintegrative process of the children's Moko Jumbie mas. In this way the children became elevated. They truly saw their music and heard their dance.

The author wishes to thank sincerely the bandleader and designer Francina Princesa Richards for all the valuable time spent in explaining the Moko Jumbie figures. She also thanks her husband, Dr. Christian Dettmers, for the Moko Jumbie photography, and her brother, Wayne Alleyne, for other interpretations, which were not so obvious at the time.

❖ ❖ ❖

CURAÇAO

19

Tambu

Afro-Curaçao's Music and Dance of Resistance

Gabri Christa

It was the case . . . nearly everywhere in the Non-European world that the coming of the white man brought forth some form of resistance.
—**Edward Said,** *Culture and Imperialism*

On a slab of concrete, between the trees of a *hofi*, I danced my first "real" tambu. Not the tambu we danced at school parties together with salsa, merengue, disco, and other dances that were popular, but a forbidden one, in a place where decent people weren't supposed to be and where a thirteen-year-old with a boyfriend six years her senior had no place at all. But I was there, where the rhythms embraced my secret escapade, and where the singing and dancing, barely lit, just kept going. Hips rotating and moving fast in counterpoint to the feet. Hips pointing back, hips grinding down, hips seducing me and convincing me that they are the basis for dance. Women and men dancing around each other without touching, while singers and drummers just kept going.

Tambu is an expression of African Curaçao, once a spiritual practice, now a popular music/dance that expresses national pride and celebration. Its lyrics often criticize the society it reflects. Basic to the music are the tambu, a big drum, and several other percussion instruments, the so-called iron works, tools to work the land. The local language, Papiamentu, contributes to the highly rhythmical lyrics and shapes much of the unique sound. Its singing style mostly reminds me of rap music and early Jamaican dancehall.

"*Si bo konose bo mes, si bo konose bo pasado, si bo konose bo historia, anto bo konose bo mes*" (Rosalia 1994, 38). [If you know yourself, if you know your past, if you know your history, that's when you know yourself.] Rosalia's quote inspired me to trace the history of tambu, my favorite dance and music form of my native island, Curaçao. Like Rosalia, I believe in understanding and knowing one's heritage. It is the foundation for who I am and what I create. Unlike him I am not a folklorist, but I do believe that folklore is "the surest key to a nation or race's thinking, for folk materials offer a true and unbiased picture of the ways in which a given people in a special locality think and act" (Harris, quoted in Adjaye and Andrews 1997, 111). So my life as a creator involves researching folklore of many forms in the societies with which I come in contact. Mixing forms such as modern dance and ballet and African Diaspora's expressions, I remain in my own mind an experimental/contemporary choreographer.

Tambu speaks to me on many levels, but my first attraction to this forbidden dance/music form at the time of my growing up was its rebellion. The cultural expressions of the African Diaspora, including tambu, were a form of resistance as well as a way of identity. Resisting the ban on playing this music, resisting the white Dutch culture through commenting on society through lyrics, resisting the ban on speaking Papiamentu by singing in the language, resisting the dominance of Roman Catholic religion by keeping tambu's religious meaning going (although this battle has been lost)—all culminated in resisting the wiping out of an African culture by holding on to the music and the dance.

Curaçao, as part of the Americas, shares with the rest of the continent and islands its history of colonialism and the wiping out of the original Indian population. Curaçao is one of the six islands that make up the Netherlands Antilles. (The Antilles are the last of the Dutch colonies and part of the Caribbean. Other Dutch islands are Aruba, which now has its independent status within the group; Bonaire; and the Leeward Islands: St. Maarten, Saba, and St. Eustatius.) After contact with Alonso de Ojeda, the islands became Spanish in 1499 and stayed under Spanish rule until 1634.

These islands with no natural resources were declared *islas inutiles*, useless islands, by Diego Colon. First, most of the Indian population was shipped to Hispaniola by the Spanish and, later, remaining people were evacuated to Venezuela by the Dutch (Martinus 1997, 4). In 1641 Curaçao was marked as a slave depot by the Dutch West India Company because its only resource, a natural deep harbor, provided a perfect place for ships to dock. The slave trade started to bloom after the conquest of the Portuguese strongholds in Angola during the reign of Peter Stuyvesant. Both the Dutch colony of New Netherlands (New York) and the islands were jointly administered by this Governor Stuyvesant between 1647 and 1664. From Curaçao the slaves were shipped to other parts of the Americas. Although it was a desert island, slaves still worked in salt mines and the few plantations. Tambu was developed by the Africans during slavery and has continued to be a major music and dance form since the abolishment of slavery in 1863.

Language

Being the child of a Surinamese man and a Dutch woman meant growing up speaking Dutch at home, the language of the *Macambas* (a derogatory word for the Dutch people living on the island). It also meant an immediate outsider status, or at least that's how I perceived it as a child. So by embracing tambu, I gained a feeling of belonging and a form for my teenage rebellion against my Surinamese/Dutch background. I embraced the forbidden nature of the expression and of Papiamentu, the language of the streets and the other people, a language that up until the 1970s wasn't spoken in the classroom, nor allowed in the schoolyards. Embracing and claiming Papiamentu as a language was an act of nationhood. The songs and dances of tambu were an important expression thereof.

Papiamentu is an Afro-Portuguese creole with many links to West African languages such as Guene and the language spoken in Cape Verde. Curaçao writer and scholar Frank Martinus (1997) traced the language back to its African connections in *The Kiss of a Slave: Papiamentu's West-African Connections*. Martinus found that the name Papiamentu itself could have derived from different origins in Saramaccan, the language and name of one of the Maroon groups in Suriname. There, *papia-papia* means small talk. In Portuguese *papear* means to chatter (Martinus 1997, 6). Papiamentu is a very rhythmic language with influences from Spanish and some from Dutch. Steadily the language's place in society is growing, being the main language of most of the newspapers and radio stations. In 1986 Papiamentu was introduced as a subject in primary schools, and children are now taught to read and write in their own language first.

Music and Dance

You could be in any Latin country when you turn on the radio in Curaçao. Venezuela's stations can be received directly and the local stations play much salsa and merengue, with songs sung in both Spanish and Papiamentu. So it is no surprise that one of the three main musical influences in Curaçaon music is from neighboring islands and the music of the nearby continent. Musicians made salsa, merengue, and bolero their own, with lyrics sung in Papiamentu, giving the music a distinctive Antillean flavor. Music with nineteenth-century European influences (and distinctive but subtle African ones) are the Curaçao waltz (danced with mobile hips) and the mazurka. All these popular forms are danced as they are elsewhere in the region.

Africa's influence can be heard in *seu, tumba, muzik di zumbi,* and tambu. Seu is a dance that can be traced back to the Bantu in Africa. It means "harvest," originating from the time when the small corn was collected. The women were helped with the harvest by neighbors and friends. While the men were cutting the stalks, the women would follow, picking up the cobs and putting them in the large baskets they carried on their heads, dancing and singing in a way that they called *wapa* on the way to the storage places. Walking back and forth they would swing their hips and dip at prescribed intervals; all the while the hips were swaying. The tambu, which is the drum; the *agan,* which is part of the plow; the *chapi,* which is the hoe, and the *bastel,* which is a bull horn or cow horn, are used for the music of seu as well as tambu. Sometimes a *karko,* a conch shell, imported from Bonaire, is used to replace the bastel.

For muzik di zumbi, or music of the spirits, the main instrument is the *benta.* This is a berimbau-like instrument that is played in the mouth. The single string of this instrument is made of a palm tree leaf, the wood support out of a twig of the karawara, a local tree. The resonating sound is made with a stick called the *maingueta.* The music has an unusual lineup of instruments that includes the tambu drum and other instruments made from a combination of iron, copper, tin, and cloth. They determine the distinctive soft and mysterious zumbi sound.

Tumba must not be confused with tambu, nor with the Cuban *tumba francesa.* Tumba evolved from the outlawed tambu at the end of the nineteenth century. Just as the British colonial regime banned African drumming and other cultural expressions in Trinidad, the Dutch authorities banned the tambu. As late as 1936, laws were being introduced that made it illegal to play or dance tambu, or even be present when it was played. So indirectly the Dutch are responsible for the development of tumba, a form derived from tambu, calypso, merengue, and cumbia.

Pre-Lenten Carnival is a twentieth-century celebration in Curaçao, and before tumba was introduced in 1971 as the Carnival music, the music of Carnival was calypso, which still is the music of Carnival in Aruba. The Tumba Festival was a deliberate move to give prominence to the tumba music. For four days singers compete to be crowned *Rei* or *Reina di Tumba*, King or Queen of Tumba. The lion's share of the prize money goes to the composer of the winning song, while the singer gets the crown, the prestige, and the road march status. The winning song will have an infectious call and response chorus and gestures and dance step.

The 1999 winning song by Harry Zimmerman, "Nos ta bibu" [We are alive], had topical lyrics that celebrated Curaçao's five hundred years of documented history that year. The call and response had a heartbeat in "padiki padiki padiki" and the crowds clenched their fists and beat their chests in time, while moving their hips. The tumba dance is fun and free. Besides being the road march dance, the tumba is danced by couples at parties. They dance together, then separate to improvise, come back together, and so on. Looking somewhat like merengue, the tumba road march and "wining" are very fast.

Tambu is a social expression with deep ritual roots. Once a strong religion like Santería, tambu has completely lost its religious aspect because of a very successful campaign to make it seem immoral, and also because of the introduction of Roman Catholicism, which, unlike its syncretizations with African religions in Haiti, Brazil, and Cuba, was never incorporated into tambu, nor vice versa. Although there are many speculations about the word *tambu*, the most likely explanation comes from the West-Kongo word *ntambu*, which also stands for a membraphone (Rosalia 1997, 32).

To the Curaçaon *tambu* has many meanings. First, it is the name of the drum itself; it is also the dance that goes with the rhythm, and it is the name of the event where the music and dance are being featured, the gathering itself. Tambu developed during slavery as one of the dances and religions of the Africans, similarly to Candomble in Brazil, Palo Monte in Cuba, Kalinda in Trinidad, and Winti in Suriname (Rosalia 1997: 30). After the abolishment of slavery in 1863, tambu became the expression of the poor black workers from the lowest working class, just as tango did in Argentina and rumba did in Cuba.

Some of the same instruments of the tambu are also found in the other music forms. The tambu drum itself is made from a little wooden container that was used to import pigtails and nails. The instrument is played with the hands and held diagonally between the knees. The tambu is the only drum. Other percussion instruments, all made from iron, are collectively called *heru*, or iron. The combination of the drum with the loud and high sounds of the *heru* makes for the original sound. The high sound is said to stimulate the intensity of the senses, to facilitate communication with the spirits, and to help heighten the intensity and energy. The *heru* will play the timeline. In tambu both the music and the dance improvise on certain rhythms. The rhythm sections have a dialogue, and the different iron sections can have a dialogue simultaneously. The melody of the song has to be in harmony with the natural tonality of the language, Papiamentu. A. M. Jones, in a study of Swahili poetry quoted by Rosalia, says, "The singer is trying to put into practice the African custom of making as far as possible the rise and fall of the tune agree with that of the spoken words" (Rosalia 1997, 57). This is the case in tambu.

The main heru instruments are the *agan*, which is part of the plow, and the chapi, the hoe, a symbol of fertility. All the instruments are played with a long nail. Other instruments are the *triangel* (triangle) and the *wiri*, a piece of ribbed metal pipe. Very skilled musicians must play, since the rhythms are very complex and fast. It is an aggressive-sounding music with nothing mellow about it. The singing, with its rapping-like rhythmical chants, adds to the intensity. The music is polyrhythmic and repetitive, with songs that can be played for hours. The four or five singers change the lead continuously and have a dialogue or comments when the others are singing. In the call and response of the tambu, improvisation is essential. Rhythmically there are pauses, parts crescendo and then quickly change to pianissimo (Rosalia 1997, 53).

I fell in love with rumba while living in Cuba, ten years after I fell in love with tambu at age thirteen. Rumba's *guaguancó* and *yambú* have many obvious similarities to tambu: a rather flirtatious dance between a man and woman who never touch, who dance to songs and drums with a particular foot pattern. My interest in the similarities was provoked when one of the older dancers at the Conjunto Folklórico Nacional commented that I, as a Curaçaon woman, logically would dance the rumba well, because she said historically the best rumba dancers were the women from Curaçao, something Fernando Ortiz is supposed to have confirmed in his writings. I am curious to know how exactly the dances influenced each other. But it is a fact that women and men from Curaçao came to Cuba after the abolishment of slavery to work in the sugarcane industry. I am sure that they, like me, spent their free moments dancing to rumba, adding a distinctive tambu "feel" to it.

The Dances

The invention of the tambu drum gave birth to the dance. As people used to say, *"baila bari,"* dance the drum. Essential is the clapping of the hands and stamping of the heels. The dancers clap as a response to the singing and when the rhythm changes in the music. As in most African dances, tambu is danced separately, without touching. The emphasis of the dance is on the hips; all movement begins there. Hips circle, move smoothly sideways or in abrupt, aggressive movements. The knees are slightly bent and the heels stamp into the floor together with the music. When you first observe the dance, it looks more like shuffling because of the subtlety of these stomps. Rosalia says that the deep and aggressive beating of the drum resonates inside the stomach and is essential for the contact between the people, the drum, and the supernatural. The higher sounds of the chapi influence the inflections of the upper torso and the head, thereby providing a symbolic balance between the spirit world and the actual world.

Emphasis is on the back of the hips, the buttocks. The dancers dance in pairs, or individually, which both men and women can do. Women can have their hands on their hips, men behind the back, but many times the arms are just free. In trance-like dancing the arms are straight up in the air. Other variations are the *bok'e indjan* (Indian-crate), which is part of the sitting dance, a seated trance dance, and the belly-roll (Rosalia 1997, 79). Many dances from the Congo area went from the hip up, or from the hip down, but everything was initiated in the pelvis. Some dances had an erect upper body, and the legs were never lifted. All the emphasis was on the hips and waist. The Cuban Kongo dances were all like that (Ortiz 1981, 217). As in the music, improvisation is important.

The buttocks are particularly important in the *tambu-di-sanka*, or the tambu of the buttocks. Although *sanka* means buttocks in Papiamentu today, the origin of the name could come from the Kongolese word *sanga*, which means to dance or to bring into ecstasy (Rosalia 1997, 82). Some women tie a piece of cloth around the buttocks to accentuate them in the tambu-di-sanka.

Tambu as a dance is rather free, dancers dance within the style in their own form and to their own ability. The singing has a call-and-response dialogue between the lead singer and the other participants. The tambu drum has a dialogue with itself, the chapi, the other musicians—in some way all participants through music or dance are connected. At a tambu one doesn't dance constantly, but shifts between listening and clapping and dancing. Structurally, the most constant and fastest playing is in the second half, which is the confirmation part, the response in the lyrics and the music to the questions raised in the rap-like chanting of the slower first section. The very rapid second part is when the dancing takes place. All other expressions such as comments, cheers, and supportive sounds are made during this second part. These slower and faster sections alternate as the tambu continues—a single tambu piece can last an hour.

When a man wants to dance with a woman who is already dancing with another man, he must follow the rules by asking, "*pidi-skina*" ("take over the dance"). Bending his knees, he dances up to the couple, who are dancing apart, and puts his arm between them to separate them. When the dancing man ignores the newcomer, it can start a *trankamentu*, a shoulder-pushing dance that develops when the newcomer doesn't accept the refusal. If the dispute isn't resolved in the dance, *sanger pa tambu* takes place. This stick fight, *kokomakaku*, starts when one of the other participants calls out, "*sanger pa tambu*" ("blood for the tambu"), and the men pick up the sticks and attack (Rosalia 1997, 84). The man who can wound the other with the stick will be the winner. The wound has to have some blood, so it can be sprinkled over the tambu. The drum is said to be the one who demands the blood. Similar stick dances can be found in Trinidadian Kalinda and in Brazilian maculele. Stick fighting is no longer common in tambu, but it still occurs, part of the hidden nature of tambu.

Although the religious reasons for tambu are gone, many spiritual reasons to dance still exist. Tambu is believed to purify the body and spirit. So people dance for hours, sometimes to protect themselves from bad luck, or sometimes to assure that the good things in life continue. One dances, in other words, to cleanse oneself, *baila pa tira fuku afo*. To dance tambu, to dance the Curaçaon beliefs, brings luck. Another belief is that tambu will make it rain.

From Curaçao the tambu also went to Bonaire around 1806. Interestingly enough, tambu also traveled to Puerto Rico when some Curaçaons immigrated there. They kept the tambu alive and integrated it with the bomba. Alonso (1988, 67), in *El Gibaro*, mentions mulattos from Curaçao dancing their *garabato* but doesn't describe it more fully. Rosalia talks about ethnomusicologist Dusfrasne-González, who in his anthology of the bomba writes about the bomba holandés, the bomba rhythm from Curaçao, the fastest of the bomba rhythms. An important version is recorded on his record "Yo oi una" [I heard a voice]. In fact, the group on the record is from Curaçao and plays tambu with the instruments of the bomba. By now this version is considered Puerto Rican.

Curaçao, like Suriname, Haiti, and Jamaica, had Maroons, but rather than staying on the island the Curaçao Maroons fled to Venezuela. Luis Arturo Dominguez (1989), in *Vivencia de un rito Loango en el Tambú*, talks about tambu in the Venezuelan cities Coro, La Vela, and Puerto Cumarebo. This tambu was brought there by Maroons, still living there since the eighteenth century. They were called *loangos* or *gente de Guinea*, since all these approximately six hundred slaves who escaped from Curaçao to Venezuela were born in Africa. Not much of this tambu is maintained.

The oldest form of tambu is *tambu telelele*. Telelele is repeated with the variations *tolol
olo* and *talalala* for telelele. I think that Brazilian maculele and its accompanying songs also come from the same region. Many meanings are found in African languages for *tele* and *lele*. In Nigeria, in the Yoruba language, tele is to gather; in the Fon language of Benin it means to revolve. In Congo lele stands for a disinclination to work, and in Bini (Nigeria) lele means to follow (Rosalia 1997, 60). This *tele* form you can find in many African Diaspora cultures.

Social Aspects and Other Meanings of Tambu

In the winter of 1996 when I went home to teach a workshop with colleague and friend, choreographer Reggie Wilson, tambu was in full swing. The tambu period is from October till January, when the activities in preparation for Carnival take over everything else. The first tambu we went to was part of a traveling tambu, a tradition at the end of the year. Originally these tambus were done by walking, then in a wooden bus; nowadays, a normal bus drives around with some people following by car.

This traveling tambu is for luck, to purify oneself and to ask for blessings. The group travels to places where a tambu is held, at the homes of family and friends or at places just along the way.

We joined the tambu at a small house in the village of Seru Fortuna. Food had been cooked, rum was served, and a lot of dancing and drumming went on. From there we went to a house for the elderly, a spontaneous, unplanned stop. Reggie and I left already exhausted, planning to join the traveling tambu that night at Banda'bou at the other end of the island. We went there with my friend "Yuchi" Javier Cordoba, a well-known percussionist. Outside, in a large compound, more than a hundred people had gathered around the musicians, who had just started playing. People started dancing, some watched, and soon we and others followed into the dance. A few hours later, as time passed and alcohol consumption grew, most of the people participated. We left to go home. It had started raining. The others kept dancing. I then knew that they were really "in" it because Curaçaons don't like getting wet.

Reggie Wilson, who calls himself a lay anthropologist as well as a choreographer, has done fieldwork in Mississippi, Trinidad, and Zimbabwe, among other places. Before we ever went to a tambu, I played the music for him as an introduction. Asked about his perceptions and comparisons later, he said,

> My first perception when hearing the music was that I had no idea what the dance would look like. It is so fast, I would do a fast jumping dance to it. The music sounded back to front to me. Seeing the dance helped me contextualize the music. There was a clear connection to other Kongo-influenced dances such as the Kumina. I also drew comparisons to the basic step of the ring shout, the closed feet, shuffling step with circular pelvic movements. I was also reminded of the Kongo-style Haitian dances. It was also obvious to me that there was a cautious dialogue between the dancers, aware that they shouldn't dance. Although a secular dance now, a more religious meaning can still be detected, in the circle form and community participation. The dance itself kept on amazing me in the context of the music: I basically never saw anybody "wine" that fast.

Besides the caravan around the island, there is the *bandera* (flag) tradition. People write short texts on little flags made of colored paper. The texts are metaphors, rhetoric, or have a double meaning. Mostly the lyrics talk about well-known local people or events, without mentioning them by name, and are sold in town on the little flags. The tambu writer can use these texts to write the songs. Some texts are displayed on the house of the person they are meant for. Rosalia mentions an example of a text in which two women fight about a man. The other woman would answer with another bandera:

Bo kuchara den bo wea
Ki mishie den mi tayo.
Your spoon has to be in your pot
What does it do on my plate? (Rosalia 1997, 91)

In other tambus you can get news from the whole island when singers from all over the island talk about their communities. In the tambu everybody from seventeen years and up can play and sing. To sing you simply put your fingers on the lips of the one who is singing, or if you want to play, you put your hand on the instrument.

The tambu plays the important role of a tribunal of the people or people's court. One's punishment is to be put in the tambu. All aspects of society—teenage pregnancy, corruption, stealing of goats—are sung about. People who are fighting sometimes use tambu to come to a solution. By singing back and forth about each other, one can "sing out the fights" and have the opportunity to voice the anger and emotions. Many people, sometimes hundreds, come to such events. Mostly the fight will be resolved.

One of the biggest roles tambu has played, and still plays, is protest. Songs have protested discrimination, the introduction of military police, the Roman Catholic church, and the Dutch government. In the big slave uprising of 1795 tambu was played as well.

Tambu today still has that protest function; other songs talk about emancipation and independence, love and relationships. The bottom line is that the singer gets to talk about what s/he needs to talk about.

It is a miracle that tambu still exists today. As early as 1710, tambu was forbidden by law and persecuted, and only in 1952 was the complete ban lifted. But immediately all kinds of rules and regulations were made, making it difficult to even hold a tambu. As late as 1996 the rules were doubled, requiring permission to hold a tambu, and adding stipulations for hours, place, drinks, and so on, thereby re-emphasizing tambu's stigma. Of course many tambus have been constantly written to criticize this. The continual repression has had its toll, though. The religious function is all but gone from tambu; the sacred female voice is replaced by that of men. Women still sing, but they mostly have gone from a leading role to a supporting role. At tambus these days there is an audience; not everybody is participating anymore. The duration of the tambu period has shortened, pushing it close to December. Women by and large watch, because a "good" woman doesn't dance the tambu.

Meanwhile tambu is being recorded, and tambu groups are formed. Their music is played on the radio stations and sold in the record stores. When I go home now, I can listen to my favorite singer, Mistika from the group Zoyoyo, on the radio, her voice embracing me back, confirming that after all I am a *Yu'di Korsow*, a child of Curaçao.

Over the last few years I have come to understand what role tambu plays in my choreography. As a choreographer, I, like a tambu singer, comment on society, on love, on politics, on events that have happened. I use choreography to create a sphere where I can rebel and comment and create my own sense of nationhood. Most of the movements, as in tambu, begin with the hips, traveling down or up and, in my case, into the space.

My heritage informs both my artistic expressions and my worldview. And if I identify myself as Caribbean/Antillean, my world is a reflection of the complexity that comes from being a member of a crossroads culture, and from the multicultural baggage that it entails. In my movement vocabulary I look for a fusion of that tradition with my own personal language, contemporary modern dance and the organic, unexpected rhythms going on in the body. For my choreography I strive to tell a story, without the urge to explain the plot, or the need for the audience to "get" it. I cherish the questions and the unexpected. I aim to give voice to an intense desire to create something new out of what is already perceived to be fact. I don't try to re-create, but rather to blend all the ingredients or influences and make something new, something Creole in its truest sense. This is where my work is most typically Caribbean.

As a member of a crossroads culture, I am constantly negotiating the links between tradition and modernity, realism and the supernatural, colonial and postcolonial. Tambu is one of the important dance forms that links me to my heritage, and the hip movements of this dance, in various forms, appear in the movement vocabulary of my choreography. Like Charles Mimic I believe that "You don't make art, you find it. You accept everything as its material" (Cosentino 1995, quoting Mimic, 27).

$\diamond$ $\diamond$ $\diamond$

UNITED STATES–
CARIBBEAN CONNECTION

20

◇ ◇ ◇

Katherine Dunham's *Tropical Revue*

VèVè A. Clark

In dance history, Katherine Dunham is remembered as one of the primary trendsetters in Afro-American concert dance. Her major works, assembled in a variety of shows on and off Broadway, combined aspects of the American musical and techniques of European ballet with forms and rhythms of traditional cultures to produce dance drama of a characteristic and noteworthy kind. Trained in social anthropology under Robert Redfield at the University of Chicago, the recipient of a bachelor's degree in anthropology, Dunham instead chose dance as a vocation over the strict academic calling that seemed to some her destiny in the 1930s.

As a *performer*, Katherine Dunham began her stage career in Chicago, where she participated in community theater and regional ballet. As a *choreographer*, she organized, early on, a group of young women who danced with her in the Illinois area. Katherine Dunham was trained in classical ballet and modern dance and was particularly influenced by teachers she met in Chicago like Ludmilla Speranzeva of the Kamerny Theatre and Mark Turbyfill and Ruth Page of the Chicago Opera. Dunham's brother, Albert Dunham, Jr., and a friend founded the Little Theatre Group of Harper Avenue in which she participated. Dunham's Negro Dance Group dates from 1934. The details of Dunham's career have been documented in biographies by Ruth Biemiller (1969), Terry Harnan (1974), and Ruth Beckford (1979).

Though her best-known choreographies never entered the canon of American dance theater, in recent years some of the Dunham works have been performed by contemporary companies, such as the Alvin Ailey and

Cleo Parker Robinson dance companies. Until the time of the Gala Concert at Carnegie Hall in 1979, Dunham's choreography remained legendary—captured only in photographs, films, and reviews, recalled now and then by the older generation of theater enthusiasts. To reconstruct in full the theatrical qualities that distinguish the Dunham style, it may be instructive to follow the choreographer at work from the point of ethnographic research in the field through to performance on stage. If one studies the evolution and structure of one of her ballets in context, a concrete image of Dunham dance drama begins to emerge.

Between 1943 and 1962, Katherine Dunham and her company enjoyed no less than four runs on Broadway, engaged in two cross-country productions in the United States and Canada, and toured Europe three times, reaching audiences in South America, Scandinavia, the Middle East, and Asia in the process. Dunham the actress gained national acclaim in 1941 when she appeared as the scandalous Georgia Brown in *Cabin in the Sky*. It was impresario Sol Hurok who catapulted Dunham and Company to prominence when he produced *Tropical Revue* at the Martin Beck Theatre in the fall of 1943.

Hurok had met Dunham a year earlier in Hollywood when Howard Skinner, director of the San Francisco Opera and Symphony, suggested that Hurok consider sponsoring Dunham's work. Hurok came to a rehearsal and sufficiently admired what he saw to add Dunham's Afro-Caribbean dance dramas to his circuit of concert success. *Tropical Revue* was an immediate hit in the Hurok tradition. To meet the demands of the public, the show was extended in New York, even moved to a nearby theater when its term ran out at the Martin Beck (Hurok and Goode 1946, 287). In late 1943, the show began two successful years of road tours throughout North America. *Tropical Revue* became a landmark on Broadway in its treatment of African and Caribbean themes in an authentic environment.

Beneath the seemingly enthusiastic response to Dunham and her work, there lurked an ambivalent reaction that surfaced over the years after the initial success of *Tropical Revue*. It was difficult for many critics, especially some of the renowned dance reviewers of the day, to reconcile the conflicting responses they had to Dunham's theater work. Some went so far as to describe Dunham derisively as "a multiple personality." They could not unite in their minds her reputation as a scholar and anthropologist with the sizzling stage image she projected. These various views were summarized in a John Martin review, "The Dance: Dunham, Schoolmarm

Turned Siren or Vice Versa in 'Bal Negre' at the Belasco," in the *New York Times*, November 17, 1946.

Part of the responsibility for the duality must fall to Dunham herself. She often wrote or spoke about the conflict in these terms, saying in essence: "Should a good, middle-class Protestant professional woman, singled out by the Rosenwald and Guggenheim Foundations, appear as Georgia Brown on Broadway?" Certainly, there were other options open to a woman of her stature, intelligence, and upbringing. The prevailing opinion seemed to be that for Dunham to engage in theater as a performer rather than, say, a director/choreographer was a form of professional slumming. And so, many critiques of the Dunham shows fall into a dialectic that originates with Dunham's own persona (serious or sexy), then apply that supposed duality to her dance technique and, by association, to the whole of then-nascent Afro-American dance. The dialectic goes something like this: (1) A serious anthropologist is not expected to play erotic theater roles in public; (2) folk dance and ballet technique do not mix; (3) folk culture should remain pure of any theatricalizing tendencies.

The fundamental conflict that characterized reviews of Dunham shows was not a new one. But, by the early 1940s, the contradiction had become a standard measure that, through constant repetition and seeming logic, reduced the novelty of Dunham's works to a peculiar enigma. In what stands as the first extended critical analysis of the Dunham oeuvre, Joyce Aschenbrenner, an anthropologist at Southern Illinois University, has demonstrated the levels of conflict apparent in the reaction to Dunham's work in particular and to the forms of Afro-American theater as well. Aschenbrenner and her editor Patricia Rowe clearly state the racial overtones that underlie the dialectic just mentioned:

> The current decade has evidenced a renaissance of appreciation for Dunham . . . [in] persisting against social opinion that viewed black dancers' anatomical structures as incapable of balletic development and their compositional subject matter as restricted to licentiousness. (Rowe in Aschenbrenner 1981, ix)

The problem faced by black artists, then, was something of a double bind. If they operated within a limited artistic scope, failing to expand their ideas and skills, they were not taken seriously. Yet, if they ventured beyond the boundaries of their accepted "place," they were criticized for "inappropriate" expression (Aschenbrenner 1981, 44).

Looking back at Dunham's long career, a former acquaintance has provided a synthesis that clarifies and unifies some of the polar opposites many of Dunham's generation perceived but could not reconcile. Anthropologist emeritus St. Clair Drake, who knew Dunham at the University of Chicago where they were both students in the social sciences, has called Dunham an applied anthropologist when she worked in the theater. He has written:

> Katherine Dunham did not reject those distinctive aspects of black life that have entertainment value when presented on the stage. Rather, through intelligent choreography and careful attention to costume and setting, she transformed every performance into an edifying experience. She accomplished this without being didactic. (Drake in Aschenbrenner 1981, xi–xii)

One might wish that she had indeed been didactic. Perhaps if she had revealed the functions that these African-derived dances held in their home environment, it would have been possible for audiences and critics to appreciate the deeper psychological meanings where they saw only flesh and flash. The tendency in American dance circles not to take Dunham's choreography seriously is not a malicious oversight. The fact remains that in 1943 few dance historians were as literate as Dunham about Caribbean art forms. Millicent Hodson, in a 1978 article titled "How She Began Her Beguine, Dunham's Dance Literacy," has pointed out the profundity and diversity of Dunham's knowledge of Caribbean and Latin dance vocabulary derived from both European and African sources (Hodson 1978, 197–199). One wonders whether Dunham, having been so advanced, should have been more pragmatic, perhaps giving cues to her audiences in program notes or feature articles.

Several barriers prevented such an approach. There was the old double bind and the more immediate social need of tempering the effects of war. For a choreographer, who was also an anthropologist, to deal seriously on stage in 1943 with questions of cultural diversity did not coincide with prevailing taste. There is another obstacle as well, recalling the scholar versus club dancer debate, that must be considered. Dunham seems to have been adamant about the difference she perceived between authentic and theatrical representations of folk culture. In her lecture demonstrations at Yale and at the Royal Anthropological Society, in her thesis and in lengthy articles, she explored the social function of dance. During a presentation titled "Caribbean Backgrounds," the Dunham Experimental

Group of the Dunham School of Dance and Theatre gave just such an authentic display of Caribbean dances. The program took place at Howard University on June 26, 1947. Among the demonstrations were dance steps that had appeared in her Broadway revues: One was the creole mazurka or mazouk, and another *l'ag'ya* (in current creole, *ladja*) or fighting dance of Martinique. Syvilla Fort and Harold Gordon danced a traditional European mazurka, followed immediately by a demonstration of the French West Indian form. In the case of l'ag'ya, Dunham showed rare footage of *savate*, a French form of fighting with feet (which some believe influenced l'ag'ya) and l'ag'ya itself as Dunham filmed it in Martinique. The film version was followed by a danced demonstration (Clark and Wilkerson 1978, 103–104).

But when it came to her ballets, the famous ones like *L'Ag'Ya*, *Rites de Passage*, and *Shango* that were on one hand composites of actual dance rituals and on the other fictitious treatments often based on a story, Dunham made no claim to be totally ethnographic. In the concert halls and theaters, she expected her audiences to be enlightened and entertained by art, not anthropology. That she consciously separated ethnographic from artistic representation is clear. How she did it is the subject at hand.

What were, then, the anthropological roots of Dunham's dance dramas? She has written elsewhere of her interest in form and function in the dance (Dunham 1941, 1947). One might assume that this same symbiotic relationship existed in her own choreographies, inspired, as they were, by folk cultures of the Caribbean, notably from the four islands she visited between 1935 and 1936—Jamaica, Haiti, Martinique, and Trinidad. For the purposes of discussion, I have chosen a Dunham first: the first ballet she created based on research gathered during her trip; it was also her first full ballet and, incidentally, her favorite. *L'Ag'Ya*, derived from the Martinican fighting dance akin to African forms of wrestling, the French savate, and the Brazilian capoeira, was the title of Dunham's ballet as well as the dance that ended this thirty-two-minute-long work.

Set in Martinique, a favorite haunt of Paul Gauguin and writer Lafcadio Hearn, *L'Ag'Ya* premiered on January 27, 1938, performed by the Federal Theater Project's Chicago Unit. Besides the ag'ya fighting dance, the ballet included other uniquely Caribbean dances like the creole mazurka, the beguine, myal, and majumba. All were woven into an elaborate village setting of bright color, realistic decor, folk-derived music, and choreography. *L'Ag'Ya*, which stayed in the Dunham repertoire for two decades, was performed in *Tropical Revue* (1944), *Bal Nègre* (1946), and

Caribbean Rhapsody (1950), the succession of composite shows that put Dunham all over the map.

The 1950 program notes from the performance at the Broadway Theatre describe the plot of *L'Ag'Ya* in this way:

> The scene is Vauclin, a tiny 18th century fishing village in Martinique. Loulouse [played by Dunham] loves and is desired by Alcide [Vanoye Aikens]. Julot [Tommy Gomez or Wilbert Bradley], the villain repulsed by Loulouse and filled with hatred and desire for revenge, decides to seek the aid of the King of the Zombies [Lenwood Morris]. Deep in the jungle, Julot fearfully enters the lair of the Zombies and witnesses their strange rites which bring the dead back to life. Frightened, but remembering his purpose, Julot pursues King Zombie and obtains from him the "cambois," powerful love charm.
>
> The following evening: it is a time of gaiety, opening with the stately "Creole Mazurka" or "Mazouk" and moving into the uninhibited excitement of the Beguine. Into this scene enters Julot, horrifying the villagers when he exposes the coveted "cambois." Even Alcide is under its spell. Now begins the "Majumba," the love dance of ancient Africa. As Loulouse defies its powers, Alcide breaks loose from the villagers who protect him, and challenges Julot to the ag'ya. In Ag'Ya and its ending is the consummation of the forces released in superstition and violence. (Program notes from the Katherine Dunham Archives, East St. Louis, Ill.)

This is the simple action of the skeleton over which Dunham masterfully constructed levels of choreographic meaning. Moreover, the dance action is at times complemented or replaced by the music composed on folk themes by Robert Sanders or by the decor and the costumes designed by John Pratt, Dunham's husband.

The form of the ballet is *creole* in every sense of the term; that is, it is born of the American sensibility and mixes African and European elements. The classical European unities of place and time are strictly observed in a linear narrative that transpires within twenty-four hours in the single village of Vauclin. However, the narrative, told in mime and dance, is by no means linear in its telling; rather it is circular, characterized by numerous repetitious gestures and movements foreshadowed from scene to scene. The story of *L'Ag'Ya* unfolds like a folktale. In many ways, its choreographic form is similar to the unfolding of a story Dunham has told in writing, *Journey to Accompong*, the story of her research findings in Jamaica.

L'Ag'Ya begins during the morning hours once the fishermen have brought home their catch. Later that day, Julot goes off to the Jungle of Zombies seeking a love charm to entice Loulouse to him. The following day, at about the same time, early afternoon, Scene Three begins. In contrast to the opening scene, the last is a day of festival when work duties are put aside for the moment. The festival seems to be a carnival celebration when life is reversed as are the roles people daily play. Dunham has used the function of carnival reversal to link each of the three scenes, which reflect one another as through a mirror. Scene One, the market scene at the shore's edge, is reversed in Scene Two, the Zombie Forest: day workers versus night workers, rhythms of the right hand (the public good) versus the left hand (magic), the conscious mind contrasted with the unconscious. Scene One is the reversal of Scene Three, the Festival. Scene Two in the forest, again, is played in reverse of Scene Three: Bossal, or ancient, African-born, rhythms are followed by creole, or New World, steps; night turns into day, and the power of magic is transformed into imitation of the political power formerly demonstrated by colonial owners and their manners.

These three tableaux are linked by movement and its repetition. Scene One sets up all of the major steps in the ballet by having them suggested *en passant*. By the time they are repeated in Scenes Two and Three, they have created a familiar kinesthetic vocabulary that binds the action and translates for us cultural patterns that are unique to Vauclin. Scene One has shown us the relevance of the mazurka and l'ag'ya in everyday life, and has suggested the roles three specific movements will play from overture to final curtain.

These three movements are the focus of attention, and function virtually as characters in the ballet. Although we come to recognize the principal performers—Loulouse, Alcide, Julot, and the Zombie King—there is no development of their roles in the piece. Essentially, except for Loulouse under the spell of the love charm, the four remain the same. Dunham has created three identities that are dance movements with a life of their own in Martinican culture. Each of the three movements is introduced in Scene One. There is the second-position plié, which in African-derived cultures represents certain social functions. It is the gesture of the palaver (meeting), of trading, and of competition. We witness this posture several times throughout the ballet, beginning with the housewives and

Julot in Scene One, the zombies of Scene Two, and the cockfight and l'ag'ya of Scene Three.

The opposite social perspective is a lifted, almost aloof position. It is literally the position of power from which the Zombie King, seated on a raised platform, surveys the action, rocking in his chair and smoking a pipe. The zombies themselves are presented on two planes. Some lie on the ground, while others are presented as larger-than-life characters dancing on stilts—an effective metaphor to describe the degree to which zombiism is the peasant's ultimate hyperbole. In a sense, the magician, with his complete control of the villagers' destinies, has replaced the former plantation owner. Ironically though, he is dressed in the remnants of the colonial era—a black, tattered suitcoat, top hat, and tie. In Scene Three, the villagers pretend to be the colonizer when, dressed in costumes from eighteenth-century France, they mimic the dances of their former owners by executing a stately, but lively, creole mazurka.

The third movement is the hip roll. It is a gesture characteristic of market women bearing loads of produce on their heads. That same gesture again appears, representing the low-life dance of fertility, the beguine that, according to Dunham, is the undoing of the villagers (interviews with Katherine Dunham, June 11–12, 1980). They begin their festival with a courtly mazurka, and when the hypnotic rhythms of the drums sound, all pretensions cast aside, the dancers automatically roll their hips and grind together the licentious national dance of Martinique, the beguine.

Scene One: Critics who had come to expect a great unleashing of energy in Afro-American dance performance found the first scene of *L'Ag'Ya* uneventful and flat (see Martin 1946). In effect, it was meant to be so. It is in this scene that, through pantomime, Dunham established the workaday rhythms of the villagers and the personality of Vauclin, the town. This scene could have occurred on any weekday in the village. The fishermen of the big and little fish bring in their catches; porteresses descend to the shore, gossiping among themselves and bargaining on the way with the housewives come to the shore's edge to buy. Fishermen are distinguished by their costumes and by the gesture of falling and rolling backward, pulling in their catch from the sea—a movement that again appears in the ag'ya section of Scene Three. Housewives dressed in white layered skirts gather in second position plié to gossip. Their roles are highlighted by the large hats and particularly the broad hand baskets in which they will carry the fish back home. The porteresses, on the other hand, are unique. Dressed in black, they reflect the image of women laborers in mourning so prevalent in Caribbean and Latin societies. (The details of choreography, lighting, and costume have been reconstructed in interviews with Katherine Dunham and John Pratt in June 1980 and May 1981 and from production-book descriptions by Giovanella Zannoni.)

The whole of the scene represents an ordered disorder characteristic of marketplaces in the Caribbean. There is a sense of safety and cohesion, of expectancy, light humor, and playfulness in this scene. That the critics were not moved by the scene, that they may even have been a little bored by it was intentional. Dunham had learned from the villagers that daily life, where so much of its living was either banned for religious reasons or disdained by custom, was monotonous. One could look for excitement, especially in the dance, only in designated areas or on official occasions set apart for festivities.

In this scene, Dunham astutely presages gestures that carry more eventful action in later scenes. When Loulouse and Alcide end their pas de deux, they execute a few mazurka steps. When Julot interrupts their musing by reaching for Loulouse's feet, he and Alcide confront each other with l'ag'ya heelsteps. These two dances figure prominently in Scene Three. Alcide and Julot would have begun to fight on the spot had not Loulouse pulled her lover offstage to the right. The scene ends with Julot in wide second position, plotting his treachery. All of the above is acted with a minimum of sound, some music, but is communicated mainly through gesture, creole dialogue, lighting, and costume. The crisp white of the costumes, the blue lighting, and the black-and-yellow costumes of the market women contrast dramatically with the decor of Scene Two.

Scene Two: John Pratt's jungle scrim is lowered behind the raised platform on which the Zombie King sits rocking in his chair. Green dominates the lighting and black the costumes. Zombie women are dressed in voile, semi-empire long dresses; the men are in white voile sailor pants and long-sleeved shirts open at the chest. Several dimensions of action are created by the raised platform, zombies on stilts, and others lying on the ground as though newly risen from the grave. These zombies lift themselves periodically with one leg extended. The theater is filled with the sound of animal cries and frightening noises intermittently joined by the cascading cackles of the Zombie King himself. Into this scene backs Julot, as though only a matter of minutes separates Scene One from Scene Two.

The stage remains semidark, lit primarily by green baby footlights and shafts of light, ominous and unreal, cutting through the jungle scrim behind.

The choreography of this scene is minimal; the action subdued. The forest comes to life, so to speak, midway into the scene during the zombie dance. The action in the dance is directed by the drum, which seems to summon these rigid bodies to dance. The zombies are entranced, and one gets the feeling that their possession is caused not only by some herbal poison but also by the hypnotic call of the resounding drum section. Dunham uses the second position once again, accompanied here by stiff elbows and quivering hands again, held at right angles to the body. The movement used is a combination of a secret dance she witnessed in Jamaica complemented by a Cuban habanera, which has been described by Kurt Sachs as "measured crossing and flexing steps with dramatic pauses in the midst of a glide" (Sachs 1937). In a June 1980 interview in East St. Louis, Dunham described the scene in this way:

> Julot is so frightened at the apparition of these zombies rising and coming toward him that he falls in one corner of the stage in what very well may be a crisis of hysteria. He lies trembling while the zombies do their dance. The zombies are in that second position, that I use a great deal . . . and they move back and forth, right and left in a hopping step. This movement came from the Myal dance of the Maroon people in Jamaica. It was one of the few old dances that I was able to see at all. This was the night when I got my only drum from the Maroons, and someone playing the drum must have brought up this particular rhythm—as you know, the use of drums was denied all over Jamaica, excepting among the shepherds of the Protestant groups. But because I had a new drum made there, they were playing it and this old woman approached a man in second position, and was actually in a trance state, and together they moved side to side. It was as though they were defying each other to get closer. I chose a habanera here, too, to add a sinister feeling to the scene. The zombies perform this habanera, a high point of the ballet, as a dance of seduction. At the end, they strangle each other and fall back to the floor once again.

The second position plié, which is fundamental to the Zombie dance, prefigures a similar act of defiance and competition in the ag'ya of Scene Three.

Scene Three: Whereas the first two scenes are limited to pantomime and a few significant dance movements, the third scene is far more lively. The ethnographic detail captured in the contrast is important, for it was only on festival days, like the one I am about to analyze, that the village of Vauclin was permitted to come alive—its inhabitants released momentarily from the routine of work rhythms. (See Katherine Dunham's stories, published under the pseudonym Kay Dunn, "La Boule Blanche" and "L'Ag'Ya of Martinique," in *Esquire* magazine, September and November 1939.) Even the zombies of Scene Two are workers of a sort, controlled by the magician. Scene Three opens in bright light to the sound of greetings and merriment.

Loulouse and Alcide have been absent since Scene One. Their presence, especially that of Loulouse, now takes prominence, and costume is particularly revealing of character here. Throughout the ballet, Loulouse has been dressed in the many petticoats, the embroidered blouse, and the madras headpiece of a young Martinican girl. On the island, headdresses, like the forms of scarification in Africa, are a mode of identification. In Martinique, the headdress serves as an indicator in mate selection. Lisa Lekis in her book, *Dancing Gods*, has shown the meaning of the custom:

> The number of points in the hat is traditional and important, for Martinique and Guadeloupe are literally the lands of the talking hats.
>
> The number of ends or points projecting from the madras tell any interested young man the exact status of the lady and may be interpreted like this:
>
> Un bout: Je suis libre, coeur à prendre. [One point: I am free, take my heart.] . . . .
>
> Deux bouts: Coeur déjà pris, tu arrives trop tard. [Two points: My heart is taken, you arrived too late.]
>
> Trois bouts: Doudou! Il y a encore de la place pour toi! [Three points: Darling! There is still room left for you.] (Lekis 1960, 157)

From the beginning of the ballet, Loulouse has worn a one point madras, which indicates to both Alcide and Julot her availability. As the ballet progresses, we know that she prefers Alcide and that Julot will attempt to seduce her by means of the bought love charm. The undoing of Loulouse is foreshadowed in Scene Three by the social undoing of the entire village. Gathered in their finest creole clothing in order to celebrate a carnival of sorts, the villagers dance a stately mazurka, bowing in rows to each other, scuffing the earth with their heels and toes. The orchestra plays a mazurka; ladies fan themselves, whirling their skirts about. Loulouse and Alcide enter from stage left to join the dance and are cheered by the villagers.

As Alcide and Loulouse finish a pas de deux, Alcide lifts Loulouse on his shoulders, and they exit stage left. In their absence, the drum changes the feel and tempo of the dance into the beguine. It is danced here in contredanse, four lines across the stage at the cardinal points. Loulouse and Alcide rejoin the cast, but stand aside not joining in. Dunham has set these two characters apart from the others. There is no explanation, but one feels that because of their mutual attraction, they are unaffected by the pretensions and the mate selection of the corps de ballet. The other members of the cast, hypnotized by the drum, allow themselves the total abandon of the smooth bump and grind of the Martinican beguine.

In her choreography, Dunham has reversed the sequence of dances that one would expect to see at the two notorious dancehalls of Fort-de-France, the Palais Schoelcher and the Boule Blanche. To cool off couples locked in the trance-like erotic rhythms of the beguine, the orchestra generally would play a mazurka or some other formal dance step (Leaf 1948, 161). In this case, Dunham has changed the order to emphasize the stripping, so to speak, of the villagers dressed up in the costumes of their former owners.

The beguine is a dance of fecundity, according to Dunham (1939b, 93), as is the ancient form of the mazurka—the scuffing of the ground represents what was once a dance of earthly salutation (Sachs 1937, 86, 440). The Polish mazurka, brought by the French to the colonies, is followed by an African version of the same ritual of fertility, men and women dancing what Dunham has described elsewhere as a dance of mate selection (Dunham 1941; 1947, 44–45, 54, 57–58). Just as the villagers have reached a point of high eroticism, Julot enters with the cambois love charm in hand, and the stage falls into a hush.

The remainder of the scene will be the undoing, literally, of Loulouse and Alcide, who dies at the very end of the ballet. The corps de ballet, entranced by the spell, remains motionless while Alcide, held by two villagers, himself falls victim to the trance. Only Loulouse and Julot are free to move about. Julot, crouched in a semifighting stance (the deep second position), encircles Loulouse who, center stage, begins to dance a majumba, a Brazilian sacred dance of possession controlled by the charm and drum. A song to Yemanjá, the goddess of fertility, is intoned in the background. As the drums gather in intensity, the formerly aloof Loulouse reveals herself by slowly removing the layers of petticoats she has been wearing since the beginning of the scene. Like her village counterparts, she too demeans herself. When she reaches the last petticoat, as Julot is about to embrace her, Alcide breaks free from the charm and separates Julot from Loulouse. The villagers call for l'ag'ya, the drum takes up the rhythm, and the two men enter into the rocking, wide second-position stance of the fighting dance. During the course of the battle, Julot jumps on Alcide's back, breaks it, and leaves Alcide to die at center stage.

As Dunham (1939a, 126) reported in her own writing such matches generally do not lead to death in Martinique. That Alcide dies as a result of the altercation means that a competition usually controlled by a singer and the beat of the drum has been overpowered by some supernatural force. Having broken with custom, Julot has become an outcast in the village and runs off in fear. The stunned villagers back away gently in a disorder that contrasts with the orderly disorder of the crowd in Scene One. Loulouse grieves over the dead body of Alcide, ending the ballet in an arabesque in relevé over his body. The lighting has returned to the original blue of the earlier scene as the curtain closes on the two lovers.

In late September of 1943 when *Tropical Revue* opened at the Martin Beck Theatre, it is curious to note that Dunham's favorite ballet, one that had never been performed in New York before this time, had been excluded from the repertoire. Hurok, the producer, who preferred a review of exotic but light materials, felt *L'Ag'Ya* was just too heavy for a wartime audience. A new ballet, upbeat and much more universal in appeal, *Rites de Passage*, became the major item during the Broadway run of *Tropical Revue*, and continued to fill that bill until December of 1944. However, it was *Rites de Passage* that caused *Tropical Revue* to be banned in Boston as the company toured. Dunham was unable to use *L'Ag'Ya* until the company performed at the Locust Street Theatre in Philadelphia in December of 1944. By that time, the entire *Tropical Revue* program had become less Hurok and more Dunham. The former variety show format of eight divisions was reduced to three: Primitive and Latin Rhythms, Creole Dances, and Plantation Dances.

L'Ag'Ya became a standard piece in the Dunham repertoire after that time. During the remainder of the *Tropical Revue* tour in 1944 and 1945, the Company underwent such a degree of external and internal turmoil that Dunham was prompted in retrospect to refer to the group as a "floating island of négritude" (interviews with Katherine Dunham, June 1980).

The cast would arrive in major American cities to find that room reservations in first-rate hotels were denied them because of their color. *Tropical Revue* left in its wake a history of lawsuits brought by Dunham against these establishments and a less well-documented story of the black boarding houses in which the company was forced to reside.

By the beginning of the third year of *Tropical Revue*, Hurok had begun his usual tactic of reducing decor and orchestra in order to capitalize on an already well-advertised show. Dunham, knowing that the accoutrements she used were central to the telling of her ballets, refused to play in front of a black velvet curtain to the sound of one or two pianos (Beckford 1979, 54). She felt it was unfair, even unethical to her audiences, who were paying to see the Company as they had appeared the year before. She offered to buy her contract from Hurok, who agreed. By 1945, Dunham and Company were on their own.

The internal metamorphosis of the Dunham Company is of primary interest regarding the evolution of their repertoire. Not only were there significant losses in the Company, notably the leave-taking of principal dancers like Talley Beatty and Tommy Gomez, but there was the constant influx of new performers who had to be trained. The Dunham School became, as of 1945, the center for Dunham's technique of dance and theater. As noted earlier, an experimental group within the Dunham School, having learned the authentic dances as Dunham had experienced them in the field, often accompanied her during lectures to demonstrate both the original folk version and the Dunham choreography that derived from it.

Dunham taught the deeper functions of African, Asian, and Caribbean dances to her Company in a variety of ways. There was, of course, the Dunham Technique of warm-ups and patterns. There were also scheduled rehearsals and an impromptu critique during each intermission of a performance. From the beginning of the Company's existence, Dunham had used the films she made during her Caribbean research trip as a teaching tool. Through film, Dunham Technique in dance, the critique of choreography, and use of authentic costuming and props, Dunham passed on her own dance education to her cast. The chasm that separated her knowledge from that of her Company and audience was significant. In the early 1940s, little had been written on the dances of the French Caribbean, for instance. It was not until 1948 and as late as 1960 that scholars other than Dunham wrote on the subject—Earl Leaf, Maya Deren, Lavinia Williams, and Lisa Lekis, to name the most well known.

The Dunham School of Dance and Theatre was also the base from which the Company toured fifty-seven countries in two decades. How the dances, particularly *L'Ag'Ya*, evolved over the years, influenced by the audiences before which they were performed, deserves future attention. At this writing, it is known that the audiences most impressed by *L'Ag'Ya* were those in Spain and Japan, where traditions of martial dance survive intact (interviews with Dunham, June 1980).

Katherine Dunham's contributions to American theater have been singled out in various writings about her life. Much of the attention she has received is as a precursor of modern black dance and as an inventor of a mass of choreography. Little has been written about her artistic contributions to American dance theater. In order to arrive at such conclusions about her work in general, one might begin with the preceding structural analysis of one particular ballet and, once the dance vocabulary is recognized, compare the stage version with an original filmed version—if it exists. In this case there is l'ag'ya that Dunham filmed in 1936. The details of the vocabulary can be studied in depth for *L'Ag'Ya* because two versions of the stage performance were also filmed—one in the United States (1944) and another in Paris (1948). (Roy Thomas, who has viewed all three of these versions of l'ag'ya, published an interesting analysis of them in "Focal Rites: New Dance Dominions" in Clark and Wilkerson 1978, 112–116.) A study of all four elements may provide an illuminating commentary on the facts of Dunham's theater artistry. The forty years since *Tropical Revue* first showed *L'Ag'Ya* will be celebrated in December of 1984. Perhaps theater scholarship will have caught up with Dunham's dance literacy by then. If the analyses are forthcoming, if Dunham succeeds in reconstructing the choreography, John Pratt the costumes and decor, and together they recreate some of the excitement of *L'Ag'Ya*, the ballet can be presented before an audience that is as well-informed as Dunham was when the ballet was originally produced.

"Katherine Dunham's *Tropical Revue*" was first published in *Black American Literature Forum*, vol. 16 (4), winter 1982, and republished in *Caribe: Special Dance Issue*, vol. 7 (1 and 2), 1983.

In December 1987 the Alvin Ailey American Dance Theater premiered its full evening program, *The Magic of Katherine Dunham*, choreographed, staged, and directed by Katherine Dunham, introducing her work to a new generation. *L'Ag'Ya*, which made up the second act, was a highlight.

21

❖ ❖ ❖

Islands Refracted

Recent Dance on Caribbean Themes in New York

Susanna Sloat

In pan-Caribbean New York City, hundreds of thousands of people from Spanish, English, and French (or Kreyol) speaking islands come together to contribute vitally to the city's vibrant cultural mix. In a city of many cultures, Caribbean people and their descendants make up perhaps a quarter of the population. Island music and dance percolate throughout—in social and religious settings, in the very streets themselves, and in the concert halls. I've been on the lookout for dance that reflects the Caribbean that finds its way to those halls, whether they're as large as City Center or the Brooklyn Center for the Performing Arts, as central to the city's dance life as the Joyce Theater, as intimate as Dance Theater Workshop, as unexpected as a cathedral. The following reports are just a sample, just the tip of the iceberg.

In discussing the dance of the islands themselves, the authors in this book seem to move immediately to the political, social, and cultural conditions that formed and are still forming the backdrop into which dance is embedded. Dance on stage, however, particularly postmodern dance with its suggestive make-up-your-own-story ethos, is presented as art in a gallery, as opposed to in a church or a well-signed museum: without context. In describing what I see, I try not to impose too much meaning, but to let meaning come out of what is shown. Sometimes, as on the stage itself, there are few clues. At other times much is suggestive, but at the same time ambiguous, open to many possible interpretations. What audiences lacking knowledge of Caribbean cultures take away from certain dances may not be what their makers intended—but that is a given under most performance conditions, one with which many artists, hoping for maximum reverberation, are comfortable.

In discussing specific dances at length I have mostly concentrated on those in which the Caribbean content is explicit, choosing works of scope and penetration, rather than dances where it is merely spice or those in which movement has been extracted from Caribbean forms. Such extractions can be a very interesting and attractive base for fresh movement forms, though because of convergences between African dance, African-American vernacular movement, and modern dance isolations with Caribbean movements, it can be difficult to assess the Caribbean content unless its use is extensive or explicit. Such convergences are common in the work of African-American as well as Caribbean dance makers. In the dances of choreographers of Caribbean background, whether of an older generation like Donald McKayle or Joan Miller or younger postmodernists such as Cynthia Oliver and Gabri Christa, both authors in this book, clear Caribbeanisms keep cropping up, sometimes in extensive sections, sometimes as persistent punctuation of or integration with modern or postmodern dance movement. Such is also the case with African-American choreographers oriented toward Caribbean dance culture such as Reggie Wilson or Jawole Willa Jo Zollar, director of Urban Bush Women. It's enjoyable to see how Zollar deploys Afro-Caribbean movement to American jazz in *C♯ Street—B♭ Avenue*, made for the Alvin Ailey company's December 1999 season—it's a slightly reordered, but applicable universe of movement, and it fits.

Puerto Rican, or Nuyorican, expression of identity in dance can take diverse and sometimes surprising forms. Sandra Rivera, whose 1993 *Ancestral Spirits* was about her Caribbean ancestry, evoked in three sections incorporating Native American, flamenco, and Afro-Caribbean movement respectively, has moved on to strikingly expressive liturgical dance at the Cathedral of St. John the Divine, in modern dance portraits of female saints and flamenco meditations, capturing both the changing moods and emotional fervor of faith. Sometimes it's all in the title. Arthur Aviles's *Puerto Rican Faggot from the South Bronx Steals Precious Object from Giuliani's East Village* is one cape-covered long swirl of a dance, until he reveals his nakedness. Yanira Castro + Company made a group dance, *laugh to the color fishes*, about postmodern movement, not identity, but which, nevertheless, seems to give us tropical fish.

Companies like Ailey or Ballet Hispanico, in which dancers are trained for it, do well by Caribbean movement, which isn't necessarily the case when modern dance companies without any special ties to Caribbean, African, or African-American movement attempt to inject something from the islands. Then it becomes clear that Caribbean torso refinements are hard to keep up and do smoothly; that the subtleties of social dances can easily escape dancers well trained in other styles. Nonetheless European American choreographers are attracted to Caribbean dance movement, particularly that of social dances, whose appearance is often a signal of or symbol for fun. So common is this that it even crops up in the work of a quirky and rigorous postmodernist like John Jasperse, who inserts a brief Latin solo dance into his 1995 *Excessories*. Much better Latin dance is an important part of a more eclectic postmodernist's *Appropriate Behavior: Further Lessons in Dance History*, in which David Neumann looks back to his own club dance history, joined by two club dancemaster collaborators, Archie Burnett and Bravo La Fortune, both of Caribbean extraction. Here we're reminded that Caribbean New York is a very important contributor to the evolution of vernacular dance in the city—not just to salsa, but to forms as disparate as the hustle and hip-hop breaking and popping and locking.

Caribbean dance can be irresistible to Europeans, too. Pina Bausch made *Danzon*, incorporating a little of that Cuban social dance form into her tanztheater. In *Paradis* the Compagnie Montalvo-Hervieu uses a hip-rolling Guadeloupe-born dancer to tie together sections from French North African hip-hoppers, a dancer from Cameroon, and European dancers trained in modern dance and ballet. Also from France, the half Cameroonian choreographer Fred Bendongué, who has dancers of Caribbean background in his Compagnie Azanie, shows how a European-based choreographer alert to the hybrid complexities of the New World can embody them in dance. In *As Seen With One Eye* [A la vue d'un seul oeil], seen in Brooklyn in June 1996, Bendongué combined capoeira, tap dance, and other African-influenced movement into an inventive modern dance that explored, with haunting depth and intensity, an escape by slaves into a Latin American or Caribbean forest.

Very substantial use of Caribbean movement is made in the works discussed below, most made by choreographers of Caribbean background, who dig into aspects of Caribbean societies they know, love, and fear for.

Spiritual Realms—Haiti

Poor and troubled, Haiti is rich in dance, and non-Haitians also like to make use of some of these riches. Choreographers are attracted especially to the Vodou dances, banda, with its bent-knees moving in and out as the dancer rolls abdomen and pelvis to suggest erotic life-giving force in the midst of death, and yanvalou, the very beautiful undulant dance of Damballah, the benign serpent deity or *loa* (*lwa* in current Kreyol). Yanvalou, in particular, turns up in some unexpected contexts, such as the ballet *Lambarena*, which Val Caniparoli made for the San Francisco Ballet and which I saw in New York in November 1995. Supposedly a mixture of the African and ballet, it incorporates as one of its highlights a richly snaking solo of yanvalou movements for a male dancer.

But banda and yanvalou are not always taken out of context and used for their special movement content alone. *The Life and Legend of Marie Le Veau*, choreographed in 1986 by Abdel Salaam for his company Forces of Nature, tells a complex story of the most celebrated nineteenth-century Vodou priestess in New Orleans through modern and African-Caribbean dance movement. With only a little mime, Salaam develops the drama in such a way that its climactic set pieces are made up of these two Vodou ritual dances, banda and yanvalou. Not that there isn't vivid dance and building drama before—priestesses make the quivering ill rise with strength; dancers with scarves or whirling legs congregate to dance in Congo Square; the lame and spastic come to be cured by Marie, danced with marvelous nuance by Dyane Harvey when I last saw the piece in September 1997.

Marie's rivals test her powers and show off their own so skillfully that she is nearly overcome. These rivals have strong dramatic presences and multiple dancing skills—from powerful modern dance to shaking-headed, flexed-kneed Haitian. Marie's final test is to raise a man whom Guede, loa of death, plans to take. Dina Wright as Guede gives us a terrific rolling-hipped, kicking-legged banda. With insouciant jumps, or wrenching but graceful convolutions of a whole, horizontal body, or a leg raised over the man with quivering power, the rivals attempt to wrest the man from death, but Guede bests them. Marie calls on the other loas before she lifts herself over and rolls over him, and pushes food, water, and life into him. Guede hits him down. Tension is maximal. In his traditional guise, Guede drinks and sprays liquid around the stage, as Marie raises her arms and the man again staggers up to life.

Her power acknowledged by the other priestesses, Marie calls on the loas Damballah Huedo and his consort Aida Huedo in thanks, and the stage fills with their beautifully supple, snaking and wave-making dance, yanvalou. Salaam choreographs a particularly lovely and elaborate group version of this dance for the white-clad dancers, the group itself curling around like a snake. With undulant backs they circle, break, and circle back. The dancers weave down until only Marie is standing, before the waves continue.

I saw another notable Haitian dance drama, Geoffrey Holder's *The Prodigal Prince*, revived by the Alvin Ailey company in December 1998, when the American Museum of Natural History's Vodou show was on, a fascinating exhibition that drew attention to the extremely complex weaving of African religions, Roman Catholicism, and other elements into the syncretized fabric of Haitian neo-African Vodou. At the museum, presentations of folkloric groups like Jean Léon Destiné's dance company and the Ibo Dancers as well as a series of lectures supplemented the exhibit, at which Haitian guides were available to explain aspects of Vodou to visitors. Destiné's show revealed a notably good choreographer, producing beautifully designed dances that capture folkloric movement, extend it with related movement, but always return to it, so that the dance is enlarged, theatricalized, yet remains essentially folkloric. Active as a choreographer since the 1940s, he is part of a generation, including Igor Moiseyev in the Soviet Union, Katherine Dunham in the United States, Beryl McBurnie in Trinidad, Ivy Baxter in Jamaica, and René Carrasco in the Dominican Republic, that brought folklore to theater stages around the world.

Different is the approach to Caribbean spiritual themes and dance taken by Geoffrey Holder, the veteran Trinidad-born choreographer, in works made for the Alvin Ailey American Dance Theater in 1968 and Dance Theatre of Harlem in 1974 and 1982, but revived in recent seasons at City Center by those two companies. These are big-stage companies with dancers with prodigious techniques, and no one fills a big stage more sumptuously than Holder. His *The Prodigal Prince* for Ailey and *Banda* for DTH integrate Haitian Vodou rhythms, loas, and dance into fabulous modern dance spectacles telling compelling stories of Haiti with the saturated colors and integrated design sense of Holder's simultaneous painter's and choreographer's eye. Holder's *Dougla* is a similarly vivacious pageant of a dance, celebrating the marriage of African and East Indian strains in Trinidad, though the Indian is hinted at and the African is as explicit here as it is in *The Prodigal Prince* and *Banda*.

The entrancing revival of *The Prodigal Prince*, which I saw in December 1998, mixes styles, combining elegant modern dance with stylized Haitian dance enlarged for the big stage. Invoking the imaginative life of Haitian painter Hector Hyppolite, it's a fabulous visionary spectacle, pulsing with color and swirling, ordered movement.

The multitalented Holder, who did the choreography, costumes, and recorded music for *The Prodigal Prince*, is also, like his subject, a painter and his painter's eye provides the washes of color and design that fill every moment of the piece. This is added to by the dramatically pictorial lighting designs and stage effects of Clifton Taylor. "Great gods cannot ride little horses," says the Haitian proverb quoted in the program and that applies not only to Hyppolite, a *houngan* or priest of Vodou ridden by or embodying the deities, the loas, but also to the spectacle and dance we see, which is not only vibrant, but also large scale. Whatever is happening, however many or few dancers are on stage, the eye feasts.

Drums play before the curtain is opened and then we hear Ave Maria. Starlight pinpricks are a backdrop until a vèvè pattern appears in the rear. By then we have been introduced to Erzulie Freda Dahomey, loa of love, here a majestic figure in turquoise robe, danced by Briana Reed. She and St. John the Baptist, Edward Franklin, imposing in green robe, dance with slow modern dance moves, every step carrying theatrical impact. But Hector Hyppolite, Matthew Rushing in red, the man whose 1943 vision these two were, is light when he jumps. Erzulie waves her arm, rolling her shoulders as she does, and as she leaves, she is sung about. Continuing "Conversation with the Gods," St. John the Baptist and Hyppolite confront each other with thrusting pelvises and dramatic, sometimes shaking or splaying hands. Rushing crouches and shivers his legs and, moving away, Franklin shivers his. Then, in a theatrical moment that is given time to sink in, St. John picks up Hyppolite. But soon Hyppolite is shaking and twisting on the floor.

Women with full white gowns with red trim roll and tumble in and form a procession carrying blue flags. St. John contracts; Hyppolite is on the floor. The percussion and song continue. Twirling the flags, the women do Afro-Caribbean steps, one leg to one side, then the other. The Mambo (priestess), Renee Robinson, presides over Hyppolite's body as St. John the Baptist stands or bends with supple shoulders and contracting thrusts. This visionary spectacle is beautiful in its colors and arrangements, with the sparkly blue flags slanted or pushed out and back like Caribbean waves. Men make quick obeisances around the body of

Hyppolite, supine in the center, with St. John and the Mambo on either side. Looking very tall, Erzulie enters, backed by a huge silvery white vèvè banner and a dancer in white with an arch of flowers. There are star points on the floor and a huge gold vèvè on the rear wall. That and the turquoise, green, red, and white costumes and the way Holder combines modern and Afro-Caribbean movement as if they belong together, make for a spectacular and truly visionary scene.

The slinky-hipped Rushing has already reached out to snatch something from Robinson, but now Franklin hoists him on his shoulders as Robinson jumps around him. When he's down, she waves a white feather over him. The principals move with striking modern dance movements. Three men in white with red knickers enter with long *rara* tubes—the horns of carnival music. Hyppolite arches back to a seated St. John the Baptist, presenting the white feather. We hear the deep horn notes and there are blue eyes on the backdrop. Dancers have brought in candles and placed them on the floor. St. John the Baptist is still making his case for Hyppolite. Bells ring as he whirls him around. Then, on the floor, Hyppolite watches St. John approach him with beautifully distinct isolations and then leave.

Erzulie, loa of love, enters in another, more primal form, wearing a headpiece of very tall feathers and a nude-seeming body suit crossed by bands of cowrie shells or painted dots resembling them, with a belt around her waist holding a box in front with a vèvè-like pattern. She is the essence of a seductive vision as Reed and Rushing dance together with slow moves and he crawls under her as she hinges back. He embraces her and she undulates. He arches back to her. She walks with a slinky shift around him. When he's upside down his pants drop to reveal a cowried dance belt with a white feather sticking up from it.

They embrace, but their visionary lovemaking will be witnessed, surrounded by more dramatic pageantry. To a new Haitian drum rhythm, a group of women in white skirts with black overrobes with white handprints on them do an Afro-Caribbean side step in and whirl out their huge red shawls, which also have red handprints. They do a high kicking dance around the lovers, who kiss. It's a moonlit scene. The Mambo returns in a pink shawl. The other women, in the rear, open and close their shawls like pulsing flowers. Hyppolite and Erzulie dance Haitian style with big kicks and undulant bodies, torsos shifting as they jump back. They skitter off, bodies shaking. An intense dreamy sensuality has pervaded their encounter.

The large-scale theater continues as dancers enter in wide yellow-orange pants, swirling huge yellow-orange stoles as they barrel turn. Their torsos are dark brown as are their fabric-covered faces, making them mysterious spirit figures as they do a strongly African-flavored dance with curling pelvises, swings, obeisances, and turns, alternating head glides and circling heads, their moves taken from folkloric dance, but bigger. Richard Witter, in a raffia costume with red ribbons, appears as the Spirit, an African ancestral figure of the type often seen in ceremonial dances. Proudly claiming his inheritance, Rushing returns, shaking his head, curving his shivery body in a Haitian way, but then he arabesques, a dancer rich and subtle in all his combined modes. All this time the women in the rear have been pulsing their red shawls. Now the others pulse their yellow-orange ones. Hyppolite jumps in; he and the Spirit and the others run in opposite circles, dancing in and out of the circle shaking heads. A procession of women appears with brown-shrouded heads and sumptuous red and gold banners that they swirl.

Everyone leaves except Hyppolite and the Spirit, though he also shakes his head and jumps off. We hear Ave Maria. Erzulie in her guise as Mary is back in turquoise and white. St. John the Baptist returns, stately in green, as Hyppolite dances with a feather. We've returned to the initial vision and its mysterious possibilities, but the communal pageantry continues with the bows. The Spirit split jumps. There are huge red umbrellas, a swirling spectacle of umbrellas, banners, shawls. The Spirit dances out to the front with big Haitian moves, then lashes out with bent-legged feats, ancestral Africa triumphant. We've been treated to a grand visionary realm, with conversations with gods, a sensual consummation with a goddess, a pulsing dream of a trip back to Africa, and a triumphant return to take up his inheritance. Folkloric dance, enlarged, has been used not to reconstruct ceremonies, but to invent visions of them. Combined with large-scale modern, the Ailey dancers, all extremely good, fill big roles with big, rich, nuanced dance. And Geoffrey Holder, in giving this to us, has been the biggest visionary of all.

Banda, which Holder made for Dance Theatre of Harlem in 1982, is another splendidly theatrical and dramatically pictorial evocation of Haitian spiritual life, mixing Haitian rhythms and Latin chant, large-scale, elastic folklore with the kicks, whirls, arabesques, and jumps of strongly etched theatrical dance. From a Catholic priest-led, cross-marked funeral procession with a child-sized coffin and a grieving mother, to the eventual entrance of Baron Samedi, emissary of Guede, who, in the person of the

Fig. 32. Matthew Rushing as Hyppolite in *The Prodigal Prince*. Choreography by Geoffrey Holder for the Alvin Ailey American Dance Theater. Photograph: Paul Kolnik. Courtesy of the Alvin Ailey American Dance Theater. Used by permission of Paul Kolnik, New York, N.Y.

superb Donald Williams, addresses the mother with a balletically sharp, clear, yet pelvically mobile, spectacular and elegant version of banda, this dramatically charged ballet is full of multiple riches.

Political Thrust—Haiti, Cuba, Puerto Rico

Staying with Haiti, let us turn to a work on a different scale, with a sharp political charge. Haitian movement as well as a tragic subject from recent Haitian history informs the second part of Eleo Pomare's striking and moving modern dance piece, *Rafts*, which premiered at Alice Tully Hall in March 1997. Much the longer section of this piece exploring the plight of immigrants, by a choreographer born in the Caribbean port of Cartegena, Colombia, "Radeau (Raft) Port au Prince to Guantanamo" is both beautiful and dire. Three women, all excellent, expressive dancers, shift, reach, revolve, collapse, and contract, searching for land on a turbulent sea. With impressive skill, Pomare takes them on a tumultuous, increasingly desperate journey that they dance for us with moves that show us the churning sea and the dimming of hope. Two men, American soldiers, front and rear, the front one nonchalantly cleaning a rifle, are utterly impassive as the women in the center struggle to stay afloat.

The program that the Conjunto Folklórico Nacional de Cuba brought to Brooklyn College in February 1996 was designed to showcase the wide range of Cuban folk music and dance, and for the most part its polished choreography followed often fascinating, but familiar folkloric troupe lines. But the last piece of the first half was unusual, not modern dance in its idiom, but nevertheless a powerful narrative, an impressive drama about the struggle against slavery built entirely from the rhythms and steps of the Afro-Cuban traditions of Arara and Palo.

Baile de los Apalencados, choreographed by Manolo Micler, inventively used ritual dances of African origin to build a drama of the fear and longing of escaped slaves (expressed in Arara) that is transformed into an assertion of strength and freedom through the dances of the Palo tradition. The dark stage had just enough light to suggest a campfire. It gave us the idea that the people, often kneeling, and down or up, shifting strong shoulders in the arm patterns of Arara—whose dance, rhythms, and chant suggest homesickness for Dahomey—were fugitives on the run.

The Palo dances of the Cuban Congo tradition are extremely emphatic, emphasizing power and masculine force with heaving chests, strong flung or pulling arms, bold speedy legs. As the company shifted into powerfully danced Palo, this assertiveness took over. It became even fiercer when the men began to dance with slashing *garabatos*, sticks that become weapons of anger and rebellion. All eyes were on the dark man with the white patch in his hair, Dionisio Paul, as he soloed with galvanizing ferocity. Another man also soloed with enormous energy and skill, becoming a worthy competitor. But it was Paul, I think, who shook his whole body until he fell to the floor. This entire dance built up into a potent surge into freedom.

Choreographers of Caribbean birth are not necessarily interested in addressing explicitly Caribbean themes, but Pepatián, the postmodern company of choreographer Merián Soto and visual artist Pepón Osorio, is—taking an angry political stance, for instance, in looking at their native Puerto Rico and its relationship to the United States in the full evening *Historias* of 1992. "Pelea de Gallos," a program of three dances that I saw both at Lincoln Center Out of Doors at the end of August 1998 and at the beginning of October 1998 at Hostos Center for the Arts and Culture in the Bronx, where the confines of the theater heightened the drama, intensity, and the fun, uses Cuban music and combined salsa, rumba, and other social dance with contemporary dance for the first two pieces, *Sacude* (Shake), a fiercely expressive solo of love for men gone awry, and *Revienta!*, a salsa carnival of a dance for seven. *Pelea de Gallos*, the concluding work, is a startling cockfight between male and female human birds that Merián Soto uses to make a vivid, fierce commentary on Puerto Rican society.

During intermission the enclosure for *Pelea de Gallos* [The Cock Fight] is set up. This 1998 piece, "brainstormed" by Merián Soto and Adal Maldonado, was directed by Soto, and choreographed by Soto with the collaboration of Niles Ford and Stephanie Tooman, though Terry Hollis danced in place of Ford. The set, designed by Maldonado, who also did the video of the cockfight that continues in back, is a cockfight arena put up with metal poles and mesh net. The net faces us, but the sides are open for entrances and exits. There are chairs for musicians and Puerto Rican drums. Milk crates at the sides are for the participatory audience. A Puerto Rican flag hangs in the rear, for this is a piece full of visceral excitement and sharp social commentary on methods of exploitation and their psychological and political consequences. With the audience of varying ages, the coaches, and betting, there's an air of stylized realism, so that *Pelea de Gallos* reflects Puerto Rican society as it criticizes it.

As lit by Roderick Murray, the set is quite beautiful. What happens at the cockfight is sometimes beautiful because the extremely accomplished dancers and their movements are, but as it progresses it becomes uglier and uglier. Stephanie Tooman is the white, female bird—sex and race are important here. She is tall, thin, and elegant in bra, shorts, and fluffy white cloth wings. She has a blue topknot on her white cap and her handler has a blue shirt, white pants, and white hat. She flutters like a cock, and he pushes her around as if he owns her, as the audience assembles and bets are made. The male cock, brown-skinned Terry Hollis, enters fluttering his feet and his white cloth wings. He, too, is tall, thin, and elegant, with a spray of bright orange atop the white cap on his head.

The Puerto Rican folkloric musicians include a clarinetist and make delightful music even as the cockfight gets more brutal. The male cock makes a series of high, bent-legged jumps as the fight begins. The handlers hold the cocks back. The two confront each other with pecking heads and flung up wings, and unison bent-legged jumps. When Tooman jumps atop Hollis she makes lots of nasty kicks as she rides his shoulders. They tumble over each other. When she falls we see that they're tied together by a string. In another confrontation she looks stunned, then he attacks her from the rear. She gets on his back and kicks him when he's down and staggers over him. Is she the winner? The referee is counting.

She preens, but it's not over. They flutter and he attacks her rear again. He staggers against her, fellow victims as the humans shout. These two elegant beings look drained as they go at each other for another round. She jumps onto his bent-over rear; he climbs her back. They fall down together and he gives her a peck. Body twisted, she struggles to get up and kicks him until he falls. They struggle, having lost their elegance—their feathers are tattered now. Their last blows are fruitless. She gets up and appears to be the winner, but then falls. Her handler looks upset, but it's certainly not out of compassion. Each cock is lifted and gets a kind of funeral procession to mournful clarinet. And then the next fight is called.

The human birds are deadly as programmed. Their moves are mimetic, but also stylized, and bear a relationship to folkloric dance. The birds are totally exploited, and Soto, a choreographer with a politically charged viewpoint, is surely thinking of other histories here—slavery, colonialism, the worst of capitalism. We see that the sense of ownership and investment means that, for the birds, victory is just as exhausting and deadly as defeat. But it's the immediacy of the piece that captures us.

Individuals and Community—Jamaica

On a program of six dances of the National Dance Theatre Company of Jamaica in May 1998 at Brooklyn College, the four by Rex Nettleford, the company's artistic director, reflected Jamaica in different ways. A protean figure in Jamaica's cultural and intellectual life, Nettleford also showed great range on this program, from the well-deployed, handsomely patterned *Drumscore* of 1979, which fuses the contracted and undulant chests and hips and shaken shoulders of Africa and the Caribbean with modern dance into a fluid, lush, big theatrical style, to the supple, slippery, slithery-hipped Jamaican vernacular that marks *Bujurama* to Buju Banton's reggae, to the company's 1971 signature folkloric spectacle on an Afro-Jamaican rite, *Kumina*, whose rich ranks of dancers gliding along in waves of tiny steps and small, precise revolutions of pelvis are led by Nettleford himself, subtlest of all in his control of tiny hip revolves and little pulses of chest. But it was *Tintinabulum*, a new piece by Nettleford, that seemed to encapsulate the largest swathe of contemporary Jamaican society in its dramatic sweep.

A complex, rich, and often beautiful and moving work, *Tintinabulum* is in an eclectic modern style with touches of Jamaican vernacular, like mobile chests, integrated into a mix that serves expansive storytelling. We hear bells to start—the title comes from one of the selections from Karl Jenkins' "Adiemus," a vocal and orchestral piece with some South African rhythms, that works well as a backdrop to this piece. With striking assemblages and richly embodied movements, we're introduced to three groups of people: three mothers in colorful dresses, three godmothers in long robes in back of them who seem to guide, and three sons.

As children the three play in a trio, box, show off acrobatic tricks, or jump up like basketball players. One whirls, jumps, and rolls on the floor. Another makes whirring-legged turns and tricky jumps on knees, whirling to the third man, who does split leaps. As adults the sons seem to have different fates, yet as they become embroiled with each other, share the same tragic one. One, the lover in red, is surrounded by a harem of four caressing women. A second in cutout black is the head of a gang of drug dealers, who seem to be looking for trouble, dancing with attitude. The third, in preacher's robe, is a minister, a peacemaker with a flock. The mothers whirl in or dance with their sons.

The drug dealers, who fight among themselves, are bad seeds within this society, setting off a chain of violence in which all the sons die. This

Fig. 33. National Dance Theatre of Jamaica in *Tintinabulum*. Choreography by Rex Nettleford. Photograph: Maria LaYacona. Used by permission of NDTC of Jamaica.

quickly escalating drama produces a shocking silence and a sad, handsome funeral scene. The three return as ghostly spirits to repeat their childhood clapping trio. Their mothers come in with undulant chests and the god-mothers are present, too, connecting with the dead they couldn't protect. *Tintinabulum* is richly and dramatically worked out, so that a whole society unfolds before us in strong group scenes, with the central figures, the sons, given enough individuality to make us grieve in shock, too.

The Afro-Caribbean, Afro-American, African, and modern converge in Jamaica-born Garth Fagan's work, just as they do in his history. As a teenager he toured with Ivy Baxter and the Jamaican National Dance Company and added to that the influences of Lavinia Williams, Pearl Primus, Martha Graham, Mary Hinkson, Alvin Ailey, and José Limon. In Garth Fagan Dance's season at the Joyce in November 1998, his choreography, in pieces from 1981 to a premier, reverberated with consolidation and mastery. Only in *Moth Dreams* from 1992 did he explicitly go back to Jamaica, with Fagan projecting the dreams of father and mother onto their son, ending with a zany, funny community scene. But the Caribbean, as well as Africa, is reflected in the inventive way Fagan makes movement, the way he follows long-held evolving balances with rapidly dislocating body parts, or has dancers swiftly reverse jumps with a twist in the air. A dancer might move across the stage contracting and twisting shoulders like an Afro-Caribbean arrow, or make a bucking jump with alternating fisted arms; bent bodies might have hips and legs that shake, or dip and undulate. Legs shimmer, snaking torsos roll, but maintain long lines.

When Fagan's master dancer and muse, Norwood Pennewell, solos to Thelonious Monk as the second part of *Moth Dreams*, "Their Dream (Son)," Pennewell's very virtuosity is nonchalant as he flings into bent-over turns, or balances into an attitude while quickly angling an arm, or jumps up with a swift twist of the body to one side or another. He keeps his cool as he moves through whatever's difficult, giving a jaunty feel that could be African American, but might just as easily be Jamaican, to this fabulous solo.

"Her Dream (Mother)" gives us characters—a hip-shifting possible bride who shifts her fur shrug with her shoulders, a hipster with a hat—a whole eleven-dancer village full of eccentrics who interact or wander this Jamaican community with springy legs and shifty, head- and shoulder-shaking, chest-jerking, jumping and spinning and flopping bodies. The assembled costumes are by Fagan, the streams of light that converge from the sides are by C. T. Oakes, and the peanut cart was donated by the Smithsonian after being in a Caribbean Festival Arts exhibition. Wynton Marsalis provides the marvelously buzzy music that sometimes sounds like bluesy Charles Mingus. Mom dreams up a community of individuals who go their own way, but even when they're flaky, they are a community and can get together. It's a lot of fun to be introduced to this dreamy, quirky Jamaican village, full of those casually elegant, shaking, and dancing characters.

Earlier on the same bill, in *Telling a Story* from 1989 to later Miles Davis, Fagan evokes home and family in his dedications—to "Jah love, Sir Miles," "For my mother and granddaughter" for a section for five women, and to "my father and grandson" for one for six men. But this is not a narrative, but a highly enjoyable piece in which Fagan shows his gift for inventing shapes and moves, displaying, repeating, and recombining them just as his dancers here shift and dislocate their body parts, then reassemble them, often while jumping or whirling. And in that approach to movement, he shows not only his own capacity for invention, but also his African Caribbean roots.

In "A Shorthand of Sensation," the women's section, Fagan uses the vocabulary he's invented for this piece like a set of cards newly dealt each time. From the opening solo through the groupings of two, three, four, or five, through a set of succeeding solo variations, through the final group of five, we see the familiar quick and slow contrasts in a varied idiom that Fagan keeps consistently fresh. Here, once again, are those long balances in which arms and legs and sometimes body move, changing the structure of the stance while the dancer stands on one foot. Three women do this at once to Miles's yearning horn, then quickly scuttle around, scuttling of various sorts being one of the motifs here. So are polyrhythmic body parts shifted rapidly. A quite amazing solo displaying those isolating parts as she flings herself around begins the series of remarkable solos in which tumbles or rolls on the floor, long extensions, and those dislocating bodies display similarities and differences in inventive new variants.

In "A Precis of Privilege," for the men, Fagan, the innovative shape maker and shape shifter, continues his body surprises, with the men dancing with great verve. To start, four men do various slow, extended, balancing moves to slow electric guitar sounds and long horn. In costumes by Zinda Williams, the women are in multicolored bras and tights and the four men are even more brightly colored figures in overshirts and tights, each in different colors, with contrasting leg warmers. The fifth man, in black, moves across the stage from left to right while the four others pose or move like spots of vibrant, childish color, toys to play with. A man in white moves past from right to left. Shaking legs, moving with flat backs, jumping with an arrow leg up or spraddle-legged, twisting with an upper torso spurting forward as the dancer moves and turns mark a series of rich, difficult solos to chugging band riffs. The men keep producing surprises of reassembly as Fagan works changes on the Afro-Caribbean dislocating body, using it in innovative, exacting ways.

Although I've concentrated on explicitly Caribbean subject matter— and the range of the fine works of dance drama I've selected is not only wide, but runs deep, burrowing into the heart of diverse aspects of Caribbean society, into the heart of the human condition—I wanted to end with that African-Caribbean dislocating body, with the sheer possibilities inherent in Caribbean movement. Other choreographers discussed use it in many different and satisfying ways; Fagan happens to be particularly inventive with it. To a dance-goer who enjoys shape-shifting, polyrhythmic bodies, and the subtleties and possibilities of the mobile torso, the potential embodied in the Caribbean's storehouse of movement is invigorating. One looks forward to its liberation and transformation by many future imaginative dancemakers.

22

◇ ◇ ◇

Teaching the People to Triumph Over Time

Notes from the World of Mambo

Robert Farris Thompson

Mambo is mid-century music. It kept the Americas dancing between 1949 and 1959. It bridged the gap between the rise of modern jazz, an art music leaving lindy in limbo, and the rise of rock dancing in the spring of 1956. In the process, it also revitalized the big band concept, which had languished in jazz, and inspired a body of music and choreography, distinguished and abiding. The music lives on, in the special hard-swinging portions of a salsa or merengue tune called the *mambo* section. And the dancing does too, in venues like Orchard Beach in New York City, or La Conga in Hollywood, or virtually anywhere in Miami. Sample its history, in a tale of four cities.

Havana

A brilliant black composer and instrumentalist, Orestes López, working in the leading danzón orchestra of Cuba in the summer of 1939, had a culturally brilliant inspiration. What would happen, he thought, if he brought one of the most important words in the classical religion of Kongo as practiced in Cuba, *mambo*, into the discourse of the dancehalls: "Orestes had observed local blacks devoted to the classical religion of Kongo [in Cuba] bring down the power of God and the force of the spirits with special altar songs called *mambos*. It was a word about words. In creolized Ki-Kongo mambo means important speech or conversation" (Thompson 1998, 10).

336

López suspected that if singing mambos in the Kongo religion of Cuba brought down spirits, then singing mambo from a bandstand might similarly activate a strong and vivid dance reaction. Which was exactly what happened, first on the bandstand—

> The syllables [of the word] first resounded in the clear, chanted strongly: *mambo! mambo! mambo! mambo!* Then, transformed into orchestral mantras, the chanted syllables traveled deep within the musicians' minds, to re-emerge as strongly syncopated two-note riffs on violins, bass, and piano. The result: *staccato incandescence.* (Thompson 1998, 10)

—and then on the dance floor itself. Couples split in two. Apart dancing in the African manner took over. This, in turn, resulted in wonderful changes in lead. The woman was free to dance around her partner and he was free to dance around her. She circles him. He circles her. She circles him right back. Mambo.

Guiding the entire orchestra into playing time, Orestes López had achieved *nothing less than the Africanization of one of the deepest conceits of the West, symphonic music, and the splitting asunder of the Western couple dance.*

Very soon thereafter other black composers, notably Arsenio Rodríguez and Dámaso Pérez Prado, were transcribing Orestes's violin riffs to trumpet (Arsenio) or to saxophone (Dámaso). When Pérez Prado moved from Havana to Mexico City in October 1949, where he had one of RCA Victor's finest recording studios at his disposal, his rich and witty mambo took on a life of its own. It made him—and the dance—world famous by the spring of 1951.

Earlier, in Cuba, mambo caused continual excitement on the dance floor. One of the mambo-inspired dances of the 1940s was "the commandos." It emerged ca. 1943 as a danced response to the allied commando raid on Dieppe on the coast of then-Nazi-occupied France. Dancers tapped out "V" for victory in Morse code, performing the commando mambo.

Then, in 1947, came another mambo dance, the *botecito* [little boat]. Winthrop Sargeant, writing for *Life* (October 6, 1947, 157), introduced North Americans to the phenomenon: "as danced in the music halls and on the streets of Havana, [*botecito*] is a thing of regimental proportions. . . . throngs of happy Cubans rock from side to side in a boat-like rhythm with their hands on their hips." Havana had translated the bounce of mambo riffing into a mirroring swing-and-sway. In addition, the challenge of the music mix—symphonic + Afro-Cuban + jazz—was countered by sass and self-confidence, indelibly communicated by arms akimbo. Meanwhile, thrilled by the all-black films of the early 1940s, *Cabin in the Sky* and *Stormy Weather*, Afro-Cuban dancers in Havana were blending lindy swing-outs and spins over the pelvic given of the rumba. That, too, was mambo. It predicted what would happen in Lima, Mexico City, and New York.

By April 1951 *Time* magazine, brash and patronizing, was reporting "a new dance craze sweeping the hemisphere. Part rumba and part jive [that is, jazz dance] with a strong dash of itching powder, the mambo had left unstormed only the tango strongholds of Argentina and the sambaland of Brazil. In all the other Americas, dancers quivered and kicked to the mambo beat" (April 9, 1951, 38).

But mambo was not a spasm. It was a revolutionary return to eternally true phrasings of the spirit. In linking up with the protocols of the classical religion of Kongo, the music revealed its history and distinction. And then, when it traveled to Peru and Mexico and Latino New York, it entered places already imbued with black cultural preparation, accelerating its acceptance and development.

Lima, 1951

In the capital of Peru, Kongo-inflected *peña* music graces the night in certain small clubs in the barrios of Miraflores and Barranco. Here that ubiquitous Kongo instrument, the *cajón* (hardwood box percussion instrument), reigns just as it does in the traditional rumbas of Havana and New York. Percussion-dominated dancing has in fact characterized Black Peru for centuries. As early as the 1790s a watercolorist was documenting black dancers in the streets of Trujillo, north of Lima. He showed them moving barefoot, in time to a creolized descendant of the Kongo scratcher, the *munkwaka*, plus Iberian guitar.

Cut to a photograph of a young man and woman mamboing in Lima, April 1951. Aware of the lindy, through film, and cognizant of bop mixed with swing in the Pérez Prado style of mambo blaring from every Lima radio, they improvise.

The young man, whose profile echoes the noble features of the Inca, "breaks" to the floor in rumba (ultimately Kongo) fashion. At the same time he wags his right forefinger in lindy "trucking" style. He leans back, way back, with head erect, relaxed and limber, showing off athletic poise and flexibility. In the process, he has combined two black styles in one, breaking and trucking. Mambo.

Meanwhile his partner, slim and ecstatic, dances with widely spread fingers and open mouth. She initiates a crossover, entirely independent of the man. She mambos with arms before her, palms in the air, as if, in her ecstasy, she is high-fiving heaven.

Mexico City, 1948

Cut to Mexico City, three years before. The classic Mexican film of 1948, *Salón México*, shows us clearly that Mexico City was aware of—and dancing to—the early danzón-mambos of Havana, hits like *Almendra* and *Sopa de Pichón*. Clearly perceptible is unmistakable mambo riffing, on piano, as Son Clave de Oro plays *Almendra*. There are tantalizing close-ups of the footwork. High heels flash and turn, in beautiful black and white.

Then something extraordinary takes place. A member of the orchestra takes his trumpet and "breaks" to the floor—like flutists in Kongo—and plays his instrument, prone on the ground. He rolls on the floor, his instrument still in his mouth. Approaching the camera, he slithers up, like Ka, the wise old serpent in the Alexander Korda film *Kipling's Jungle Book*. He is dancing his mambo while playing it on trumpet, in a deliberate confusion of roles recalling the totalizing performance rules of Central Africa.

Cut to 1949. By this time the incomparable Afro-Cuban *sonero* Beny Moré and the remarkable Afro-Cuban lyricist Justi Barretto are living on Meave Street, the mini-Harlem of Mexico City. There is a remarkable photograph from that year. It shows Justi and other black colleagues playing mambo on a stage in Mexico City. Beny Moré is with them. He points to a black Cuban, Silvestre, who is suavely "breaking" to the floor. Silvestre deep bends his right knee, while shooting out his left foot with capoeira-like assertion. Meanwhile, his partner, Amalia Aguilar, holds his left hand and smilingly supports him.

Who knew that in 1955, during the filming of *Mambo Madness* in New York, the entire orchestra of Tito Rodriguez would "break" and play their mambo in the prone. They took the culturally linked tendencies of Kongo, Lima, and Mexico City as far out as they could.

What these vignettes show us is that mambo clearly prepared the way for downrock (media term: "break dancing") in hip-hop. B-boyin' or downrock, as the dancers themselves call "breaking," perennially reflects a certain aspect of Puerto Rican New York mambo. Just look at the names in hip-hop choreography: Clemente, Molina, et al.

The New York Palladium: The Capital of Mambo in the 1950s

But "breaking" was a single aspect. Many styles form Latino New York mambo, a logical consequence of colliding mainland black and Caribbean modes of motion. The masters were Cubans and Puerto Ricans who had lived in New York for some time, who were fluent in two kinds of language. Recall that Brancusi was Rumanian and Picasso Spanish. Both moved to Paris, learned French, and found their true expression. Similarly, ambitious musicians, like Machito and Mario Bauzá, and ambitious dancers, like Anibal Vásquez, trekked up from Cuba and Puerto Rico to New York to find recognition in the "city of ambition." Their mambo was mambo, the Latin dance supreme.

How fortunate that Anatole Broyard, the brilliant African-American writer, caught fragments of their early work. In Broyard's (1993) phrasing, Cuban and Puerto Rican dancers taught New York how to "throw an arm around life and move with it."

Watching the dancers at the Park Plaza dance hall, Broyard sensed an extraordinary release, from sameness and restraint:

> Everybody in the Park Plaza—and there must have been two hundred people there—knew how to dance. In Afro-Cuban dancing one dragged the beat, like postponing orgasm, withholding assent, resisting, buying time. Nobody danced on the beat—nothing was ever that simple. Here at the Park Plaza, everyone skillfully toyed with the rhythm and *it was exciting to see so many people triumphing over time* [my italics]. (Broyard 1993: 116)

In the process, Broyard saw a man "break." He thought he fell. Then, noting an ending with a flourish, concluded that "he hadn't fallen at all."

The distance in mambo from the original sacred music that named and propelled it is never far. Broyard saw that, too. He witnessed a duet, between bongo and conga in the great band of Machito. This caused some dancers to fall to the floor, kneel there, eyes closed in ecstasy, and shout out to the players, *no! no!*, meaning please don't stop.

By 1950 all-out mambo moved from the Park Plaza to the Palladium at Broadway and 53rd. Mura Dehn was there in 1951 and promptly pronounced it "the most glamorous popular dance hall in New York." She saw amazing concentric circles of class and focus, an outer circle of rich visitors and celebrities seated at tables by the side of the dance floor, an inner circle of Latino and black dancing connoisseurs seated on the floor communally, and, in the sovereign center, the star dancers themselves. Such was the spatial logic of Palladium during Wednesday night contests and performances.

But even on Fridays, Saturdays, and Sundays, whenever the best dancers improvised, in the "corner of the experts," the southwest area reserved for the masters, African-like handclapping circles of standing admirers spontaneously took shape around them. Where and whenever these structures blossomed, they formed the ultimate accolade of mambo. "I cause circles," a Puerto Rican mamboist named Tommy Díaz pridefully told me in 1959, "when we dance people form a circle around us, me and my partner, clapping their hands, to drive us on to more."

Christopher Rand, in his book, *The Puerto Ricans*, wrote about the Palladium. He was impressed, too:

> In general I felt the Palladium had more gaiety and spirit than the run of New York night clubs, and my partner on excursions there agreed. The Puerto Ricans dominate the place, but there is usually a sprinkling of mainland whites and a goodly number of mainland [blacks]. (Rand 1958, 28)

Rand came to see the Wednesday night battles of dance:

> Sometimes there is a contest, staged with dramatic spotlighting, and several couples take part in it. Each couple has only an instant to show their stuff. Then the master of ceremonies [Joe Piro] holds a handkerchief over their heads, the crowd votes by clapping or booing; and the next couple comes on, lickety-split. (Rand 1958, 29)

But the central attraction was not the amateur contests, but watching spotlit house stars unfurl their mambo. They danced as couples, first together, then in two solos, then together again as finale. These stars of New York mambo—the Mambo Aces, Andrew Jerrick, Cuban Pete and Millie, the Cha-Cha Taps, Ernie Ensley and Dotty Adams—*they* were the magnets for stage and film celebrities who turned up on Wednesdays. Marlon Brando came often. Later, in 1955, he showed off an over-the-hip spin of his partner, learned from Palladium stylists, in the film *Guys and Dolls*.

Kim Novak, another film star, insisted on dancing with the finest mamboist, Anibal Vásquez. Vásquez said yes. But first he chivalrously took the precaution of surrounding their mambo with bodyguards, lest someone unwanted cut in and embarrass her. Queen Soraya, of then friendly Iran, came twice in 1958. I watched her mambo with a strong, silent type while someone shouted, "well, *that* should take her mind off the king." (The Shah had just divorced her, on grounds of infertility.) Black intelligentsia composed the most loyal audience—Amiri Baraka, Katherine Dunham, Geoffrey Holder, Harry Belafonte, and many, many others. In 1972 when I asked Baraka why he came so often to the Palladium he replied, "Why, man, mambo was what was happening."

What was happening on the dance floor was critical and revolutionary: demolition of the conviction that only in ballet do we have an art history; demolition of remains of a Western academic argument to the effect that styles of "the folk" operate in some sort of immanence transcending the individual; demolition of thinking that "folk" dancing is different from "high." The evaporating nonsense could be summed up in a phrase: everyone knows who Nijinsky is, but folk dancers dance without names—it's art without artists, moves without masters.

In truth New York mambo comprised a complex interaction of known personalities out of which a classic style emerged. Palladium art history was *not* anonymous. It reflected conscious choices, by named creative women and named creative men, interacting with further conscious choices by other named creative people—dancers, musicians, and singers, all equal in the creative process.

Mambo showed what happens when a popular style gets on its feet. In other works, on mambo art history, I retell the rise and achievement of all this. Here, for brevity, I give cameo renderings. The two most influential male masters were Anibal Vásquez, a black Puerto Rican, and Andrew Jerrick, a mainland black. Vásquez pioneered "the four corners" mambo that he called *la perfecta*. He marvelously mamboized flamenco stampings and postures by pulling them down into the hips of the rumba. Hitting four corners with tightly webbed fingers, smooth as silk, his mambo perfecta by 1959 was danced by everyone. But all the stylists knew who invented it. He also mamboized mimes à la Chaplin and takeoffs on the stars of stage and film.

Andrew Jerrick began to attract attention around 1955. He was, and is, an incredible stylist. The movie *Mambo Madness* documents him in action, punching the air with his hands, carving out bas-reliefs, predicting King Tut, snapping on invisible currents of electricity. Indeed, the electric boogie was trying to be born in his body. He could draw tiny circles, with the tips of his shoes, while counter-drawing with his arms and hands. He could swim, he could walk, he could grimace, he could freeze. Alexander Pope, it is said, was so talented he could write blank verse in heroic couplets. Jerrick, similarly, could write over box-steps with ballet and sports and mime in a personalized cubism that "zooted" his trunk and "reeted" his arms.

The Rosa Parks of mambo was Jackie "La Negra" Danois. This talented black woman broke the color bar in Broadway dance halls in the 1940s. She opened the way for the coming to the Palladium of mainland and Caribbean blacks. She also danced barefoot, flaunting her roots and the insights of the barrios, decades before two American black athletes stood in stocking feet at the Mexico City Olympics to make similar points about pride.

Part of the forte of Millie Donay, Italian-American partner of Cuban Pete (Pedro Aguilar), was a gift for sensing how a black-influenced move, from another country, could fit into mambo. She fashioned the tango fan, a staccato version of the *quebrada* break of that Argentine dance. She was fluent in gesture, especially the Kongo pose, left hand on hip, right hand forward. So was Barbara Boyce, a black woman from Brooklyn, who in 1962 was mixing mambo with twist and the freeze, framing her face with her hands at each sudden pose, in a way that presaged voguing.

Teresita Perez found herself dancing one night at the Palladium with someone *antipático*. She signaled to friends on the sidelines, the story goes, to cut in and save her by drawing down, from time to time, an invisible window shade between her and her partner. Dotty Adams invented a similar step one night, covering her eyes with her right hand and pushing out with her left, the get-outta-my-face mambo. Adams was also famous for a signature leap with a shimmy. She, too, danced barefoot and in a classic photograph from around 1960, you see her reaching for the sky with a flamenco-like gesture while her partner, Ernest Ensley, touches the earth with the palm of his hand in a break. Spain within Kongo within the twinkling of an eye. Mambo.

An important step of womanist mambo was "the head"—standing in place, weaving one hand in space, then the other, while rattling the head with puppet-like suddenness. This is the move that announces the aura, of the coming of the spirit, among priestesses of the traditional religion of the Akan of Ghana. I have seen it rattle the heads of possession women in Agogo, in northern Asante, in a way very close to the Palladium. The mamboists have a theory as to how it came to New York: it stems from

Katherine Dunham's incomparable knowledge, of motion and dance in Africa, entering mambo when several Palladium dancers studied with her in the 1950s to deepen their fluency in blackness.

But this was not the only link between mambo and black religion. Time and again I saw Tito Puente trace a circle around his head with his drumstick, only to be mirrored by a man on the dance floor tossing *his* hand in a circle around *his* head. To Anglos in the house it was "showmanship." But to knowing Latinos, it was self-purification, a *limpieza*, in the name of God and the spirits.

GLOSSARY

Places and numbers in parentheses refer to the chapter for which the glossary entry was submitted and were defined by the author of that chapter, with a second place occasionally added if that is where the term originated. Words without chapter citations are terms widely used throughout. Words within definitions that have their own glossary entries are in boldface. Often an entry is particular to an island, but some terms have much wider currency; for some of these there is more than one entry, reflecting other meanings or different points of view.

Abakuá (Cuba 3)—Only surviving masked dance/music tradition in Cuba from secret societies of Calabar River region; also called **Carabalí** and **Ñáñigo** in Cuba.

Aficionado(s) (Cuba 3)—Amateur(s), lovers of the dance, the arts, etc.; not very professionally trained.

AfroCubanismo (Cuba 3)—African and African-based predominance within Cuban culture.

Agan (Curaçao 19)—Musical percussion instrument, part of the plow, used in **Tambu.**

Aguinaldo (Puerto Rico 12)—Puerto Rican folk song related to the **seis**; usually sung during Christmastime.

Anansyism (Trinidad and Tobago 18)—Tricks, especially by political or public figures; from the stories from Ghana about Anansi, the spider.

Arará (Cuba 3)—Major dance/music tradition in Cuba from West African ethnic groups with corresponding religious system; shoulder movements and cylindrical drums characterize the family of dances.

Areíto (Cuba 3)—Indigenous dance and song ritual of Cuba, Jamaica, Hispaniola, and Puerto Rico; also related to **mitotes** and **batocos** of Mexico and South America.

Atabal (Dominican Republic 10)—A Dominican term for the long-drum, generally synonymous with **palo.**

Babylon (Jamaica 7)—Biblical derivation of an oppressive state of being.

Bachata (Dominican Republic 10)—Traditionally a raucous backyard dance party of the lower social sector of the capital city and environs, accompanied by metal-stringed instruments, principally the guitar. In the past twenty years, the term for its music and dance as a genre, increasingly commercial. Derived from the Cuban **son** and danced similarly.

Baile (Puerto Rico 12)—Popular dance. The word **danza** is used for performance dance.

Baile de palos (Dominican Republic 10)—The couple dance accompanied by the Dominican long-drums (**palos** or **atabales**), traditionally performed unembraced as a "dance of respect" because of the sacred association of the long-drums with Afro-Dominican religious brotherhoods.

Balakadri (French Caribbean 16)—Guadeloupean popular balls during which **quadrilles** were the main genre performed.

Bal boutché (French Caribbean 16)—Martinican dance party for members of a community. At the end of the ball, a bouquet was thrown and the person who received it was responsible for organizing the next party. **Quadrille, biguine, maziouk,** and waltz were the only genres performed in a bal boutché.

Ballet (Cuba 3)—Derived concert dance form from nineteenth-century Europe.

Balsié (Dominican Republic 10)—The term for two different types of medium-sized Dominican drums of two different types of instrumental ensembles, both called **priprí,** that accompany social dances of the eastern/central-southern and southwestern regions, respectively.

Bamboula (Virgin Islands 15)—An African-derived dance. The term was applied to dance as well as to a drum from various islands in the eighteenth and nineteenth centuries. It is now used for a revived dance in the Virgin Islands.

Bambulá (Dominican Republic 10)—A recreational Dominican dance of Haitian origin. Characterized by a caller (**bastonero**) and accompanied by long-drums played horizontally, lain on the ground with the drummer seated atop. Formerly more widely known in the Dominican Republic, but today performed only in the Samaná peninsula; undoubtedly imported by Haitian homesteaders in 1824–25.

Banco (Dominican Republic 10)—The anniversary-of-death ritual (more generally called **cabo de año**) of the Afro-Dominican Brotherhood of the Holy Spirit of greater Villa Mella for deceased adult members.

Banda—Dance of the **Guedes** or Gedes, a division within the pantheon of Haitian **Vodou** spirits. Characterized by erotic hip movement.

Bandolas (Cuba 3)—European string instrument that was associated with **son** music.

Bandurria (Cuba 3)—String instrument of Europe that was brought to Cuba.

Bantú (Cuba 3)—In Cuba, refers to **Kongo, Kongo-Angolan,** or Central African descent; in Cuba more than a linguistic term for Bantu speakers, though elsewhere, in Africa and the United States, for example, the term more often refers to related linguistic groups of central and southern Africa. Also another name for Central African religion that developed in Cuba (**Palo** and **Palo Monte**).

Barril (Puerto Rico 14)—A goatskin barrel drum that is the basic instrument of Puerto Rican **bomba** music.

Barrio (Puerto Rico 12)—A district or neighborhood, urban or rural.

Bas (Haiti 9)—A low-pitched, handheld frame drum. Provides a bass sound in a **Vodou** drum ensemble.

Bass Pipe (Virgin Islands 15)—Also known as the "ass pipe" or "tail pipe," a rhythm and percussion instrument made out of an actual metal tubing or exhaust pipe from an automobile.

Bastel (Curaçao 19)—Bull or cow horn used as a musical instrument.

Bastonero (Puerto Rico 12)—Director or caller of a dance. (Dominican Republic 10)—The caller in certain Dominican social dances such as the southwestern **carabiné** and the **bambulá** of Samana.

Batarumba (Cuba 3)—A combination of Yoruba *Batá* drumming with Cuban **rumba** drumming; a combination of **Yoruba,** Cuban rumba, and **casino** dance movements.

Batey (Dominican Republic 10)—An indigenous community surrounded by land, adopted as the term for the Dominican sugarcane community, surrounded by cane fields.

Batocos (Cuba 3)—Indigenous dance and song of Mexico, Caribbean, and South America; related to **areítos** and **mitotes.**

Batty (Jamaica 7)—Buttocks. Other Jamaican patois: *bwoy*—boy; *couda*—can do; *fi*—for; *mek*—make/allow; *mi*—my.

Bele or **Bel air** (Trinidad and Tobago 17)—A social dance found among the African/French (Creole slaves) in Haiti, Martinique, and other islands. It is maintained in folk celebrations in Trinidad and Tobago.

Bele linò (French Caribbean 16)—African-derived set dance of northern Martinique. The set comprises the *bélia*, the *gwanbèlè*, and the *bidjin bele*.

Bele lisid (French Caribbean 16)—African-derived set dance of southern Martinique. The set comprises the *bele* and the *gwanbele*.

Bele twapa (French Caribbean 16)—Martinican rural dance to the sound of the bele drum, rarely included in **bele linò** set.

Benta (Curaçao 19)—A one-stringed instrument played with the mouth and a stick called the *maingueta*. (Jamaica 6)—a bamboo instrument played at Jamaican wakes.

Biguine (French Caribbean 16)—A syncopated two-beat dance from the French Caribbean islands characterized by a light, elastic, spring-like motion in the knees on or between each beat. The rhythm of biguine is derived from rural *bidjin bele* and resembles that of Haitian **banda.** Danced with hands on hips or in couples.

Bolero (Cuba 3)—Slow, romantic song form in Cuban song complex, la **canción cubana;** also slow couple dance. (Puerto Rico 12)—Boleros traveled to Mexico and spread to the rest of Latin America, peaking in popularity in the 1940s and 1950s. They still epitomize romantic love throughout the region.

Bomba (Puerto Rico 14)—An Afromestizo drum-dance genre of Puerto Rico that incorporates **call and response** singing, drumming, and percussive dancing in which dancers' movements are interpreted by a lead drummer or **subidor.** Also a name for the **barril** drum basic to bomba music.

Bombazo (Puerto Rico 14)—A communal **bomba** party. A new word devised for the current revival of bomba.

Bongo (Trinidad and Tobago 17)—A dance of strength, virility, and agility, the bongo is another wake dance that arouses great excitement among the participants and onlookers alike. The basic movements closely resemble the Russian Cossack dances.

Bossale (French Caribbean 16)—An African enslaved in the French Caribbean who was not yet baptized. **Bozal** (Dominican Republic 10)—The same in colonial Santo Domingo.

Boula—The smallest, highest-pitched drum in a **Vodou** drum ensemble. Usually played with two sticks.

Bula (French Caribbean 16)—Guadeloupean drum for **gwoka** music. It provides the rhythmic background for the **makè.**

Buleador (Puerto Rico 14)—The low drum used in **bomba** music; also the person who plays the basic rhythm on this drum.

Buroo drums (Jamaica 7)—The rocking drums accompanying **Pocomania** rites.

Cabildo(s) (Cuba 3)—Both religious and ethnic organization of enslaved Africans in Cuba; storage structure for unique music and dance traditions over centuries, as well as repository of African beliefs and customs.

Cabo de año (Dominican Republic 10)—The Dominican folk–Catholic ritual held for the first anniversary of death.

Calenda (French Caribbean 16)—The term was often used in the past to refer to African dance in the New World. Today in Martinique, there are three genres called calenda, two in the northeast and one in the southwest.

Calinda (Cuba 3)—An ambiguous dance form mentioned in writings from the sixteenth to nineteenth centuries that on the one hand signaled a dance of a couple in flirtatious sensuality, but also referred to a martial dance form. (ed.)—This term, also spelled **calenda** and kalenda or **kalinda,** was used historically to refer to dance of different types on many islands.

Call and response—see **voye/reponn.**

Callao (Dominican Republic 10)—An unaccompanied segment of the **zapateo** dances of **sarambo** in the Cibao (north) and **guarap**o in the eastern city of El Seybo, in which virtuosic turns and flourishes (*flores*) are performed.

Calypso (Cuba 3, Trinidad and Tobago)—A type of protest song with a standard accompanying rhythm that originated in Trinidad and developed also in Jamaica; a major popular music form of the Anglophone Caribbean.

Campesino (Cuba 3)—A Cuban country farm worker; the name for the country folk music/dance tradition of western and central Cuba, with closest roots in European dance of Spain; also called **punto guajiro.**

Canboulay (Trinidad and Tobago 18)—A colorful march through the streets, depicting what actually took place on estates when the sugarcane fields were being burned prior to harvest to remove trash and insects; the name comes from the French *cannes brulée*, burning of the sugar canes.

Canción cubana (Cuba 3)—A large family or tradition of sung repertoire in Cuba that does not involve dancing the music, but concentrates on varied structures of singing, dramatic speaking, and instrumental accompaniment; Cuban song complex.

Capoeira (Cuba 3, Brazil)—A Brazilian martial arts form with **Kongo-Angolan** roots.

Carabalí(s) (Cuba 3)—A major music/dance tradition of Cuba with roots in Cameroon and Nigeria along the Calabar River; another name for **Abakuá** or **Ñáñigo** culture in Cuba.

Carabiné (Dominican Republic 10)—A Dominican social dance of the southwestern region in duple tempo, characterized by a caller (**bastonero**), with no fewer than six couples. Today played in the southwest in a triptych with the **mangulina** and the valse or **danza**.

Cariso (Virgin Islands 15, Trinidad and Tobago)—Also called *caruso*, a song form sung a cappella or accompanied by music. Mostly performed by women, it can express protest, political commentary, or gossip.

Casas de cultura (Cuba 3)—Municipal, provincial, and national culture houses of Cuba. Places where artists, writers, poets, and dramatists present their artistry and where the Cuban public has access to the arts at minimal cost.

Casino (Cuba 3)—Cuban **salsa;** dance type in **son** family.

Casino de la rueda (Cuba 3)—A circle form of **casino** or group **salsa** dancing in Cuba.

Cassé corps (Cuba 3, Haiti)—Literally, "broken body" in French; to dance as if the dancer had no spine, dancing fully and expressively in all body parts.

Catá (Cuba 3)—A cylindrical wooden or bamboo instrument, played on a stand with sticks; characteristic in **rumba,** also called **guagua.**

Chachachá (Cuba 3)—Popular twentieth-century Cuban dance; identified by three quick running steps, followed by two slow steps; performed by dancing couples to **charanga** and **son** music.

Changüi (Cuba 3)—A regional form of **son** from the eastern provinces of Cuba.

Chapi (Curaçao 19)—Percussion instrument made from a hoe.

Charanga (Cuba 3)—Cuban orchestra type of the nineteenth and twentieth centuries that emphasized the piano, violin, and flute with Cuban percussion instruments, **güiros,** and **maracas;** also called **orquesta típica,** *orquesta típica francesa.*

Chay o pye—Literally, "foot charge." Danced by the **majò jon** (baton major) in **Rara**, it is a display of intricate footwork.

Chenche matriculado (Dominican Republic 10)—A nineteenth-century Dominican folkdance in supposed imitation of the schottische as danced by the occupying Spanish troops during the Spanish Annexation of 1861–65.

Chipping (Trinidad and Tobago 18)—Shuffle-type dancing. Usually one steps in time to the music, but slowly, with the weight on the toes. The name came from the chip, chip sound that shuffling feet make.

Chivo (Dominican Republic 10)—A type of **merengue** of the Samaná peninsula.

Chutney—Current popular dance and music of Trinidadians and Guyanese with ancestors from the Indian subcontinent. The dance is mostly **wining,** but may incorporate Indian hand gestures or other Indian or Middle Eastern influences; it can be danced to **soca** or the hybrid *chutney-soca* or to Indian-influenced music played on North Indian instruments.

Clave(s) (Cuba 3)—A pair of sticks used as a musical instrument; also the name of the organizing rhythmic patterns of Cuban music.

Cofradía (Dominican Republic 10)—In southern Spain and Catholic Latin America, a lay religious brotherhood. The Afro–Latin American versions serve as mutual aid and burial societies. The Dominican version is not parish-associated, is symbolized by long-drums (**palos**) and their music, and is characteristically led by a woman.

Columbia (Cuba 3)—The traditional male form of Cuban **rumba** that is fast and exceedingly virtuosic, sometimes danced with knives or around bottles; originated in the rural areas of Matanzas and Havana provinces during the early nineteenth century.

Commandeur (French Caribbean 16)—A man who calls the steps and dance routine in the **quadrilles** of the French Caribbean.

Comparsa(s) (Cuba 3)—A Cuban processional dance form; also called **conga(s);** common during provincial and national carnivals and at the Day of the Kings celebration on January 6th in Cuba.

Complejo (Cuba 3)—The Spanish term for "complex" and the basis of classification of the five large divisions of Cuban dance/music.

Conga(s) (Cuba 3)—Processional dance and music or a **comparsa** in Cuba; also a group of barrel-shaped drums from Kongo-Angolan heritage, called alternately **tumbadores.**

Congos (Cuba 3)—Central African groups with similar cultures; also **Kongo** or **Kongo-Angolan** cultures.

Congos (Dominican Republic 10)—The Dominican long-drum variant ensemble associated with the Brotherhood of the Holy Spirit in Villa Mella and environs; unique to this region.

Conquistadores (Cuba 3)—European explorers who exploited indigenous

Native Americans and initiated the forced migration of Africans to work the mines, farms, and plantations of the emerging economies within the Americas.

Continentals (Virgin Islands 15)—The term customarily used for people of the continental United States; North Americans, most often whites.

Contradanza (Cuba 3)—A popular Cuban dance at the turn of the nineteenth century that mixed French court figure dances with Cuban percussion; also called *contradanza cubana*, part of the **Danzón** dance/music complex.

Contradanza (Puerto Rico 12)—A type of figure dance of the eighteenth century that originated in Britain as country dance and became popular throughout Europe, especially in France. It was introduced to Spain and brought to Latin America during the colonial period. Modified by Africans and Creoles in the Caribbean, it was influential in the development of Puerto Rican (**danza**), Cuban, and Haitian musical/dance forms.

Contredanse (Cuba 3)—A group of French court dances, originally evolved from the English country dance and taken to Cuba with French and Haitian colonists and their European families; males and females in dancing lines performing set figures to European instruments; also *contradanza francesa*.

Coro (Cuba 3)—Chorus; answering or responding group of singers who respond to a lead singer.

Créolité (French Caribbean 16)—A poetic movement that promotes self-investigation of all the cultural and racial components of the *métis* (mixed) society of the Caribbean, in an attempt to recompose their fragmented identity. Créolité is at the foundation of the composite Caribbean identity and results from the abrupt encounter of a variety of cultures on the same territory.

Crucian (Virgin Islands 15)—Something/someone native to St. Croix.

Cuadrilla (Dominican Republic 10)—**Quadrille** dance.

Cuaresma Chiquita (Dominican Republic 10)—The fifty-day period between Easter and Pentecost. Within a couple of Afro-Dominican religious brotherhoods, this period, especially its seven Fridays, includes significant ritual moments and builds up to a big event on the Friday before Pentecost.

Cuatro (Puerto Rico 12)—A Puerto Rican musical instrument that evolved from the Spanish guitar. It is the main instrument of **plena** and *jíbaro* (country farmer) music.

Cultural music (Virgin Islands 15)—Local or Caribbean music.

Cumbia (Cuba 3, Colombia)—A Colombian dance of African and Spanish heritage, related to **son.**

Cumfa (Jamaica 6, Guyana)—An African-derived possession dance from Guyana.

Dance culture (Cuba 3)—A continuum of dance traditions with distinctive types from specific geographical areas and usually among distinct groups of people.

Dancehall (Congolese 2, Jamaica)—Jamaican popular music and dance form evolving from **reggae** that often uses samples from rap or rhythm and blues.

Dans (Haiti 9)—Generally, "dance." Specifically, the full-scale **Vodou** ceremony that invokes the complete pantheon.

Danza (Cuba 3)—A Cuban concert form, called in the United States modern dance. Also, a salon dance that developed in the formation of the nineteenth-century **danzón** complex, the first in which a couple danced in each other's arms.

Danza (Puerto Rico 12)—A Creole musical/dance form that evolved from the European **contradanza** into a new synthesis incorporating African elements. Although the genesis of the form was the result of complex cross-fertilizations, in Puerto Rico the danza became one of the most popular social dances of the upper classes and, more importantly, was adopted by the elite as the national music.

Danzón (Cuba 3)—The national dance of Cuba in the nineteenth century, identified by alternation of walking and dancing patterns and by soft, elegant instrumental sound; the name of a Cuban music/dance complex.

Danzonete (Cuba 3)—An elegant salon couple dance in the nineteenth century **danzón** complex in Cuba, mainly differentiated by the variation of lead instruments in the rondo-like musical organization.

Danzonchá (Cuba 3)—Part of the **danzón** complex; mainly differentiated by the addition of a vocal lead within the third section of the musical organization; elegant salon couple dance of nineteenth-century Cuba.

Décima (Cuba 3)—A literary form from Spain with a 10-syllable line in a 10-line verse; basis of Cuban and Puerto Rican song formation.

Diablitos (Cuba 3)—Literally, "little devils," but another name for the masked spirit dancers of the **Abakuá** society; also called **Íremes** and **Ñáñigos.**

Dinkimini (Jamaica 6)—An African-derived dance danced at Jamaican wakes.

Djouba, Djuba (Haiti 9)—Dance of the Djouba division within the **Vodou** pantheon. Its spirits represent the earth and the peasantry. Some movements mimic those of farmers at work or at play.

Dub (Jamaica 7)—**Reggae** beat.

Enkríkamo (Cuba 3)—The small invoking drum of the **Abakuá** spirit dancers or **íremes.**

Enlazadas (Cuba 3)—Locked or laced together in dancing couple position.

Etu (Jamaica 6)—A **Yoruba**-derived dance in Jamaica.

Flag Corps—see **kò drapo.**

Flamenco (Puerto Rico 12, Spain)—The most important song and dance expression of the province of Andalucía in southern Spain. Evolved from many diverse sources, it incorporates Arabic, Jewish, Christian, and Gypsy elements. Flamenco consists of singing (*cante*), dancing (**baile**) that includes intricately rhythmic footwork (**zapateado**) and guitar playing, accompanied by hand clapping (*palmas*) and verbal encouragement (*jaleo*).

Foklò (Haiti 9)—Folklore. The term may refer to Afro-Haitian culture in general, or more specifically to the representation of that culture in modern theatrical contexts.

Folklórico (Cuba 3)—The dance/music traditions that comprise the varied roots of Cuban dance culture in their historical and classic manifestations; also the name of the Cuban national dance company that specializes in Cuban folk and popular dance.

French quadrille (French Caribbean 16)—Most popular ballroom dance in France from the early nineteenth century. Derived from **contredanse,** it is a set dance composed of five numbers: *le pantalon, l'été, la poule, la trénise,* and the *finale.*

Fwapé (French Caribbean 16)—A step in which each foot is alternately raised knee-high and sideways, then immediately lowered as the dancer strikes the ground vigorously with both feet.

Gagá (Dominican Republic 10)—A Lenten **Vodou**-like, ritual society dedicated to a deity of the **Petwo** family, and the society's music and dance, imported by Haitian seasonal workers to Dominican sugarcane communities.

Ganja (Jamaica 7)—Marijuana.

Gayap (Trinidad and Tobago 17)—A coming together of village folk to accomplish a communal task for the benefit of an individual or group, also called *Lend Hand*. Camaraderie and feasting lighten the tasks, while binding the people closer.

Gerreh (Jamaica 6)—A dance danced at Jamaican "dead-yard" ceremonies or wakes.

Groun'ation (Groundation) (Jamaica 7)—A ceremonial schooling in the tenets of **Rastafari.**

Guagua (Cuba 3)—A small cylindrical musical instrument played with sticks on a stand, also called *catá*.

Guaguancó (Cuba 3)—The most popular type of **rumba,** in which the male dancer chases the female and makes the *vacunao* gesture; also a particular **rumba clave.**

Guaracha (Puerto Rico 12, Cuba)—Cuban musical/dance genre associated with light, humorous lyrics and stimulating dancing.

Guarapo (Dominican Republic 10)—A type of **zapateo** dance of El Seybo, danced unembraced. A balancing step alternates with one of ritual pursuit in constant movement; the man's arms hang at his sides while the woman holds her skirts.

Guateque (Cuba 3)—A type and style of **son** from the central region of Cuba; in the western region, a gathering of rural families with country music (**punto guajiro**), in which instruments include the **laud.**

Guedes, Gedes (Haiti 8)—Spirits of death. Most belong to the **Rada** rite.

Güira (Dominican Republic 10)—The Dominican metal version of the gourd scraper, the **güiro,** common throughout the Caribbean region.

Güiro (Puerto Rico 12)—A Puerto Rican musical instrument inherited from the indigenous Taíno culture. Made of a gourd and scraped to create a particular sound commonly found in **plenas, seises,** and **aguinaldos. Guiro** (Virgin Islands 15)—rhythm instrument made from a dried gourd with grooved sides, played with a wire comb.

Gwoka (French Caribbean 16)—African-derived set dance of Guadeloupe; also, drums that play **léwoz** music.

Habanera (Puerto Rico 12, Cuba)—Cuban Creole rhythm derived from the European **contradanza** in combination with rhythms of African and Arabic origins. It became popular in the nineteenth century in all of Latin America as well as in Spain and Europe.

Haute-taille (French Caribbean 16)—**Quadrille** of southern Martinique.

Heru (Curaçao 19)—Iron; in this context the collective name of the percussion instruments, all made of iron, used in **tambu.**

Higher Heights (Jamaica 7)—A lofty place of being (Rastafarian).

Hispanidad (Dominican Republic 10)—A cultural policy promoted by Dominican dictator Rafael Trujillo (1930–61) and his mastermind and successor, President Joaquín Balaguer, in which Hispanic racial and cultural purity was promoted as the epitome of the most authentically Dominican, in juxtaposition with black and African influences via Haiti, viewed as contaminants of Dominicanness.

Hofi (Curaçao 19)—A name for a former plantation now used for social activities; also a garden, orchard, courtyard, or vegetable garden.

Holandés (Puerto Rico 14)—A **bomba** rhythm, brought by slaves from Curaçao, played very fast and in 2/4 time.

Hounfor (Haiti 8)—**Vodou** temple. In current Kreyol spelled **oufò**.

Ibo—Dance of the Ibo division within the **Vodou** pantheon. Dramatizes the pride, sometimes extreme, of the Ibo people (originally of Nigeria), who bore a reputation for resistance to slavery.

Íremes (Cuba 3)—Masked spirit dancers from **Carabalí** (**Abakuá** or **Ñáñigo**) tradition in Cuba.

Ital (Jamaica 7)—Pure.

Jaleo (Dominican Republic 10)—In the orchestrated **merengue,** the third of three sections, characterized by virtuosic turns and figures.

Jouvert (Virgin Islands 15, Trinidad and Tobago)—Carnival tramp behind band before break of dawn.

Juba (Djouba) (Dominican Republic 10)—A widely spread social couples dance in the colonial Caribbean, characterized by a medium-sized drum, the juba drum. The Dominican retention is the **priprí** of the east.

Juego de maní (Cuba 3)—"Peanut butter game," the martial art form of Cuba with **Kongo-Angolan** heritage.

Kadans, Cadence—An early stage in the evolution of **konpa** music, from the 1950s.

Kalinda (Trinidad and Tobago 17)—Dance game/fight with sticks, done at wakes.

Kanaval—Carnival. Public festival held between the end of the Christmas season and the beginning of Lent. Traditionally, bands of many kinds challenge the social order.

Kanzo—**Vodou** initiation rites.

Karko (Curaçao 19)—Conch shell imported from Bonaire, used to replace the **bastel.**

Kase, Cassé—"Break." In Haitian traditional rhythm and dance, a pattern in direct opposition to the main pattern. In Vodou, the kase stimulates possession. In stage performance, it delineates form.

Kaseko (Cuba 3, Surinam)—A popular dance/music of Surinam and also Francophone Caribbean nations.

Kè—Chorus in **call and response** singing.

Kò drapo (Haiti 9)—Flag Corps. The military-style parading of a **Vodou** society's sequined flags. Flags are oriented to the four cardinal points of the cosmos.

Kokomakaku (Curaçao 19)—Stick dance, a form of **Tambu.**

Konbit, Coumbite—A labor cooperative, found primarily in rural Haiti. A favorite subject of folklore troupes, since music accompanies both the work and the feast that follows.

Kongo, Congo (Cuba 3)—A major amalgam of Central African cultures in Cuba; also called **Kongo-Angolan** or **Bantú** in Cuba and refers to a dance/music tradition. Also, a dance of the Kongo division within the **Vodou** pantheon. A gently seductive hip movement has made the dance popular in secular as well as sacred contexts.

Konpa, Compas—A dance made popular by commercial dance bands in Haiti since the 1950s. Synthesizes elements of Haitian **twoubadou** music and Dominican and Cuban secular styles.

Koregrafi (Haiti 9)—In Haiti, a stylized representation of a folk dance, complete with floor design and movement elaborated for the public.

Kouri lawond (French Caribbean 16)—At the beginning and end of a Martinican **bele linò** set, the dancers circle the dance area clockwise, then counterclockwise to the sound of the drum. This is called kouri lawond.

Kreyol (Haiti 9)—One of the two official languages of Haiti (since 1987) and the language of most Haitians. An amalgam of a number of different languages, including European, indigenous, and African, with a largely French vocabulary, but structured differently than French. Now spelled in a standardized phonetic way, reflected in Haitian (9) entries in this glossary.

Kriyè (French Caribbean 16)—Lead singer (shouter) in African-derived music of Martinique.

Kumina (Jamaica 6)—A danced **Kongo**-derived Jamaican rite of ancestral worship.

Ladja (French Caribbean 16)—Fight dance of Martinique that bears a strong resemblance to the *kadjia* of Benin. Also called *damié* and formerly spelled *l'ag'ya*.

Lalinklè (French Caribbean 16)—In northeast Martinique, a series of dances performed at night, at funeral wakes and **swaré bele.** The dances are: *karesé-yo, bénézuel, woulé mango, ting-bang, mabélo,* and *kanigwé.*

Lanflanmansyon (French Caribbean 16)—Creole for "the ignition." Nickname by which **quadrille** dancers call the *finale,* because it is in a very fast tempo.

Laplas—Vodou sword-bearer. Nearly always a man, he dances between the two flag-bearers in the **Flag Corps.**

Latin Jazz (Cuba 3)—A major division of jazz music that integrates basic structures of Cuban music, including **clave** organization and the use of percussion in the full range of the African traditions of Cuba.

Laúd (Cuba 3)—A string instrument with rounded back from North Africa via Spain, played characteristically in *punto libre* or freestyle song form in the western region of Cuba.

Leggo (Virgin Islands 15)—"Let go"; to let go of all inhibitions, be free to behave in any way one feels without the fear of consequence or reputation.

Léwoz (French Caribbean 16)—African-derived set dance of Guadeloupe. The set comprises *tumblak, kaladja, kadjenbel, graj, woulé, léwoz,* and *menndé.* It is called *léwoz-au-commandement* when performed with a caller.

Libertos (Puerto Rico 12)—Men and women freed from slavery.

Limbo (Trinidad and Tobago 17)—A competitive dance originally seen at Waking ceremonies for the dead, passed to the realm of entertainment. Passing below a bar held by two individuals progressed in nightclub acts to the "human limbo," with the dancers' bodies replacing the bar.

Lucumí(s) (Cuba 3)—An African ethnic group that has come to be synonymous with **Yoruba** in Cuba; the name of an African religion in Cuba; the name of an African language in Cuba; the name of a dance/music tradition that is also called **Yoruba, Oricha,** or **Santería** in Cuba.

Lwa (Haiti 9)—A **Vodou** spirit. The older spelling is **loa.**

Madruga (Cuba 3)—A metal cross-shaped shaker instrument, used in **rumba** to set the pace and assist the division between singing and dancing sequences.

Majò jon (Haiti 9)—Baton major. Costumed in a cloak made up of sequins or bits of mirror, and sporting sunglasses, he twirls his baton and dances the **chay o pye.**

Makè (French Caribbean 16)—The dominant drum in a Guadeloupean **gwoka** ensemble. It plays the rhythmic variations in response to the dancers' movements.

Makuta (Cuba 3)—A **Kongo-Angolan** dance that survives in Cuba.

Mambo (Cuba 3)—A twentieth-century type of **son** music with two variations in the dance: a bouncy, playful quality in Cuba, a smooth and suave quality elsewhere; also a section of the son music where brass instruments take the lead and make improvisational developments.

Manbo, Mambo—A **Vodou** priestess.

Mangulina (Dominican Republic 10)—A Dominican social dance of the southwestern region in 3/8 time, perhaps derived from the Andalusian *seguidilla*. Today performed in a triptych with the **carabiné** and the valse or **danza.**

Maní (Dominican Republic 10)—A spiritualist party of Dominican **Vodú** that celebrates initiation, healing, or a patrons saint's day. Traditionally public and characterized by music and dance with either **palos** or, in the central-south, **salves** ensembles.

Manman—The "mother" drum of the **Vodou** ensemble, played by the master drummer. Largest and lowest-pitched, it executes the **kase** and leads conversations with the **segon** drum.

Maraca(s) (Cuba 3)—Handheld shaker, musical instrument usually played in pairs.

Marímbula (Cuba 3)—A percussion instrument with metal prongs over an opening of a wooden or gourd structure that is plucked or hit with music sticks. (Dominican Republic 10)—**Marimba** is the Dominican term for the same instrument (not to be confused with the wooden xylophone widely known as a marimba), the Cuban-originated adaptation of the African thumb-piano or *mbira* in giant form. Developed to serve as a bass instrument in a social dance ensemble.

Maroons (ed.)—Escaped slaves who formed their own communities.

Mas (Trinidad and Tobago 18)—The Carnival costume; from *masquerade.*

Maskawon—Dance associated with a prominent Carnival band. Displays a trembling of the shoulders.

Masumba (Jamaica 6)—Jamaican Maroon form of the **limbo** dance.

Mayi, Mahi—One of the dances associated with the **Rada** division within the **Vodou** pantheon. Named after the Mahis of West Africa, it uses a kind of backward pedaling foot movement.

Mayoacán (Dominican Republic 10)—The wooden, horizontal slit-gong that accompanied the Taíno **areíto** song-dance ritual.

Maziouk (French Caribbean 16)—Mazurka. European-derived dance of Martinique. Similar to the Lakonmèt *pitché* of St. Lucia. In the past decade a new version has developed, called the *maziouk-zouk* because it has borrowed rhythmic elements from **zouk.**

Mazouk (Cuba 3)—A contemporary mazurka with Caribbean instrumentation, in 3/4 meter.

Mereng (Haiti 9)—In French, **méringue,** a frothy pastry that possibly gave its name to a popular dance around the time of Haitian independence. Represents a fusion of slave dances and French ballroom forms.

Merengue (Dominican Republic 10)—Currently the most popular Dominican social dance. It is the variant of the northern Cibao region that has become nationally popular, and there the original guitar family instruments of the nineteenth century were replaced by the accordion starting around the 1880s. In the early twentieth century a process of adaptation to the ballroom began, leading to the development of a commercial, orchestrated merengue, which diverged from the folkloric *merengue típico* (also known as **perico ripiao**), with which it now coexists. Both are in 2/4 meter.

Minuetes (Cuba 3)—Minuets; court dance form of sixteenth and seventeenth centuries in Europe, performed by colonists in the Americas up to the nineteenth century.

Mitotes (Cuba 3)—Ancient indigenous dance/music form in Mexico and South America; resembles native dance descriptions in Cuba at time of contact; see **areítos** and **batocos.**

Mizik rasin—Literally, "roots music." A late twentieth-century Haitian commercial music style influenced by 1970s rock and **reggae.** Tends to use the rhythms of **Rara.**

Moko Jumbie (Trinidad and Tobago 18)—Carnival masquerader on stilts.

Mulato/a (Cuba 3)—A person of mixed African and European heritage; formerly a somewhat privileged class in Cuba.

Musique tipique (Cuba 3, West Africa)—Mainly **son** but also **rumba** or Caribbean music in West Africa.

Muzik di zumbi (Curaçao 19)—Literally, "music of the spirits"; Curaçaon music form.

Myal (Jamaica 7)—An African-derived ceremony honoring the ancestors (the inner sanctum of **Kumina**).

Nago (Haiti 9)—Dance of the Nago or **Yoruba** division within the **Vodou** pantheon. Powerful, like the spirits it dramatizes (the several *Ogous* or *Oguns*), it utilizes thrusting chest movements.

Ñáñigo(s) (Cuba 3)—Another name for **Carabalí** cultures from Africa that survived in Cuba; like **Abakuá** and **íremes,** refers to the masked spirit dancers and their stories.

Nasyon—"Nation." A division of the **Vodou** pantheon, sometimes directly associated with an ethnic group from Africa. Each nation shows a unique temperament, or ethos.

Ni' Night (Jamaica 7)—Ninth Night postdeath ceremony. Ninth Night ceremonies are held on a number of islands.

Novena (Dominican Republic 10)—The nine-night ritual for the Virgin (i.e., a saint's festival) or for the dead; the final event is the largest and longest of the sequence.

Nyabinghi (Jamaica 7)—Warrior; Rastafarian term derived from Jomo Kenyatta's Nyabinghi fighters; the name of a three-part drum ensemble, and the drumming, chants, and ceremony at which they are played.

Ogan—Metal percussion instrument in **Arará** dance/music tradition of Cuba; functions as organizer of rhythm instruments in ceremony or performance. (Haiti 9)—A small iron gong, sometimes a flattened, clapperless bell, sometimes a hoe blade, or sometimes a machine part. The basic timekeeper of the **Vodou** drum ensemble.

Oricha(s) (Cuba 3)—The divinities, divine spirits of **Yoruba** belief who manifest through dancing; a name of the Yoruba-based religion also called **Santería, Lucumí,** or **Yoruba** in Cuba; also *Orisa, Orisha* (usual spelling in the United States), or *Orixa* (Brazil).

Orisha religious system or **Shango** (Trinidad and Tobago 17)—The early anthropologists registered the common terms for African religious retentions found in Trinidad. Shango became the popular term for the predominantly **Yoruba** system inherited and maintained by adherents who follow the tenets of the ancestors.

Orquesta típica (Cuba 3)—The name for the musical ensemble of European trio of violin, piano, and flute with added African percussion and rhythms for **danzón** complex dances of the nineteenth century; also called *charanga francesa* during different periods; in twentieth century involves the sweet, elegant sound of a Cuban or Latin orchestra for **chachachá** and **son.**

Ougan, Houngan (Haiti 9)—A **Vodou** priest.

Ougjenikon, Houngenikon—**Vodou** song specialist. Leads in **call and response** singing.

Ousi, Hounsis—A **Vodou** initiate. One who has gone through a **kanzo.**

Palo, Palo Monte (Cuba 3)—A **Kongo-Angolan** or Central African–based religion of Cuba.

Palo (Dominican Republic 10)—The Afro-Dominican drum made from a hollowed-out tree trunk. Also called **atabal** in many areas. Associated with extra-official religious brotherhoods and saints' festivals. Played in ensembles of two or three.

Palo abajo, palo arriba (Dominican Republic 10)—Two rhythms of the south-central region. Originally played for the dead, but also may be danced by the living in some areas. Palo abajo has a triple meter and lugubrious tempo; palo arriba is in duple meter with faster tempo.

Pambiche (Dominican Republic 10)—A variant rhythm and dance of the *merengue típico* that developed in Puerto Plata. Consists of the **jaleo** section only, allegedly an adaptation of the dance-style ineptitude of the U.S. Marines during the first occupation by U.S. troops (1916–19).

Pandero—A Dominican hand drum like a tambourine. Accompanies non-liturgical **salves,** altar music of saints' festivals. Generally a woman's instrument.

Papiamentu (Curaçao 19)—Language spoken in Curaçao, Aruba, and Bonaire.

Parang or **Parranda** (Trinidad and Tobago 18)—The first is Trinidadian creole, the second Spanish for the old Spanish-type songs that came from Venezuela, performed at Christmastime.

Parigol—One of the dances of the **Rada** division within the **Vodou** pantheon. Like a slow, graceful **mayi.** Some call it *twa rigol,* or three streams.

Pasadía (Dominican Republic 10)—A daylong dance party held at a local bar or pub for the enjoyment of any and all.

Paseo (Puerto Rico 14)—The stylized walk steps used at the beginning and end of a **bomba** dance solo. (ed.)—Also, the walking section of certain social dances from Spanish-speaking islands, including **danza** (Puerto Rico), **merengue** (Dominican Republic), and **danzón** (Cuba). (Dominican Republic 10)—The first part of the orchestrated **merengue,** allegedly derived from the polka, adopted from other ballroom dance to make the merengue acceptable in the dancehall. Played for the purpose of the man's selection of a dance partner and their positioning on the dance floor.

Pasodoble (Dominican Republic 10, Spain)—A Spanish popular dance, the two-step, characteristic of bullfighting music as well as the dance hall.

Perico ripiao (Dominican Republic 10)—Synonymous with, and the more popular term for, the Dominican **merengue típico.**

Peristyle (Haiti 8)—The front part of a **Vodou** temple (**hounfor**) where the public ceremonies are held.

Petwo, Petro (Haiti 9)—The hot dance of the Petwo division (one of the two main divisions) within the **Vodou** pantheon. The chest trembles, the feet execute a kind of disjointed movement with respect to each other.

Pique (Trinidad and Tobago 17)—A spicier version of the **bele** or **bel air** with much coquetry and accented hip movements. Drums and chants accompany the dancers in both dances.

Piquete (Puerto Rico 14)—The improvised movements of the **bomba** dancer that are to be interpreted musically by the lead drummer (**subidor**).

Pitché (French Caribbean 16)—Variable step with a lift on 3, 5, or 6, toes pointing down.

Playing mas (Trinidad and Tobago 18)—The actual enactment and performance of a Carnival costume; also, to don a costume and participate in the competitions at Carnival time.

Plena (Puerto Rico 12)—Developed in Ponce toward the end of the nineteenth century, the plena integrates African and European elements. Traditionally accompanied by the accordion or the *armónica* (harmonica), the **güiro,** and the *pandereta* (hand drum or tambourine without jingles), the plena has a contagious rhythm and a vivacious dance step. Its lyrics serve as joyful social commentaries and newsletters.

Pocomania, Pukkumina (Jamaica 7)—A Jamaican religious rite fusing Baptist and African rituals.

Polka-la-poule (French Caribbean 16)—Last figure of the Martinican version of the French **quadrille.**

Pòt drapo—One of two flag bearers in the **Vodou Flag Corps.**

Poto-mitan (Haiti 9)—The centerpost of a **Vodou peristyle,** around which initiates dance. It is a channel through which the **lwa** enter the material world.

Pot-pourri (French Caribbean 16)—Small suite of two or three French **contredanses.** The contredanses en pot-pourri were very fashionable in the French salons at the end of the eighteenth century.

Premye chanté—Lead singer in **call and response** singing, whether in **Vodou,** Carnival, or folklore representations.

Priprí (Dominican Republic 10)—The social dance ensembles and accompanying dances of the eastern and southwestern regions of the Dominican Republic, each with different types of ensembles and music.

Profesionales (Cuba 3)—Generally, trained, fully accredited workers in Cuba; concert level among artists.

Pueblo (Cuba 3)—The people, the public.

Pukkumina, Pocomania (Jamaica 6)—An African Jamaican possession ritual dance-rite syncretized with Christianity.

Punto guajiro (Cuba 3)—The rural, country music/dance complex of Cuba; also called **campesino.**

Quadrille (Virgin Islands 15)—Eighteenth- and nineteenth-century French set dance widely danced in the Caribbean. See **French quadrille** for the form set in early nineteenth century; see chapter 15, Virgin Islands, and chapter 16, French Caribbean, for modern continuations.

Quelbe (Virgin Islands 15)—Also called *fungi* and *scratch*. A distinctive Virgin Islands musical tradition; an essential accompaniment to St. Croix **quadrille.**

Quinto (Cuba 3)—Soprano or high-voiced **tumbador,** a small barrel-shaped drum.

Rabòday—A Carnival or **Rara** band and the dance associated with it. Makes use of much hip and foot movement.

Rada (Haiti 9)—A major division of the **Vodou** pantheon. Derived from Arada, a people from Dahomey (now Benin). The other major division is **Petwo.**

Rancheros (Cuba 3, Mexico)—Contemporary rural couple dances of Mexican farm workers; related to **son** and **punto guajiro** in Cuba.

Rara (Haiti 9)—Public festival held throughout Lent in Haiti. Special features include hocketing bamboo trumpets and a baton major costumed in shimmering sequins or bits of mirror.

Rastafari (Jamaica 7)—A religious concept developed in Jamaica by Leonard P. Howell in the 1930s.

Reggae (Jamaica 7)—Indigenous popular music of Jamaica developed in the 1960s.

Reto (Puerto Rico 14)—The challenge that a dancer makes to the lead drummer in **bomba,** to make sounds on the drum that correspond to the dancer's improvised movements.

Rezo (Dominican Republic 10)—Term in the Afro-Dominican religious brotherhood of Villa Mella for the last and longest (all night or all day) prayer ritual of the nine nights following burial. The rezo includes drumming, and dance by the spirit of the deceased, who possesses a relative of the opposite sex.

Ritmo de habanera, ritmo de tango (Cuba 3)—A rhythmic pattern of five pulses sounded within three beats; also called *cinquillo*.

Rocksteady (Jamaica 7)—A slow ballad-tempo counterpoint to **ska.**

Rumba (Cuba 3)—A Cuban dance/music creation of the nineteenth century that continues in the present; the name of a dance/music family of dances or complex from the mixtures of African and European cultures in Cuba; percussion, human voice, and improvisation within a set structure of dance and of instruments.

Rumba, Rhumba (International—ed. in consultation with Y. D.)—A social dance, distinct from the Cuban **rumba** defined above, that follows a basic **son** step pattern and first became popular in the 1930s in the United States and elsewhere outside of Cuba.

Rumba clave (Cuba 3)—The organizing rhythmic pattern of **rumba;** varies by one-half a beat from **son clave;** a stretched syncopated rhythm from **Carabalí** music/dance tradition that helped to identify the new creation in Cuba.

Rumberos (Cuba 3)—True **rumba** performers.

Salsa (Cuba 3)—A type of **son** music and dance of the twentieth century; a fast, constantly turning, couple dance in virtuoso display; developed by Puerto Rican and other Caribbean musicians in the United States. (Puerto Rico 12)—Music/dance phenomenon originating in New York City in the late 1960s. Salsa is not a new rhythm, but a new way of making music, a new way of freely combining diverse Afro-Caribbean rhythms.

Salve (Dominican Republic 10)—Altar and procession/pilgrimage song genre of Dominican folk Catholicism. The genre includes: (1) the sacred, liturgical *salve de la Virgen*, sung antiphonally and unaccompanied, in groups of three, during a saint's festival of personal sponsorship and during processions and pilgrimages; (2) the African-influenced, accompanied *salve con versos* of the East and yet more African-influenced *salve con panderos* (with hand drums) or *salve con palos* (with long-drums) of the central south. This nonliturgical salve is performed at the altar after the salve de la Virgen and is structured in **call and response** form. The term *versos*, in addition to meaning extra text in reference to the salve prayer, is also a generic term for all folk-Catholic songs that are not salves.

Samba (Cuba 3, Brazil)—A Brazilian dance from **Kongo-Angolan** heritage with a gestural naval bumping; related to **rumba** in Cuba.

Sanba—Poet or composer of the people. Leads Carnival and **Rara** bands, as well as the bands that accompany cooperative work (**konbit**).

Santería (Cuba 3)—The **Yoruba**-based religion of Cuba; discussed often in terms of "syncretism" or the interpenetration of African and Catholic beliefs; today is discussed in terms of the range of African beliefs beneath an "umbrella" of Catholic symbols during the period of slavery and other oppressive times in Cuba.

Sarambo (Dominican Republic 10)—A Dominican social dance of the Cibao region, and El Seybo, where it is called **guarapo,** in a fast 6/8 tempo. Based on the **zapateo.**

Sarandunga (Dominican Republic 10)—The music and dance of the Afro-Dominican religious brotherhood of St. John the Baptist in or near Baní. According to oral history, originally from Port-au-Prince, Haiti, and associated with a Dominican extended family. The music and instruments are unique variants of **palos.** The dance is similar in pattern to **baile de palos,** but the male role is much more virtuosic.

Segon—Second drum of the **Vodou** ensemble. Engages in musical conversations with the mother drum.

Segundo (Cuba 3)—The second **tumbador** or mid-range, barrel-shaped drum.

Seis (Puerto Rico 12)—One of Puerto Rico's most important folk musical genres, preserving the Spanish 10-line stanza poetic form, the **décima.** Known as *música jíbara* or *campesino*, it evolved among peasants. The songs are composed in a strict music and rhyme scheme and are frequently improvised by *trovadores*. The dance evolved from the six-couple Spanish seises.

Seu (Curaçao 19)—Music and dance form from Curaçao; original word means "harvest" in Bantu.

Shouters or **Spiritual Baptists** (Trinidad and Tobago 17)—A belief system that blends Old Testament Judaism with modern Christianity while retaining fundamental aspects of African religious practices.

Sicá (Puerto Rico 14)—A **bomba** rhythm complex with twelve known variants [see chapter for names and details], played in 2/4 time.

Siyak (French Caribbean 16)—Scraper made out of bamboo and used in most **quadrille** bands of the French Caribbean.

Ska (Jamaica 7)—An indigenous up-tempo Jamaican pop music.

Soberao (Puerto Rico 14)—The dance circle that is formed in **bomba.**

Soca—As a party music, the older calypso has been succeeded in many locales by the hard-driving, **wining**-inducing *soca* (standing for soul-calypso), developed from calypso, and, like it, originating in Trinidad and now widely popular on many English-speaking islands.

Son (Cuba 3)—The name of a Cuban dance/music complex that surfaced in the sixteenth century and has evolved to permeate folk, popular, and symphonic music of Cuba, the Caribbean, Latin America, Africa, Europe and perhaps other places in the twenty-first century; a popular blend of European and African concepts of dancing and music-making.

Son clave (Cuba 3)—An organizing rhythmic pattern for **son** music and dance.

Spliff (Jamaica 7)—Marijuana cigarette.

Steelband or **Pan**—The percussive but melodic metal orchestra of Trinidad, originally made from oil drums.

Subidor (Puerto Rico 14)—The high drum used in **bomba** music; also the lead drummer who plays this drum while interpreting the movements of the bomba dancer.

Sucu-sucu (Cuba 3)—A type of **son** music/dance from the western region of Cuba.

Swaré bele (French Caribbean 16)—From the French *soirée*. Martinican **bele** dance parties that take place during the evening and part of the night.

Tambora (Dominican Republic 10)—The drum associated with the Dominican **merengue**. A medium-sized, double-headed drum, held horizontally by a cord around the neck and beaten on one head by a stick and on the other by the hand.

Tambu (Curaçao)—African-Curaçao's ritual-derived music and dance, and the name of the event where it takes place; also, the name of a drum.

Tambu (Jamaica 6)—An African Jamaican ritual dance.

Tanbou—Collective name for all drums.

Tanbouwinè—Drummer.

Tibwa (French Caribbean 16)—Pair of sticks that sets the tempo in all musical genres of Martinique. In the north, the tibwa is played on the side of the bele drum; in the rest of the island, on a bamboo branch.

Ticano (French Caribbean 16)—Other name for **calenda** danced only in northeastern Martinique.

Timba (Cuba 3)—A contemporary, highly improvisational musical organization of Cuban, Caribbean, and Latin American music, based in **son**

and contemporary jazz and funk sounds; evolving from "happenings" or spontaneous gatherings with free-form improvisation.

Tiple (Cuba 3)—A Spanish instrument of the colonial period in Cuba.

Toast (Jamaica 7)—DJ's banter.

Toeheel (Congolese 2, Jamaica)—Popular dance to Jamaican **dancehall** that looks like a slow **samba.**

Trankamentu (Curaçao 19)—Shoulder-pushing dance (after cutting in on a partner) by men in **Tambu.**

Tres (Cuba 3)—A small Cuban-style, double-stringed guitar.

Tumba (Curaçao)—Carnival music and dance from Curaçao.

Tumba francesa (Cuba 3)—The dance/music tradition of French Haitians of African descent who arrived in Cuba at the end of the eighteenth century; continues today in the eastern provinces.

Tumbadores (Cuba 3)—The barrel-shaped drums of **Kongo-Angolan** heritage, also called **congas.**

Twoubadou—From the French *troubadour.* A secular music style developed by itinerant Haitian workers returning from Cuba and the Dominican Republic. Impacted the evolution of **konpa.**

Vaksin (Haiti 9)—One of a set of bamboo trumpets. Deliberately dissonant, they intone in hocket fashion while players strike the sides of the instruments with sticks.

Velación (Dominican Republic 10)—The all-night Dominican saint's festival held at the homestead of an individual who offers this devotional act in payment of a vow for divine healing. Includes rosaries and altar music (**salves, versos**); may include drumming and drum dance; may also include social dance.

Versos—see **salves.**

Vèvè—A cosmogram traced on the floor of a **Vodou peristyle.** Each vèvè both represents and invokes a spirit.

Virgen de la Altagracia (Dominican Republic 10)—The extra-official, but most venerated deity of Dominican Catholicism and folk Catholicism. Her date of celebration, January 21, draws vow-based pilgrims to Higüey from throughout the country, even from Haiti. The secondary pilgrimage is August 14.

Vodou (Haiti 9)—In the Fongbe language of Benin, it means "spirit." In Haiti, it has come to signify Afro-Haitian spirituality and the rituals it entails.

Vodú (Dominican Republic 10)—The Dominican version of Haitian **Vodou,** with its own characteristics as well as regional variants. Like

Vodou, it is a religious society for healing and divination, characterized by spirit possession by African-derived and Afro-New World deities. Vodú includes both private consultations as well as public celebrations, the latter including music (**palos** or **salves**) and dance (embraced drum dance or similar). Dominican practitioners avoid the term Vodú and prefer to refer to altars of *los misterios*, and to their leader or medium as *Servidor* or *Servidora de misterios*.

Voye/reponn—Literally, "send and respond." Better translated as "call and response." Refers to antiphony, that is, a chorus responding to the lead of a solo singer.

Wapa (Curaçao)—A name for the way women sang and danced in **seu**.

Wining (Cuba 3)—A hip gyrating dance of the Anglophone Caribbean; common to Carnival dance movements and **comparsa** dancing in Cuba.

Wiri (Curaçao 19)—A piece of ribbed metal pipe used as a musical instrument.

Wukkin' up (Virgin Islands 15)—"Working up"; a thrusting of the hips as though the dancer is practicing sexual moves.

Yanvalou (Haiti 9)—One of the dances in honor of the **Rada** division of the **Vodou** pantheon. Famous for its undulating spine, evocative of Danbala, the serpent god. Fongbe for "praise."

Yoruba (Cuba 3)—An African ethnic group, sometimes including the neighboring **Lucumí;** an African language; a music/dance tradition in Cuba; also an alternate name for the **Oricha, Santería,** or **Lucumí** religion.

Yubá (Puerto Rico 14)—A **bomba** rhythm complex, played in 6/8 time.

Yuca (Dominican Republic 10)—A Dominican social dance of the Cibao region, possibly related to the **merengue**. It consists of the **paseo** and a short conventional dance section followed by an elaborate **jaleo** section, characterized by many turns, made more complex if danced by two interacting couples.

Yuka (Cuba 3)—A **Kongo-Angolan** dance that survives in Cuba; antecedent of Cuban **rumba**.

Zapateado (Cuba 3)—The rhythmic foot and heel patterns in the dancing tradition of Spanish **flamenco;** the **zapateo** dancing part of **punto guajiro** complex.

Zapateo (Cuba 3)—Flat-foot, heel-stomping dance style from Spain; part of identifying characteristic of rural dance in Cuba, the **zapateado** dancing part of **punto guajiro** complex.

Zèpol, Zépaules (Haiti 9)—Named after the French *les épaules,* "shoulders," because of its characteristic movement. A **Rada** dance that usually follows **Yanvalou,** bringing it to a heated conclusion.

Zouk (French Caribbean 16)—Social dance of the French Caribbean. Up to the late 1970s, used in reference to private nighttime dance parties only; since the mid-1980s, also applies to a new musical genre that draws heavily on Carnival rhythms. The slow-tempo zouk, called *zouk love,* is danced by a couple in close embrace and emphasizes undulant hips. The faster *zouk béton* or "hard zouk" is for individual jump-up.

BIBLIOGRAPHY

Acosta, Leonardo. 1983. *Del Tambor al Sintetizador.* Havana: Editorial Letras Cubanas.

Adjaye, Joseph K., and Adrianne R. Andrews, eds. 1997. *Language, Rhythm, & Sound: Black Popular Cultures into the Twenty-First Century.* Pittsburgh: University of Pittsburgh Press.

Ahye, Molly. 1983. *Cradle of Caribbean Dance: Beryl McBurnie and the Little Carib Theatre.* Port of Spain: Heritage Cultures.

———. 1978. *Golden Heritage: The Dance in Trinidad and Tobago.* Port of Spain: Heritage Cultures.

Ajayi, Omofolabo Soyinka. 1998. "In Contest: The Dynamics of African Religious Dances." *African Dance: An Artistic, Historical and Philosophical Inquiry,* ed. Kariamu Welsh Asante, 183–202. Trenton, N.J.: Africa World Press.

Alberti, Luis. 1975. *De música y orquestas bailables dominicanas, 1910–1959.* Santo Domingo: Museo del Hombre Dominicano.

Alén, Olavo. 1994. *De lo Afrocubano a la salsa: Géneros Músicales de Cuba.* Havana: Ediciones ARTEX, S.A.

———. 1987. *La música de las sociedades de tumba francesa en Cuba.* Havana: Casa de las Américas.

Alleyne-Dettmers, Patricia T. 1998. "Ancestral Voices. Trevini—A Case Study of Meta-Masking on the Notting Hill Carnival." *Journal of Material Culture* 3(2): 201–221.

———. 1993. "Jump! Jump and Play Mas!" Ph.D. diss. Ann Arbor, Mich.: University Microfilms.

Alonso, Manuel A. [1849] 1988. *El Gíbaro: Cuadro de Costumbres de la Isla de Puerto Rico.* San Juan: Instituto de Cultura Puertorriqueña.

Anderson, Benedict. 1995. *Imagined Communities.* Reprint. New York: Verso.

Anderson, Michelle. 1982. "Authentic Voodoo Is Synthetic." *The Drama Review,* 26(2): 89–110.

Andrade, Manuel J. 1930. *Folklore from the Dominican Republic.* Memoirs of the American Folklore Society, vol. 23. New York: American Folklore Society. Spanish language edition: 1930. *Folklore de la República Dominicana.* Santo Domingo: Universidad de Santo Domingo.

Appiah, Kwame Anthony, and Henry Louis Gates, Jr., eds. 1999. *Africana: The Encyclopedia of the African and African American Experience*. New York: Basic Civitas Books.

Aretz, Isabel, and Luis Felipe Rámon y Rivera. 1963. "Reseña de un viaje a la República Dominicana." *Boletín del Instituto de Folklore* 4(4): 157–204. Caracas: Ministerio de Educacíon, Dirección de Cultura y Bellas Artes.

Arzeno, Julio. 1927. *Del folk-lore musical dominicano*. Santo Domingo: Imprenta "La cuna de América," Roques Román, Hnos.

Aschenbrenner, Joyce. 1981. "Katherine Dunham: Reflections of the Social and Political Contexts of Afro-American Dance." *Congress on Research in Dance Annual* 12: 4, 41–59.

Austerlitz, Paul. 1997. *Merengue: Dominican Music and Dominican Identity*. Philadelphia: Temple University Press.

Baez, Josefina. 2000. *Dominicanish*. New York: I Ombe.

Bailey, Marilynn. 1999. "Bamboula: A Special Link." *Virgin Islands Daily News* special, *The Times of Our Lives: 100 Years in the Virgin Islands, 1900–1999*.

Barnes, Clive. "Jamaica Opens Dance Season." *New York Post*, September 16, 1983: 48.

Barnett, Sheila. 1979. "Jonkonnu and the Creolisation Process in Jamaica: A Study in Cultural Dynamics." Master's thesis, Antioch International University.

———. 1979. "Jonkonnu: Pitchy Patchy." *Jamaica Journal* 43 (March): 18–32.

Barton, Halbert. 2002. "The Bombazo Movement in Puerto Rico during the 1990's." In *Con Ton y Son: Ensayos de Musica, Cultura y Sociedad Puertorriqueña (Un Homenaje a Amaury Veray Torregrosa)*, ed. Edgardo Diaz Diaz and Xavier Totti Veray. Rio Piedras: University of Puerto Rico Press.

———. 2000. "A Thousand Soberaos: Social Space as a Drum," part. 2. In *Caribbean 2000 Symposium Proceedings*, ed. Lowell Fiet and Janette Becerra, vol. 4. Rio Piedras: University of Puerto Rico Press.

———. 1999. "El Espacio Social Como Tambor: Bomba en la época postpatriacal." In *Caribbean 2000 Symposium Proceedings*, ed. Lowell Fiet and Janette Becerra, vol. 3. Rio Piedras: University of Puerto Rico Press.

———. 1995. "The Drum-Dance Challenge: An Anthropological Study of the Gender, Race and Class Marginalization of Bomba in Puerto Rico." Ph.D. diss., Cornell University.

———. 1995. "The Puerto Ricanization of the Americas: A View from Gringolandia." *Chicano/Latino Research News* (fall). University of California–Santa Cruz.

Bastide, Roger. 1972. *African Civilizations in the New World*. Trans. Peter Green. New York: Harper Row.

Baxter, Ivy. 1970. *The Arts of an Island: The development of the culture and of the folk and creative arts in Jamaica, 1494–1962 (Independence)*. Metuchen, N.J.: Scarecrow Press.

Beckford, Ruth. 1979. *Katherine Dunham: A Biography.* New York: Marcel Dekker.

Benoist, Jean. 1975. "Les composantes raciales de la Martinique." In *Les sociétés antillaises: études anthropologiques.* Fonds St.-Jacques, Martinique: Centre de recherches caraïbes, Université de Montréal.

Bentley, Rev. W. Holman. [1887] 1967. *Dictionary and Grammar of the Kongo Language as spoken at San Salvador.* Farnborough, Hants, England: Gregg Press.

Bettleheim, Judith. 1988. "Jonkonnu and other Christmas Masquerades." In *Caribbean Festival Arts: Each and Every Bit a Difference,* ed. Judith Bettleheim and John Nunley. Seattle: University of Washington Press.

———. 1985. "The Jonkonnu Festival in Jamaica." *Journal of Ethnic Studies* 13(3): 85–105.

———. 1979. "The Afro-Jamaican Jonkonnu Festival: Playing the Forces and Operating the Cloth." Ph.D. diss., Yale University.

———. 1976. "The Jonkonnu Festival: Its Relation to Caribbean and African Masquerades." *Jamaica Journal* 10(2–4): 21–27.

Bettleheim, Judith and John Nunley. 1988a. "Masquerade Mix-up in Trinidadian Carnival: Live Once, Die Forever." In *Caribbean Festival Arts: Each and Every Bit a Difference,* ed. Judith Bettleheim and John Nunley. Seattle: University of Washington Press.

———, eds. 1988b. *Caribbean Festival Arts: Each and Every Bit a Difference.* Seattle: University of Washington Press.

Biemiller, Ruth. 1969. *Dance: The Story of Katherine Dunham.* New York: Doubleday.

Bleiberg, Laura. 2000. "A Passage from India." *Dance Magazine* 74(6): 48–51, 80.

Bob, June. 1998. *Beating a Restless Drum: The Poetics of Kamau Braithwaite and Derek Walcott.* Trenton, N.J.: Africa World Press.

Bólivar, Natalia. 1990. *Los orichas en Cuba.* Havana: Ediciones Union.

Bourgeois, J.-J. 1958. *Martinique et Guadeloupe terres français des Antilles.* Paris: Horizons de France.

Bouton, Jacques. 1640. *Relation de l'établissement des François depuis l'an 1635, l'isle de la Martinique, l'une des Antilles de l'Amérique, des moeurs des sauvages, de la situation et des autres singularités de l'isle.* Paris: Cramoisi.

Bowser, Frederick Park. 1974. *The African Slave in Colonial Perú: 1545–1650.* Stanford: Stanford University Press.

Boyer, William. 1983. *America's Virgin Islands: A History of Human Rights and Wrongs.* Durham, N.C.: Carolina Academic Press.

Brandon, George. 1993. *Santería from Africa to the New World: The Dead Sell Memories.* Bloomington: Indiana University Press.

Brenneker, Paul. 1976. *Sambumbu: volkskunde van Curaçao, Aruba en Bonaire,* vols. 1, 2, 3, 6, 7, 10. Willemstad: Uitgeverij van Dorp.

Brito Ureña, Luis Manuel. 1987. *El merengue y la realidad existencial del hombre dominicano.* Santo Domingo: Universidad Autónoma de Santo Domingo.

Broyard, Anatole. 1993. *Kafka Was the Rage*. New York: Vintage.

Cabrera, Lydia. 1958. *La sociedad secreta Abakuá*. Reprint, Miami: Ediciones C.R., 1970.

Caillois, Roger. 1984. "Mimicry and Legendary Psychasthenia." Translated by John Spheley. *October* 1 (Winter): 16–32.

Campbell, Joseph. 1988. *The Power of Myth*. With Bill Moyers. New York: Bantam Doubleday.

Canizares, Raúl. 1993. *Cuban Santería: Walking with the Night*. Rochester, Vt.: Destiny Books.

Carrasco, René. [1970s]. "Album: Museo de la Cueva Colonial," vol. 2. Santo Domingo. Mimeographed.

———. [1960s–1970s]. "Enciclopedia." Manuscript.

Carty, Hilary S. 1988. *Folk Dances of Jamaica: An Insight: A study of five folk dances of Jamaica with regard to the origins, history, development, contemporary setting, and dance technique of each*. London: Dance Books.

Cashion, Susan V. 1989. "Educating the Dancer in Cuba." In *Dance: Current Selected Research*, edited by Lynnette Overby and James H. Humphrey, vol. 1, 165–85. New York: AMS Press.

Castro Ríos, Andrés. 1975. "Algo sobre nuestra danza." *Nosotros* 2 (2), July–September.

Chao Carbonero, Graciela. 1980. *Bailes Yorubas de Cuba*. Havana: Editorial Pueblo y Educación.

Chao Carbonero, Graciela, and Sara Lamerán. 1982. *Folklore Cubano, I, II, III, IV*. Havana: Editorial Pueblo y Educación.

Chatterjee, Partha. 1993. *The Nation and Its Fragments*. Princeton, N.J.: Princeton University Press.

Christopher, Mary Ann Golden. 1999. "Modern Dancers Revive the Bamboula." *Virgin Islands Daily News* special, *The Times of Our Lives: 100 Years in the Virgin Islands 1900–1999*.

Chujoy, Anatole, and P. W. Manchester. 1967. *The Dance Encyclopedia*, revised ed. New York: Simon and Schuster.

Clark, VèVè. 1994. "Performing the Memory of Difference in Afro-Caribbean Dance: Katherine Dunham's Choreography." In *History and Memory in African-American Culture, 1938–87*, edited by Robert O'Meally and Geneviève Fabre, 188–204. New York: Oxford University Press.

Clark, VèVè, and Margaret B. Wilkerson, eds. 1978. *Kaiso: Katherine Dunham: An Anthology of Writings*. Berkeley: University of California Institute for the Study of Social Change.

Clarke, Dennis, ed. 1989. *The Penguin Encyclopedia of Popular Music*. London: Viking Penguin.

Compan, Charles. 1787. *Dictionnaire de la danse, contenant l'histoire, les règles et les principes de cet art avec des réflexions critiques et des anecdotes curieuses concernant la danse ancienne et moderne*. Paris: Cailleau.

Coopersmith, J. M. 1949. *Music and Musicians of the Dominican Republic/Música y músicos de la República Dominicana.* Music Series, no. 15. Washington, D.C.: Pan American Union.

Corvington, Georges. 1991. *Port-au-Prince au cours des ans: La ville contemporaine, 1934–1950.* Port-au-Prince: Imprimerie Henri Deschamps.

Cosentino, Donald J., ed. 1995. *Sacred Arts of Haitian Vodou.* Los Angeles: UCLA Fowler Museum.

Courlander, Harold. 1960. *The Drum and the Hoe: Life and Lore of the Haitian People.* Reprint, Los Angeles: University of California Press, 1985.

Cowley, John. 1997. "Slavery, Jonkonnu and Carnival: Continuities and Contrasts." Unpublished paper.

———. 1991. "Carnival and Other Seasonal Festivals in the West Indies, USA & Britain: A Selected Bibliographical Index." In *Bibliographies in Ethnic Relations,* no. 10. Coventry: Coventry Center for Research in Ethnic Relations.

Craven, Henry, and John Brafield. [1883] 1971. *English-Congo and Congo-English Dictionary.* Freeport, N.Y.: Books for Libraries Press.

Crowley, Daniel J. 1956. "Traditional Masques of Carnival." *Caribbean Quarterly* 4(3,4): 198.

Cuisse (de La), maître de danse. 1762. *Le (1er) répertoire des bals ou théorie pratique des contredanses décrites d'une manière aisée avec des figures démonstratives pour les pouvoir danser facilement auxquelles on a rajouté les airs notés.* Paris: Cailleau.

Curtin, Philip D. 1969. *The Atlantic Slave Trade; A Census.* Madison: University of Wisconsin Press.

Cyrille, Dominique. 1996. "Recherche sur la musique rurale de la Martinique." Ph.D. diss., Université Paris-IV-Sorbonne.

———. 1989. "Quadrilles Nègres: Contribution à l'étude des musiques et danses d'origine européenne, introduites à la Martinique entre 1780 et 1840." Master's thesis, Université Paris-IV-Sorbonne.

Daget, Serge. 1990. *La traite des Noirs: Bastilles négrières et vélléités abolitionnistes.* Rennes: Editions Ouest-France.

Daniel, Yvonne. Forthcoming. "Articulate Movement: Sacred Performance in Vodun, Santería, and Candomble."

———. 1995. *Rumba: Dance and Social Change in Contemporary Cuba.* Bloomington: Indiana University Press.

———. 1989. "Ethnography of Rumba." Ph.D. diss., Berkeley: University of California.

David, Bernard. 1973. *Les origines de la population martiniquaise au fil du temps 1635–1902.* Fort-de-France: Société d'Histoire de la Martinique.

Davis, Martha Ellen. 1998a. "Dominican Republic." In *International Encyclopedia of Dance,* vol. 2: 429–33. New York: Oxford University Press.

———. 1998b. "The Dominican Republic." In *The Garland Encyclopedia of World Music,* vol. 2: 845–63. New York: Garland Publishing.

———. 1994a. "'Bi-Musicality' in the Cultural Configurations of the Caribbean." *Black Music Research Journal* 14(2): 145–160.

———. 1994b. "Music and Black Ethnicity in the Dominican Republic." In *Music and Black Ethnicity in the Caribbean and South America*, edited by Gerard Béhague, 119–55. Miami: University of Miami North-South Center.

———. 1976. "'The Drum Dance ("El Baile de Palos"),' Afro-Dominican Religious Brotherhoods: Structure, Ritual, and Music." Ph.D. diss., University of Illinois.

Debien, Gabriel. 1974. *Les esclaves aux Antilles Françaises XVII et XVIIIe siècles*. Fort-de-France: Société d'Histoire de la Martinique.

Delawarde, Jean-Baptiste. 1937. *La vie paysanne à la Martinique; essai de géographie humaine*. Fort-de-France: Imprimerie Officielle.

Del Castillo, José, and Manuel García Arévalo. 1992. *Antoʾogía del Merengue/Anthology of the Merengue*. Santo Domingo: Editora Corripio.

Delgado, Celeste Fraser, and José Esteban Muñoz. 1997. "Rebellions of Everynight Life." In *Everynight Life: Culture and Dance in Latin/o America*, edited by Celeste Fraser Delgado and José Esteban Muñoz, 9–32. Durham, N.C.: Duke University Press.

Denis, Lorimer, and François Duvalier. 1944. *L'Evolution Stadale du Vodou*. Port-au-Prince: Le Bulletin du Bureau d'Ethnologie.

Deren, Maya. 1953. *Divine Horsemen: The Living Gods of Haiti*. New York: Thames and Hudson. 1991. Reprint, New Paltz, N.Y.: McPherson.

Dessalles, Pierre. [1834] 1987. *La vie d'un colon à la Martinique au XIXe siècle*. Montrouge, France: Désormeaux.

Dirección Política de las FAR. 1972. *Historia de Cuba*, vol. 1. Havana: Instituto Cubano del Libro.

Dominguez, Luis Arturo. 1989. *Vivencia de un rito Loango en el Tambú*. Caracas: Hijos de Ramírez Paz.

Dookhan, Isaac. 1974. *A History of the Virgin Islands of the United States*. Epping, England: College of the Virgin Islands Caribbean University Press with Bowker Publishing.

———. 1996. "Dossier Gilda Navarra." *Postdata* 12 (May): 73–108. San Juan.

Drewal, Henry, John Pemberton, and Rowland Abiodun. 1989. *Yoruba: Nine Centuries of African Art and Thought*. New York: Center for African Art.

Drewal, Margaret Thompson. 1989. "Bade Ajuwón—Dancing for Ogun in Yorubaland and in Brazil." In *Africa's Ogun: Old World and New*, edited by Sandra Barnes. Bloomington: Indiana University Press.

Dufrasne-González, José Emanuel. 1994. *Puerto Rico también tiene tambó*. Rio Grande: Paracumbé.

Dunham, Katherine. 1983. *Dances of Haiti*, revised ed. Los Angeles: Center for Afro-American Studies, University of California, Los Angeles. French edition: 1957. *Les Danses de Haiti*. Paris: Fasquel Press.

———. 1969. *Island Possessed*. Garden City, N.Y.: Doubleday.

———. 1947. "The Dances of Haiti." *Acta Anthropologica* 2 (November): 5–61.

———. 1946. *Journey to Accompong*. New York: Henry Holt.

———. 1941. "Form and Function in Primitive Dance." *Educational Dance* (October): 2–4.

———[Kaye Dunn]. 1939a. "L'Ag'Ya of Martinique." *Esquire*, November, 84–85, 126.

———[Kaye Dunn]. 1939b. "La Boule Blanche." *Esquire*, September, 92–93, 158.

Dutertre, R. P. 1973. *Histoire Générale des isles habitées par les François (1661–1671)*. Fort-de-France: Edition des Horizons Caraibes.

Elder, Jacob D. 1969a. *From Congo Drum to Steelband: A Socio- Historical Account of the Emergence of the Trinidad Steel Orchestra*. St. Augustine: University of the West Indies.

———. 1969b. *The Yoruba Ancestor Cult in Gasparillo: Its Structure, Organization, and Social Function in Community Cohesion*. St. Augustine: University of the West Indies.

Emery, Lynne Fauley. 1988. *Black Dance in the United States from 1619 to 1970*, 2d ed. Princeton, N.J.: Princeton Book Company.

———. 1972. *Black Dance in the United States from 1619 to 1970*. Palo Alto, Calif.: National Press Books. Second, revised edition. 1988. Princeton, N.J.: Princeton Book Company.

"Encuentro con el Merengue," proceedings. 1978. Santo Domingo.

Fernández de Oviedo, Gonzalo. 1851–55. *Historia general y natural de las Indias, Islas y tierra-firme del Mar Oceano*, 4 vols. Madrid: Réal Academia de la Historia.

Figueroa, Frank. 1994. *Encyclopedia of Latin American Music in New York*. St. Petersburg, Fla.: Pillar Productions.

Flores, Juan. 1993. "Puerto Rican and Proud, Boyee: Rap, Roots and Amnesia." *Centro de Estudios Puertorriqueños Bulletin* 5(1): 22–32.

Floyd, Samuel. 1998. "Toussaint Rhythm." Public lecture, Northwestern University, April.

Fouchard, Jean. 1973. *La Meringue, Danse Nationale d'Haiti*. Montreal: Leméac.

Franck, Harry A. 1920. *Roaming through the West Indies*. New York: Century.

Frank, Henry. 1998. "Haitian Ritual and Secular Dance." In *International Encyclopedia of Dance*. New York: Oxford University Press.

———. 1982. "African Religion in the Caribbean: Santeria and Voodoo." *Caribbean Magazine* 2(1).

García Canclini, Néstor. 1995. *Hybrid Cultures: Strategies for Entering and Leaving Modernity*. Translated by Christopher L. Chiappari and Silvia L. López. Minneapolis: University of Minnesota Press.

Garrido de Boggs, Edna. 1961. "Panorama del folklore dominicano." *Folklore Américas* 21(1–2): 1–23.

———. 1955. *Folklore infantil de Santo Domingo*. Madrid: Cultura Hispánica. Reprint, Santo Domingo: Sociedad Dominicana de Bibliófilos, 1980.

———. 1950. "La sarandunga." *Cuadernos dominicanos de la cultura* 7(77): 1–18.

Gates, Henry Louis, Jr. 1988. *The Signifying Monkey: A Theory of African-American Literary Criticism.* New York: Oxford University Press.

Gay, Geneva, and Willie L. Baber, eds. 1987. *Expressively Black: The Cultural Basis of Ethnic Identity.* New York: Praeger.

Glasser, Ruth. 1995. *My Music Is My Flag: Musicians and Their New York Communities (1917–1940).* Berkeley: University of California Press.

Goldberg, Alan Bruce. 1981. "Commercial Folklore and Voodoo in Haiti: International Tourism and the Sale of Culture." Ph.D. diss., Indiana University.

Gottschild, Brenda Dixon. 2000. *Waltzing in the Dark: African American Vaudeville and Race Politics in the Swing Era.* New York: St. Martin's.

———. 1996, 1998. *Digging the Africanist Presence in American Performance: Dance and Other Contexts.* Westport, Conn.: Greenwood Press, Praeger Publishers.

Granier de Cassagnac. 1844. *Voyages aux Antilles Françaises, Anglaises.* Paris.

Green, Doris. 1998. "Traditional Dances in Africa." In *African Dance: An Artistic, Historical and Philosophical Inquiry,* edited by Kariamu Welsh Asante, 13–28. Trenton, N.J.: Africa World Press.

Guerra, Ramiro. 1999. *Coordenadas Danzarias.* Havana: Ediciones Union.

———. 1989. *Teatralizacíon del folklore y otros esayos.* Havana: Editorial Lettras Cubana.

Guilcher, Jean-Michel. 1969. *La contredanse et les renouvellements de la danse française.* Paris: Mouton.

Guillard, Yves. ca. 1988. *Le quadrille tel qu'il se dansait à ses origines et son évolution au cours du XIXe siècle.* Cahiers de Recherche. Le Mans: Fricassée.

Guillaume and La Haute, maîtres de danse. 1769. *Almanach dansant ou positions et attitudes de l'allemande avec un discours préliminaire sur l'origine et l'utilité de la danse.* Paris.

Hall, Neville A. T. 1992. *Slave Society in the Danish West Indies.* Mona, Jamaica: University of the West Indies Press.

Harnan, Terry. 1974. *African Rhythm, American Dance.* New York: Knopf.

Harris, Joseph E. 1993. *Global Dimensions of the African Diaspora.* Washington, D.C.: Howard University Press.

Hartog, J. 1973. *Tula: Verlangen naar vrijheid.* Curaçao: Uitgegeven door het Eilandsbestuur van Curaçao.

Hazzard-Donald, Katrina. 1996. "Dance in Hip Hop Culture." In *Droppin' Science: Critical Essays on Rap Music and Hip Hop Culture,* edited by William Eric Perkins. Philadelphia: Temple University Press.

Hernández, Julio Alberto. 1969. *Música tradicional dominicana.* Santo Domingo: Postigo.

———. 1964. *Música folklórica y popular de la República Dominicana.* Santo Domingo: n.p.

———. 1927. *Album musical.* Santo Domingo: Tipografía del Carmen.

Hernández, María del Carmen. 1980. *Historia de la danza en Cuba.* Havana: Editorial Pueblo y Educacíon.

Herskovits, Melville. 1990. *The Myth of the Negro Past*. Boston: New Beacon Press.

———. 1964. *Life in a Haitian Valley*. 1937. Reprint, New York: Octagon Books.

Higman, Barry W. 1984. *Slave Populations of the British Caribbean: 1807–1834*. Baltimore: Johns Hopkins University Press.

———. 1979. "African and Creole Slave Family Patterns in Trinidad." In *Africa and the Caribbean: The Legacies of a Link*, edited by Margaret Craham and Franklin Knight. Baltimore: Johns Hopkins University Press.

Hill, Errol. 1972. *Trinidad Carnival: Mandate for a National Theatre*. Austin: University of Texas Press.

Hodson, Millicent. 1978. "How She Began Her Beguine, Dunham's Dance Literacy." In *Kaiso: Katherine Dunham*, edited by VèVè Clark and Margaret B. Wilkerson. Berkeley: University of California Institute for the Study of Social Change.

Honorat, Michel Lamartinière. 1955. *Les Danses Folkloriques Haïtiennes*. Port-au-Prince: Imprimerie de l'État.

Hurbon, Laennec. 1972. *Dieu dans le Vodou Haitien*. Paris: Payot.

Hurok, Sol, and Ruth Goode. 1946. *Impresario*. New York: Random House.

Jahn, Janheinz. 1961. *Muntu*. Translated by Marjorie Grene. New York: Grove.

Jarvis, Antonio. 1952. *Folk Dancing in the Virgin Islands*. San Juan. Booklet prepared for the Caribbean Festival, August 1–10.

———. 1944. *The Virgin Islands and Their People*. Philadelphia: Dorrance.

John, Suki. 1998. "Cuba: Modern Dance." In *International Encyclopedia of Dance*. New York: Oxford University Press.

Jones, Duane L., ed. 1983. *Caribe: Special Dance Issue* 7(1 and 2).

Jones, Leroi [Amiri Baraka]. 1963. *Blues People*. New York: William Morrow.

Knight, Franklin W. 1978. *The Caribbean: The Genesis of a Fragmented Nationalism*. New York: Oxford University Press.

———. 1970. *Slave Society in Cuba during the Nineteenth Century*. Madison: University of Wisconsin Press.

Kraus, Richard. 1969. *History of the Dance in Art and Education*. Englewood Cliffs, N.J.: Prentice-Hall.

Kubik, Gerhard. 1994. "Ethnicity, Cultural Identity and the Psychology of Culture Contact." In *Music and Black Ethnicity: The Caribbean and Latin America*. Miami: University of Miami North South Center Press.

Kunene, Masisi. 1981. *Anthems of the Decades*. London: Heinemann.

Labat, Jean-Baptiste. 1722. *Nouveau voyage aux isles de l'Amerique . . .*, vol. 4. Paris: Giffart.

Labat, R. P. 1724. *Nouveaux Voyages aux Iles Françoises de l'Amérique*. Paris: Delespine.

Lafontaine, Marie-Céline. 1982. *Musique et société aux Antilles*, vol. 121–22. Paris: Presence africaine.

Lafontaine, Marie-Céline, and Carnot. 1986. *Alors ma chère, moi. Carnot par lui-même*. Paris: Editions Caribbéennes.

Leaf, Earl. 1948. *Isles of Rhythm*. New York: A. S. Barnes.

Le Herissé, A. 1911. *L'Ancien Royaume du Dahomey*. Paris: Larose.

Lekis, Lisa. 1960. *Dancing Gods*. Metuchen, N.J.: Scarecrow Press.

León, Algeliers. 1984. *Del canto y el tiempo*. Havana: Editorial Letras Cubanas.

Lewis, Gordon K. 1972. *The Virgin Islands: A Caribbean Lilliput*. Evanston, Ill.: Northwestern University Press.

Lewisohn, Florence. 1970. *St. Croix under Seven Flags*. Hollywood, Fla.: Dukane Press.

Linares, María Teresa. 1979. *La Música y el Pueblo*. Havana: Editorial Pueblo y Educacíon.

Liverpool, Hollis. 1998. "Origins of Rituals and Customs in the Trinidadian Carnival: African or European?" *The Drama Review* 42(3): 24–38.

———. 1993. "Rituals of Power and Rebellion: The Carnival Tradition in Trinidad & Tobago." Ph.D. diss., University of Michigan.

Lizardo, Fradique. 1975a. *Danzas y bailes folklóricos dominicanos*. Santo Domingo: Museo del Hombre Dominicano and Fundación García-Arévalo.

———. 1975b. *Metodología de la danza: Elementos de coreografía aplicados a los bailes folklóricos dominicanos*. Santo Domingo: Editora Taller.

Lloyd, Margaret. 1949. *The Borzoi Book of Modern Dance*. Brooklyn, N.Y.: Dance Horizons.

Lohr, Lynda. 1999. "Don't Even Try to Stop the Carnival." *Virgin Islands Daily News* special, *The Times of Our Lives: 100 Years in the Virgin Islands 1900–1999*.

Long, Richard. 1989. *The Black Tradition in American Dance*. New York: Rizzoli.

Manuel, Peter. 1995. *Caribbean Currents: Caribbean Music from Rumba to Reggae*. Philadelphia: Temple University Press.

Mars, Louis. 1946. *La Crise de Possession dans le Vaudou*. Port-au-Prince: L'Imprimerie de l'État.

———. 1977. *The Crisis of Possession in Voodoo*. Translated by Kathleen Collins. New York: Reed, Cannon, and Johnson.

Martin, John. 1946. "The Dance: Dunham, Schoolmarm Turned Siren or Vice Versa in 'Bel Negre' at the Belasco." *New York Times*, November 17, section 2: 9.

Martinus, Frank Efraim. 1997. *The Kiss of a Slave: Papiamentu's West-African Connections*. Willemstad: Drukkerij De Curaçaose Courant.

Mason, John. 1992. *Orin Orisa*. Brooklyn, N.Y.: Yoruba Theological Archministry.

Maultsby, Portia K. 1990. "Africanisms in African American Music." In *Africanisms in American Culture*, edited by J. E. Holloway, 185–210. Bloomington: Indiana University Press.

Maximilien, Louis. 1945. *Le Vodou Haitien*. Port-au-Prince: L'Imprimerie de l'État.

McAlister, Elizabeth. 1995. "'Men Mou Yo,' 'Here Are the People': Rara Festivals and Transnational Popular Culture in Haiti and New York City." Ph.D. diss., Yale University.

McCoy, James A. 1968. "The Bomba and Aguinaldo of Puerto Rico as They Have Evolved from Indigenous African and European Cultures." Ph.D. diss., Florida State University.

McDaniel, Lorna. 1998. *The Big Drum Dance of Carriacou: Praise Songs in Rememory of Flight.* Gainesville: University Press of Florida.

McKayle, Donald. 1966. "The Negro Dancer in Our Time." In *The Dance Has Many Faces,* 2d ed., edited by Walter Sorrell, 187–92. New York: Columbia University Press.

McLane, Daisann. 1991. "Dance-Till-You-Drop Merengue." *New York Times,* January 6: 28, 38.

Metraux, Alfred. [1958, French edition] 1959. *Voodoo in Haiti.* Translated by Hugo Charteris. London: A. Deutsch. Reprint, 1972, New York: Schocken Books.

Michalon, Josy. 1987. *Le ladja origines et pratique.* Paris: Editions Caribbéennes.

Minshall, Peter. 1998. "A Voice to Add to the Song of the Universe: An Interview by Richard Schechner and Milla C. Riggio." *The Drama Review* 42(3): 170–93.

Moore, Lillian. 1946. "Moreau de Saint-Méry and 'Danse.'" In *Dance Index,* vol. 5 (October): 232–60. New York: Arno Press.

Moreau de Saint-Méry, M.L.E. 1802. "De la danse." In *Notions coloniales: Rédigé au commencement de l'année 1792.* Parma: Bodoni. Original publication: 1796. *Danse.* Philadelphia: self-published.

———. [1797–1798] 1984. *Description Topographique, physique, civile, politique et historique de la partie française de l'île de Saint Domingue.* Paris: Société d'histoire d'Outre mer.

Murphy, Joseph. 1988. *Santería: An African Religion in America.* Boston: Beacon Press.

"Música." 1978. *Enciclopedia Dominicana,* 2d ed., vol. 5: 75–88. Santo Domingo: Enciclopedia Dominicana, S.A.

Navarra, Gilda. 1988. *Polimnia: Taller de Histriones 1971–1985.* San Juan: Gilda Navarra and Instituto de Cultura Puertorriqueña.

Nettleford, Rex. 1990. "Afro-Caribbean Dance." *Dancing Times,* Dance Study supplement 8, London.

———. 1985. *Dance Jamaica: Cultural Definitions and Artistic Discovery: The National Dance Theatre Company of Jamaica, 1962–1983.* New York: Grove Press.

———. 1969. *Roots and Rhythms: Jamaica's National Dance Theatre.* London: Andre Deutsch; New York: Hill and Wang.

Nicolas, Armand. 1996. *Histoire de la Martinique.* 3 vols. Paris: L'Harmattan.

Nkétia, Kwabena J. H. 1968. *Our Drums, Our Drummers.* Accra: Ghana Publishers House.

———. 1965. *Music, Dance, and Drama: A Review of the Performing Arts of Ghana.* Legon: Institute of African Studies.

Nolasco, Flérida de. 1956. *Santo Domingo en el folklore universal.* Ciudad Trujillo: Impresora Dominicana.

———. 1948. *Vibraciones en el tiempo.* Ciudad Trujillo: Montalvo.

———. 1946. "El carabiné." *Boletín del Folklore Dominicano* 1(1): 19–24.

———. 1939. *La música en Santo Domingo y otros ensayos*. Ciudad Trujillo: Montalvo.

Olalquiaga, Celeste. 1992. *Megalopolis: Contemporary Cultural Sensibilities*. Minneapolis: University of Minnesota Press.

Oliver, Cynthia. 1995. "St. Croix Dancing: The Contemporary and Historical Path of Dance on the U.S. Virgin Island of St. Croix." Master's thesis, New York University.

Omari, Mikelle. 1984. *From the Inside to the Outside: The Art and Ritual of Bahian Candomble*. Los Angeles: Museum of Cultural History, University of California.

Oriol, Jacques, Michel Aubourg, and Leonce Viaud. 1952. *Le mouvement folklorique en Haiti*. Port-au-Prince: Imprimerie de l'État.

Ortiz, Fernando. 1951 (1981, 1985). *Los bailes y el teatro de los negros en el folklore de Cuba*. Havana: Editorial Letras Cubanas.

Pacini Hernández, Deborah. 1995. *Bachata: A Social History of a Dominican Popular Music*. Philadelphia: Temple University Press.

Paiewonsky, Isidor. 1989. *Eyewitness Accounts of Slavery in the Danish West Indies*. New York: Fordham University Press.

Pajares Santiesteban, Fidel. 1993. *Ramiro Guerra y la danza en Cuba*. Quito: Casa de la Cultura Ecuatoriana.

Paul, Emmanuel C. 1962. *Panorama du Folklore Haïtien (Présence Africaine en Haïti)*. Port-au-Prince: Imprimerie de l'État.

Paulino, Julio César. 1992. "Apuntes para la historia: Un merengue llamado pambiche durante la intervención del 1916." *Listín Diario*, "La Tarde Alegre." September 7: 6.

———. 1987. "El pambiche." *Listín Diario*, Suplemento. November 2: 9.

Pérez, Jorge. 1991. "La plena puertorriqueña: de la expresión popular a la comercialización muscial." *Centro de Estudios Puertorriqueños Bulletin* 3(2): 50–55.

Perez, Louis A. 1988 (1995). *Cuba: Between Reform and Revolution*. New York: Oxford University Press.

Perkins, William Eric. 1996. *Droppin' Science: Critical Essays on Rap Music and Hip Hop Culture*. Philadelphia: Temple University Press.

Pollack, Barbara. 1993. *Dance Is a Moment: A Portrait of José Limon in Words and Pictures*. Pennington, N.J.: Princeton Book Company.

Primus, Pearl. 1998. "African Dance." In *African Dance: An Artistic, Historical and Philosophical Inquiry*, edited by Kariamu Welsh Asante, 3–11. Trenton, N.J.: Africa World Press.

Quintero-Rivera, Angel. 1998. *Salsa, sabor y control: sociología de la música tropical*. Mexico City: Siglo XXI.

Ramos, Arturo. 1954. *O Folclore Negro do Brasil: Demopsicologia e Psicanálise*. Rio de Janeiro: Livraria-Editoria da Casa do Esudante do Brasil.

———. 1940. *O Negro Brasileiro*. Rio de Janeiro: Companhia Editoria Nacional.

Ramsey, Kate. 1997. "Vodou, Nationalism, and Performance: The Staging of

Folklore in Mid-Twentieth Century Haiti." In *Meaning in Motion: New Cultural Studies of Dance*, edited by Jane C. Desmond, 345–78. Durham, N.C.: Duke University Press.

Rand, Christopher. 1958. *The Puerto Ricans*. New York: Oxford University Press.

"Resolution sur le folklore." 1947. *Bulletin du Bureau d'Ethnologie* (March): 37–38. Port-au-Prince.

Riggio, Milla C. 1998. "Resistance and Identity: Carnival in Trinidad and Tobago." *The Drama Review* 42(3): 7–23.

Ríos-Colón, Nydia A. 1980. *Bailes de Puerto Rico: apuntes para un estudio*. San Juan: Inter-American University of Puerto Rico.

Rivera, Raquel Z. 1993. "Rap Music in Puerto Rico: Mass Consumption or Social Resistance?" *Centro de Estudios Puertorriqueños Bulletin* 5(1): 52–65.

Rivera González, Luis. 1961? *Antología musical de la era de Trujillo, 1930–1969*, 4 vols. Ciudad Trujillo: Secretaría del Estado de Educación y Bellas Artes.

Roberts, John Storm. 1999. *The Latin Tinge*, 2d ed. New York: Oxford University Press.

———. 1998. *Black Music of Two Worlds*, 2d ed. New York: Prentice-Hall.

———. 1979. *The Latin Tinge*. Tivoli, N.Y.: Original Music.

———. 1973. *Black Music of Two Worlds*. London: Allen Lane.

Rodríguez, Demorizi, Emilio. 1971. *Música y baile en Santo Domingo*. Santo Domingo: Librería Hispaniola.

Rodriguez, Victoria E. 1994. "Cuban Music and Ethnicity: Historical Considerations." In *Music and Black Ethnicity: The Caribbean and Latin America*, 91–108. Miami: University of Miami North South Center Press.

Rogers, Rod. 1967. "For the Celebration of Our Blackness." *Dance Scope*, spring.

Rohlehr, Gordon. 1999. "The Rehumanizing of History: Regeneration of Spirit, Apocalypse and Revolution in Braithwaite's *The Arrivants* and *X/Self*." In *The Shape of That Hurt & Other Essays*. Port of Spain: Longman.

Rondón, César Miguel. 1980. *El libro de la salsa: crónica de la música del Caribe urbano*. Caracas: Editorial Arte.

Rosalia, Rene V. 1997. *Tambu: De legale en kerkelijke repressie van Afro-Curaçaose volksuitingen*. Zutphen, Netherlands: Uitgeversmaatschappij Walburg Pers.

———. 1994. *Tambu di Siglo 20: kuater epoka kuater genero, 20 aña zoyoyo I su grupo*. Curaçao: Instituo Stripan.

Ryman, Cheryl. 1984. "Jonkonnu: A Neo-African Form," parts 1 and 2. *Jamaica Journal* 17(1): 13–23, 17(2): 50–61.

———. 1983. "Dance as a Major Source and Stimulus for Communicating Africanisms in Order to Effect a Process of Self-Actualization." Master's thesis. Antioch International University.

Sachs, Kurt. 1937. *World History of the Dance*. New York: Norton.

Said, Edward W. 1993. *Culture and Imperialism*. New York: Knopf.

Sands, Rosita. 1989. "The Musical Culture of Junkanoo." *The Wooster Review* 9: 143–53.

Schmiderer, Stephanie. 1990. "Dancing for the Loas to Make the Loas Dance: Haitian Ritual Dance and Its Translation to Theatrical Performance (Haiti, New York)." In *Ay Bobo: Afro-Karibische Religionen, Teil 2, Voodoo*. Vienna: Institut für Völkerkunde der Universität Wien.

Schrader, Richard A., Sr. 1994. *Maufe, Quelbe and t'ing: a calabash of stories*. St. Croix: Antilles Graphic Arts.

Thomas, Hugh. 1997. *The Slave Trade: The Story of the Atlantic Slave Trade: 1440–1870*. New York: Simon and Schuster.

Thomas, Roy. 1978. "Focal Rites: New Dance Dominions." In *Kaiso: Katherine Dunham: An Anthology of Writings*, edited by VèVè Clark and Margaret B. Wilkerson. Berkeley: University of California Institute for the Study of Social Change.

Thompson, Robert Farris. 1998. "Notes on Mambo." *First of the Month* 1(1): 10.

———. 1988. "Recapturing Heaven's Glamour: Afro-Caribbean Festivalizing Arts." In *Caribbean Festival Arts: Each and Every Bit a Difference*, edited by Judith Bettleheim and John Nunley. Seattle: University of Washington Press.

———. 1983. *Flash of the Spirit: African and Afro-American Art and Philosophy*. New York: Random House.

———. 1974. *African Art in Motion*. Los Angeles: University of California Press.

———. 1966. "An Aesthetic of the Cool: West African Dance." *African Forum* 2(2): 85–102.

Uri, Alex, and Françoise Uri. 1991. *Le chant du Karukéra: Musique et musiciens de la Guadeloupe*. Paris: Con Brio.

Urfé, Odilio. 1984. "Music and Dance in Cuba." In *Africa in Latin America: Essays on History, Culture and Socialization*, edited by Manuel Moreno Fraginals. New York: Holmes and Meier.

Vega Drouet, Héctor. 2000. "Puerto Rico." In *The Garland Handbook of Latin American Music*, edited by Dale Olsen and Daniel Sheehy. New York: Garland Publishing.

———. 1983. "The Bomba and the Plena: Africa Retained in Music and Dance in Puerto Rico." *Caribe* 7(1 and 2): 42–43.

———. 1979. "Historical and Ethnological Survey on Probable African Origins of the Puerto Rican Bomba, Including a Description of Santiago Apostol." Ph.D. diss., Wesleyan University.

Vinueza, María Elena. 1986. *Presencia Arará en la música folclórica de Matanzas*. Havana: Casa de las Américas.

Vogel, Susan. 1986. *Aesthetics of African Art*. New York: Center for African Art.

Walker, Sheila S. 1972. *Ceremonial Spirit Possession in Africa and Afro-America: Forms, Meanings, and Functional Significance for Individuals and Social Groups*. Leiden, Netherlands: Brill.

Warner-Lewis, Maureen. 1994. *Yoruba Songs of Trinidad*. London: Karnak House.

Weeks, John H. [1882] 1914. *Among the Primitive Bakongo: Record of Thirty Years of*

Close Intercourse with the Bakongo and Other Tribes of Equatorial Africa. London: Seely, Service.

Welsh Asante, Kariamu, ed. 1998. *African Dance: An Artistic, Historical and Philosophical Inquiry.* Trenton, N.J.: Africa World Press.

———. 1985. "Commonalities in African Dance." In *African Culture: The Rhythms of Unity,* edited by Molefi Kete Asante and Kariamu Welsh Asante. Westport, Conn.: Greenwood Press.

Wilcken, Lois. 1998. "The Changing Hats of Haitian Folklore in New York." In *Island Sounds in the Global City: Caribbean Popular Music and Identity in New York,* edited by Lois Wilcken and Ray Allen, 162–83. New York/Urbana: Institute for Studies in American Music/University of Illinois Press.

———. 1992. *The Drums of Vodou.* Tempe, Arizona : Whitecliffs Media.

———. 1991. "Music Folklore among Haitians in New York: Staged Representations and the Negotiation of Identity." Ph.D. diss., Columbia University.

———. 1983. "The Music and Dance of Haitian Vodou in the Urban Environment: Case Study of a Dance Troupe." Paper presented to the International Council for Traditional Music, New York, August 11. Archived in the NYPL Dance Collection.

Williams-Yarborough, Lavinia. 1959. *Haiti-Dance.* Frankfurt-am- Main: Brönners Druckerei.

Willocks, Harold W. L. 1995. *The Umbilical Cord: The History of the United States Virgin Islands from Pre-Columbian Era to the Present.* Christiansted, St. Croix.

Young, Sir William. 1793. "Tour through the Islands of Barbados, St. Vincent, Antigua, Tobago and Grenada in 1791 and 1792." In *The Civil and Commercial History of the British Colonies in the West Indies,* edited by Bryan Edwards. London: John Stockdale.

Film and Video

"The Americans." 1993. Part 10 of *The Americas.* Boston: WGBH.

Biberman, Abner. 1954. *The Golden Mistress.* Film featuring André Narcisse and La Troupe Folklorique Nationale. Distributed by Englewood Entertainment, LLC (888–573–5490). Hollywood: United Artists.

Dancing. 1993. Video series. New York: WNET-Thirteen. Distributor: Chicago: Home Vision.

Daniel, Yvonne, producer. 1997. *Public Vodun Ceremonies in Haiti.* Video. Distributor: New York: Insight Media.

———. 1991. *Cuban Rumba.* Video. Distributor: New York: Insight Media.

———. 1990. *Cuban Dance Examples.* Video. Distributor: New York: Insight Media.

Deren, Maya. 1977. *Divine Horsemen: The Living Gods of Haiti.* Videocassette: 1985. New York: Mystic Fire Video M101.

JVC Anthology of World Music and Dance. 1988. Video series. Tokyo: Victor Company of Japan. Distributors: 1990. Cambridge, Mass.: Rounder Records; 1996. Washington D.C.: Folkways—Smithsonian.

Limbo. 1983. Television documentary. Port of Spain: Banyon Productions.

Music and Dance of the Americas. 1995. Video series. Washington, D.C.: JVC—Smithsonian Institute.

Discography

Dominican Republic (field and documentary recordings)

Afro-Dominican Music from San Cristóbal, Dominican Republic. Folkways FE 4285.

Caribbean Island Music: Songs and Dances of Haiti, the Dominican Republic, and Jamaica. Nonesuch Explorer Series 72047–2.

Caribbean Revels: Haitian Rara and Dominican Gaga. Smithsonian Folkways SF 40402.

Gillis, Verna, and Gage Averill. 1991. *Caribbean Revels: Haitian Rara and Dominican Gaga.* Notes for compact disc. Smithsonian Folkways CD 40202.

Merengue: Dominican Music and Dominican Identity. Rounder CD 1130.

Merengues from the Dominican Republic. Lyrichord LLST 7351.

Music from the Dominican Republic, vols. 1–4. Folkways FE 4281–84.

Root Music/Música Raíz, vol. 1. Santo Domingo: Fundación Cultural Bayhonda.

Singers of the Cibao. Tivoli, N.Y.: Original Music. (audiocassette) OML 403CC

Martinique

Anthologie de la Musique Antillaise, vol. 1. CMAC. Fort-de-France.

Le Bélia des alliés, musique traditionnelle de la Martinique. Bel Alians. BA 93.

Chants et musique négro-martiniquais/Le Sud. AM4, vol. 2. Compact disc DIR 243.

Les frères Rastocle. Sully Cally Productions. Compact disc FR 93.

Rigolé mé pa mò. Chants et musique négro-martiniquais, vol 4. Compact disc AM4. 04.

Soirée Leroz à Cacao/à Jabrun. Ocora Radio France. Compact disc LCD 7035.

Ti-Emile et son groupe of Sainte Marie, Martinique. Sonovox Records. SLP 305 or compact disc SC 93.

Virgin Islands

Derima, Tony. 1999. "Bounce to de Ounce." Compact disc: *Rhythmorphisis.* Performed by Dee and Tony. Produced and arranged by Al Baptiste, Jr. Executive director, Al Baptiste, Sr. V.I. Manufacturing 340–513–7290.

Onyan. 1999. "Swim." CD: *Jouvert.* Producer, Toriano Edwards. Executive producer, Dr. Prince Ramsey. New York: Crystal Sounds Recording.

ABOUT THE CONTRIBUTORS

Molly Ahye, author of *Golden Heritage: The Dance in Trinidad and Tobago* (1978) and *Cradle of Caribbean Dance: Beryl McBurnie and the Little Carib Theatre* (1983), knows Trinidad's dance and spiritual life inside and out as an ethnologist, the artistic director of a dance troupe, and as Chief Iyalorisha-Opa Orisha (Shango) of Trinidad and Tobago. She holds a Ph.D. from New York University.

Trinidadian-born Patricia Tamara Alleyne-Dettmers is a linguistic anthropologist who has studied Trinidadian Carnival for more than ten years, and continues to research Carnival in Great Britain, from the perspective of the native masquerader and from the outside as a professional anthropologist. She was commissioned by the Arts Council of England to develop the first national Carnival database for British Carnivalists and is an honorary research fellow in the Department of Anthropology at University College, London, a foundation member of the Carnival in Arts Education Steering Committee (Goldsmith's College), and a visiting professor, Department of Sociology, at the University of Hamburg, Germany.

Halbert Barton is assistant professor of anthropology at Long Island University–Brooklyn. He was awarded a Rockefeller postdoctoral fellowship in the humanities in 1998 for his community development research with young Puerto Rican bomba performers. He is cofounder and development director of CICRE (Centro de Investigación Cultural Raices Eternas), a nonprofit community arts organization based in Carolina, Puerto Rico, which sponsors the group's "Bombazo de Puerto Rico" tour. He also is an accomplished bomba dancer, having performed extensively throughout Puerto Rico, New York, and the Pacific Northwest over the past several years as a lead dancer, percussionist, and artistic director.

Gabri Christa, born and raised in Curaçao, arrived in New York from Puerto Rico, via the Netherlands and Cuba. She choreographed and danced for a few years in Cuba, where she was one of the founders of Danzabierta de Cuba. In the United States she has been a dancer with Bill T. Jones/Arnie Zane Dance Company. She holds a degree from the School for New Dance Development in Amsterdam and taught at and received an M.F.A. from the University of Washington. A 1999 Guggenheim Fellow, she directs her own company, whose work has been seen throughout the United States, the Caribbean, Latin America, and the Netherlands.

VèVè A. Clark is associate professor of African and Caribbean literatures and cultures in the African American Studies Department at the University of California, Berkeley. She has published widely on numerous subjects, including Haitian theater, Katherine Dunham's dance works, Caribbean literature, and critical feminisms.

Independent scholar, teacher, choreographer, and dancer, Alma Concepción is a graduate in literary studies from the University of Puerto Rico and was a member of Gilda Navarra's Taller de Histriones throughout its existence. Currently the assistant director of People and Stories, a grassroots literature program sponsored by the New Jersey Council for the Humanities, she is also the founder and director of Taller de Danza, a volunteer organization dedicated to introducing children in Trenton's Hispanic community to movement through the creation of story-dances. She teaches at Fordham University and Ballet Hispánico in New York and at Princeton University and Rutgers University and the Princeton Ballet School in New Jersey.

Nathaniel Hamilton Crowell, Jr., is a candidate for a Ph.D. in cultural anthropology at Yale University. He has traveled extensively in West Africa and West Central Africa as well as in the Caribbean and South America, has studied a range of African and Afro-American music and dance with master musicians and dancers for more than sixteen years, and has performed African and Afro-American music and dance semiprofessionally for just as long. He currently dances with Malaki Ma Kongo, a Congolese dance troupe in New York City, and prior to that apprenticed with its sister company, Fua Dia Congo in California.

Dominique Cyrille received her doctorate in musicology from the Université Paris IV, Sorbonne. As a specialist in the music of Martinique, her native island, she is the author of several articles, has been invited for lectures in the Caribbean, France, and the United States, and is presently an adjunct assistant professor in the Department of Black Studies at Lehman College, City University of New York.

Yvonne Daniel teaches dance and anthropology at Smith College. She holds a Ph.D. in anthropology from University of California, Berkeley, an M.A. in dance, and a B.A. in music. She is a Ford Fellow and has been studying Cuban dance forms since she began her field work in Cuba in 1985. Daniel is the author of *Rumba: Dance and Social Change in Contemporary Cuba* and has produced three videos on Caribbean dance culture.

Martha Ellen Davis, anthropologist and ethnomusicologist, has been doing field research in the Dominican Republic, her primary field site, since 1972. She has served as a professor at the country's public university, the Universidad Autónoma de Santo Domingo, a curator of sociocultural anthropology at the Museo del Hombre Dominicano, and a researcher at the Archivo Nacional de Música. Her book *La otra ciencia: el vodú dominicano como religión y medicina populares* received the Dominican national nonfiction award. She is currently on the faculty at the University of Florida.

Henry Frank is a Haitian anthropologist who has lectured and consulted widely on Vodou and other Haitian subjects and was for nine years assistant director of Caribbean studies in the education department of the American Museum of Natural History. Much involved in the Haitian community in New York in a variety of roles, he was Haitian consul general in 1990 and is currently executive director of the Haitian Centers Council.

Brenda Dixon Gottschild is professor emeritus of dance at Temple University, where she teaches performance history, theory, and criticism. She is the Philadelphia critic for *Dance Magazine*, author of the final chapter of *Black Dance from 1619 to Today* (revised edition), coauthor of the third edition of *The History of Dance in Art and Education*, and author of *Digging the Africanist Presence in American Performance: Dance and Other Contexts*. Her latest book is *Waltzing in the Dark: African American Vaudeville and Race Politics in the Swing Era*.

Suki John is a choreographer, teacher, and dance writer in New York and Havana. She and her husband, Horacio Cocchi, founded the group ANDANDO as an intercultural and humanitarian exchange between Cuba and the United States.

Melinda Mousouris is a freelance journalist based in New York City. Her articles on the arts and Cuba have appeared in *American Theatre Magazine, Attitude, Dance Magazine, Dance Teacher Now,* the *New York Times,* and the *Village Voice.*

Rex Nettleford is vice chancellor of the University of the West Indies, where he has taught as professor of continuing studies and is responsible for the University's Cultural Studies Initiative Programme. He is also the founder, artistic director, and principal choreographer of the National Dance Theatre Company of Jamaica (NDTC).

Cynthia Oliver is an award winning choreographer/performing artist working in New York and abroad. She is a doctoral candidate at New York University's Department of Performance Studies, where her scholarship has centered around performance in the Caribbean, specifically the United States Virgin Islands. She is currently an assistant professor of dance at the University of Illinois, Urbana-Champaign.

Thomas Osha Pinnock is an award winning choreographer/performance artist/writer. He has been involved in Caribbean dance-theater for over thirty years.

Ramón Rivera-Servera is a doctoral student in the Department of Theater and Dance at the University of Texas at Austin, where he holds a Ford Foundation predoctoral fellowship. He has taught at the Department of Modern Languages and Cultures at the University of Rochester, N.Y., the Department of Speech and Theater at John Jay College, and the Department of Women's Studies at Hunter College. His research focuses on U.S. Latina/o and Caribbean performance.

Susanna Sloat is a writer, editor, and arts consultant in New York City. As an associate editor of *Attitude — The Dancers' Magazine,* she has written extensively on modern, postmodern, and many kinds of world dance.

Robert Farris Thompson is Colonel John Trumbull Professor of the History of Art at Yale University. He is the author of many books including *African Art in Motion*, *The Four Moments of the Sun: Kongo Art in Two Worlds*, and *Flash of the Spirit*, and numerous, much anthologized articles on topics ranging from the influence of African art on U.S. sports and drama to the black impact on John Cage's prepared piano and Martha Graham's stance. He lectures widely and in 1995 received the Leadership Award of the Arts Council of the United States African Studies Association for distinguished contributions to scholarship in the field of African and African-American art.

Dr. Lois Wilcken, ethnomusicologist, has researched the music and dance of the spirits in Port-au-Prince and New York City's Haitian neighborhoods. She is executive director of La Troupe Makandal, a company that mystically demystifies Haitian folk music and dance. Dr. Wilcken has written *The Drums of Vodou* (1992) and co-edited *Island Sounds in the Global City* (1998); her forthcoming book is *Crossroads, a Teacher's Guide to the Folk Arts of Haiti*.

INDEX